When the Scorpion Stings

First published in 2002

Allen & Unwin
83 Alexander Street
Crows Nest NSW 2065
Australia
Phone: (61 2) 8425 0100
Fax: (61 2) 9906 2218
Email: info@allenandunwin.com
Web: www.allenandunwin.com

National Library of Australia
Cataloguing-in-Publication entry:

Anderson, Paul.
When the scorpion stings: the history of the 3rd Cavalry Regiment, South Vietnam, 1965–72.

Bibliography.
Includes Index.
ISBN 1 86508 743 2.

1. Australia. Army. Cavalry Regiment, 3rd—History.
2. Vietnamese Conflict, 1961–1975—Participation, Australian.
I. Title.

355.310994

Map of Vietnam on page xvi supplied by MAPgraphics. All other maps drawn by Paul Anderson.
Index compiled by Jo Rudd
Typeset in 10.5 on 11.5 pt Garamond by Midland Typesetters, Maryborough
Printed in Australia by McPherson's Printing Group

10 9 8 7 6 5 4 3 2 1

When the Scorpion Stings

The history of the 3rd Cavalry Regiment, South Vietnam, 1965–1972

Paul Anderson

ALLEN&UNWIN

Foreword

Lieutenant Colonel R.K. Hill, MC
Commanding Officer, 1 APC Troop, 1965–66

When the Scorpion Stings tells the proud story of the part played by the cavalrymen and their Armoured Personnel Carriers during offensive operations in South Vietnam over the period 1965–72.

The units involved, in chronological sequence, were 1 Troop of A Squadron (ARA), 4th/9th Prince of Wales' Light Horse Regiment, 1st Armoured Personnel Carrier Squadron and the 3rd Cavalry Regiment A and B Squadrons.

This book explains the role and the tasks of the Cavalry unit and how it supported its principle customer, the Australian Infantry, during operations. In the greater majority of the search and clear missions, the APCs were used in their primary role—the transportation of infantry, and as such were under the command of the Infantry. As a consequence, any enemy casualties inflicted by the cavalrymen with their .50 cal. machine guns were automatically claimed as casualties inflicted by the Infantry. Needless to say, some umbrage was noted on occasion, particularly when enemy anti-armour mines were a constant threat to the armoured vehicles. Infantry men were, at times, not particularly enthusiastic when invited to ride inside the APCs—much to the cynical amusement of the crewmen.

The deaths and injuries suffered by so many of those cavalrymen in a war to which they had been committed by their country is a sad reflection of the final result of the campaign.

The late Paul Anderson researched his subject with great thoroughness. His book is indeed an effective profile of operations as seen by the cavalrymen of the Royal Australian Armoured Corps.

Robert Hill

This history is dedicated to the families who waited at home while their men served. For they truly knew what it meant to wait.

ONLY A SOLDIER'S GRAVE

Only a soldier's grave! Pass by,
For soldiers, like other mortals, die.
Parents had he—they are far away;
No sister weeps o'er the soldier's clay;
No brother comes, with tearful eye;
It's only a soldier's grave—pass by.

Yet, we should mark it—the soldier's grave,
Someone may seek him in hope to save!
Some of the dear ones, far away,
Would bear him home to his native clay:
'twere sad, indeed, should they wander nigh,
Find not the hillock, and pass him by.

S.A. Jones

Contents

The B Squadron 3rd/4th Cavalry Regiment Museum was founded a number of years ago to conserve, interpret and exhibit armoured fighting vehicle (AFV) relics, artefacts and memorabilia, as well as historical information relating to the 3rd and 4th Cavalry Regiments. Through commemorating the unit's heritage, the Museum aims to foster understanding and support for today's members and to continue the ethos of the 3rd Cavalry Regiment. The Officer Commanding (OC) extends a personal welcome to all ex-members to visit and have a drink at the 'Scorpion Club' with the custodians of their legacy.

Please direct enquiries to the Squadron Sergeant Major (SSM) or Curator at the Museum:

B Squadron 3rd/4th Cavalry Regiment
Lavarack Barracks
Townsville QLD 4813

Telephone: 07 4771 7298

The 3rd Cavalry Regiment (Vietnam) Association was established in 1992 to bring together veterans of the Vietnam War who served with the 3rd Cavalry Regiment, to preserve the memories and comradeship of those who returned safely and, above all, to remember those who made the supreme sacrifice. Please contact:

Kevin Ortlipp 0438 759 733 (National Secretary)
Dallas Burrage 02 6658 7339 (Treasurer/Editor)

Acknowledgments

Special thanks must be given to certain people and organisations without whose support the compilation of this history would have been extremely difficult.

First I must thank the Australian Army History Unit in Canberra, which provided both financial and intellectual support for the project. I would especially like to thank Bill Houston for his advice and support.

I also acknowledge the support of the Armoured Corps Museum at Puckapunyal in providing information. Special mention must be made of Major Paul Handel and Sergeant Barry Marriott.

For assisting with photographs I would like to thank Socrates Lecatis from the 3/4 Cavalry Regiment Museum, Rick Wells and Kevin Ortlipp from the 3rd Cavalry Regiment (Vietnam) Association, and Geoff Murray.

I would like to acknowledge John Batchelor as the illustrator of the APC diagram on page 301.

To Bob Field and Ann Holgate who assisted with editing the text, I also express my gratitude.

Finally, I must acknowledge those ex-members of the Regiment who contacted me and kindly and graciously provided me with information and material.

Preface

This history of the 3rd Cavalry Regiment's role in the Vietnam War outlines a number of engagements in which the Squadrons of the Regiment were involved. Because the unit served a period of approximately six years it is beyond the scope of this book to record every incident, movement and operation in which it was involved. However, in writing the history of the Regiment in South Vietnam I have attempted to research and document as much as possible what I believe to be the most important actions in which the members of the Regiment were involved. It is not intended to be a definitive work, although the many events and actions in which the unit participated and which are recorded in this history reflect the type of roles that were undertaken by members of the Regiment and the conditions under which they served and operated.

The fact that this history has been written some 34 years after the first involvement by the Regiment in the Vietnam War has meant that many otherwise valuable sources of information from members who served have already been lost. A large number of the Regiment's members who served in Vietnam have already died, and memories fade with time and age. In writing my history I found the actual account of events by the people involved invaluable. That said, I have deliberately refrained canvassing ex-members to relate their memories of events and actions, as this may inadvertently have caused distress to those who would prefer to forget. In spite of my intentions, some ex-members of the Regiment did contact me, and I am most grateful for their account of events. Their kindness, sincerity and encouragement were overwhelming. It would of course have been preferable for the unit's complete history to be compiled earlier, to take into account these and other personal testimonies of events, but I have made every attempt to research and reconstruct the events diligently and accurately from the various documents and resources that have been made available to me. At least now a history of the service of the 3rd Cavalry Regiment's role in South Vietnam will have been recorded and the Regiment's role in the Vietnam War acknowledged for its more than considerable contribution to Australia's military history.

Numerous histories of units that served in South Vietnam have existed for many years, and it is entirely appropriate that the service of the members of the 3rd Cavalry Regiment and their contribution to Australia's military history now be more fully recognised. With few exceptions, the histories to date have tended to adopt a rather superficial view of the Cavalry's efforts, without seemingly appreciating or understanding the role played by the Regiment and its enormous contribution to the Australian Task Force in South Vietnam. A fact often overlooked is that the Regiment was the first unit involved in the establishment of the Task Force at Nui Dat and the last to leave when the Task Force was disbanded. Thus, this history consistently presents the 3rd Cavalry Regiment as one of Australia's foremost combat units in the Vietnam War. The book focuses exclusively on the 3rd Cavalry Regiment's participation in the Vietnam War. As the history of many other units that served with the 3rd Cavalry Regiment have already been recorded, it is not intended to include their participation in the events, actions and operations that have been outlined.

An important factor that has undoubtedly prevented the Regiment's full activities in the Vietnam War from ever being properly recognised is that contacts initiated by Australian armoured units were often never reported by the infantry units under which they served. Major Peter Badman RAAC recognised this in early 1971, when he expressed his concern at an analysis of Australian Army contacts in South Vietnam. He correctly pointed out that past analyses had not been very illuminating: 'The main reason for this is the fact that many contacts in which Armour is involved are reported on by the infantry unit to which Armour is allotted under operational control and the full facts relating to Armour are not always recorded'.[1] A perfect case in point is the Regiment's involvement in the action in the Long Tan rubber plantation on the evening of 18 August 1966. Nowhere in the after-action report relating to this substantial action is 1 APC Squadron mentioned, although much embarrassment and criticism would have accrued to the Australian Army's high command and politicians had the men of 1 APC Squadron not intervened that evening in August 1966. I have devoted Chapter 2 to the unit's considerable involvement in that action. This chapter highlights what the after-action report writers failed to acknowledge—that a troop of cavalry played a major role in saving an entire Australian infantry company from annihilation. I hope this will once and for all dispel the misconceptions and prejudices that would not allow the 1 APC Squadron to be named in this important report or at least have an appropriate citation publicly acknowledged.

The number of men who served with the Regiment during the Vietnam War was small compared with many of the other corps or units. Its establishment of 169 men in August 1971 was the largest contingent of the Regiment at any one time in South Vietnam. Yet what the Squadrons achieved during their tours of duty in Vietnam was an invaluable contribution to the Australian Task Force's overall war effort. The Regiment's emblem was a scorpion, which appropriately reflected the unit's small size but extremely dangerous capabilities each time it went into action.

Let there be no mistake: this unit suffered more than most. Twenty of its members never returned home alive, and a further 110 men suffered serious wounds in the service of their country. This meant that for every seven members of the Regiment's Squadrons serving in Vietnam, at least one could expect to become a battle casualty. Despite these statistics, the Regiment carried out its dangerous tasks in a dedicated and professional manner.

The Squadrons became a highly mobile force, being able to move over large areas at speed despite the armoured characteristics of the M113A1 vehicles. Their operational charter meant the APCs from the Squadron were continually deployed, making them Australia's most versatile and busiest unit in the Vietnam War. The M113A1 presented to other Australian troops a high degree of security through the simple knowledge that these highly armed vehicles, manned by the men of the 3rd Cavalry Regiment, would be at their side when the need arose.

Members of the Squadron took substantial risks when it was necessary to provide urgent assistance to other Australian units. As no amount of planning could cover every contingency, engineering mine specialists were eventually added to every APC section each time they deployed, to reduce the possibility of hitting a mine. Such was the role of the Regiment that a mine attack or enemy ambush was a distinct possibility every time APC crews mounted their vehicles. But the APCs were fighting vehicles, and the men who crewed them could only rely on their training and skill to mitigate the considerable risks they faced.

A main determinant in my recording this history was the vexed issue surrounding the award of an Armoured Combat badge. In some quarters there is a mistaken belief that the Cavalry acted as purely an armoured transport unit, or as 'battlefield taxis'. Nothing could be further from the truth. The combat role undertaken by the men who fought with the 3rd Cavalry Regiment and the 1st Armoured Regiment on many occasions surpassed that of other combat units, albeit from a mounted armour perspective. And the fact that numerous actions in which both regiments fought were not reported certainly has not helped to advance the case for such an award. Perhaps once this book is read and noted by the institutions and parties that in the past have sought to deny the award, they will intercede and have this anomaly in Australia's military history correctly acknowledged.

Both theatre and battle honours were won by the Regiment for its performance in Vietnam. The battle honours appearing on the guidon that was presented to the 3rd Cavalry Regiment by Her Majesty, Queen Elizabeth II, are 'Vietnam 1965–1972', 'Long Tan' and 'Coral–Balmoral'. Battle honours were also awarded to the Regiment for the role it played in Bien Hoa, Hat Dich and Binh Ba. Additionally, the Squadron participated in every major Australian Task Force operation, including the Battle of Long Tan in 1966, the Tet Offensive in 1968, the Battle of Binh Ba in 1969 and the Battle for Fire Support Bases Coral and Balmoral.

Like the helicopter, the M113A1 APC added a new dimension to the way in which wars could be fought and at the same time, directly and indirectly, saved the lives of hundreds of the Australian troops serving in South Vietnam. The APCs were often called in to resolve combat situations in which serious Australian troop losses might have occurred. I hope with this history to instil in the reader an appreciation of the efforts of those who served with the 3rd Cavalry Regiment and recognition of the sacrifices they made. Some may view the work as a tribute to those who served; others may see it as an informative document. Whatever their reason for reading it, I would like to include a tribute to the men who served with the 3rd Cavalry Regiment in South Vietnam. The poem on page viii, from the American Civil War, reflects the truism that if we forget those who served, we ourselves will be forgotten. The 3rd Cavalry Regiment's record of service in South Vietnam is too rich and valuable to be forgotten.

NORTH VIETNAM
SOUTH CHINA SEA
LAOS
THAILAND
CAMBODIA
SOUTH VIETNAM
Mekong
River
Mouths of the Mekong
Quang Tri
Thua Thien
Quang Nam
Quang Tin
Quang Ngai
Kontum
Binh Dinh
Pleiku
Phu Bon
Phu Yen
Darlac
Khanh Hoa
Quang Duc
Tuyen Duc
Da Lat
Cam Ranh
Binh Long
Phuoc Long
Ninh Thuan
Tay Ninh
Lam Dong
Binh Duong
Long Khanh
Binh Tuy
Binh Thuan
Bien Hoa
Hau Nghia
Kien Phong
Kien Tuong
SAIGON
Chau Doc
Long An
Phuoc Tuy
Gia Dinh
NUI DAT
Dinh Tuong
An Giang
Sa Dec
Go Cong
Vinh Long
Kien Hoa
Kien Giang
Phong Dinh
Vinh Binh
Chuong Thien
Ba Xuyen
Bac Lieu
An Xuyen
N
0
100 km

1

The beginning

The evolution of the Regiment's history of service in South Vietnam lies in the 4th/19th Prince of Wales' Light Horse (PWLH) Regiment, whose historical origin was the Victorian Mounted Rifles. This Regiment and its predecessors were derived and manned predominantly from throughout regional Victoria, and their rich histories are documented in David Holloway's book, *Hooves, Wheels & Tracks*. While the 3rd Cavalry Regiment cannot claim formal lineal descent from the 4th/19th PWLH Regiment, the units acknowledge a fond association with and mutual regard for each other. Given that the 4th/19th PWLH Regiment's history has already been recorded, it is sufficient to say that that Regiment served in the Boer War, World Wars I and II, and in South Vietnam from 1965 to 1966, with bravery and distinction.

For many years Armour had been regarded as the 'ugly duckling' of the Australian Army, primarily because many of those in the Army's High Command had very little knowledge of the operations and tactics associated with Armour. It is said that those commanding troops in Vietnam had reservations about the role of the M113A1 armoured personnel carrier (APC) and how it should be employed. This mindset probably harks back to the last time Australian Armour was employed—in World War II, in the jungles of New Guinea and in the southwest Pacific. The attack on Slater's Knoll in New Guinea by the Australian Matilda tanks had highlighted the considerable benefits and value of having Armour lead an assault on heavily defended jungle positions, with infantry accompanying to assist in the 'mop-up' of the remaining enemy.

The M113A1 was not a tank, but the value of the role that the 'new' M113A1 APC could play had been quickly recognised by the Australian

Command in Vietnam. Already the APCs of 1 Troop 4th/19th PWLH had achieved considerable success in their operations with 1 RAR and its allied forces in Bien Hoa province. Its ability to deliver troops quickly to an operations area and then use sustained fire power to support those troops was widely acknowledged. Thus the role of the Royal Australian Armoured Corps was to be expanded in Australia's contribution to the war effort.

1 Troop A Squadron 4th/19th PWLH had been in South Vietnam since June 1965, as part of Australia's commitment to the war effort. This unit, under the command of Lieutenant R.K. Hill MC (later promoted to Captain), together with the First Battalion Royal Australian Regiment (1 RAR) and other ancillary units, operated under the command of the US forces in an area known as War Zone 'D'. This area was northwest of the yet to be established Australian Task Force base at Nui Dat in Phuoc Tuy province.

In March 1966, 1 Troop 4th/19th PWLH was redesignated 1 APC Troop and subsequently completed its tour of duty under that title, returning to Australia in May 1966. It is at this point that the history of the 3rd Cavalry Regiment commences.

The 1st APC Squadron was raised on 1 July 1965 at Puckapunyal in Victoria, with the specific purpose of relieving 1 APC Troop on completion of its tour of duty in South Vietnam. In January 1966, 'A' Squadron of the 4th/19th PWLH and 2nd/14th Queensland Mounted Infantry were reorganised and designated 'A' and 'B' Squadrons 1st Cavalry Regiment. A Squadron had a full complement of 156 personnel, while B Squadron was restricted to 76 personnel.[1]

Because of confusion within Army Command, there existed a 1st Armoured Regiment and a 1st Cavalry Regiment. The Director of Armour at the time believed that the Regular Army unit identity should be ascribed to the many APC subunits that were starting to evolve. Eventually the Chief of General Staff indicated that there should be a Regular Army cavalry regiment and that all Regular Army armoured units, like their predecessors in the Light Horse, should be sequentially numbered. This led to the 1st Cavalry Regiment being renumbered the 2nd Cavalry Regiment minus A Squadron, which was the Regular Army's new Armoured Personnel Carrier Regiment and would later be redesignated the 3rd Cavalry Regiment.[2]

On 9 March 1966 the Australian government announced that its commitment to the Australian force in Vietnam would be increased to a task force consisting of two battalions, and include a squadron of armoured personnel carriers among the ancillary troops. The Squadron was to be restricted to 50% of full strength and would be the only armoured unit supporting the Tasks Force's efforts. Additionally, the

Australian government announced that the Australian Task Force would now operate as an independent force and had been assigned an operational area of responsibility within Phuoc Tuy province, approximately 35 kilometres southeast of Saigon.

1 APC Squadron was commanded by Major R.E. Hagerty, who had already served in South Vietnam with the AATTV at Hiep Khanh between March 1962 and November 1963 and was an experienced officer. Members of 3 Troop under the command of the Squadron's two troop leaders, Lieutenants Ross Guymer and Adrian Roberts, were to fly to South Vietnam and arrange the takeover of carriers of 1 APC Troop in late May 1966. The rest of the Squadron would travel on HMAS *Sydney*, and were scheduled to arrive in South Vietnam on 6 June 1966. The Squadron consisted of seven officers and 109 other ranks. A substantial portion of the Squadron were National Servicemen from the first and second National Service intakes. The officers and NCOs were recruited from the 1st Armoured Regiment and A Squadron 4th/19th PWLH. The formation of the Squadron was a totally new concept, and the men were hand-picked.

Armoured Personnel Carriers

The Squadron drew its newly arrived APCs, which the Regiment would use in South Vietnam, from the Army's Ordinance Depot at Bandiana in Victoria. 3 Troop, who were to take over the vehicles from 1 Troop on arrival in South Vietnam, had a slight advantage inasmuch as their vehicles had intercom facilities and all had been fitted with steel MG shields to protect the crew commanders. However, whereas the other troops had acquired new vehicles, the carriers in South Vietnam were in dire need of a major overhaul.

The APCs were the American diesel-fuelled, tracked M113A1 vehicles. They were powered by a GM Detroit 6V53 diesel engine and were first manufactured in 1964. The body was made of aluminium and when fully laden weighed 11 515 kg. It could accommodate 10 fully equipped infantry, together with a crew of driver and crew commander. The initial APCs came with a pintle mount on the crew commander's cupola, which accommodated a .50 cal. Browning M2HB machine gun. A .50 MG shield was later added, and eventually the T50 turret was fitted to most of the vehicles in service in South Vietnam.

Other members of the M113A1 family in the Squadron's makeup included the M125A1 mortar carrier. A rotating mortar baseplate was attached to the floor on which the infantry could mount their 81 mm mortar tubes. The mortar base limited the number of troops that could be carried in the back of the carrier. It carried the same armaments as

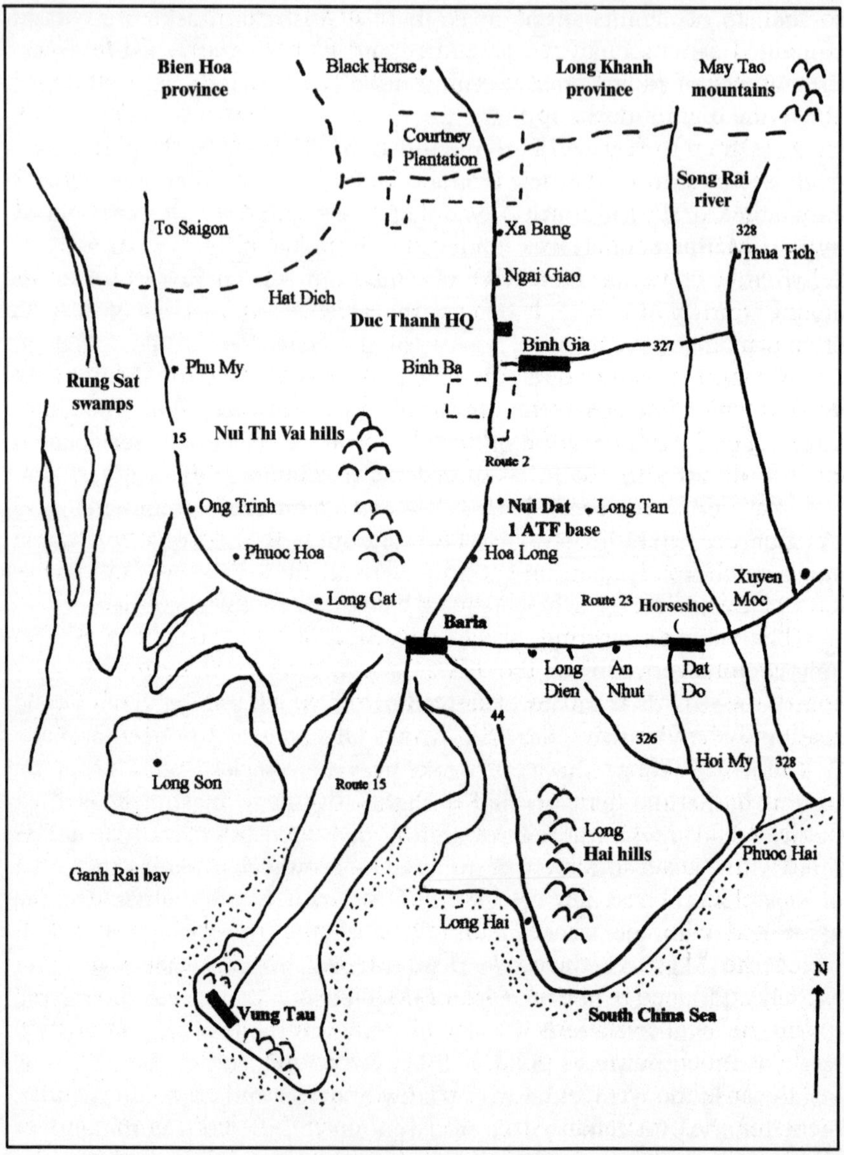

Phuoc Tuy province

the other M113A1 vehicles in the Squadron, but when not carrying mortar crews was used in cavalry-type roles, as its capacity to undertake APC tasks was limited by its internal configuration. The M577A1 armoured command vehicle (ACV), which did not see service with the Australian Task Force until some time later, had its hull height extended so that its occupants could work in relative comfort. These vehicles contained a number of radios and map-viewing facilities. To facilitate the number of radios operating in the ACV, a generator was mounted above the engine deck, opposite the driver's compartment. The ACVs were assigned to HQ 1ATF command and were normally based in relatively secured areas, as their size and lack of armaments presented an easy target for enemy attack. The M113A1 repair fitters' carrier (crewed by RAEME personnel) was fitted out as a mobile armoured workshop. A hydraulic crane was attached to the deck and was capable of lifting an engine from an M113A1. It also carried a .50 calibre machine gun as its main armament.[3]

A common feature of all these vehicles was a rear ramp for the easy deployment of troops from the back of the carrier. The raising and lowering of the ramp was based on a hydraulic oil system attached to the engine, allowing troops to be dismounted while the vehicle was either stationary or in motion. Mounted on the rear ramp was a hatch that obviated the need to continually lower and raise the ramp. A substantial cargo hatch was located on the back deck of the APC and was usually left open while the vehicle was being driven, to enhance ventilation.

The vehicle's steering system consisted of two sets of levers. The long lateral levers allowed the driver to turn the vehicle right or left. At speed, the drivers learnt to balance the vehicle against the pitch of the road and thereby drive the APC using only one of the lateral levers. A second set of levers, called pivots, allowed the vehicle a much smaller turning radius and to pivot on its own axis. The pivot steering was essential to the M113A1 water-borne operations. Each vehicle's engine was fitted with a governor box prior to leaving Australia to regulate the speed of the vehicle. These devices were considered necessary given the risks associated with the tracked running configuration and the speed at which the M113A1 travelled. However, the first 'modification' (not entirely condoned by the authorities) made by the crews to their vehicles to suit the local conditions was usually the removal of the governor box, to get as much power as possible from the engine.

Because the M113A1 was a relatively new piece of military equipment for the Australian Army and had been 'hurried' into service in Vietnam, it did have some problems. On 11 March 1966 Captain R.K. Hill, commanding 1 APC Troop, wrote to Major G.J. Murphy at Army Headquarters in Canberra outlining some of its shortcomings and the problems that his troop had experienced with the M113A1 over the previous nine months of operations:[4]

1. The generator pulleys were gripping the spines and causing abnormal wear. An incident report had been submitted in relation to this defect.

2. The generator mounting brackets were cracking at an abnormal rate, which was attributed to too soft a metal in the manufacturing process. However, it had been decided to replace these brackets with a locally made steel bracket.
3. The troop had to replace 11 blower drive shafts. This had meant that after every 1000 miles (1600 km) travelled by an APC the LAD were required to extract these drive shafts and carry out a thorough inspection. Any shafts showing signs of wear were automatically replaced.

Hill was also critical of the radios used in the carriers at that time, stating that they were unsuitable for M113A1 operations. Conversely, he applauded the .50 cal. machine guns that had been fitted to each carrier. The .50 cal. MG was a heavier gun, capable of firing through rubber trees, therefore invaluable in a fire fight, especially one in which the enemy used heavy foliage and trees for protection. The M60 MG, which was predominantly used by the Australian Infantry and the USA, did not have this capability.

There were a total of 18 carriers in South Vietnam at the time Hill made his report, and these would be handed over to 1 APC Squadron on its arrival in South Vietnam. The original 10 carriers had travelled a total of 41 898 kilometres, or an average of 4190 kilometres per carrier, while the remaining eight 'newer' carriers had completed a total of 17 947 kilometres, or 2243 kilometres per carrier. On this basis, several of the carriers due to be taken over by 1 APC Squadron were deemed to be due for a major overhaul.

Major problems encountered by Hagerty prior to the departure of the Squadron were the shortage of NCOs to be trained as crew commanders and the lack of radio equipment for the carriers. The 'new' VRC 12 radio sets which were to be installed in the carriers, and were integral to the Squadron's communications, had been delayed. This prevented any meaningful field exercises, as radios are a vital component in armoured fighting vehicles, the noise created by which is so great that it is impossible for crews to communicate with each other by word of mouth. Additionally, in any armoured unit there is a requirement that the activity and movement of vehicles be closely coordinated with other vehicles in the section/troop as well as other members of the Squadron.

As well as the lack of radio communication, the Squadron had not undertaken any training with infantry. The training on the Puckapunyal driving range consisted of organising an intricate system of hand signals between carriers to overcome the lack of radio communication. Each troop was not entirely without radio communications, as every troop leader's vehicle had a '25' radio set strapped to the deck behind the crew commander's hatch. Messages were relayed from troop to troop, then passed on to individual members of the troop by the troop leader using hand signals.

The Squadron under Major Hagerty's command was organised with a Squadron HQ, an administration troop, two APC troops (numbered 2 and 3 Troops) together with elements of a support troop and supporting arms. The supporting arms included a contingent from the Royal Australian Electrical and Mechanical Engineers (RAEME), who were incorporated in the unit and would provide the Light Aid Detachment (LAD) so necessary for the maintenance of the Squadron's vehicles. The Squadron's command structure when it arrived in South Vietnam would see 2 Troop commanded by Lieutenant Ross Guymer, while Lieutenant Adrian Roberts would lead 3 Troop. The Support Troop was commanded by Lieutenant Ian Bryant and would later be redesignated 4 Troop. The Liaison Officer/Quartermaster was Lieutenant A.F. King and the SSM was Warrant Officer A.L. Cabban.

To facilitate the Squadron's communication system each vehicle within the troop had radio callsigns designated so that each vehicle could be easily identified. The assignment of callsigns was as follows.

Callsign 9(Squadron OC)
Callsign 9(Echo SSM)

No 2 Troop Callsigns	**No 3 Troop Callsigns**	**Support Troop**
20Alpha (Troop Leader)	30Alpha (Troop Leader)	81Alpa
20Bravo (Troop Officer)	30Bravo (Troop Officer)	81Bravo
20Juliet (Troop Sergeant)	30Juliet (Troop Sergeant)	
20Mike (Ambulance)	30Mike (Ambulance)	
21 Section Callsigns	**31 Section Callsigns**	
21Alpha	31Alpha	82Alpha
21(Section Sergeant)	31(Section Sergeant)	82Bravo
21Bravo	31Bravo	
22 Section Callsigns	**32 Section Callsigns**	
22Alpha	32Alpha	83Alpha
22(Section Sergeant)	32(Section Sergeant)	83Bravo
22Bravo	32Bravo	
23 Section Callsigns	**33 Section Callsigns**	**Support Troop**
23Alpha	33Alpha	84Alpha
23(Section Sergeant)	33(Section Sergeant)	84Bravo
23Bravo	33Bravo	

Each section's callsign commenced with Alpha followed by the Section's principal number, then Bravo. This is because when the troops were deployed in tactical formation, the leading APC was crewed by the most experienced corporal and driver in the section. The section leader (usually the rank of sergeant) remained between the Alpha and Bravo carriers for control purposes. The same would occur when the whole troop was deployed: the Troop Headquarters would follow the leading Section so that the troop leader could control every section within the troop.

ARRIVAL AT SOUTH VIETNAM

The Squadron, which had travelled to South Vietnam on board HMAS *Sydney*, landed at Vung Tau on 6 June 1966, where US landing barges were used to ferry the Squadron's APCs from the *Sydney* to the beach. An advance party moved to an area to the north of the airfield at Vung Tau near Route 15 and secured an area for the main body of the Squadron. The Squadron remained at Vung Tau for two days before setting off north to Nui Dat, where it was reunited with Adrian Roberts, now redesignated 3 Troop. On arrival at Nui Dat on 9 June 1966, the Squadron, together with the 5th Battalion RAR (5 RAR) and 105 Battery RAA, proceeded to establish a base for the Australian Task Force. Adrian Roberts and Ross Guymer, who had assumed command of 1 Troop from Captain R.K. Hill, had earlier moved down to the proposed new Task Force area from Bien Hoa province with the US 173rd Airborne Brigade. This force had carried out a clearing operation to prepare for the arrival of the main elements of the Task Force. This move allowed Adrian Roberts, who had accompanied Guymer, to obtain a very good knowledge of the area surrounding the Task Force base and the river crossings of the Suoi Da Bang creek, an experience that was to prove invaluable in later operations.

Phuoc Tuy, which means 'prosperous and peaceful', had long been a 'hotbed' of Viet Cong guerilla activity; its security was vital because of the communication and transport links with the developing port and large airbase at Vung Tau. The province was divided into five districts, consisting of Long Le, Long Dien, Dat Do, Duc Than and Xuyen Moc. The major portion of Phuoc Tuy's population was located in the southern portion of the province. The enemy forces on the other hand operated a number of enemy bases in the jungles of the May Tao mountains in the northeastern sector of the province. Several of these bases had been established since the Viet Minh war against the French in the 1950s. In the southeast were the Long Hai hills, which housed the Viet Cong's Minh Dam 'secret zone'. This zone was named after two

The members of 1 APC Squadron on the deck of HMAS *Sydney*, en route to South Vietnam, May 1966. (3rd Cavalry Regiment (Vietnam) Association)

brothers and their sister who came from the village of An Nhut and had been leaders of the local Viet Minh cadre in their conquest of the colonial French. In the west was the Hat Dich base area while in the southwest were the Rung Sat swamps and waterways, which provide excellent transport and communication facilities for the enemy.

At the time the Australian Task Force arrived, Phuoc Tuy province was defended by one battalion of largely untrained and ill-equipped Army of the Republic of Vietnam (ARVN) troops. In addition, the popular force and local militia undertook the task of providing protection for the various villages and hamlets throughout the province. This ragtag army, which had been administered by a military government for a number of years, had been unable to cope with the constant demand of defending the population. In fact, the government had little control over the province, and the Viet Cong were able to operate freely. The town of Xuyen Moc in the northeast of the province had been cut off for a number of years, and the vitally important Route 15 between Saigon and Vung Tau was often closed by the enemy. This disrupted supplies and communications between the capital and its closest seaport and had had a destabilising effect on the government in Saigon. In light of the formidable Viet Cong and North Vietnamese forces occupying

The newly arrived vehicles from 1 APC Squadron preparing to move from Vung Tau to establish the Task Force base at Nui Dat, early June 1966. (3rd Cavalry Regiment (Vietnam) Association)

the province, the strategic decision to place the Australian Task Force in the geographic centre of the province was meant to challenge directly the enemy's entrenched occupation.

When the Australian Task Force moved into Phuoc Tuy, the enemy forces consisted of approximately 6000 men from the 5th Division's 274 and 275 Regiments. Additionally, a local mobile provincial force known as D445, consisting of 550 men, had operated virtually unchallenged throughout the province for a number of years. In November 1965 the enemy had ambushed and almost destroyed the crack 52nd ARVN Ranger Battalion near Binh Gia on Route 2. Just prior to the Task Force moving into its base at Nui Dat (1 ATF), the US 173rd Brigade suffered heavy casualties when it undertook a clearing operation of the area. The villages of Long Phuoc and Long Tan had been heavily fortified Viet Cong positions, and clearing them and surrounding areas had seen the Americans lose 23 of their men killed in action and a further 160 wounded.

The base was 8 kilometres north of the provincial capital of Baria (also known as Phuoc Le but more commonly referred to as Baria), and sat astride the important Route 2 running north to Long Khanh province. Nui Dat was a jungle-covered knoll, surrounded by an abandoned rubber plantation of about 4000 square metres. On arrival at Nui Dat the Australian troops undertook considerable work in preparing the base area, which required the clearance of secondary growth. They also commenced the erection of defensive perimeters around the base in which areas of defence responsibility for each unit were allocated.

During the first nights of the Australians occupying the newly formed base, and while the defences were being developed, Viet Cong probing parties were sent to 'test' the defensive structures. To show they were more than irritated by the Australian's presence at Nui Dat, the Viet Cong stepped up their harassment and on 12 June 1966 bombarded the base area with mortars.

To counter this attack, 3 Troop was deployed the following day on a reconnaissance patrol to try to locate the mortar position that had been used by the enemy to attack the base. As the troop moved to the west of the base it came under enemy fire, and Trooper Terrence Johnson was reported as sustaining wounds in the encounter and had to be evacuated. The enemy's mortar firing location could not be determined and the troop returned to Nui Dat that evening. The first phase of the establishment of the Task Force base was completed on 14 June 1966 when 6 RAR moved to Nui Dat. Earlier in the day 2 Troop had been deployed to again attempt to locate the position that the enemy had been using to bombard the base with its mortars. The position was eventually located, and the troop officer reported it as being approximately 1.5 kilometres northwest of the base; the location was logged for possible action by the artillery later that evening.[5]

The Squadron had been assigned an area of responsibility on the defence perimeter, northwest of the Nui Dat feature occupied by D Company 5 RAR and later to become known as SAS hill. The Squadron's defence positions were astride Route 2 near the entrance/exit to the Task Force base, with Squadron HQ located on the western side of the road. Initially Route 2 ran through the Task Force base; however, for security purposes the road was later redirected so that it bypassed the base. Accommodation and administration lines consisting of canvas tents surrounded by sandbags were established under the rubber trees that proliferated in the area. These structures were in later years replaced with corrugated iron huts on concrete slabs, which necessitated the removal of the rubber trees. In later months and years these defences were further developed into more complex arrangements, when it was realised that the enemy were prepared to attack the base. The Squadron's area was eventually surrounded with an earthen bank, approximately 2 metres high, interspersed with defensive machine gun bunkers. Barbed wire entanglements extended out past this bank by a further 30 metres into a 'dummy' minefield.

EARLY OPERATIONAL TASKS

The initial primary operational task assigned to the Task Force was to ensure that the main road between Vung Tau and Saigon remained open. To achieve this task the local Viet Cong strongholds had to be closed down, using cordon-and-search operations of the villages and hamlets around Nui Dat that for so long had harboured the enemy. The Task Force commander established an operational strategy based on keeping one battalion at Nui Dat to protect the base when the other infantry battalion was engaged on major operational tasks. To assist with the cordon-and-search operations one of the troops of APCs was assigned to the operational battalion, while the other troops remained at Nui Dat and carried out the general support tasks.

Such was the demand for the Squadron services in the early days of the establishment of the base that the APC became the workhorse of the Task Force, being affectionately named 'road runner' by other units. The multifunctional nature of the APC allowed it to be used in dual operational roles. Accordingly, the Squadron could be called on to act as cavalry or as armoured personnel carriers, undertaking many of the tasks requiring armoured transport. The roles that could be undertaken by the Squadron were classified as follows:[6]

The Squadron lines in the early days of the establishment of the Task Force base at Nui Dat. (3rd Cavalry Regiment (Vietnam) Association)

As APCs:

- infantry insertions, redeployment and extractions, almost always in heavy jungle and often under fire;
- ready reaction force;
- deployment of artillery;
- insertion of SAS patrols;
- logistics tasks, including resupplying infantry and the evacuation of captured personnel and stores;
- armoured ambulance.

As cavalry:

- accurate and sustained machine gun fire;
- mobile mortar base;
- convoy protection;
- reconnaissance;
- cordon-and-search operations;
- flank protection;
- perimeter defence;
- armoured command vehicle duty.

On 21 June 1966 3 Troop was deployed with 6th Battalion RAR to assist in a search-and-destroy operation, codenamed Operation ENOGGERA. The early phase of the operation was centred on the village of Long Phuoc, which had for years been notorious for its Viet Cong activity. Long Phuoc lay approximately 2 kilometres south of Nui Dat and had been heavily fortified by the Viet Cong prior to its clearance by the US 173rd Brigade earlier in the year. The operation proved very successful, with 3 Troop quickly delivering the troops from 6 RAR and then moving off to surround the village in a cordon. The result of this manoeuvre saw four Viet Cong killed and one captured.

It was during Operation ENOGGERA on 21 June 1966 that Callsign 22Alpha from the Squadron's 2 Troop had the dubious distinction of detonating the first anti-tank mine. The incident occurred at 8.15 am on Route 2, approximately 2 kilometres north of the Task Force base, as 22 Section was returning to Nui Dat with a captured rice cache. The damage to the vehicle was minimal and none of the crew was reported as sustaining serious wounds from the explosion. A more serious mine incident occurred on the afternoon of 28 June 1966, when 2nd Lieutenant Ian Savage, Troop Officer of 3 Troop, detonated a mine near Long Phuoc. The carrier was heavily damaged and the crew were saved by a load of rice that had been found by 6 RAR and was being transported back to Nui Dat. The rice, which had been stowed in the back of the carrier, had acted to nullify the explosion and prevent serious wounds to the crew. The carrier, which had been loaned to Savage by his counterpart in 2 Troop, Lieutenant David Watts, was, much to his consternation, written off. Although other Viet Cong anti-tank mines caused only comparatively light damage to the APCs in the first few months of their arrival in South Vietnam, by November 1966 more powerful mines were being brought into use which would cause considerable concern. Anti-tank mines that had been manufactured from plastic explosives or unexploded bombs and shells could make a crater in excess of 6 metres in diameter and, despite precautions, were to account for numerous losses to the Regiment in personnel and equipment during its years of service in South Vietnam.

The cordon-and-search operations were to become most important in the 1 APC Squadron's early period in Phuoc Tuy province. The objective of this type of operation was to discourage Viet Cong sympathisers among the population obtaining supplies and cash, and to cut off recruitment and information sources. The APCs had proven successful here because of their ability to deliver troops at high speed when establishing a cordon or to divert the enemy's attention from the intended area of operation.[7]

The Squadron suffered its first death on 7 July 1966. Trooper Tony Holland was cleaning his Owen machine gun when it accidentally discharged. He was taken to the 36th US Evac Hospital in Vung Tau but died at 4.30 that afternoon.

Four days later, on 11 July, the Squadron almost suffered a further loss when a .50 cal. MG round exploded in the face of Lance Corporal John Wilson while he was servicing his vehicle's machine gun. After his wounds were treated at the 36th US Evac Hospital at Vung Tau he was able to return to the Squadron.

The Squadron was still experiencing problems with its communications system, as the radio sets that had been ordered several months previously had still not arrived. To overcome intervehicle communications problems, some crew commanders were forced to tie strings to their drivers' epaulets so the crew could then operate on a 'horse and cart' steering system. Major Hagerty was later to institute a policy of declaring an APC 'non-operational' if its radio and associated intercom system were not working: modern armoured vehicles, with their speed and associated weapons, were dangerous to all concerned without adequate communications systems.

Additionally, the majority of the carriers in the Squadron were still without steel MG shields, which left the crew commander extremely vulnerable to enemy small arms fire. Many of the crew commanders had placed a piece of timber across the hatch which they used as a seat to lower their profile as well as obtain a degree of comfort while travelling. The crew commander on top of a carrier was likely to be blown off the carrier rather than be caught inside the vehicle with the explosion in the event of the carrier hitting a mine. Unfortunately, while the driver then had greater protection from small arms fire, he could not be protected from injuries caused by anti-tank mine detonations. In fact, the question of some form of driver protection from anti-tank mines was not addressed until the latter years of the war.

OPERATION GAUNTLET

In the months after the establishment of the Task Force base, the Squadron was called on to undertake numerous tasks to ensure security. At this time the Task Force had been concentrating on extending its artillery coverage surrounding the base area. A typical example of the tasks undertaken by the Squadron at this time to support the Task Force's objectives can be seen in the execution of Operation GAUNTLET. This operation required the transfer of a battery of US artillery from Long Binh in Bien Hoa province to Nui Dat to boost its defences. Intelligence reports from agents had recently indicated that the Viet Cong were planning to ambush a convoy somewhere along Route 15, between Baria and northwards through Bien Hoa.

As a preliminary to Operation GAUNTLET, the Squadron had the previous week participated in Operation BRISBANE with 6 RAR to clear areas adjacent to Route 15. Intelligence reports stated that there were numerous telltale signs of extensive enemy activity in the vicinity, confirming the agents' reports of the enemy's intention to ambush Route 15. The Squadron initially transported 6 RAR and 161 Field Battery (RNZA) to FSB Cook, some 6 kilometres west of the provincial capital of Baria and adjacent to Route 15. This move required the Squadron to make two trips from Nui Dat to deploy the Task Force troops in the area of operation. On completion of the move, a troop from the Squadron remained at FSB Cook to support 6 RAR as they continued to search the area.

Operation GAUNTLET commenced on 22 July 1966 and required the Squadron to undertake the escort of US 'A' Battery 2/35 Artillery from Long Binh to Nui Dat. The convoy was particularly large, consisting of 75 trucks and 35 APCs from the Squadron. Two sections of APCs, comprising six carriers, were interspersed between every 15 trucks to give security coverage. The spacing between each serial (two APC sections and 15 trucks) was 200 metres so as to minimise the effects of an ambush on the entire convoy. Squadron HQ, consisting of eight APCs, was placed in the middle of the convoy, allowing Major Hagerty, the escort commander, to control the movement. Four infantry platoons were dispersed on the APCs as an additional counter-ambush measure, while an infantry mortar platoon was deployed with Squadron HQ's mortar carriers.

The operation consisted of four phases over a two-day period. On 22 July, the Squadron was to move to Long Binh with infantry on board and meet the US artillery unit, and escort the US artillery unit to Nui Dat. On 23 July, the Squadron was to escort the returning vehicles (minus guns and personnel) to Long Binh, and return to Nui Dat. Each phase of the operation consisted of a travel distance of approximately 65 kilometres. Part of the considerable planning saw the provision of complete artillery coverage between Nui Dat and Long Binh. To facilitate this coverage, four different artillery coverage areas along the route were required. Also, an aircraft (FAC) was deployed to clear the route of travel before each phase of the operation was carried out.

Operations BRISBANE and GAUNTLET demonstrate the contrasting roles undertaken by the Squadron during this initial period of the Task Force. Operation BRISBANE was typical of the Squadron's armoured personnel carrier role, while Operation GAUNTLET was an excellent example of a cavalry deployment. These and previous

An APC from the Squadron escorting locals to Hoa Long along Route 2, below SAS hill, shortly before a monsoonal storm hit the Task Force base. (3rd Cavalry Regiment (Vietnam) Association)

operations were instrumental in cementing a relationship between the cavalry and the infantry. More importantly, the Squadron had established an understanding in the minds of the two newly arrived infantry battalions that the APCs would be a valuable resource.

While the Squadron continued with other tasks in support of the Task Force's operations, development of the Squadron's area within the Task Force base continued. On 27 July Squadron HQ commenced the construction of bunkers and further development of defensive positions. 3 and Support Troop assisted by laying two rows of barbed wire lines around the Squadron's perimeter. While the other troops developed the Squadron's area, 2 Troop was deployed to assist the Task Force on Operation HOBART, to the east of the base. This operation was generally uneventful; however, the troop suffered the loss of Callsign 20Bravo (albeit subsequently recovered), which sank while crossing the Suoi Da Bang creek.

The next two weeks were quiet for the Squadron, although intelligence reports were suggesting considerable enemy movement and activity occurring around the Task Force's immediate area of operation. These reports were confirmed in mid-August 1966, when Support

Troop reported a contact with the enemy. As well as supporting Australian troops, the Squadron had commenced operations to support the Republic of South Vietnam Army (ARVN). These operations proved valuable in improving local knowledge, and on 15 August Support Troop was deployed to support the 48th ARVN Battalion on a road to the north of Long Dien. To the surprise of the Troop Leader, Lieutenant Ian Bryant, the ARVN battalion commander suddenly and surprisingly identified a group of peasants working in a paddy field as Viet Cong. Callsign 84 immediately engaged a party of six (whom the ARVN commander had identified) with machine gun fire to cut off their escape. Ian Bryant then ordered the other carriers in his troop to drive into the field, where they surrounded the workers and took six Viet Cong prisoner.[8]

The outcome of this contact and subsequent confirmation of the prisoners as Viet Cong indicated that the enemy numbers in the Task Force's immediate area were substantial. It seemed clear that the enemy were about to conduct a major operation against the Australians and their fast-developing base at Nui Dat. This was the start of an action that within a matter of days would test the Squadron's capabilities to the fullest.

2

Long Tan, 1966

The establishment of the Task Force base at Nui Dat had infuriated the local enemy command, whose forces up to that point had operated at will within the province. The prospects of the Viet Cong had suddenly become bleak, as the actions of the Australian Task Force were a serious threat to their efforts at extorting, taxing and recruiting from the local population.

To counter this threat, the enemy command made a decision to inflict a blow on the Task Force which it was hoped would destabilise the Australians' effort and allow them to re-establish their now diminished powers in the province. Intelligence reports were being received at Task Force HQ stating that Local Force D445 and the 5th VC Division were in the area in large numbers and that a sizeable operation against the base at Nui Dat could be expected.

On the evening and early morning of 16/17 August 1966, the Task Force base headquarters and the engineers' area were heavily bombarded with mortar shells. Damage to the base was moderate, but 24 men were wounded. During the bombardment the Squadron was placed on immediate 'stand to', where they remained until morning as it was thought that an attack on the base was imminent. The following morning, Task Force Commander Brigadier Jackson ordered B Company 6 RAR to locate the enemy mortar firing position. When the position had been located, B Company was ordered to return to Nui Dat and was replaced in the field by D Company 6 RAR, which was ordered to locate the enemy that had mortared the Task Force base. Unbeknown to the Australians, the bombardment of Nui Dat was a deliberate ploy by the enemy to draw them out of the base and into a large and well-organised ambush.

At 3.40 pm on 18 August, D Company was moving through the Long Tan rubber plantation, approximately 4 kilometres east of the Task Force base, when it encountered a large enemy force. D Company became pinned down by sustained enemy fire and was unable to counterattack the enemy positions. Then one of the platoons became virtually isolated from the rest of the company and the platoon commander as well as several of his men were killed. The whole company continued to experience heavy and sustained small arms and rocket fire; the wounded could not be evacuated and the company was running desperately low on ammunition. A violent monsoonal storm prevented any air cover. The only support that could be given was an artillery bombardment of the estimated enemy positions from Australian and New Zealand 105 mm gun batteries in Nui Dat. The gunners continued their non-stop fire missions in an effort to keep the enemy at bay and stop them overrunning D Company's position. The indications were that D Company had run into a main force VC unit whose instructions were to completely destroy them and then move on to Nui Dat for an all-out assault on the Australian Task Force base.

Back at Nui Dat, the Australian troops, including members of the Squadron, had been attending a Col Joye concert, but the noise and the amount of artillery fire leaving the base made it obvious to all that there was a substantial battle being fought. At 4.40 pm 1 APC Squadron was placed on 15 minutes' notice to lift a company from the 6 RAR lines within Nui Dat and transport them to assist D Company. The following account of the Squadron's involvement in the relief of D Company 6 RAR in the Long Tan rubber plantation is paraphrased from an address given by Lieutenant Adrian Roberts to a group of army officers while he was still a serving member of the Australian Defence Forces. Lieutenant Roberts' account of events has been interspersed with supporting and factual information supplied by his troop officer and since retired 2nd Lieutenant Ian Savage.

The Squadron at Long Tan

The task of relieving D Company was given to 3 Troop, commanded by Lieutenant Adrian Roberts, who, together with his troop, had that afternoon attended the concert. Not knowing he would be deployed he had allowed troop officer Ian Savage to take his carrier and transport the entertainers, Little Patti and Col Joye and the Joy Boys, from the entertainment area to the airfield and a waiting helicopter. To win a bet, Ian Savage drove Little Patti, who was sitting on the driver's hatch through the Squadron's lines, to much amusement and 'ribbing'. At 4.50 pm Roberts, minus his vehicle, was summoned by Squadron Leader Major

Hagerty and told he was to report immediately to a Major Passey at the 6 RAR lines. Savage had just arrived at the helipad when he received an urgent radio call to return to the Squadron's lines where he immediately mounted his own vehicle, Callsign 30Bravo. All the carriers had already been fully fuelled and armed, and set off for the 6 RAR lines shortly before 5 pm.

At that time the troop was made up of 13 vehicles, of which most were the originals used by 1 Troop PWLH when they arrived in South Vietnam in 1965. Although old and well worn, they had reasonable radios and were equipped with steel MG shields. As a number of the troop's vehicles were unserviceable, the Squadron's CO, Bob Hagerty, decided to allocate a section of 2 Troop to Roberts' troop, thus making a composite troop of 10 vehicles. Unfortunately the 2 Troop vehicles did not have gun shields, which was to prove costly later that night. Ian Savage states that all the carriers had radios, which meant crews were able to communicate on the troop net and intercom facilities. Adrian Roberts' vehicle also had a radio tuned to the Squadron's net.

Deployment

On arrival at A Company 6 RAR lines, Adrian Roberts left to meet the battalion's second in command, Major Brian Passey. Passey had a map of the Long Tan area in front of him and directed Roberts' attention to a large circle on the map where it was thought the battalion's D Company was deployed, giving him an order to drive A Company to that area. No precise grid reference as to D Company's location was available and there was a lack of information on D Company's situation—all making for a confusing and highly dangerous situation.

Compounding these difficulties was the fact that A Company had just returned to Nui Dat from deployment, and the men were looking forward to a barbecue and a couple of beers when the order came that they were to be redeployed. It is most important (in view of later criticism) to understand that at this time the carriers of 3 Troop were lined up and waiting in A Company's lines shortly after 5 pm. Until that stage the men of A Company had been relaxing after being out in the bush for the past three days. To be called on to don their equipment for an urgent deployment must have been especially confusing, not knowing the full extent of D Company's plight at that stage. The men of A Company hurriedly found something to eat and re-equipped themselves after the carriers arrived at their lines. Records show that the APCs of 3 Troop departed A Company's lines at 5.35 pm. This means that it took at least half an hour to board the infantry, a task that would normally take two minutes with the infantry troops lined up and ready to embark (as Roberts had anticipated). Ian Savage states that the troop would otherwise have been ready to move immediately. A Company 6 RAR that evening was under its second in command, Captain Charles Mollison. It should be noted that 6 RAR had had little or no training with the APCs which resulted in a lack of appreciation of the cavalry's operational requirements when deploying with infantry. Many members of the troop found some of the infantry's commanders' inability to recognise the necessity for close cavalry/infantry cooperation frustrating. This issue might easily have been avoided had some training in Australia been devoted to this facet of operational procedures.

Given the urgency of the evolving situation, Roberts decided to head for the battle area via the most direct overland route. This involved travelling southeast from Nui Dat until they reached the Suoi Da Bang creek, where a crossing was to be attempted before heading north. However, a delay was experienced at a closed gap in the Task Force base wire defences, where they were to exit. An engineer had to be located to allow an exit from the base. At this stage, the commanding officer of 6 RAR belatedly decided that he wanted to accompany his A Company to the battle area. Roberts requested his second in command, Ian Savage, on 30Bravo driven by Trooper Geoff Newman, together with Corporal Jock Fotrills, 33Alpha, to return to the 6 RAR lines. On arrival the commanding officer of 6 RAR, Lieutenant Colonel Townsend, and his HQ group were boarded and the two APCs set out in pursuit of the eight carriers that had already left the base. Townsend had his own radio communications and was in contact with D Company during the journey to Long Tan. This additional communication source proved valuable, as Ian Savage was able to relay messages from the battalion commander to his troop leader.

The next obstacle that confronted Adrian Roberts was the continuing torrential monsoonal storm and the flooded Suoi Da Bang creek, which needed to be crossed to meet up with a road running north into the Long Tan rubber plantation. Roberts was familiar with the area, having previously conducted operations along the creekline in conjunction with the establishment of the Task Force base area. It was intended to cross the creek to the south of where D Company was located. In the meantime a message had been received requesting Roberts to wait at the crossing point for the 6 RAR HQ group on board 30Bravo and 33Alpha. However, while monitoring the Squadron's radio, Roberts saw that D Company's situation was becoming desperate and decided to push on. At the crossing point selected by Roberts there was a dam, which prevented the carriers from being swept downstream in the flooded and fast-flowing Suoi Da Bang creek. Several of the carriers were without their pivot steering, an essential element for M113A1

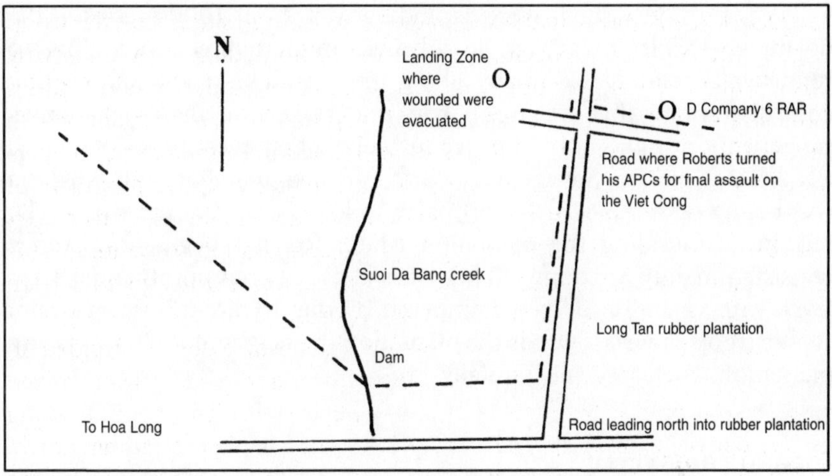

Route taken by 3 Troop on the evening 18 August 1966 to relieve D Company 6 RAR

water-borne operations, and the crews experienced extreme difficulty in the crossing.

By the time the troop had crossed the Suoi Da Bang creek and were on the road leading into the Long Tan rubber plantation, daylight had begun to fade. Roberts saw that with the coming darkness an all-out assault on D Company's position by the enemy was his most immediate problem. The overall situation was confused, with both D Company and enemy positions guessed at rather than known. There was no opportunity to undertake a reconnaissance of the area. Radio reports from D Company indicated that they were experiencing assaults, primarily from the southeast but also from the east, west and north. The enemy were clearly 'tightening the noose' on D Company, and they faced the prospect of being overrun.

Roberts therefore decided to press on towards D Company's position. It was decided that one carrier commanded by Lance Corporal J.J. (Tiny) O'Shea would be left to guard the creek crossing while the remaining seven carriers that had crossed the creek advanced. Roberts lined his understrength troop in 'two-up' assault formation with his own carrier astride the northern road. The three carriers on the right-hand side were commanded by Sergeant R.E. Richards while the left was commanded by Sergeant J.T. O'Reilly. Each section leader's vehicle was between the two other carriers in the section for control purposes, while Roberts in the centre of the two sections had overall control of the seven vehicles. Roberts had estimated that the point where the artillery shells were exploding was about 1000 metres to the north, so the troop started to advance in that direction hoping to rendezvous with D Company along the way. The troop and section control training that the troop had undertaken on the Puckapunyal range without radios would prove invaluable that evening.

Meanwhile Ian Savage, on board 30Bravo, together with 33Alpha was racing with the 6 RAR HQ party to join the rest of the troop. The terrain surrounding the plantation where Roberts began to advance consisted mainly of young rubber trees at about crew commander's eye level, with visibility severely hampered by the driving monsoonal rain. As the troop moved towards the plantation the height of the now mature plantation stock rose substantially.

JOINING THE BATTLE

As the line of APCs from 3 Troop advanced, first contact was made with the enemy on the right-hand side of the formation. The unit commander's log records that first contact was made at 6.05 pm with an enemy of at least company-sized strength. At first it was thought they had suddenly come across D Company's position, by virtue of the number of men sighted and the disciplined manner in which they were moving. This illusion was quickly shattered when Corporal R.J. Gross, the crew commander on Callsign 32Bravo, commenced firing his machine gun at the enemy after recognising camouflaged clothing items not carried by Australian infantry. The troop had come across an enemy company of about 100 men moving across their front from east to west. Once Gross, who was on the right-hand side of the advance, had opened fire, the rest of the troop engaged the enemy with their .50 cal. machine guns while continuing to advance. The enemy were taken completely by surprise because the rain was so heavy it had muffled the sound of the APCs' engines. This allowed the troop an advantage as they intercepted the enemy column. Another large group of enemy troops were engaged as they attempted to withdraw to the north. The commander's log records that the troop killed at least 25 enemy during this contact. Without stopping, the troop pressed northwards—sweeping through the rubber trees and dispatching the enemy as they went. It was later disclosed that the enemy troops were from the D445 Battalion and were headed to assist with the encirclement of D Company. From the troop's radio net, Ian Savage could tell that the fighting between the seven APCs ahead of him and the enemy was extremely fierce.

Corporal J.A. Carter on board Callsign 39Mike (fitted out as an ambulance but without the red cross), which was also on the right-hand side of the troop's formation, detected men in what appeared to be green uniforms. Aware that they might be D Company he hesitated briefly, but immediately came under fire. Roberts observed a .57 mm recoilless anti-tank rifle team attacking Carter's carrier. Both radio antennas on Carter's vehicle were shot away after two rounds fired by the RCL team exploded in a rubber tree next to his carrier. Despite this Carter opened fire with his .50 cal. machine gun, which subsequently jammed. Carter instructed his driver, Trooper P.S. McNamara, to stop the vehicle, and calmly climbed out of the crew commander's hatch with McNamara's Owen machine gun. With total disregard for his own safety Carter engaged the enemy, killing the RCL team just before another round was fired at his carrier. The round exploded, dazing McNamara and the infantry on board the carrier. Undeterred, Carter continued to engage the enemy while McNamara threw ammunition magazines to him, enabling him to kill a further five. Carter's action effectively drew attention away from other members of the troop, who continued to advance to the north.

Roberts was aware that the enemy troops who operated the RCL weapons usually worked in teams of two, so he again halted the advance and looked for the other anti-tank team. The acting company commander of A Company 6 RAR, Captain Mollison, who up to this stage had been riding down inside Roberts' carrier to monitor the 'radio traffic', emerged and urged him to continue. After what he described as a heated exchange, Roberts refused Mollison's request and elected to wait until he was certain there were no more RCL teams in the area. Roberts was aware of the Viet Cong ploy of deliberately creating maximum confusion and then ambushing troops as they tried to recover the situation. Here it should be pointed out that a protocol had previously been established which dictated that, while infantry were on board the APCs, the troop leader had overall authority, even if the APC commander was outranked by the infantry commander on board his vehicle.

Compounding this problem was the action of some members of A Company, who had taken it on themselves to dismount from their carriers once the fighting had started, adding to Roberts' annoyance at the issues raised by Mollison. The infantrymen dismounting had added to the confusion confronting the troop leader. The members of A Company up to this stage had been in the back of the carriers, and were totally disoriented when they emerged. Their actions, while admirable, only impeded the crew commanders' ability to fire their .50 cal. machine guns without hitting infantrymen on the ground. Additionally, it had slowed up the progress of the troop to its objective. The instructions given to Roberts by Major Passey were to take A Company to relieve D Company; how he got the men there was his problem. At no time was an order given by either Roberts or the infantry command to dismount the infantry before they reached D Company's position.

On the left-hand side of the road, between the rubber plantation and the Suoi Da Bang creek, the section being led by Sergeant O'Reilly, Callsign 23, was receiving continued heavy enemy small arms fire. O'Reilly, whose section was on loan to 3 Troop from 2 Troop, was knocked unconscious when he was grazed on the head by a small arms round fired by the enemy. At that stage O'Reilly's driver, Trooper P.E. 'Boots' Turner, was unaware that Adrian Roberts had been attempting to contact his crew commander on the troop radio net. Further out, on the left-hand side of O'Reilly's section, Corporal Peter Clements on board 23Bravo had been seriously wounded when he was shot in the stomach and fell down into the carrier. His driver, undeterred, drove the APC over the enemy machine gun crew that had wounded his crew commander.

Roberts, realising that Clements' carrier was in serious trouble, requested his troop sergeant, Sergeant Noel Lowes, who had been travelling on board his carrier, to take command of Clements' carrier. This meant that Lowes had to run about 200 metres across open ground under sustained enemy fire. Lowes, whose complexion Roberts describes as almost Asian in appearance, was almost shot by one of the infantrymen on Clements' carrier as he raced over the ground. On reaching the APC, Noel Lowes reported that Peter Clements' wounds were very serious. Roberts immediately ordered Lowes to withdraw the carrier with Clements and two other wounded infantrymen, so he swung back to the west. Despite Lowes' incredible act of bravery his feat was never recognised, regardless of a recommendation by Roberts and Savage. Unbeknown to Roberts, Clements' carrier contained part of A Company's HQ which was carried back with the wounded Clements. Roberts' compassionate stance in ordering Noel Lowes to withdraw the carrier was criticised by the acting commander of A Company, Captain Mollison, a criticism Roberts later acknowledged. However, it was noted that not one of the troops in the Company HQ on board the vehicle made any attempt to disembark from the carrier before it withdrew. It might also be noted that Peter Clements' carrier was one of the 2 Troop carriers 'on loan' to Roberts that evening, and that Roberts may thus have felt some added responsibility to evacuate him.

On the left-hand side of the advance the enemy had brought the carriers to a halt. A bullet had jammed in the barrel of one of the carriers .50 cal. machine guns. This necessitated the APC crew's changing the barrel under the direct observation of the enemy. The two crew members felt that the best option in the circumstances was to pretend the enemy could not see them, so they hastily changed the barrel in full view of the enemy troops but under cover of the infantry on board. Fortunately, the enemy did not have a commander on the spot or the capability to take advantage of the situation, and as soon as the barrel was changed the crew again opened fire on the enemy.

The section on the right-hand side of the advance, not knowing what had happened on the left, continued the advance to the north and by this time had reached the point just short of where the Australian artillery shells were falling. Adrian Roberts had attempted to 'turn off' the barrage along the line which the troop were using to try to reach D Company, but the message was misinterpreted and the wrong barrage was stopped. The noise created by the exploding shell bursts was being muffled by the rain and the crew's radio headsets, although the troop were aware of the constant grey and brown explosions of the shells in front of and around them. The APCs from Sergeant Richard's section on the right-hand side of the advance raced through the artillery barrage and the Viet Cong lines, with guns firing, and fortuitously almost drove into the right-hand extremity of D Company HQ's position. Realising that Roberts and the others were still some distance back, the section wheeled east past the now cheering infantrymen and in a looping manoeuvre raced back through the artillery barrage to Roberts' position.

It was now about 6.45 pm and Ian Savage, who had returned to Nui Dat to collect the commanding officer of 6 RAR, had caught up with Roberts. In his haste to catch up, Geoff Newman, the driver of 30Bravo, drove straight at the Suoi Da Bang creek without stopping to push out the vehicle's trim vane. He did this while the vehicle was at full speed and in mid-air, just before it hit the water. The driver of 33Alpha, taking his cue from Geoff Newman, did the same, and both carriers hit the water at the same time. Once the two carriers were on the other side of the creek they were joined by 'Tiny' O'Shea and his crew, who had awaited their arrival anxiously on board 33Bravo. The three carriers linked up and again set off in pursuit of the rest of the troop. As Ian Savage's section approached the edge of the artillery barrage zone where the other carriers were now located, Lt Colonel Townsend received a message from Major Harry Smith, company commander of D Company 6 RAR, stating that the enemy were lining up for an all-out assault on their position and he was doubtful that the company could sustain this attack; he felt they would probably be overrun. Ian Savage distinctly recalls Townsend instructing him to relay an urgent message to Adrian Roberts, alerting him to the enemy's intention and telling him to get to the company as soon as possible and break up the enemy attack. Roberts then wheeled his troop right and started moving to the east along a road that traversed the plantation.

The enemy had been continuously probing D Company's defensive perimeter, determining the strength of the Australians. The forward elements of the enemy were repeatedly calling out information on D Company's locations and estimated strength to their commanders in the rear. They knew that the Australians could not sustain an all-out assault given their superior numbers, and were now preparing an assault intended to completely overrun D Company. Fortunately, the monsoonal storm had hidden the sound of the approaching APCs and the enemy were not aware that 3 Troop were now close by. Ian Savage attributes the troop's ability to get so close to the enemy's position not only to the sound of the rain but more importantly to the fact that the carriers had not yet turned on their headlights despite the darkness now engulfing the area.

The troop now proceeded at a much-reduced pace, owing to the fact that Roberts was not aware of the precise position of D Company's three platoons and the Company HQ. Additionally, Roberts was mindful of the fire power of the APC's main armament, the .50 cal. machine gun, and was cautious not to overshoot the enemy's position, knowing that D Company was now close by. Ian Savage recalls manoeuvring his carrier behind and to one side of his troop leader's vehicle. He says he had great admiration for the way Adrian Roberts was conducting himself and especially the calm and confident manner in which he was controlling the troop over the radio net.

As the troop moved slowly forward towards D Company's position the carriers began to receive continuous and heavy enemy fire. It is said that the Viet Cong command, on becoming aware of 3 Troop's position, had issued instructions that the APCs were not to be allowed to reach D Company. However, the darkness and the continuing monsoonal storm confused and hindered the Viet Cong's dangerous RCL teams from effectively stopping the push of the troop vehicles. As the carriers made their approach on and past D Company's position the infantrymen observed the APCs rolling straight over a number of enemy positions, crushing the hapless victims who had never before encountered armour used to this effect.

Roberts had instructed his driver Bill O'Rourke to head for a small hut on the eastern side of the plantation, around which two D Company platoons had positioned themselves. On reaching this objective, Ian Savage states, the troop continued the assault to the east, driving the enemy back from D Company's defensive perimeter. Very heavy enemy machine gun and small arms fire was received as the troop continued the assault. Roberts saw enemy tracer rounds coming straight at the carriers, and thought he could swerve to avoid the rounds. In reality the enemy were aiming their weapons too high, and the troop was lucky to avoid any further casualties. Ian Savage recalls firing his .50 cal. machine guns between Adrian Roberts' carrier and another APC, but was told by Roberts to check his fire because of its closeness. Despite this, the APCs continued to charge the enemy who had no answer to these tactics and were finally forced to retreat as the attack was broken.

Roberts finally broke off his troop's engagement at the request of the commanding officer of 6 RAR, and returned to D Company HQ's position where a protective cordon was formed. A Company were finally disembarked and placed between the carriers as added protection. Two of the platoons from D Company flanked Company HQ; however, the third D Company platoon (11 Platoon), which was to the east at that stage, had still not been accounted for and had been termed 'lost'. The troop waited in the darkness for the expected enemy counter-assault although, despite some sniper fire, this did not eventuate. A hasty orders group was organised by Lt Colonel Townsend once it became obvious that the enemy had retreated. It was decided that the Australian dead and wounded would be loaded onto the APCs and then with D Company on board move to the west. On the western edge of the rubber plantation a landing zone was to be established and the dead and wounded evacuated. The dead infantrymen were gathered together under the supervision of D Company's Company Sergeant Major WO2 Kirby, then loaded onto the first carrier with the wounded following in the other carriers. At that stage 11 Platoon remained isolated, and it was presumed that all its members had been killed.

By this time darkness had fallen, and the night was pitch black. The commanding officer of D Company 6 RAR had asked Roberts to facilitate the task of coordinating the withdrawal of the dead and dustoff flights for his wounded men. The APCs were manoeuvred around without lights and formed up in a single line facing west. Ian Savage states that during this move his carrier ended up as the lead vehicle and that most of the dead were loaded onto the back of his carrier. Adrian Roberts still did not know where the enemy were and whether they would ambush the carriers as they left the battlefield, so it was decided that they should leave the area as quickly as possible. To facilitate this Roberts gave an order over the troop net that all carriers were to start their engines and switch on their headlights simultaneously, then make a dash through the rubber trees to the plantation's western perimeter. In fact, this was the first time the carriers had turned on their headlights that evening. Ian Savage says that it was a frightening experience, but pays tribute to his driver for leading the column away from the battle area as he steered at full speed through the rubber trees.

On reaching the western side of the rubber plantation, Roberts formed his APCs into a large protective square to make a landing zone for the helicopters. He then instructed his crews to switch on the red illumination lights inside the back of the carriers. The red glow from the interior of the APCs through the open cargo hatches identified the landing zone for the aircrews of the helicopters, who were then able to land their aircraft in the middle of the square and load the dead and wounded.

(As a sideline, at this point of his talk Roberts points out that the men of D Company 6 RAR were understandably reluctant to handle their own dead, so this task was left to the men from 3 Troop. He goes on to state that when Ian Savage's carrier in which the dead had been transported was cleaned out, the area under the carrier's floor boards was awash with blood and rainwater. From that point on whenever the crew mounted the vehicle they would sense the stench that remained in the carrier.)

By this time B Company 6 RAR, which had also been deployed on foot, had reached the area in which the landing zone had been established. The troop, together with the infantry, were stood-to all night awaiting further attacks by the enemy, which fortunately never eventuated. Roberts and the others who had been attached to his carrier spent the night in the back of the carrier, staring at each other in what he describes as 'dazed shock'.

Meanwhile, back at the Squadron's base in Nui Dat, warning orders were issued to 2 Troop together with Callsigns 8, 98 and 9Echo that they were to prepare to move at 6 am the next day to support 3 Troop on Operation SMITHFIELD, as the deployment was to become known.

The next morning at 6 am 2 Troop with Callsigns 8, 98 and 9Echo left the Task Force base to join 3 Troop on the edge of the Long Tan rubber plantation. 3 Troop was given the task of transporting D Company 6 RAR back to the scene of the battle to look for 11 Platoon, which had been 'lost' the previous evening. The platoon was located, with all its members dead except one. The eerie sound of the platoon's radio which had remained on squelch broke the silence that engulfed the area as they approached the platoon's position.

Later, on the morning of 19 August 1966, Ian Savage, together with Corporal John Carter and Corporal Paul Fottrill, were charged with undertaking the grim task of battlefield clearance. Together with a section from A Company 6 RAR they returned to the area where 3 Troop had fought their way through to D Company the previous evening, in order to collect the enemy's dead. On reaching this area the infantry dismounted and came into contact with three enemy. After a brief fire fight two enemy were killed and one was taken prisoner. Later,

Callsign 39Mike being used to clear casualties on 19 August 1966, the day after Long Tan. This carrier was commanded by Corporal John Carter and was attacked by Viet Cong RCL teams the previous evening as 3 Troop moved to relieve D Company 6 RAR. (3rd Cavalry Regiment (Vietnam) Association)

John Carter was able to recover a number of the weapons that had been fired at him during the previous evening.

The troop then set out to sweep to the south, but one of the carriers turned over on its side when it accidentally drove into an old trench. The rest of the day was spent attempting to get it upright. At 4 am Callsign 9Echo with Major Bob Hagerty on board was recalled to Nui Dat to organise the defence of the Task Force base, as another attack by the enemy was expected. The exhausted members of 3 Troop eventually returned to the contact area, where they spent the night and were able to get some sleep for the first time in 48 hours, many still in shock at the events of the previous evening. The troop returned to the Task Force base the next day, and thus ended the Squadron's role in one of the most decisive battles fought during the Vietnam War.[1]

The larger context

The action by the cavalry was a truly remarkable effort considering the adversity in which Roberts' men had to operate. Not least was the fact that the vehicles had been in South Vietnam for over 12 months and were in need of a complete overhaul. Compounding this was the limited radio facilities on board. It has not been appreciated that the crossing of the flooded Suoi Da Bang creek in itself was a major feat, as was manoeuvring a troop of fully laden 13-ton armoured vehicles. Roberts had identified the urgent need to get to the battle area quickly, and a person with any knowledge of the M113A1 will appreciate the considerable risk that Roberts took in achieving this objective. Not least was the fact that the vehicles might have sunk in the flooded creek, and that a less direct route would have taken considerably longer, thus delaying their arrival. Also, the monsoonal storm and lack of detailed orders

Callsign 32 provides protection on the edge of the Long Tan rubber plantation as battlefield clearance is undertaken the day after Long Tan. (3rd Cavalry Regiment (Vietnam) Association)

made navigation and determining the precise position of D Company extremely difficult.

Well might the men of D Company 6 RAR have cheered the arrival of the cavalry. Just before the arrival of the APCs, the Viet Cong commanders were marshalling their troops for an all-out assault to overrun D Company's position. At that stage D Company was running low on ammunition, had a large number of their men either killed or wounded, and could not be evacuated. Given the massed enemy troops and counterfire that the troop members encountered as they approached D Company's position, the rescue was never going to be easy. Also, to get to D Company, 3 Troop had to drive through their own artillery barrage, which was firing continuously around D Company's position to keep the enemy at bay.

Historians to date have largely tended to focus on the Battle of Long Tan (as it became known) in terms of the survival of D Company 6 RAR, which faced untold adversity against a larger enemy force—and rightly so. However, what is seen as a historic military victory, because of the heroic efforts of the men of 3 Troop 1 APC Squadron in relieving the beleaguered D Company, could have turned out to be one of Australia's worst military defeats. Additionally, irreparable damage would have been caused to the Australian Task Force's reputation. The advantage the enemy would have gained had they been able to overrun D Company 6 RAR would have placed the Australians in an invidious position. The political effect would have most likely seen future offensive operations seriously inhibited. Then, not only would the local enemy forces' morale have been boosted, but further large-scale ambushing operations on the Australians would probably have closely followed.

It is important to realise that the cavalry played the critical role that evening, and their action should not in any way be viewed as subordinate to other units in the overall context of this battle. Perhaps the saddest indictment on those in the command structure who did know of 3 Troop's efforts was the fact that no mention was ever made of 1 APC Squadron in 6 RAR's after-action report. This lack of recognition by those in command has been noted by many, including the men of D Company 6 RAR. Adrian Roberts and Ian Savage were invited by Major Harry Smith to join him and his officers in their mess for a few beers as an act of appreciation on 20 August 1966. Both Roberts and Savage were afforded honorary membership of the mess in recognition of the troop's efforts.

While Adrian Roberts was subsequently criticised for taking too long to get to the battle area, he maintains that no orders were ever given to him and that he was unable to receive any. The only order he received was the obscure one from Major Passey of 6 RAR to drive A Company to an ambiguous area on the map in the Long Tan rubber plantation. Added to this was the fact that the troop were forced to wait at least half an hour to mount A Company 6 RAR. All other actions taken by Roberts were on his own initiative, which for a junior officer thrust into such a situation were both thoughtful and courageous. On balance and from the evidence now available, the criticism that was levelled at Roberts at that time is inappropriate and unwarranted.

Casualties inflicted on the enemy included 245 dead, several hundred wounded and large amounts of arms and ammunition captured. Australian infantry losses included 17 killed and 22 wounded in action.

From 3 Troop, Corporal P.E. Clements, who had serious gunshot wounds from the action, died on 27 August 1966 of his wounds, despite Roberts' compassionate stance in immediately evacuating him from the battle area.

Corporal J.A. Carter was awarded the Distinguished Conduct Medal for his action in neutralising the anti-tank weapon crew. The citation for his award reads:[2]

> When contact was made with the enemy, Corporal Carter's vehicle was engaged by fire from .57 millimetre recoilless rifle, machine gun and small arms fire. The projectile from the .57 millimetre recoilless rifle missed his vehicle and exploded against a rubber tree. Corporal Carter returned fire using his .50 calibre machine gun. The gun jammed. He then grabbed the driver's Owen Machine Carbine and without hesitation leapt onto the top of his vehicle and returned fire, killing the .57 Recoilless Rifle team a fraction after another .57 millimetre round had been fired. This round exploded and dazed the crew and passengers. Corporal Carter still undeterred continued to fire, killing five other enemy.
>
> By his action Corporal Carter also drew additional fire onto himself enabling the other vehicles of the Troop to advance.
>
> Through the action that was fought at very close range, Corporal Carter showed outstanding courage, initiative and determination. His actions were an inspiration to all his comrades and contributed greatly to the success of the assault by the relief force, the heavy casualties inflicted on the enemy, and immediately afterwards, the relief of 'D' company, 6 Battalion, Royal Australian Regiment.

Lieutenant F.A. Roberts received the award of Mentioned in Dispatches for his leadership of 3 Troop in the battle. The citation for his award reads:[3]

> Lieutenant Roberts' personal conduct in commanding and controlling his Troop was of the highest order. While moving to the 'D' Company location, the Troop encounted an enemy company equipped with anti-tank weapons, and at this time the Troop consisted of only seven armoured personnel carriers. After a short action the enemy withdrew to the east.
>
> Continuing the advance the Troop moved through supporting artillery fire, as the fire could not be stopped due to a temporary loss of radio communications.
>
> One Crew Commander was seriously wounded in the chest and was evacuated. The Troop carried out a final assault and forced the enemy to withdraw from the 'D' Company position.
>
> Later, during the night in pitch blackness the Troop assisted evacuating 'D' Company and its casualties to a helicopter landing zone. Lieutenant Roberts, under orders from the Officer Commanding 'D' Company, acted as controller for the helicopters.
>
> At all times Lieutenant Roberts acted with skill and judgement and led his Troop with determination and courage. The action was accomplished in spite of the poor radio communications existing in the No 3 Troop vehicles, and in spite of heavy torrential rain and poor light during the enemy contacts.

The Australian Task Force had demonstrated to the enemy that they were more than capable of matching them tactically, and that they were willing to stand up and fight despite the overwhelming numbers opposing them. Furthermore, the enemy now realised that the Australians would not be so easily intimidated as their high command had anticipated.

The Cavalry had once and for all proven their resourcefulness and how invaluable the unit was to the Task Force. However, it is said that the Task Force Commander, Brigadier Jackson, deliberated long and hard about whether the APCs should be deployed, given the seriousness of the situation confronting him. There were two main issues he needed to consider. First, at the time a decision had to be made, Jackson was facing the strong possibility of losing an entire infantry company. Second, the APCs as relief force would undoubtedly be confronted by a large enemy force, including numerous anti-tank RCL teams. He feared that several of the APCs would be 'knocked out' in the fading light in which the battle was being fought. Fortunately there was an RAAC officer (believed to be Captain R.V. Musgrove) at Jackson's 1 ATF HQ who understood the capabilities of the M113A1 and the tactics they could employ to retrieve the situation confronting D Company 6 RAR. This officer argued that the APCs should at least initially be sent to the battle area; if substantial damage or losses to the APCs and their crews arose they could always be withdrawn from the action. The notion of the APCs as mere 'battlefield taxis' was still held by some in Australia's High Command, with many unable to come to terms with the idea that the M113A1 was a fighting vehicle. The action of this RAAC officer in persuading the Task Force commander to send the carriers from 3 Troop was perhaps the most critical decision that Jackson made that afternoon.

Because the cavalry had made it abundantly clear to the Viet Cong that they should not take on the more heavily armed APCs directly, they decided that more lethal devices would be needed. Accordingly, more devastating and powerful anti-tank mines were now to be manufactured for specific use against the Australian APCs. The Soviet-produced RPG2 and RPG7 anti-armour rocket-propelled grenade launcher would also be employed against the APCs. What's more, the enemy would learn to become more judicious in their development of these weapons, and therefore APC targets would become more selective and the damage more destructive.

The final words belong to Lieutenant Roberts, as he pays tribute to his men's bravery and dedication to duty: 'Not one member of the Troop backed off that afternoon.'

3

1966–67

In the week following the Battle of Long Tan the Squadron supported both 5 and 6 RAR to clear the entire Long Tan area. The Squadron also undertook numerous clearing patrols around the Task Force base during this time to validate the security of the area. However, the mauling that the enemy had received at the hands of the Australians had seen them lie low to 'lick their wounds' before again taking on a large force. On 27 August 1966 the Squadron was given the sad news that at 11.30 that morning Corporal Peter Clements had died of his wounds. To ensure the enemy were not contemplating another offensive, 2 Troop was deployed to the Long Tan area on 24 September for a further search of the area. While 2 Troop searched the plantation, 3 Troop and Support Troop moved to a blocking position about 3 kilometres south of the Long Tan plantation. No further evidence of the enemy was found during this deployment, so the Squadron moved back to the Task Force area later that afternoon.

Around this time the Australian Task Force undertook a program of building trust among the local communities, and the Squadron undertook a visit to the village of Hoa Long on 29 September. During this visit members of the Squadron helped organise the children's annual school party and took the children for rides in the carriers.[1]

At the end of September 1966, 3 Troop was in Nui Dat and deployed as the Task Force's Ready Reaction Force; this was to facilitate each section in the troop being sent to Vung Tau having their radios converted to the type currently used by the other vehicles in the Squadron. While these conversions were taking place, 2 and Support Troops undertook another cavalry role when they combined with infantry from 5 RAR on Operation CROWS NEST. During this operation large tracts of land on either side of Route 2 around the Duc Than area were successfully swept for enemy positions. Operation CROWS NEST was focused specifically on securing Route 2, the major road leading north into Long Khanh province and of strategic importance to the Australian Task Force area. As the operation continued, a section of APCs from the Squadron came into contact with three enemy troops on the northern outskirts of Ngai Giao village at 11.50 am on 1 October. The enemy were engaged with the Squadron's mortar carriers, but results of the contact could not be determined. Two days after the mortar carriers had engaged the enemy to the north of Ngai Giao, Callsign 81Bravo detonated an anti-tank mine adjacent to Route 2. The site of the attack was about 1 kilometre west of Ngai Giao village. Although there were no casualties among the crew, the APC was extensively damaged and needed to be recovered back to the Squadron's base at Nui Dat.

In a subsequent deployment during Operation CANBERRA, conducted between 6 and 10 October, the Squadron again operated with and accompanied 5 RAR in a sweep of Route 15. At the conclusion of this operation on 10 October, and as they began to lift the battalion from the area, two carriers from 2 Troop suffered damage when anti-tank mines were detonated. The first mine attack was against Callsign 20Alpha, which detonated an anti-tank mine at 11.40 am approximately 4 kilometres south of Phu My. A further attack occurred at 12.37 pm against another carrier some 300 metres south of the attack earlier that morning. The extent of damage to the carriers was not reported, although one of the carriers needed recovery to enable it to return to Nui Dat. The other APC was reported to be repaired at the site of the attack, and was able to resume operations with the troop later that afternoon. Ian Savage notes from his personal diaries that the detonation of these two mines brought the total number of carriers from the Squadron involved in anti-tank mine attacks to six.

The following day, 2 Troop had moved further south and was in an area some 10 kilometres west of Baria to assist in preparation for the next Task Force deployment, which was to be Operation ROBIN. At 12.39 pm Callsign 20Alpha reported receiving sniper fire. After receiving seven well-aimed rounds from the enemy the troop leader made a decision to withdraw from the area, as the sniper's position could not be determined and his accuracy was improving with each shot. 2 Troop and Support Troop commenced Operation ROBIN on 15 October, while 3 Troop remained at the Task Force's base as Ready Reaction Force. Operation ROBIN was one of a series of four 'mini-operations' that were carried out with 5 RAR to secure Route 15 running north to Long Binh. The

Squadron's role in these operations was to clear and secure Route 15 for a newly arrived American brigade, which was moving north to the base at Bear Cat. The Squadron's primary task in ROBIN was to cruise along the road supporting the various infantry units with the APCs' speed and fire power. Occasionally, infantry patrols were transported across swampy areas as the search operations continued.

Towards the end of October 1966 the Squadron was again deployed with 5 RAR, this time to the nearby Nui Thi Vai hills overlooking Route 15. In this deployment the Squadron's role was to undertake simulated patrol operations while in fact ferrying troops into the jungle hides of the Viet Cong. This operation caught the enemy by surprise—10 Viet Cong were reported killed—and highlighted the degree of skill that the Squadron, and specifically 5 RAR, were attaining in these types of surprise cordon-and-search deployments.[2]

By this time, Squadron Commanding Officer Major Hagerty had realised that the original structure of the Squadron was inadequate for the tasks that it was being asked to perform, so he set about reorganising the Squadron into a more operative form. On 17 October the two previous APC troops and Support Troop were converted into three troops: 2, 3 and 4 Troops. This brought the number of vehicles in each troop to 11 APCs, with Callsigns 29Juliet, 29Mike, 39Juliet and 39Mike being transferred to 4 Troop. Callsigns 81Alpha, 81Bravo, 82Alpha and 82Bravo were transferred to Squadron HQ to form the Squadron's first Support Section. This meant that the carriers now in Support Section were mortar carriers. Although the mortar carriers that had reverted to Squadron HQ's Support Section were fitted out to take infantry mortars, they were used only occasionally in this role.

These changes meant that the Squadron could now lift three infantry companies. Squadron HQ, which now contained Callsigns 9 and 9Echo together with the Support Section of carriers, was strong enough to act independently if needed. This made the Squadron's cavalry role much more flexible and allowed each troop and the support section to be divided into four separate units. By including the troop leader or the troop officer in one of the sections, a small, powerfully armed unit was created. In total, A Squadron now had 37 fully operational vehicles in service.

Additionally, to improve and promote greater understanding between the cavalry and infantry, some training was carried out with the mortar carriers and the infantry. However, this proved ineffective, as the infantry units were in an operation theatre and did not really like training in such an environment.

Mortar tracks near Xuyen Moc. (3/4 Cavalry Regiment Museum)

Operation YASS

On 1 November 1966 the whole Squadron returned to Nui Dat, where much-needed and long-overdue maintenance and reconditioning of the vehicles were carried out before the next series of operations. The Squadron again deployed in force on 11 November on Operation YASS. Squadron HQ, 2 and 4 Troops travelled to the area of operation some 9 kilometres east of the Task Force base, where shortly after their arrival at 9.25 am they were engaged by a sizeable enemy force. After the ensuing fire fight with the enemy force, seven Viet Cong were taken prisoner of war. One of the POWs subsequently volunteered to lead the Squadron to the force's main base camp, which he identified as being nearby. The camp was attacked a short time later resulting in two enemy killed and one wounded and evacuated for medical treatment.

The Squadron then moved further south of the area in which Operation YASS was being conducted and on 21 November came into contact with two Viet Cong, who were engaged with machine gun fire. Results of the contact could not be determined. The following day 2 Troop was deployed in an area some 15 kilometres directly east of the Task Force base and 8 kilometres west of Xuyen Moc. Early that morning they began an extended search of the area and located a 400-pound rice cache. Shortly afterwards, at 9.10 am, they were engaged by six Viet Cong troops. The results of the contact could not be determined as the enemy immediately retreated once the troop opened fire with machine guns. The troop again pressed on with its search of the area and shortly afterwards located another 1000-pound rice cache and a substantial supply of medical equipment. Blood trails leading from the area indicated that the troop had inflicted a number of casualties on the enemy during its contact earlier that morning.

On the 23 November, 2 Troop moved slightly south of the area it had been searching the previous day and found one of the largest enemy caches of the war. The cache consisted of many thousands of pounds of rice and a large amount of other logistical supplies. The troop had uncovered one of the enemy's main logistical supply areas, and the discovery was to have dire consequences on the Viet Cong's immediate war effort in the province. The area in which the troop was operating was obviously a major support facility and contained a number of the enemy's supply dumps, so the search of the area continued. On 24 November, while 2 Troop continued its search of the area, it sighted and engaged five Viet Cong troops. The enemy fled as soon as they came under fire from the troop's machine guns but the results of the contact could not be determined. The following morning, 2 Troop was deployed along the banks of the Suoi Rai river. As it moved along the western bank of the river approximately 7 kilometres southwest of Xuyen Moc, it was engaged by an enemy force. The enemy, who had been waiting for the troop to approach, fired command-detonated mines at the APCs. Callsigns 20Bravo and 22 immediately returned fire on the enemy's position, killing two. No members of the troop sustained wounds as a result of the attack, nor were any of the APCs seriously damaged, so the troop continued its search of the area. Later that afternoon the troop was again ambushed by the enemy, who again directed command-detonated mines at the APCs. As a result of this attack, three infantrymen on board the carriers were wounded and one of the APCs sustained some damage to its hatches.

During this part of the operation 4 Troop had been deployed to the north of where 2 Troop had been operating, and on 28 November fired on two enemy troops with unknown results. The following morning at 10.45, 2 Troop contacted a large Viet Cong group consisting of over 30 troops who were moving in a westerly direction. The troop attacked with machine guns, but the enemy immediately fled into dense jungle in an attempt to retreat to the east. To cut off their escape route, 3 and 4 Troops were directed to move to blocking positions to the east of where 2 Troop had initiated the contact. 2 Troop remained close to the location where the contact had been initiated in case the enemy attempted to turn back on their intended escape route. The Squadron's attempts to block the enemy's escape proved fruitless: the enemy were masters at avoiding cordons in jungle conditions and had managed to slip through the blocking positions. One of the enemy troops who had been wounded in the contact earlier that day was later taken prisoner as the Squadron continued to sweep the area.[3]

The start of December saw 3 and 4 Troops deployed on operations with A and C Companies 6 RAR, while Squadron HQ and 2 Troop were deployed to the west of the Suoi Rai river approximately 8 kilometres east of Dat Do. On 3 December, 2 Troop was redeployed with the 43rd ARVN Battalion approximately 4 kilometres west of the previous deployment area. The ARVN Battalion had been pursuing a sizeable enemy force consisting of two companies of Viet Cong northwards, and

Callsign 21Alpha edges into the water as it begins to cross the Son Don Nai river during Operation INGRAM. (3/4 Cavalry Regiment Museum)

had requested the support of the Squadron which had become highly regarded by the 43rd. However, much to the frustration of 2 Troop, the pursuit had to be called off when the APCs encountered the flooded and swollen Song Ba Dap river, which could not be crossed. Despite this the troop, who had sighted part of the enemy force, fired machine guns across the river at the escaping enemy. The Troop then returned to the Task Force base at Nui Dat.

The Squadron carried out its normal support tasks over the following two weeks. Infantry units were ferried to new areas of operation and patrols were carried out to maintain security around the Task Force's area. Christmas Day was no different for the Squadron, with deployments continuing despite obervation of the holiday by several of the Task Force's units. The commander's log notes that the Squadron was deployed at 1.30 pm when they boarded A Company 5 RAR, and proceeded to spend the afternoon patrolling an area some 3 kilometres to the northwest of the Task Force base. The Squadron returned to Nui Dat at 5.45 pm after a long, hot day in the scrub thinking of their families and friends back home in Australia.

The following day, Boxing Day, saw no let-up for the troops, with the Squadron tasked to lift elements of 6 RAR and 101 Battery to Dat Do. At 12.45 pm, as the Squadron moved along Route 23 some 4 kilometres west of Dat Do it was engaged with sniper fire. Because the area in which the attack occurred was heavily populated, fire could not be returned for fear of hitting some of the local residents. The only option available to the APC crews was to increase speed and race past the snipers' position to avoid casualties. The following day, on Route 44 to the north of Phuoc Hai village on the eastern side of the Long Hai peninsula, Support Section was engaged by the enemy with a command-detonated mine. Callsign 81 received the force of the mine explosion and the vehicle's crew commander, Corporal Alan Buckingham, was wounded as a result. The vehicle was reported to have sustained some damage, but this was mainly confined to the hatches.[4]

Lengthy delays in rectifying the Squadron's communications problems were still being experienced, despite an order for the supply of radios being approved by AHQ in 1965. When the radios eventually arrived several of the sets were unserviceable, and brackets and leads were not available. The problems were finally overcome in late 1966, when every carrier in the Squadron was fitted out with an AN/VRC-12 and an AN/GRC-125 series radio by 101 Field Workshop.[5] 3 Troop had been sent down to Vung Tau on 1 October 1966 to have its radios converted to the 12 and 125 sets, having previously operated with the original radios inherited from 1 Troop when it took over its vehicles on arrival in Vietnam in May 1966.

During the year two members of the Squadron had been killed and another four wounded or injured.

1967: The 3rd Cavalry Regiment is born

The start of 1967 saw several important changes to the Regiment, in both South Vietnam and Australia. On 15 January the numbering policy for regular RAAC units was implemented. Accordingly, the 1st Cavalry Regiment, was redesignated the 2nd Cavalry Regiment, and the 1st APC Squadron in Vietnam became A Squadron 3rd Cavalry Regiment. The Squadron's establishment in South Vietnam now totalled 117 men, consisting of 10 officers, 14 warrant officers/ sergeants, and 93 other ranks.

In early 1967 a decision was made to have the Squadron's detachment at Puckapunyal moved to Holsworthy, where it was designated B Squadron 3rd Cavalry Regiment. The number of members of B Squadron was expanded, with a specific charter to provide a full relief for A Squadron on active service in South Vietnam. When armoured crew trainees completed their course in the operation of the M113A1 at the Armoured Training Centre at Puckapunyal, sufficient numbers were posted to B Squadron and placed on draft to South Vietnam. A man-for-man replacement system would henceforth operate, so that when a member in South Vietnam completed his tour of duty a man from the Squadron in Australia would be sent to replace him. This system meant that there was always a large percentage of Regiment members in South Vietnam with experience, who could train the new arrivals in the Squadron's operating procedures. The National Servicemen serving with the Squadron in early 1967 comprised approximately 65% of its strength, giving the Squadron a mixture of experience and youthful vibrance. It is said that while the National Servicemen were more uninhibited and enterprising, they needed more coaching and needed to know why something was required to be done in a certain manner. Regular soldiers were said to be more experienced and better trained but were more passive and less likely to question or reason.

It is said that when the Regiment was redesignated the 3rd Cavalry Regiment its members were quietly jubilant, as it was felt that the term 'Cavalry' more accurately reflected the role with which it had been charged. Coinciding with this news was a visit to the Squadron by the South Vietnamese Premier, Nguyen Cao Ky, on 12 January. Members of the Squadron gave the Premier an impromptu driving lesson on board Callsign 9, following which he was presented with a 'licence' to drive the M113A1.[6]

While B Squadron (referred to at the time as 'Detachment' A Squadron) established itself at Holsworthy, A Squadron continued its role in supporting the Task Force. January 1967 turned out to be a relatively quiet time, and no major contacts with the enemy were reported. However, if any members of the Squadron had developed a false sense of security because of the respite they had been experiencing, this was soon to change. On 5 February two APCs detonated anti-tank mines in an area that had been selected by the enemy to attack the Australian cavalry unit. The attacks were against 3 Troop, which had been operating in an area 3 kilometres north of Route 23 and 9 kilometres east of Dat Do. The first attack was against Callsign 33Bravo, with the explosion breaking the right-hand track and destroying the suspension arm. The crew were unharmed. The second attack was against Callsign 32Bravo, and occurred some 2000 metres directly north of the earlier attack. The left-hand track was broken and the suspension wrecked. Again the crew were not harmed and the vehicle was able to be repaired in the field. These two attacks prompted the troop leader to request extra engineers for support while the troop's deployment in that particular area continued. There was considerable enemy activity where the mine attacks occurred, and the following day D Company 6 RAR engaged a large enemy force. This contact occurred some 4 kilometres south of the area where 3 Troop had been operating the previous day, which prompted the Squadron to race to the area to assist D Company. It was reported that the entire Squadron subsequently moved to the area and engaged the enemy with heavy fire with both .30 and .50 cal. machine guns.

OPERATIONS BEAUMARIS, BRIBIE AND RENMARK

In an excellent example of cooperation between the Cavalry Squadron and 5 RAR, a well-planned and coordinated cordon-and-search operation took place in the village of An Nhut between Long Dien and Dat Do on 13 and 14 February. The operation had been named BEAUMARIS, and considerable planning and detail went into ensuring complete surprise. This was to be Major R.E. Hagerty's last operation and he had been joined by his replacement, Major G.J. Murphy, who acted as observer for the manoeuvre. The first part of the operation involved two troops of APCs from the Squadron transporting two companies from 5 RAR in daylight to the northern edge of the Long Hai hills, to the vicinity of the village of Tam Phuoc and the Dinh Co monastery. This was to be a disguised move and was to suggest to the enemy that a move would be made by the Australians on the Long Hai hills, a well-established Viet Cong stronghold. The Dinh Co monastery was approximately 5 kilometres from An Nhut, which would be reached by the APCs under the cover of darkness. Later that afternoon the remainder of 5 RAR were taken by the APCs to the Dat Do airfield, where they remained concealed inside the carriers, which by this time were hot and cramped. Under cover of darkness the infantry were unloaded, then had a meal before moving on foot into their cordon positions.

The APCs from the Squadron waited until dawn, then in a cavalry role created a diversion by patrolling along the scrub line on the north-eastern and eastern slopes of the Long Hai hills. A number of Viet Cong were subsequently taken prisoner by the 'net' that had been created by the APCs and 5 RAR. Operation BEAUMARIS had obviously confused the Viet Cong because two days later on 16 February, as Support Section moved to an area some 3 kilometres north of the village of An Nhut with B Company 5 RAR, they engaged a sizeable enemy force. Support Section thus required immediate support, and so 3 Troop was directed to the area to assist the infantrymen in a sweep of

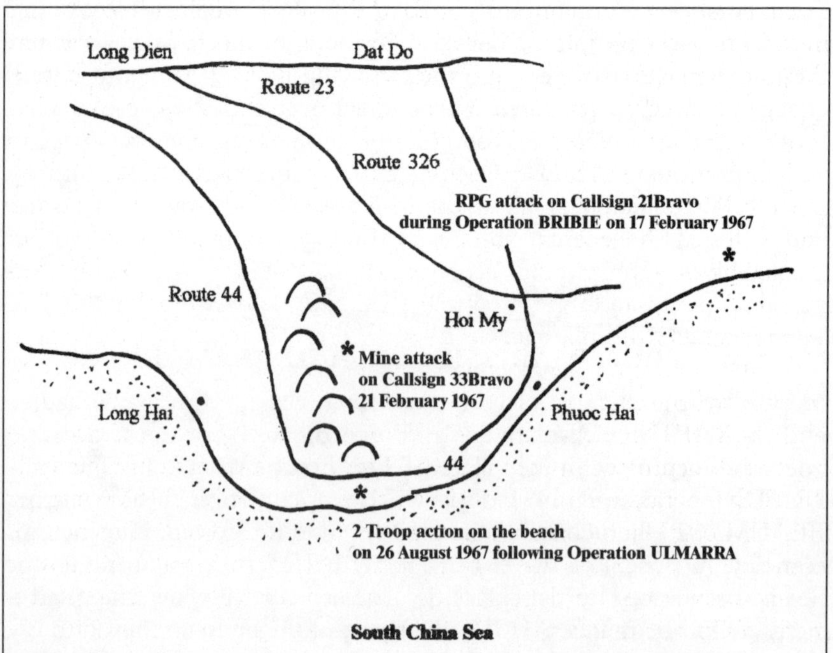

The Long Hai hills and surrounds

the area. Operation BEAUMARIS had again demonstrated the degree of skill that had been achieved by the Squadron in conjunction with 5 RAR in successfully mounting cordon-and-search operations.

The last day of Major Hagerty's command of the Squadron was 16 February. Hagerty had done a magnificent job in forming the Squadron and leading it in the unit's first year of operations in South Vietnam. His replacement, Major G.J. Murphy, who had been in South Vietnam for about one week, assumed command at one minute past midnight on 17 February. Unfortunately for Murphy this proved to be a most unwelcoming occasion, as reports were being received at Task Force HQ at 2.20 am that the Viet Cong had made an attack on the regional post at Lang Phuoc Hai, a fishing village on the Long Hai peninsula to the southeast of the Task Force base at Nui Dat. Apart from the fact that the enemy had used recoilless rifles to attack the base, little information was available.

Further reports received at Task Force Headquarters indicated that a large Viet Cong force was concentrated at Lang Phuoc Hai and that an ARVN company reaction force was starting to move down Route 44 from Dat Do. When reports of the attack on Phuoc Hai were originally received, a company-sized reaction force from 5 RAR was put on notice for deployment. At 4.45 am the Squadron was put on 15 minutes' notice to lift the company from 5 RAR; however, when the size of the enemy force that had attacked Phuoc Hai became known, it was decided to deploy the whole of the 6th Battalion with the 3rd Cavalry Regiment under operational command. Major Murphy had previously appealed to the Task Force commander when he realised the risks involved in moving his force in darkness along the roads directly to Phuoc Hai via Dat Do. While his caution was not based on any knowledge of a large enemy force in the area, he was concerned that reacting in such a predictable manner would be an open invitation to any competent guerilla force to ambush or mine the route to be taken by his vehicles. The recoilless rifles that had been used against Lang Phuoc Hai hinted at main force unit involvement (probably D445) with associated support weapons.

The Task Force commander decided to heed Murphy's advice, and by 5 am Murphy was involved in the Task Force planning of Operation BRIBIE. Operation RENMARK, which was to involve 5 RAR moving into the Long Hai hills, had originally been scheduled to commence the next day, 18 February, but in view of the developments at Lang Phuoc Hai it was decided to delay this deployment. Prior to the commencement of Operation RENMARK a substantial B52 raid on the Long Hai hills was to take place, and the Task Force commander now thought this raid might be used against the forces that had attacked Lang Phuoc Hai.

It was anticipated that the enemy would move to the north and north-east as they made their escape once the Squadron and 6 RAR commenced Operation BRIBIE, and if the Australians could shepherd them into the Long Hai hills the B52s would hit them there as they sought shelter.

At 9.45 am the Squadron was placed on 15 minutes' warning for Operation BRIBIE. The operation required the Squadron to transport C Company 6 RAR and secure a landing zone so that the remainder of the battalion could be flown in by helicopter to the east of Route 44. (The area to the west of Route 44 was said to be occupied by the enemy.) The four mortar carriers from Support Section were also dispatched to add fire power to the reaction force. The decision to deploy to the east of the enemy position was to allow the Squadron and 6 RAR to drive the enemy forces towards the Long Hai hills. It was hoped that the enemy force would encounter further trouble as they moved towards the Long Hais, when Operation RENMARK commenced the following day with an opening bombardment by the B52s.

The operation began badly, as delays were encountered through the necessity to check for mines, putting the Squadron some 30 minutes behind the time that the landing zone was to have been secured. Because the intended landing zone was well away from where it was thought the Viet Cong were located, and there was adequate artillery support available, a decision was made at Task Force Headquarters to proceed with the helicopter landing in the unsecured area. A Company 6 RAR landed at approximately 1.45 pm and after it moved into the scrubby jungle began to receive heavy enemy fire from a sizeable enemy force. The enemy had set up a number of machine gun posts well inside the jungle adjacent to the landing zone, and after A Company had moved about 50 metres into the jungle when the enemy opened fire. The enemy that A Company had encountered were elements of D445, who were performing some sort of reserve or security tasks and were not part of the main force that had attacked Phuoc Hai.

The Squadron was still running behind time, and had raced through Long Dien and into the paddy fields parallel to Route 326 to avoid enemy anti-tank mines. Route 44 was crossed at Hoi My, about 4 kilometres from their final destination. It was subsequently revealed that the enemy had set up a linear ambush along Route 44 between Hoi My and Lang Phuoc Hai that comprised two main force battalions. Twenty-nine command-detonated mines had been set up in an effort to catch the reaction force if it moved along Route 44, as had been anticipated (and rejected by Murphy when it was originally proposed to send a reaction force). It is also said that the main Viet Cong Headquarters was located just to the south of Hoi My. Numerous villagers had moved out of the houses for their own safety as they had anticipated trouble, and having nowhere to go had gone into the open paddy fields.

Murphy realised it was vital that he get his Squadron to the 6 RAR location as quickly as possible, as it was becoming apparent that they were in serious trouble. The Squadron's leader thus decided to compromise safety and took the most direct route, which was a track adjacent to Route 326. Route 326, which was in fact a meandering dirt-cart track, had very probably been mined, but the adjacent track proved harder to negotiate than Murphy had anticipated. The APCs raced down the edge of the overgrown track at full speed, which dislodged overhanging branches that had encroached on the track. The APCs' radio antennas in turn clipped the branches of overhanging trees, sending showers of enraged red ants into the carriers and making life uncomfortable for the occupants. As the Squadron was arriving at the landing zone, helicopters were landing B Company, which immediately went into action to support A Company. Both companies were being hard-pressed by the enemy, who continued to fire from their jungle hides.

From a tactical standpoint the situation that confronted the Squadron was complex and, as any military tactician will attest, a defended position in the jungle is extremely difficult to attack, especially from open ground. The problem confronting the cavalry was that the M113A1 is a lightly armoured vehicle—quite unlike the heavy armour carried by the centurion tanks that were not posted to Vietnam until 12 months later. To attack the enemy position would mean exposure to anti-tank weaponry, such as the 75 mm recoilless rifle and RPGs, (whose rounds could easily pierce the armour of the M113A1), in broad daylight. In New Guinea during World War II, tactics allowed the tanks to assault machine gun positions, with infantry following behind. The tank's armour was able to absorb and sustain the fire from the enemy machine guns and in turn destroy them with their heavier guns. This allowed the infantry to 'mop up' a residual enemy force once the tanks had passed their position. However, with the advent of more powerful weapons such as RCLs and RPGs, these tactics became more hazardous for lightly armoured vehicles such as the M113A1.

On arrival, the Squadron deployed in a line running north to south in an area covering approximately 1.5 kilometres. Squadron HQ and 2 Troop were in the centre, 3 Troop to the north and 4 Troop to the south. First contact with the enemy was made by 2 Troop at 2.05 pm and, despite the lack of armour protection, the troop on two occasions attempted to give support to the infantry. The section led by Sergeant F.S. Graham first moved off, as a request had been received by the infantry for their wounded to be collected and transported to the landing zone for evacuation. Great difficulty was encountered navigating the area of contact: a map reference was of no use on this occasion, given that the APCs could be within 10 metres of the infantry which the thickness of the scrub prevented being sighted. Eventually, Graham's section was directed to move to a point where there was a fire burning, but the smoke that the APCs could see from outside the scrub was from another fire and Graham's section moved off in the wrong direction. As he drove towards what he thought was his objective the section was attacked with two recoilless rifle rounds. Fortunately, both rounds missed the APCs and, thinking that he was near the 6 RAR position, Graham held his fire. In reality, Graham had almost come across the headquarter elements of D445, who were opposing the Australian force. Once it was apparent that the infantry were not in the intended location, Graham withdrew on the premise that he had been fired on and was unable to return fire.

Murphy was upset at the inefficient use of his APCs and insisted that, if he was to direct his carriers into the scrub, the infantry provide a guide to the area where they were needed (at that stage the infantry commanders did not understand how 'blind' his APCs were in the thick jungle). Once a guide was provided Murphy ordered the whole of 2 Troop, led by 2nd Lieutenant D.J. Watts who had since been joined

Mortar tracks: Callsign 82Alpha in action near Lang Phuoc Hai during Operation BRIBIE, 18 February 1967. (3rd Cavalry Regiment (Vietnam) Association)

by Graham's section, to again move into the jungle. Together with B Company, 2 Troop formed a junction, from where it attempted to advance on the enemy positions. However, the infantry immediately came under intense machine gun fire and were unable to advance from their position.

It was now almost 4.30 pm, and with only an hour left before dusk, decisions were being made to extract the infantry from their positions. The priority was to evacuate the wounded, and Callsign 21Bravo was requested to undertake this task. While the other members of the troop attempted to assist B Company the wounded were loaded on board Callsign 21Bravo. As the carrier with the wounded infantrymen on board started to move back through the thick jungle towards the clearing which would be the evacuation point, it was hit with a 75 mm recoilless rifle round. Crew Commander Corporal Geoff Strachan was severely wounded by the blast; he was assisted from the carrier by crew members from a nearby APC and placed on the ground. A number of the wounded infantry riding in the back were also hit by molten metal fragments from the recoilless rifle round. Meanwhile the explosion had wounded the driver, Trooper Victor Pomroy; being a particularly tall man, it was difficult for him to move from his compartment. Before the rest of the section could react to his plight, the enemy fired another 75 mm recoilless rifle round at the disabled carrier which killed the driver instantly.

The situation was compounded by the fact that some of the men from B Company were unsighted and in front of 2 Troop's location. The other APCs in the troop immediately opened fire on the enemy's position, but Major Murphy estimated that no more than 50 rounds were fired by his APCs before they were ordered to cease for fear of hitting the Australian infantry. This was despite the crew's having sighted the position from which the recoilless rifle rounds had been fired by the enemy and the assumption that there were other recoilless rifle teams in the area waiting to attack the APCs. Sustained machine gun suppression fire was the troop's only defence against the 75 mm recoilless rifle teams. The infantry later acknowledged that the battle changed once the APCs opened fire. Those enemy soldiers previously above ground were either dead or had retreated into their bunkers. The sniper fire directed at the infantry ceased, and the enemy's fire in general became less accurate, with some weapons only being raised above the bunkers and fired wildly.

The troop was eventually able to retrieve the situation, but nothing more could be achieved by the APCs once the dead and wounded had been taken from the area. The crew of Callsign 22Bravo recovered much equipment from the wrecked 21Bravo, but the radios and the guns were jammed in their mountings. What equipment could be recovered was taken out of the carrier, and the remainder rendered useless. In the meantime the infantry had evacuated their wounded troops from the damaged carrier, taking with them Geoff Strachan. This fact was at first unknown to the other members of the troop, who were concerned that Strachan may have been missing in action.

The Australians had been in continual action all afternoon, and as night began to fall the infantrymen were at last able to fall back to a defensive position, covered by 2 Troop. Later that evening the APCs continued to resupply the companies of 6 RAR with sufficient ammunition to continue the fight by traversing enemy country at great risk. A difficult and perhaps heart-rending decision had to be made in relation to the wrecked carrier Callsign 21Bravo, which had been hit by the RCL rounds earlier in the afternoon. Recovery of the wrecked carrier was impossible so the only option available was to set the hull alight and destroy it where it had been hit. This was achieved by throwing white phosphorus grenades into the hull, which ignited the ruptured fuel lines. Hand grenades had been attached to the machine guns and detonated, rendering them inoperable so that none of the components could be recovered by the enemy. Later that evening two of the LAD members came to Major Murphy and demanded to be allowed to go back and recover the vehicle such was their dedication. Despite his admiration for their action, Murphy had to give them a direct order to remain with their vehicle.

That night the enemy position was continually bombarded by artillery, mortar and air strikes to keep them at arm's length and 'soften them up' for a further assault by the Australians the next day. At times the air strikes were only 400 metres from the carriers' night harbour position. The fire from the phosphorus grenades placed in the wrecked hull of 21Bravo made a macabre sight, its silhouette clearly observed by the Australian troops as it continued to burn for the greater part of the night. It did, however, make an excellent reference point for the air strikes. During the early hours of the following morning, 18 February, the whole Squadron was roused by hearing the rumble and seeing vivid flashes of the B52 airstrike on the Long Hai hills. The ground shook as the giant US planes dropped their bomb loads to commence Operation RENMARK. Then came the flash flares as the post-strike photo reconnaissance plane bathed the whole area in flickering light.

It was later realised that the failed ambush along Route 44 had occurred because of a deliberate ploy by the Viet Cong to draw the Task Force into a position where they could inflict maximum damage. The enemy's tactics in drawing the Australians away from the Task Force base was not dissimilar to what had happened the previous year at Long

Tan. However, their plan failed because the APCs and the infantry had blocked the Viet Cong's intended withdrawal route to the east. 6 RAR suffered seven of its men killed in action and 26 wounded. Casualties inflicted on the enemy were unknown: the Viet Cong went to great lengths to prevent this information from being revealed and made every attempt to carry away their dead and wounded from the battlefield.

At 8.05 am the next day the Squadron and 6 RAR prepared to again assault the enemy position, but once in the area from which they had withdrawn the previous evening, they realised the enemy had already retreated. When Callsign 21Bravo, in which Victor Pomroy had been killed the previous day, was recovered the Australians were shocked to find that the Viet Cong had daubed obscene graffiti on the side of the now burnt-out carrier. Its destruction was then completed and at 10.35 am the Squadron undertook a thorough search of the surrounding area. The Squadron, with a company of infantry minus 2 Troop, was released to undertake a 'hook' to the south of the BRIBIE area. It was intended that the APCs would follow a jungle track towards the swamps along the Song Rai river and try to catch up with the damaged elements of the withdrawing enemy. The APCs set off at

The wreck of Callsign 21Bravo which was destroyed during Operation BRIBIE. The APC was hit with two RCL rounds, killing the driver, Trooper Victor Pomroy, and wounding the crew commander. Corporal Geoff Strachan, and several passengers. (3 Cavalry Regiment (Vietnam) Association)

breakneck speed in their pursuit of the enemy, but despite their efforts no contact was made.

The members of the Squadron who took part in Operation BRIBIE acquitted themselves well, and through sustained fire power from their machine guns averted what might have turned into a disastrous situation for the infantry. The Viet Cong had learnt the lessons of the Battle of Long Tan well: don't take on a large Australian force in a head-to-head battle. By resorting to ambush tactics from jungle hides, the Viet Cong had clearly accepted that the Australians were going to be a different proposition from what they had become accustomed to. The operation was completed at 8.10 that evening when the last of the carriers from the Squadron returned to Nui Dat. Earlier in the day Major Murphy had requested that the hulk of 21Bravo be recovered. A flatbed trailer transported it back to Nui Dat; Murphy had no intention of leaving it close to an inhabited area as a monument to the Viet Cong's prowess.[7]

Operation RENMARK, which had originally been scheduled to commence on 18 February, had been delayed because of the events surrounding Operation BRIBIE. The operation had involved considerable planning to facilitate an attempt to clear the enemy from the strongly defended area around the Long Hai hills, and was rescheduled to start on 20 February. Intelligence reports subsequently indicated that the attack on Phuoc Hai village the previous day had been designed specifically to disrupt the Task Force's preparations to move into the adjacent Long Hai hills area. Elements from 5 RAR had already been in the area clearing approaches into the area of operation, and up to that point the operation had been uneventful. At 7.30 am on 21 February the Squadron, minus 4 Troop, moved to FSB Arrow, which had been established on the northeast side of the Long Hai hills on Route 326, where they were to assist with the operation.

A new area of operation within the Long Hai hills was assigned to B company 5 RAR; together with the Squadron's 3 Troop commanded by 1st Lieutenant John Howard, it was ordered to search and clear the new area some 5 kilometres south of FSB Arrow. 3 Troop had picked up B Company 5 RAR, which had 'harboured up' in an old coffee plantation the previous evening. The pickup was made on Route 44, a road running all the way from Baria down the Long Hai peninsula and back up past Phuoc Hai to Dat Do. The troop with B Company on board moved along Route 44 until it came to a track leading to the two features at the bottom of the Long Hai hills. After travelling a short distance along this track, Kevin Mitchinson, the crew commander of

33Bravo who was leading the column, came to a series of barbed wire obstacles on which were attached notices written in both Vietnamese and English warning that the area contained a minefield. Mitchinson immediately stopped his carrier and reported this to Howard. Dean Branson from 1 Field Squadron, an engineer specialising in mine clearance, was travelling on the carrier behind Mitchinson. Branson, who was attached to B Company 5 RAR, had been monitoring the radio net as he expected to receive instructions to sweep the area for mines before the troop proceeded. It has since been revealed that during Operation BEAUMARIS, which involved a cordon-and-search of An Nhut on 13 and 14 February, most of the vehicles in the Squadron had travelled down the same track that 3 Troop was now traversing. It was later discovered that all the vehicles had run over a Soviet anti-tank mine that had been planted in the middle of the track but had not detonated because of sand clogging the striker plate.

After Mitchinson located a break in the wire a little further along the obstacle he drove his carrier through and continued along a track for about 2 kilometres towards two small hills, where B Company was to be offloaded. At 2.05 pm, as Mitchinson's carrier (with view obstructed) edged slowly forward to determine his position, he detonated a very powerful anti-tank mine. The carrier was flung 4 metres into the air and landed on its side, killing both the crew commander, Lance Corporal Mitchinson, and the driver, Trooper Robert Wilsen. Two of the passengers on board were also killed and the remaining troops severely wounded. Dean Branson recalls one of the tracks from the vehicle being flung through the air and landing behind the carrier on which he was travelling, a distance of some 30–40 metres.

After detonation of the mine the other APCs in the troop immediately slewed left and right in a counterambush procedure, covering the surrounding area with their machine guns. When no movement was detected, the infantry officers and other ranks immediately jumped off their vehicles and ran to assist the medics, who had moved forward and were already treating the surviving wounded troops in the lead carrier. Unfortunately, as they moved down the left-hand side of the track towards the wrecked carrier, they in turn detonated a series of M16 anti-personnel mines. Within four minutes most of the medics already treating the wounded and Company HQ were either killed or seriously wounded. Because of the concern held by the Australian troops for their mates and their anxiety to get forward and render assistance, normal mine-contact procedures had not been observed. The engineer mine-clearance specialists now started calling out to the troops that they were in a minefield and to stand still. They then set about clearing paths and marking them with backpacks so the wounded could be evacuated.

In the meantime, a medical officer was lowered into the mine area by helicopter and set about treating the wounded without fear for his own life. He had to be reminded that his action in moving into uncleared areas was endangering the lives of others, as a further mine detonation would render even further havoc. The dustoff flights were starting to arrive at the scene of the catastrophe but were initially reluctant to land their crafts for fear of setting off further mines. The landing zone, in an area of low scrub, was established to the rear right of where the mine attacks had occurred. As soon as the area had been cleared by the engineers one of the members of the troop gripped a machete, raced into the area and started cutting down the scrub. Another donned an air recognition jacket and stood in the cleared zone to indicate the landing area. To convince the aircrews that the landing zone had been cleared, another of the Australian troops tied a rope to a couple of SLR rifles and commenced to drag them over the area. The whole area in which this action took place was later found to be full of anti-personnel mines, demonstrating that the enemy had anticipated the reaction of the Australian troops to detonation of the anti-tank mine on the APC.

The final casualty list amounted to seven Australians killed and 22 wounded. So horrendous was the number of casualties that the 36th US Evacuation Hospital at Vung Tau was overflowing and a special RAAF medical flight had to be arranged to evacuate a number of the wounded back to Australia. Operation RENMARK was called off shortly after this event when the Viet Cong made a concerted attack on the Task Force base at Nui Dat, and 5 RAR was compelled to return and assist in driving off the enemy force and restoring the situation. The decision to deploy the troop into this area is difficult to explain in light of the clearly defined minefield in the area (albeit supposedly cleared). It must be remembered that, at this stage of the Squadron's service in the war, engineering mine specialists had not been specifically deployed with APCs. In fact, the engineering 'mini-teams', as they were to become known, were not deployed with the Squadron until late 1967.

The carrier being crewed by Kevin Mitchinson and Robert Wilsen was so badly damaged by the anti-tank mine, estimated to have contained approximately 80 pounds of high explosive, that it was later destroyed by engineers at the location where it had detonated the mine. The explosion had ripped through the driver's compartment, destroying the engine, dislodging the gun from its mountings and leaving insufficient roadwheels on the vehicle to allow it to be recovered.

In the after-action report compiled by 1 Field Squadron RAE two important observations were made. First, that the incidence of enemy mining activities in the province had increased in an effort to counter the movement of the Squadron's APCs. This was in line with the prediction made following the battle in the Long Tan rubber plantation in August 1966. Second, that engineering 'combat teams' should in future be attached to the Squadron for mine clearance when they were deployed, and this should become standard procedure.

From the Squadron's perspective, the incident and the casualties that had been sustained had taught the commanders some valuable lessons. The most important was that in future the practice of following tracks was to be avoided at all costs. The alternative was that each track should be cleared by combat engineers before the APCs travelled on them. Obviously, each deployment by the Squadron in these types of operations would then require more time, something that was not readily appreciated by the staff officers' planning operations. Major Murphy later tried to emphasise this point, especially with new staff officers who could not grasp the need to allow the Squadron time for mine clearance when his APCs were to be deployed in known mined areas. Murphy stated:

> I would openly invite the officers who planned these operations to demonstrate their confidence that the area in which we were to be deployed was free of anti-tank mines. This could easily be achieved by them riding on the lead carrier when they were to be deployed in an area containing uncleared tracks on which they expected my APCs to travel.

The Viet Cong remained active in the Long Hai region, and their 5th Division again tried to catch part of the Australian Task Force in an ambush on 21 March. An attack was made on the government outpost at Lo Gom between the village of Hoi My and the coast, on Route 44, in an attempt to lure the Australians into the area. This was close to where the Viet Cong had earlier in the year ambushed the Australians in Operation BRIBIE, but the Viet Cong were caught in a freshly laid minefield which disrupted their attack. Australian sappers had previously surrounded the outpost at Lo Gom with a minefield and the Vietnamese defenders had stubbornly resisted attacks by the Viet Cong. It was this resistance that frustrated the enemy and eventually led them to attack it; although they failed, it was clearly an attempt to entice the Australians into another ambush.

Operation PORTSEA

Unbeknown to the enemy, a large Task Force operation known as Operation PORTSEA was scheduled to commence at 7 am that same day. This operation was intended to finally free Xuyen Moc from the enemy, who for a number of years had isolated it from the remainder of the province. The Squadron allocated 2 and 3 Troops to support this operation, with 4 Troop remaining at Nui Dat as a ready reaction force. In a preliminary move, 2 Troop carried B Company 6 RAR in a move to the northeast along the beach on the Long Hai peninsula parallel with Route 44. It was intended to cut across the withdrawal route of the Viet Cong ambushing force. The enemy had prepared vast numbers of weapon pits inside the jungle edge and facing the clearing along the Ba Dap creek, which was thought to be the likely approach for the APCs as they entered the area. At 11 am, 2 Troop and B Company 6 RAR were engaged in contact with troops from the enemy's 275 Regiment. Because of the elusive nature of the enemy, and wishing to avoid another BRIBIE situation, it was decided to call in a large air strike. This proved preferable to the APCs having to contend with a number of hidden enemy RPG teams in broad daylight. The result of the air strike was a large casualty count inflicted on the enemy, with minimal damage to the Australian force.

Early on 22 March and approximately 2.5 kilometres northeast of where they had contacted 275 Regiment the previous day, four enemy sampans were engaged as they tried to flee the area. In this contact two of the vessels were sunk and two others severely damaged. At 5.20 pm, 3 Troop had moved some 6 kilometres further up the coast from 2 Troop's position, where it located a large Viet Cong hospital. 2 Troop and B Company 6 RAR continued to search their area and on 23 March at 9.40 am located a large Viet Cong base camp. Meanwhile, 3 Troop, still operating to the northeast of 2 Troop, discovered a large number of .75 mm RCL weapon pits close to the area where the enemy had performed its ambush in the old Operation BRIBIE area. On 24 March, 3 Troop was engaged by four Viet Cong. The troop returned fire but the outcome of the fire fight could not be determined. 3 Troop returned to Nui Dat that afternoon while 2 Troop continued its deployment with B Company 6 RAR.[9]

Operation PORTSEA proved an enormous success, as the area along Route 23 from Dat Do to Xuyen Moc was finally freed from Viet Cong control and never returned to enemy domination while the Australian Task Force was in the province. Joining the Squadron in this operation were tanks and APCs from the US 1st Squadron 11th Armoured Cavalry Regiment. In all, over 100 armoured vehicles from the 3rd Cavalry Regiment and the US 11th Armoured Cavalry Regiment (ACR), from their Black Horse base in Long Khanh province, were involved in this operation as they swept over large tracts of land. Many enemy bases and caches were destroyed during the operation, and engineers reconstructed all the bridges along Route 23. The substantial

An APC from the 11th US Armoured Cavalry Regiment which was located at the Black Horse base in Long Khanh province. This regiment was the 3rd Cavalry Regiment's counterpart in the adjoining province. (3/4 Cavalry Regiment Museum)

logistical losses inflicted on the enemy by Operation PORTSEA meant that in order to mount further operations of any size they would require substantial replacements for the supplies that they lost. They would also need to build up their reserves, which would take considerable time. As a prologue to this operation, on 12 April Route 23 from Dat Do to Xuyen Moc was officially opened. To help celebrate this great achievement the Vietnamese District Chief Colonel Dat travelled the route, with security being provided by 2 Troop from the Squadron.

By the end of April 1967 Major G.J. Murphy, who had been with the Squadron for about two months, had the following appointments made to his command structure on 26 April: Captain J.M. Oxenham, Second in Command; 2nd Lieutenant G.N. Quint, Adjutant; 2nd Lieutenant D.G. Cribb, Quartermaster; Lieutenant C.R. Campbell, Troop Commander 1 Troop; 2nd Lieutenant K.H. McAndrew, Troop Officer

1 Troop; Captain Graham Ayre, Troop Officer 2 Troop; 2nd Lieutenant R.L. Tingley, Troop Officer 3 Troop; Lieutenant G.K. Howard, Troop Commander 3 Troop; 2nd Lieutenant L.M. Herron, Troop Officer 3 Troop. Additionally, Squadron Sergeant Major WO2 Laurie Cabban handed over to WO2 R.S. 'Slim' Kennard. Both were said to be excellent NCOs and made a considerable contribution to the Squadron's success. (Major Murphy recalls on one occasion SSM Cabban leading the Squadron advance when he thought the lead troop was being too cautious and not headed in the right direction.) As well as the above changes in the command structure, 4 Troop was redesignated 1 Troop, as the designation of 1 APC Troop had since become redundant.

While the Squadron undertook a proactive role in supporting the Task Force's operational role between the beginning of January and April 1967, it was engaged in numerous other tasks. For example, the Squadron provided almost daily convoy escorts between Vung Tau, Nui Dat and the 'Horseshoe', where a number of the Task Force's operations were being conducted at that time. (The Horseshoe is an eroded extinct volcano, approximately 60 metres high. Believed to have originally been used as a fort by the French, it was established as a permanent company FSB in March 1967.) The negative outcome of these escort tasks provided the greatest success for the Squadron, inasmuch as the enemy chose not to attack these important convoys. The Australian lines of supplies and communications were thus allowed to operate unhindered.[10]

Operations LISMORE, LEETON, BROKEN HILL, GERALDTON

During May 1967 the Squadron continued to undertake both operational and support tasks for the Task Force. A major operation in which the Squadron was involved was LISMORE, which was carried out between 2 and 8 May and was a search-and-destroy mission in the Long Green area. As well as supporting the Task Force's units it extensively supported the local ARVN forces within the province. On the morning of 15 May the Squadron undertook a one-day search-and-destroy operation with the local 43rd ARVN Battalion approximately 5.5 kilometres east of the Long Tan rubber plantation. Several bunkers were located and a large cache of rice discovered. The Squadron returned to the Task Force base at 6 pm after a short but effective deployment with their Vietnamese allies. Major Murphy attributed the success of this operation to the province chief, Colonel Le Duc Dat, who accompanied him on his vehicle during the operation to 'to make sure the Battalion did what Major Murphy wanted'.

The Squadron had occupied its defensive area in Nui Dat for almost 12 months, and its growing role dictated some re-siting of the original Squadron lines within the Task Force base area. This task was undertaken on 20 May, when Squadron HQ moved to the west of Route 2. The tactical elements of Squadron HQ including the SSM, tents, vehicles and crews had previously moved to the west of Route 2 when Murphy had assumed command of the Squadron in mid-February earlier that year. The relocation of Squadron HQ meant that the Squadron's command would be closer to the three troops and the Support Section, giving it a far greater degree of control. As well as the relocation of Squadron HQ, further modifications were made to the Squadron's defensive perimeter fortifications. To streamline the Squadron's workshop facilities, the LAD moved into the area vacated by Squadron HQ on the eastern side of Route 2.

On 24 May the newly arrived 7 RAR commenced Operation LEETON. 2 Troop and 1 Section of 1 Troop were deployed with the fresh infantry battalion to assist them with the operation, which consisted of the completing of a minefield stretching from Dat Do to Phuoc Hai on the coast. The role of the Squadron in this operation was to provide a troop to transport the infantry to the beach near Phuoc Hai, where they were to construct a barbed wire fence to obstruct the enemy. Once the infantry had been landed, the troop was charged with providing of protection as the work was completed. However, a new role was discovered for the M113s when it was found that running it out the back of the vehicle was an excellent method of dispensing barbed wire for the infantry. The infantry could then simply lift the wire onto the star pickets that had been placed in the ground, which greatly sped up construction of the fence. 2 Troop, which had played a key role in completing this task, returned to the Task Force base on 1 June.[11] On its return a welcome decision had been made to allow crews to remove the heavy rubber shrouds covering the APCs tracks. The shrouds were used to enhance the vehicles' performance in water-borne operations, but the heavy ground and foliage in South Vietnam often tore them off. From then on, when they needed to cross a river the shrouds were replaced, then removed on completion of the task.

Between 7 and 13 June the Squadron assisted the Task Force with Operation BROKEN HILL in the Binh Ba area. Initially one of the troops from the Squadron transported C Company 7 RAR to the Binh Ba airfield. The remainder of the Squadron provided security for 106 Field Battery while FSB Leopard was established. The Squadron remained detached to this operation until 8 June.

On the morning of 15 June, Squadron HQ, 2 and 3 Troops were deployed to assist with the ongoing Operation GERALDTON. In keeping with Task Force strategy of always keeping one of the Squadron's troops at the Task Force base, 1 Troop remained at Nui Dat as Ready Reaction Force. On 17 June the Squadron, while operating approximately 1 kilometre south of Route 23, halfway between Dat Do and Xuyen Moc, discovered a large bunker complex in which 50 pounds of TNT explosive, four hand grenades, a sampan and 100 pounds of rice were located and later destroyed. Two days later a large rice storage area was discovered by 2 Troop near the coast approximately 5 kilometres northeast of Phuoc Hai. On 26 June the whole Squadron including 1 Troop, which had remained in Nui Dat as a Ready Reaction Force, deployed from Nui Dat on a one-day operation and moved to an area around FSB Wilton, some 9 kilometres east of Ngai Giao on Route 2. A large number of bunkers were located, and all were either blown up with explosives or crushed by the APCs before the Squadron returned to Nui Dat at 5.30 that afternoon.

On 29 June the Squadron was informed that in addition to the M113A1 APCs, a troop of M108SP 105 mm mobile howitzers would shortly be temporarily attached to the Squadron. This troop was to be designated 6 Troop and was initially commanded by 2nd Lieutenant Kevin McAndrew, who at that time was Troop Officer 1 Troop and subsequently handed command of that troop over to Captain Colin Campbell. The six M108 vehicles that had been allocated to the Squadron were to be crewed by members of other units from the Task Force as well as some Squadron members, who were to be specially trained in their operations.

The M108 was a tracked armoured vehicle with a 105 mm howitzer gun mounted on the deck, and was on loan to the Australians from the US Army. The M108s were to provide protection for the base defence using splintex ammunition, as their fire power was heavier than that afforded by the machine guns on the Australian M113A1 APC. The M108s were specifically forbidden for use in patrolling and escort tasks; however, when they were stationed at the Horseshoe, without the Task Force being informed, the company commander did use them in that role (albeit without much success).[12]

Major Murphy had argued that the guns on the M108 could also be used for direct fire from the Horseshoe against Viet Cong supply parties moving at night, as his troops could often see the light from the spirit lamps that the enemy wore around their necks. Whenever ordinary indirect or mortar fire approached the enemy they would disperse, douse their lights and move on. The M108s' high explosive shells, on the other hand, would be among them before they could react.

Callsign 21Bravo moving through water soaked country east of Xuyen Moc in June 1967. The crew commander is Corporal 'Curley' Petteit and the driver Trooper Larry Warren. (3rd Cavalry Regiment (Vietnam) Association)

Murphy also tried to deploy the M108s from the top of the Nui Dat hill, but his plans were foiled when it was thought that their role might usurp that of the artillery. Perhaps the greatest contribution of the M108s to the Task Force was the fact that the enemy mistook them for tanks. The M108s were often rotated around the Task Force base—especially those areas occupied by the battalions, which were regularly absent from the base on operations. A captured Viet Cong map showed 20 tanks meticulously marked at various positions, although there were no tanks at the base at that time. The regular rotation of the M108s had obviously confused the enemy and may have acted as a deterrent against attacks on the base.[13]

By July 1967 the enemy had again become proactive, and in response to intelligence reports of extensive enemy activity 3 Troop was deployed to the Duc Than area adjacent to Route 2 on 19 July. An ARVN post was being established at Xa Bang, further north, and the garrison at Duc Than was to cover the new post during its 'settling-in' period. 3 Troop was given the task of manning the fixed fortifications at Duc Than during the absence of its ARVN counterparts. At 2 am the next day the enemy commenced bombarding 3 Troop's position with 60 mm mortar rounds. The attack on Duc Than was thought to be a ploy to keep the troop occupied while a much larger attack was launched on the newly established base at Xa Bang. While several of the rounds landed close to the carriers no casualties were reported among the troop members, nor did any of the carriers sustain any serious damage. The artillery forward observer with the troop found that the only guns in range to support the troop were at Nui Dat. He quickly got a bearing on the mortar fire and ordered his guns to commence firing. After the first round the Viet Cong mortars fell silent. In response to this attack the troop was deployed early the next morning to patrol the area and search for the site from which the enemy had fired their mortars. By this time the enemy had left the area and the firing position could not be located. 3 Troop was eventually replaced and returned to Nui Dat to prepare for a move south to the mouth of the Song Rai river on 29 July. Here the troop supported 2 RAR in a series of ambushes along the coastline until the end of the month.

Earlier in the month the M108SP 105 mm howitzers had been handed over by the US Army to the Squadron. The vehicles had been landed at Vung Tau, and 2 Troop moved to Baria on 21 July to escort the Squadron's latest acquisition back to the Task Force base, where training on the new weapons would commence.[14] A number of RAAC NCOs who had taught centurion tank gunnery at Armoured Centre in Puckapunyal were invaluable in the M108 gunnery training, despite the fact that the 105 mm guns on the M108 were different from the 20-pounders on the centurion tank.

Enemy activity around Duc Than was ongoing, which necessitated the Squadron's maintaining a troop in the area following the mortar attack on 3 Troop on the morning of 20 July. At 10.10 pm on 7 August, 1 Troop, which was deployed at Duc Than, reported that the enemy had fired two M79 grenades at its vehicles. However, both rounds missed their targets and there were no casualties among the troop. Meanwhile, back at the Task Force base, the crews from 6 Troop, who had been undertaking familiarisation training with the M108s, were making good progress. It was anticipated that they would shortly become fully operational, as they had conducted their first practice shoot outside the wire adjacent to the 2 RAR area on 12 August.

Operations MOSMAN, COOPOROO, ULMARRA

On 18 August 1967, 1 Troop moved with 7 RAR to the area around Hoa Long where Operation MOSMAN was to take place. This was a search-and-destroy task aimed at again clearing enemy threats to the Task Force base. On 23 August, intelligence reports indicated that the Viet Cong were massing troops in the Long Hai region from where they planned to mount a substantial attack on Nui Dat. To counter this threat 1 Troop was deployed to Dinh Co on the northern side of the Long Hai hills. The next day at 1.50 am, 1 Troop's position at Dinh Co was bombarded with enemy mortar fire, but there were no casualties sustained by the troop. The decision to deploy 1 Troop into the Viet Cong's staging area had proven to be correct, and the immediate threat to the Task Force base subsided.

By now the Squadron's operational capabilities were being fully utilised by the Task Force. As well as LISMORE, LEETON, BROKEN HILL and MOSMAN the Squadron participated in several other Task Force operations, including COOPOROO between 23 June and 1 July, which involved a sweep of the east of the Song Rai river in a search-and-destroy type of operation. The Squadron's role in these operations was to act as a blocking force for the infantry. After dropping the infantry off in their operational area the APCs would move to a selected location in an attempt to cut off the enemy's expected path of retreat. However, their deployment by the Task Force command was at times ill-conceived, with little thought given to the consequences of the tasks assigned to the Squadron. An example of this can be seen at the conclusion of Operation ULMARRA. Undertaken by 7 RAR and supported by elements from the Squadron, it involved a cordon-and-search operation on the village of

A M108SP gun in action on the wire at Nui Dat. A number of these vehicles were 'acquired' from US forces and operated by A Squadron for an extended period of time until the Task Force commander discovered them, ordering their return. (3/4 Cavalry Regiment Museum)

Phuoc Hai on the eastern side of the Long Hai peninsula. At the commencement of this operation on 25 August the carriers of 3 Troop were deployed to the village of Phuoc Hai, where the APC of 2nd Lieutenant Roger Tingley was attacked by four M16 mines. Tingley received shrapnel wounds to his back and neck and was taken to the 36th Evac Hospital at Vung Tau. The APC received only superficial damage, and was able to be driven after the incident.

At the conclusion of Operation ULMARRA on 26 August 2 Troop, led by Lieutenant Rodney Earle, who had joined the Squadron the previous month, was requested by the Task Force to lend support to 'some other units' to recover two US Navy motor launches that had been stolen by the Viet Cong. The craft were Boston whalers and were crewed by US Marines, who had come from Danang to demonstrate them to the US Navy at Vung Tau because it was thought they might be useful in the Rung Sat 'Special Zone'. Nobody knew quite how to treat the marines at Vung Tau, and this probably encouraged them to 'go for a picnic' on the beach at the southeastern end of the Long Hais. The two marines were subsequently captured by the Viet Cong, who took them to a cave high in the Long Hai hills where they were left guarded by an enemy soldier with an M1 carbine. The same guard remained on duty for two days and nights; when he eventually fell asleep the marines grabbed his rifle and shot him. The marines escaped by running barefoot at full speed down the side of the hill before reaching Long Hai town. It was their story that led to the operation to recover the two Boston whalers. At 12.40 pm Earle deployed his troop along the beach on the eastern side of the Long Hai peninsula about 4 kilometres south-west of Phuoc Hai.

Earle, not realising the launches were some 7 metres in length, had taken the orders direct from Task Force HQ. He was under the impression that the boats were to be 'procured' for the Task Force's own activities. The manner in which the orders had been given was highly irregular, as the normal Squadron command structural procedures had been completely bypassed and the Task Force had not informed the Squadron of Earle's movement. 7 RAR had already returned to Nui Dat in helicopters leaving D&E Platoon from Task Force HQ to accompany Earle's 2 Troop. No-one at Task Force HQ had arranged artillery support for this deployment, and in any case the area was probably out of range.

As the troop rounded a bend on the beach about 500 metres from where they had deployed that morning they came under fire from enemy in the hills and high ground running down to the beach along which the troop was travelling. Trooper Kevin Ortlipp recalls seeing an old temple from which puffs of smoke were coming, and suddenly realised that the troop was under fire; he reported this fact to his crew commander, Sergeant Frank Beattie. At this stage 21 and 22 Section were in a direct line of enemy fire with 23 Section a little further down the beach, and all had set up defensive formations on the edge of the beach with their backs facing the South China Sea. The men from D&E Platoon, who had already dismounted to conduct a search for the two launches, had reported successfully locating the two vessels. However, they also stated that both boats had already had their engines and fuel cells stripped by the enemy. In the meantime, the APCs on the beach were experiencing heavy small arms and machine gun fire from the enemy, who had moved down to the beach and were using abandoned villas and hedges as cover. The troop responded to the enemy move by directing .50 cal. machine gun fire into the enemy position, and managed to keep them at bay.

When the Squadron's CO, Major Murphy, was informed of the troop's plight he immediately arranged for a Sioux helicopter to fly him down to 2 Troop's location from the Task Force base to assess the situation. As radio communications had to be relayed via the Horseshoe Murphy did not at first realise that there was a fire fight going on, and blithely flew along the edge of the cliffs looking for foot tracks. Murphy and his pilot Major George Constable soon 'got the picture' and asked for artillery support. As soon as he realised that the Task Force had not arranged any artillery coverage for 2 Troop he ordered two of his 81 mm mortar carriers commanded by Corporal 'Big Robbie' Robinson that were stationed at the Horseshoe to scramble to the area. When the mortar carriers arrived they were positioned about 1200 metres to the east of where 2 Troop was deployed. In the interim Murphy's helicopter began to run low on fuel, and he was forced to return to Nui Dat for a quick refuel. The troop and D&E Platoon were going about their task competently and Murphy assessed that, provided the enemy were not reinforced, no major problems could be anticipated.

However, during his absence and to compound the situation confronting Earle, a short time later a seaborne force comprising 100 Vietnamese naval forces from Vung Tau stormed the beach where the troop was in heavy contact with the enemy. The Vietnamese were dressed in black pyjama suits with red scarves and carrying old US weapons. To all intents the forces were dressed and looked the same as Viet Cong soldiers. The Vietnamese naval force had been joined by the Australian RAN diving team from Vung Tau, on their second day in country, who had decided to come along 'for the ride'. Seemingly this force had also been assigned to assist in the recovery of the launches from the enemy, although no-one at Task Force HQ knew how the force was to arrive at the location. The sight of these men struggling ashore in a heavy sea in full battle kit and then running up the beach and past the APCs towards the enemy's position astounded the cavalrymen. Kevin Ortlipp vividly recalls the utter confusion surrounding the incident.

Callsign 21, crewed by Sergeant Frank Beattie, Trooper Kevin Ortlipp and Geoff Willoughby, was being especially targeted by the enemy with their machine guns. The vehicle's driver, Kevin Ortlipp, was hit in the head by bullet fragments and the blood from the wounds impeded his sight. Radio operator Geoff Willoughby was able to remove Ortlipp from his compartment and place him in the back of the vehicle to receive first aid. Next to him one of the Vietnamese naval force members lay dying, having been shot through the heart; another who had been shot in the arm was also receiving treatment. During the course of the ensuing battle Callsign 21 was said to have fired over 4500 rounds of .50 cal. machine gun ammunition at the enemy. Further down the beach, Chad Sutton's 23 Section continued to support the other two sections with machine gun fire.

By this stage Earle was trying to determine how he could extricate his troop and the other forces from their predicament. His troop was being exposed to heavy and constant enemy fire; he had a naval force on the ground whose commander was unknown, and their command appeared non-existent. Also, the majority of the naval force troops did not speak or understand English, so communication was proving difficult. Nine members of the combined naval force had been either killed or wounded and because of the volume of enemy fire could not immediately be evacuated.

In the meantime, the Squadron's Commanding Officer Major Gordon Murphy had returned to the scene of the battle in a helicopter and witnessed two motorised junks that were being swamped in the surf on the beach. Also, a corvette and a patrol boat which had a 40 mm Bofors gun were firing intermittently and indiscriminately at the troop's position in support of their colleagues, without any regard for the APCs on the beach. The artillery were unable to provide any support because of the trajectory the guns required to fire their rounds over the Long Hais. Despite this, the commander's log notes that Mortar Section, which had been scrambled to the area via Route 44, had arrived at its assigned location to the east of where 2 Troop was positioned and went into action at 3.15 pm with a fire mission to give support to those on the beach. Murphy says that he did what seemed most useful at the time, and from his helicopter started calling in the mortars and controlling their fire. At the troop's request Murphy undertook a fast and low run along the beach in the helicopter in an effort to locate a sniper who had been peppering the troop with fire. A tall Vietnamese soldier was located with a red scarf firing his rifle in a suspicious direction, and while he was not challenged by Murphy several fresh bullet marks were found in the side of the mortar carrier.

By this time Earle had decided to take matters into his own hands, and assumed command of the combined naval force, much to the relief of everyone involved. If the troop were to remain on the beach that evening, they would be forced to endure certain enemy attacks in the darkness, with their only avenue of escape the rough ocean at their rear. Earle therefore ordered everyone on the beach to board the carriers, which provided a greater degree of security than the open beach and its surrounds.

The commander's diary notes that at 3.45 pm the mortar carriers again went into action and commenced firing at the enemy's position to give cover to the troop as they commenced their withdrawal along the beach. Once everyone was on board the now seriously overcrowded carriers, Earle ordered the troop to move off to the east along the beach at full speed. To escape the enemy's fire the troop moved as far along the beach as possible before reaching an outcrop of rocks jutting into the sea. The rocks blocked further travel along the sand, and the carriers were required to 'swim' around them to the beach on the other side.

Unfortunately, as the lead carrier of Sergeant Chad Sutton's section raced into the surf at full speed it was hit by the waves of the incoming tide. The carrier lurched to one side and a wave engulfed the vehicle, killing the engine and swamping the interior. At this stage the troop was still within enemy firing range and was continuing to experience heavy fire from the Viet Cong's hidden positions.

As the rest of the carriers were wading in the surf, Earle turned his attention to rescuing the 'downed' APC. Corporal D.C. 'Bleep' Singletary on Callsign 22Alpha had already manoeuvred his carrier close to Sutton's carrier, and was able to attach a towline and haul it onto the beach. The occupants of the APC were then dispersed among the carriers that had assisted with its recovery. This manoeuvre was carried out without further casualties and the 'downed' APC was towed across a nearby swollen creek emptying into the ocean and out of range of the enemy's fire. At 5.25 pm it was reported that both the troop and Mortar Section had been extracted and were now in the relative safety of open country away from the beach. By this time dustoff flights had been able to evacuate both the wounded and dead to Vung Tau.

The two Boston whalers that the troop had been sent to recover were destroyed, while the two junks that had been swamped on the beach were riddled with .50 cal. machine gun fire from the APCs to render them unusable. A day or so later a US destroyer came in close to the beach and fired 5-inch rounds until they were satisfied that the junks and whalers had all been destroyed. In general this deployment had proven a fiasco: little or no planning had put 2 Troop at great risk. The fact that Earle was not told that the launches were 7 metres long but was given instructions to 'load them on top of the carriers' would indicate that command at Task Force HQ had given no thought to the folly they were committing the troop to. On the information available, this was an ill-conceived venture on the part of both command at Task Force HQ and Allied Naval Forces Command. The troop had been extremely fortunate that the enemy did not possess anti-tank weaponry such as RCLs or RPGs which would have had a devastating impact on the APCs and their crews.[15]

Operations AINSLIE, KENMORE and SANTA FE

The next major Task Force operation the Squadron became involved in was Operation AINSLIE. The Squadron involvement commenced on 4 September 1967, with 3 Troop charged with the responsibility of moving to an area west of Route 2 between Binh Ba and Ngai Giao to secure the ground for the establishment of FSB Barbara. This was a month-long operation with both 2 and 7 RAR participating; the

Squadron's responsibility was the security of Route 2. On 25 September the Squadron concluded its role in Operation AINSLIE and Squadron HQ, 2 and 3 Troops moved down to Baria to test the APCs for seaworthiness and undertake water-borne training in preparation for Operation KENMORE. The results of these tests were less than satisfactory when two carriers 'drowned' and three others were found to be unseaworthy. The following day 1 Troop moved to Vung Tau, where it also undertook water-borne training. The main problem encountered with the APCs in the water-borne training exercises was that when they attempted to steer to port, the front of the carrier would dip and water would rush into the engine via the radiator louvres, flooding the engine compartment. This was to have serious consequences when the carriers had to 'swim' at the start of the operation.

On 29 September the Squadron was deployed to assist with Operation KENMORE, which was to be conducted in the southeastern sector of the province. The Squadron at this time was under the Command of Captain Oxenham, as Major Murphy had been seconded to join the US 11th Cavalry at its Black Horse base in Long Khanh province to assess the operation of tanks in Vietnam for possible deployment by an Australian tank unit to the Task Force. The Squadron initially moved to Phuoc Hai, where A Company 7 RAR were boarded. They then drove along the beach some 10 kilometres, crossing the Song Rai river without incident. A defensive position was established to await the arrival of Task Force HQ the following day. On 30 September the Squadron moved to the Ho Tran cape area to secure a landing zone for Task Force HQ and the artillery so that they could establish FSB Spear. On Monday 2 October at 7 am, 2 Troop was deployed to the west of FSB Spear where they were required to cross the mouth of the Song Rai river. Callsign 21Bravo, crewed by Corporal Bob Hunter and Trooper Stretton Joel, was one of the last carriers to cross and got caught by the river's fast-flowing tide as it emptied into the South China Sea. The driver instinctively tried to correct the direction of the vehicle, but the port side immediately dipped and water raced in and flooded the engine compartment. Stretton Joel in the driver's compartment was wearing a flak jacket which caught on the controls and was pulled down with the carrier as it sank. While under water he was able to free himself of the cumbersome jacket and eventually struggle to the surface, where he and his crew commander managed to stand on the submerged vehicle until rescued.

The carrier had only recently undergone a full overhaul and refit but all attempts to salvage it proved fruitless. The flow of the current at the mouth of the river was strong and attempts to attach a towline failed. The sharks downstream and crocodiles upstream made members of the

Squadron wary about entering the water, but about 20 men entered the deep water in an attempt to drag a line to the drowned carrier. The vehicle was eventually recovered on 6 October by members of the Australian Naval clearance diving team in 4 metres of water. (The RAN diving team, which had been extracted from the beach following Operation ULMARRA, had previously expressed their gratitude by telling Major Murphy not to hesitate to contact them if he ever needed assistance.) The USS *Nation*, a naval recovery vessel, was used to lift the vehicle and deliver it to the beach. The floor of the carrier was covered with sand in which a couple of stingrays had made their home. After recovery, the vehicle was returned for another complete overhaul and refit.[16] Operation KENMORE concluded on 11 October, and the Squadron returned to Nui Dat by again crossing the Song Rai river without incident.

Meanwhile, 6 Troop had commenced active deployment. On 25 October the troop moved to the southeast of Phu My in the western sector of the province, where they engaged targets on the western side of the Nui Ti Vai hills. The next day the Squadron was again deployed on Operation SANTA FE. The Squadron had moved to 2 RAR lines in Nui Dat at 12.50 pm and transported that battalion to an assembly area in the Gallia rubber plantation adjacent to Route 2. Once the infantry were in position the Squadron moved approximately 10 kilometres to the northeast and secured the area to allow the establishment of FSB Wilton. Then 3 troop was deployed to the north of FSB Wilton where it was to act as a blocking force for 7 RAR, which would attempt to drive the enemy back to the southwest towards 3 Troop's blocking position. However, on this occasion no contact with the enemy was reported.[17]

On 1 November the Squadron moved to Thua Tich in the northeast sector of the province, where FSB Lion was established to support a two-week Task Force operation. That evening at 11.50 three Viet Cong were observed on the wire surrounding the base, but fire could not be directed at them as the guns from the artillery unit in the base were in the APCs line of fire. On 5 November at 6 am a clearing patrol was sent out to investigate movement detected outside the Squadron's area at FSB Lion the previous evening. It was later discovered that the enemy had managed to crawl close to the wire surrounding the base and set up a series of claymore mines, which were directed at the base. Fortunately, when the enemy attempted to detonate the mines they had misfired, leaving the banks of claymores intact although dangerous. Following their discovery 1 and 3 Troops were requested to make a sweep of the area around the base. The troops commenced their search at 7 am, but with no result. The

11 Section moving out through the wire on an early morning clearing patrol in late 1967. (3rd Cavalry Regiment (Vietnam) Association)

following evening the enemy attacked 2 Troop's position within FSB Lion with small arms fire. The troop countered by firing M79 rounds at the enemy's position. The enemy continued to probe the wire outside the Squadron's area and a short time later commenced bombarding the base with a mortar barrage. Fortunately, none of the members of the troop was harmed by the mortars crashing into the base. The next day at 7 am, 1 Troop was deployed to locate the enemy's position for the previous night's activities, again without success.

The following week elements of the Squadron were deployed 5 kilometres south of FSB Lion and into a new area of operation, while the remainder of the Squadron stayed at FSB Lion. To facilitate and support the troops operating in the new area of operation, FSB Ben was established adjacent to Route 328. The APCs that had moved into FSB Ben immediately deployed with the infantry and began providing security by searching an area 2000 metres surrounding the base. Meanwhile the OC's Callsign 9, which was travelling along Route 328 approximately 5 kilometres south of FSB Ben, detonated an anti-tank mine. This was an improvised mine consisting of four unexploded bomblets, which acted as the trigger mechanism, and a 155 mm HE projectile. Only two of the bomblets detonated; the larger 155 shell beneath them failed to detonate. The vehicle was being commanded by

Captain John Oxenham; his men were not wounded and the vehicle sustained only light damage. Later that day a large tunnel and bunker complex was discovered in the surrounding area and destroyed. As operations in the Thua Tich area started to wind down a decision was made to withdraw from FSB Lion on 16 November. A platoon from the US 3/5 Cavalry who had been attached to 1 Troop during their deployment around FSB Lion accompanied the troop as it moved to approximately 5 kilometres from the Route 23/Route 328 junction. Here they harboured for the night and continued to provide security for other returning vehicles the following day. An air strike on likely enemy positions and a light fire team were also deployed to cover the remaining troops withdrawing from the area. The operation concluded at 5 pm on 17 November when the last APCs finally moved back onto Route 23 and returned to the Task Force base. That evening the platoon from the US 3/5 Cavalry were guests of the Squadron, and spent the night with the unit before returning to their base.

The Australian government had in October 1967 indicated that the 1st Armoured Regiment would be deployed to South Vietnam to support its increasing effort in the war. On 26 November, Squadron HQ took the 1st Armoured Regiment's officer, Major Peter Badman, who would command the Squadron when it arrived in Vietnam, for a run down to Phuoc Hai to give him an appreciation of the country in which it was expected that his tanks would be operating. The following day intelligence reports indicated that there had been substantial enemy movement to the north of the Task Force base. 1 Troop, the Ready Reaction Force, was immediately dispatched to the Binh Ba and Duc Than rubber plantations, where it carried out an extensive reconnaissance patrol without contact.[18]

On the morning of 1 December as 3 Troop moved along Route 15 they were engaged with enemy small arms fire. No damage was inflicted on the troop and they continued their task after reporting the contact. The remainder of December was reasonably quiet but saw the Squadron undertaking numerous tasks by providing convoy escorts and protective patrols in support of Operation FORREST and a number of subsidiary operations, including OODNADATTA, SHEPPARTON, DIMBOOLA, MELBOURNE, LORNE and LAWLEY. Participation in these operations helped the Squadron live up to its reputation as the workhorse of the Task Force. Additionally, the Squadron helped to secure landing zones in the new areas of operation that were being opened up and ferried infantry forward while protecting the entry and exit routes with cavalry-type patrols. In previous conflicts in which Australian troops had been involved, the infantry were required to walk to the area where the conflict was being fought. With the advent of M113A1 armoured personnel carriers a new dimension had been added to the way infantry could be assisted in their operations. The APCs could transport troops quickly and directly to the battle area, and if required support the infantry with sustained fire power from their machine guns.

The end of 1967 remained reasonably quiet, as Christmas and New Year's Day had been declared a truce, and the Squadron took advantage of the break. Each member of the unit received a gift-wrapped package of 100 cigarettes from an Australian manufacturer. Then an elaborate Christmas dinner, including ham, turkey and Christmas pudding, was served in the messes. Christmas Day was not without its problems, as Major Murphy was ordered to send a troop to an area just to the south of the Task Force base to sort out a problem reported by a small Vietnamese garrison. The report received at Task Force HQ indicated that some New Zealand artillerymen had gone to a small hamlet outside the base and were said to be behaving poorly. Of concern to Murphy was the fact that the New Zealanders were reported to be armed. However, it turned out that the New Zealanders were all drunk and that their only weapon was a ukelele.

While the year ended on a relatively quiet note, the coming year was to test the Squadron to its fullest capacity. During 1967 three members of the Squadron had been killed in action, while another 10 were reported wounded or injured.[19]

4

The Tet Offensive, 1968

The Australian government's decision in October 1967 to commit a squadron of centurion tanks to the Task Force as well as another infantry battalion revolved around the thinking that the infantry could become more effective in their pursuit of entrenched Viet Cong if they were given the close fire support that a tank could afford. A strategy of mixed tank, APC and infantry would prove more potent in taking the fight to the enemy.

To facilitate deployment of the tanks to the war effort, the Squadron's Commanding Officer, Major G.J. Murphy, undertook a visit to various US armoured units—first the 1st US Marine Tank Battalion at Danang, then the 1/69th US Army Armor Battalion at Pleiku and finally the US 11th Cavalry Regiment HQ at Black Horse in Long Khanh province, from 24 September to 3 October 1967. The 11th Cavalry Regiment 1st Squadron (ACR)(US) was the US armoured 'counterpart' in neighbouring Long Khanh province. As well as the M113 APCs they deployed M48A2 tanks as part of their operational charter. Murphy's role was to advise on problems that the Australian centurion tanks might encounter before they were deployed in South Vietnam. To this end Murphy became actively involved in the M48A2 tanks of the 1st Squadron 11th Cavalry Regiment (US) and deployed on operations as a crew commander to assess their role. During his previous deployment with the Americans on Operation PORTSEA, Murphy came to have great admiration for the commanding officer of the 1st Squadron, Lieutenant Colonel 'Tiger' Howell, whom he described as handling his troops and a large range of support forces (including helicopter gunships and artillery) during an enemy contact like 'a conductor leading a well coordinated orchestra'.

From A Squadron's point of view, the addition of the more heavily armoured centurion tank would be very welcome, as until that time the Squadron, with its lightly armoured vehicles, had performed a role that was not entirely within its tactical charter or capability. This was especially so when it was required to assault heavily defended and hidden enemy positions, such as the ones the Squadron had encountered during Operation BRIBIE. The M113A1 was capable of withstanding small arms fire and giving protection from grenade and mortar fire. However, the enemy's RPGs left the APCs crew and its passengers vulnerable when one of these projectiles hit. A round from an RPG was capable of slicing through the M113A1 armour and exploding into molten hot metal fragments in the interior of the vehicle. The heavier armour of the centurion tank was thought to be able to withstand these blasts, unless the projectile was aimed accurately at specific weak points in its structure.

Given the growing numbers of Australian troops now being committed to the war effort, A Squadron was also enlarged. By December 1967, serving with the Squadron in South Vietnam were 12 officers, 18 warrant officers/sergeants and 117 other ranks. By April 1968, A Squadron's numbers were further increased to 158, with the inclusion of one officer, one sergeant and nine other ranks. The demand for trained APC crews grew to cater for the increasing number of members being posted to South Vietnam. Armoured Centre increased its training intake numbers and B Squadron in Australia was expanded to facilitate the growing numbers of personnel awaiting draft to A Squadron in South Vietnam.

Throughout the year the number of APCs in service grew to a total of 48 fully operational vehicles. As had happened in early 1967, when the Squadron's role was expanded to support the increasing part being played by the Australian Task Force in the war effort, the number of vehicles in each troop was expanded. The number of vehicles in Support Section was also expanded to enable the Squadron to cater for the increased operational role now required, especially with the addition of another infantry battalion to the Task Force.

In the Buddhist culture of Vietnam, the traditional holiday period of the Chinese Lunar New Year is known as Tet. In early 1968 the Viet Cong and the North Vietnamese Army made an all-out strike across South Vietnam, in an attempt to catch the government's forces and its allies during the holiday period. Many of the South Vietnamese forces had taken advantage of the holiday to stand down their troops, leaving many posts on half-strength. This was in the mistaken belief that a truce would

APCs from 3 Troop moving into a clearing near Thua Tich in early 1968. (3/4 Cavalry Regiment Museum)

be observed by the enemy, who were also said to be taking advantage of the Tet to stand down their troops. However, US intelligence sources indicated that the enemy would break the truce. It was also believed that Phuoc Tuy was not of strategic importance from the enemy's perspective, and the defence of the approaches to Saigon were a US priority at that time. But the enemy did have plans for Phuoc Tuy and especially its provincial capital, Baria, which lay approximately 10 kilometres south of the Task Force base at Nui Dat.

Evidence of the enemy's intention to step up their activities was revealed early in the year when they started to probe the wire around the Squadron's area at the Task Force base. On the evening of 2 January 1968 an enemy force of undetermined strength was fired on by pickets in the Squadron's bunkers on the defence perimeter. The enemy again probed the wire around the unit's area on 18 January and were engaged with a defensive artillery fire mission. Earlier that day 1 Troop, which had been deployed in the northern sector of the province, discovered a large bunker system approximately 5 kilometres south of the Courtney rubber plantation on the western side of Route 2. The following day, while deployed on a patrol some 3.5 kilometres northwest of the Task Force base, 2 Troop located a cache of hand grenades and an M16 rifle.

While the newly arrived 3 RAR remained at Nui Dat to strengthen its defences, the greater part of the Australian Task Force moved to the north and into Bien Hoa province. Intelligence reports had indicated that the enemy would move through the Task Force's western neighbouring province of Bien Hoa in order to attack the nation's capital of Saigon. Of more concern to the Task Force was the enemy's intention to attack the Bien Hoa airbase (the busiest in the world at the time) and the Long Binh complex, which contained vital ARVN and US headquarters It was expected that these attacks would come from the north and northwest. As the time approached, the Australian Task Force had highly detailed and reliable intelligence about the approach of enemy main force units. While the tank squadron settled in, A Squadron 3rd Cavalry Regiment continued to do all the armoured tasks required by the Task Force.

In the early hours of 31 January the enemy launched a series of attacks against the Long Binh and Bien Hoa US military complexes. Earlier in the month, on 24 January, the Task Force had commenced Operation COBURG to support its US allies. The entire Australian Task Force minus the newly arrived 3 RAR was initially sent to the large US base at Long Binh and the Airforce base at Bien Hoa to assist in its defence. The Squadron had deployed with Squadron HQ, 1 and 2 Troops to transport 2 and 7 RAR to their new areas of operations. 3 Troop remained at Nui Dat as the Ready Reaction Force. The Squadron arrived at two newly established fire support bases called Anderson and Harrison, which had been allocated to the Australians during Operation COBURG. FSB Anderson was located on a hill devoid of vegetation and had been strategically sited with the specific purpose of 'blocking' enemy activities. FSB Anderson was positioned approximately 800 metres north of Trang Bom village in Bien Hoa province with easy access to National Route 1, and was one of a series of FSBs that had been established in the area. FSB Harrison was located to the west of FSB Anderson, and was positioned so that each base could support the other in the event of an enemy attack. This act by the Australians and its allies, which had effectively cut the enemy's communications links to their troops around the Saigon area, so infuriated the enemy that they made plans to overrun the base. On arrival at FSB Anderson at 12.30 pm the Squadron set about establishing themselves and setting up defensive positions. On the afternoon of 25 January, while 2 Troop remained in the base, 1 Troop began patrolling the area north of the base before moving to FSB Harrison.

In total there were about 500 Australian and American troops eventually assigned to defending the base. As events were to turn out, FSB Anderson was to be what some would refer to as a 'mini Khe Sanh'. Khe Sanh was a legendary fire support base in one of the northern provinces in South Vietnam and had been defended by US Marines against overwhelming numbers of enemy forces over a period of several months. Geoff Murray, who was a member of 2 Troop, recalls on the night of 25 January being on guard duty in the turret of his carrier at the fire support base and seeing several lights outside the defensive perimeter. (The commander's log reports numerous lights sighted at 11 pm on the eastern boundary of the base.) He alerted his troop leader, Bruce Richards, and an artillery barrage was directed from FSB Harrison. The accuracy of the artillery fire was confirmed the next day when several enemy bodies were located. That the enemy were prepared to deploy in such a manner reflected their audacious attitude and the large numbers of enemy troops in the area preparing to take part in the Tet Offensive. More importantly, it confirmed a belief that FSB Anderson was about to be attacked by a large enemy force which was determined to capture this strategic piece of ground to ensure that the attack on Saigon would proceed successfully.

1 Troop departed FSB Anderson on escort duty on the morning of 26 January and returned to Nui Dat, while 2 Troop remained and patrolled the area south of the base. In addition to the Squadron's APCs an infantry company from 3 RAR had arrived, as well as a battery of heavy US 155 mm guns and a battery of New Zealand 105 mm guns. 1 Troop returned to FSB Anderson from Nui Dat on 27 January before again moving to FSB Harrison to help defend that base. One of the continuing deployments required to be carried out by the Squadron's vehicles was the almost daily run that was made between the two FSBs and Long Binh in order to replenish the ammunition being used by the US 155 mm battery. Because of enemy activity around the area in which the Squadron was operating, these resupply runs were undertaken at different times each day so as not to provide the enemy with an established routine. The enemy had one evening mined the route over which the APCs normally travelled, expecting the APCs to be the first vehicles to use the roads the following morning. The APCs decided to delay their run to Long Binh until later that morning, and a Vietnamese school bus full of schoolchildren was the first vehicle to use the road, detonating the mine with hideous results.

On 30 January at 4 pm, 2 Troop was requested to carry out a reconnaissance patrol of the village of Trang Bom, as reports had been received that the enemy had moved into the village. The patrol reported that the village appeared deserted, that most of the civilians had left, and that the ARVN post seemed to be deserted. Once this information had been conveyed to Task Force HQ the troop returned to FSB Anderson. It was subsequently determined that an enemy force had taken over the village of Trang Bom, and at 9.30 am on 31 January Captain Bruce Richard's 2 Troop was ordered to deploy its APCs with D Company 2 RAR against the large enemy force now occupying the village. After a fierce fire fight which included street fighting, the village was retaken from the enemy by 2 Troop and the infantrymen from 2 RAR. The troop had initially been engaged by the enemy at 11.20 am, who fired several RPG rounds that fortunately missed the APCs they were aimed at. At 11.40 am the troop reported drawing heavy enemy fire from the village but had not sustained any casualties. The enemy were proving hard to dislodge, so at 12.26 pm a light fire team was called in to engage the enemy from the air. Geoff Murray recalls that the pilots of the helicopter gunships were Australians who were attached to a US Airforce unit. This seemingly made it easier for members of the troop to communicate with them as they made their rocket attack runs on the enemy positions. The gunships had the desired effect on the enemy's positions, and at 4.30 pm the troop was able to enter the village to assess the damage. It was reported that the village had suffered substantial damage, with some houses still burning and large amounts of ammunition exploding in the flames, making for an extremely dangerous situation.[1]

On 1 February, and with most of the Australian Task Force still deployed in Bien Hoa province, the Viet Cong had unexpectedly infiltrated Baria and attacked. Task Force HQ was advised of the attack at approximately 5 am with a vague report that the ARVN at Baria were having 'a bit of trouble' with a couple of platoons of Viet Cong. In fact, a force consisting of several companies of Viet Cong had attacked the Regional Forces' administration and ammunition storage compound in the northeastern sector of the town. In the centre of town another two companies of Viet Cong had entered Sector HQ, the Security Forces compound, the Police Offices and the American advisers' (CIA) compound. Another enemy company had moved off to attack the main bridge on the western approaches to the town. The airfield adjacent to the National Training Centre of Van Kiep on the eastern side of the town was taken over by the enemy at 7 am. In addition to the enemy forces in Baria it was thought that a battalion was stationed to the north of the town and another two companies located to the south. It was initially estimated that 600 of the local force, D445 Viet Cong Battalion, had been deployed against Baria.

To assist, Task Force HQ responded by advising the US and government forces in Baria that it was deploying its Ready Reaction Force. This force consisted of nine carriers from a depleted 3 Troop, to be accompanied by A Company 3 RAR. 3 Troop was commanded by 2nd Lieutenant Roger Tingley, who had been with the Squadron since April 1967. The previous evening the Task Force base had been mortared by the enemy, and at 6.10 the following morning the troop was deployed to locate the position from where the enemy had fired its mortars. However, when the call for assistance from Baria came it was decided to redeploy the Ready Reaction Force, so the troop returned to Nui Dat to make hasty preparations for its redeployment. Tingley drove to Task Force HQ where he was briefed by the deputy Task Force commander, who had been in the country less than 24 hours. While he was being briefed the rest of the troop drove to the 3 RAR lines and boarded A Company before proceeding to the main gate, where they were to meet up with the troop leader. To save time and while still at Task Force HQ, Tingley briefed his troop and A Company in detail regarding the situation in Baria on the APCs' radio speakers.

The situation that confronted Tingley was that 3 RAR had only just arrived in the country, and he again briefed the troop on this point. It

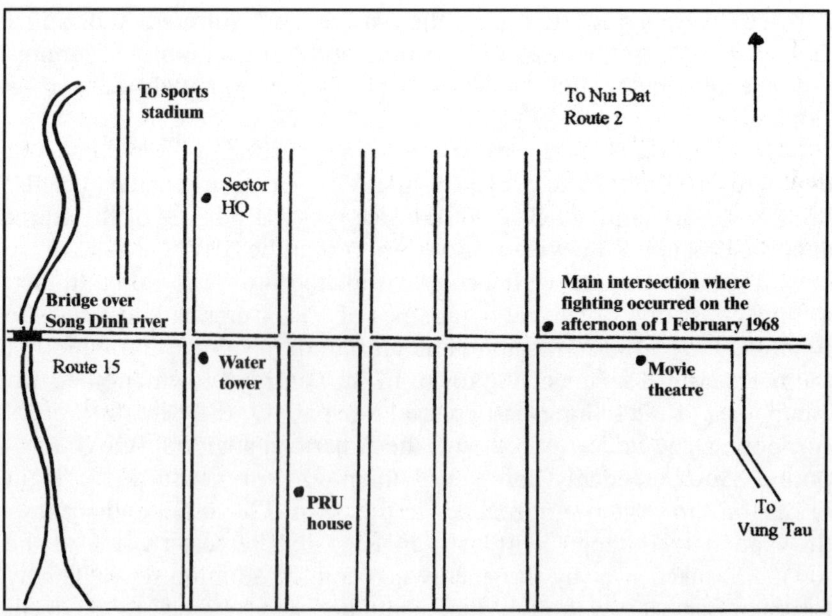

The main precincts of Baria

was felt that, given the circumstances, A Company should be afforded as much protection as possible, and the troop might have to accept some damage or loss of vehicles to achieve this objective. The troop agreed, even though several members were shortly due to return to Australia, having completed their tour of duty. They departed Nui Dat at 8.10 am and, with A Company 3 RAR on board, raced towards Baria, where it was noted that substantial air activity was occurring over the provincial capital as gunships and F5 jets made bombing and strafing runs. As the troop travelled south along Route 2, the enemy made a token attempt to inflict damage on any relief forces that the Australian Task Force might send to their South Vietnamese allies. Ian Bates, who was Roger Tingley's driver, recalls puffs of dust on the road as the enemy fired their weapons at the carriers. One RPG round was fired at the troop which missed its target, and the APCs were able to push through the enemy fire leaving the ambushing force in its wake.

As the troop approached the western confines of Baria at approximately 9 am, an enemy group estimated to be at least half a company were sighted heading in a northerly direction. While the troop experienced some small arms fire from this group it was decided not to attack, as they were not seen as a priority at that stage. However, as the troop made a right-hand turn towards Sector HQ, Callsign 33Bravo, the last carrier in the column to intersect the enemy troops, saw one of their number running to the east. Corporal 'Red' Webb opened fire on the enemy, killing him.

The situation that greeted Tingley in Baria was chaotic, with the local ARVN forces being hard-pressed by their Viet Cong attackers. On arrival at Sector HQ the troop formed a covering circle around the compound, while the Senior US Adviser in Baria, Colonel Austin, gave a briefing to Major Howard, the OC of A Company 3 RAR. Roger Tingley was not involved in the briefing, and on his return Major Howard informed him that he was to split the troop to undertake various tasks. While Tingley was anxious about having to split the troop, especially in the prevailing circumstances, it was agreed that guides would be allocated to each of the sections so that the APCs could reach their destinations quickly. It was also decided that Tingley's Callsign 30Alpha and 31 Section would be assigned 2 Platoon, and were charged with protecting Sector HQ as well as protecting and rescuing a group of civilians from their houses. 32 Section were to carry 1 Platoon and 3 RAR A Company HQ to the sports stadium while 33 Section would carry 3 Platoon to the transport and ammunition compound.

As the three APC sections moved off, Sergeant John Murphy on Callsign 31 reported that the troop was under fire from several snipers and that one member of the troop had been wounded. He also reported two RPG teams as being sighted in the area. Murphy's section had moved only 100 metres to the south of Sector HQ when it was attacked by snipers at an intersection, prompting Murphy to again report that both he and Callsign 31Bravo were unable to move due to sniper fire from surrounding houses. This prompted Tingley to join 31 Section, whose APC was also attacked with five RPG rounds as he moved towards the intersection where 31 Section was pinned down. The RPGs aimed at the troop leader's vehicle were fired from a distance of between 15 and 30 metres, all of which fortunately missed their target. The sniper's position at the intersection was identified as an adjacent two-storey building which was occupied by some civilians. This prevented the immediate use of machine gun fire by the APCs. Fire was eventually returned at the lower floor of the building by the APCs' .50 cal. machine guns, which put an end to the enemy's sniper activity.

At this stage 31 Section and Tingley's 30Alpha were deployed between the Sector HQ and the American compound and, with the assistance of A Company 3 RAR, had set about the task of rescuing aid workers from that compound (who were thought to be held as hostages by the enemy). At 9.25 am Murphy again reported a large number of Viet Cong in the sports stadium, and his section was drawing heavy fire. As the APC group moved to support the infantrymen, Tingley observed two tree snipers who were blocking the platoon's escape route from the area. He fired his machine gun, killing them both and clearing the intersection. Given the number of enemy troops in the area Tingley decided to protect his withdrawal route, but as he could not afford to dedicate one of his APCs to this task he decided to leave one of the members of the troop in a culvert in the side of the road with an M60 machine gun, with orders to shoot anybody in an arc of fire he had defined. This unenviable task fell to Barry Pitt, who was a surplus member of the troop at that stage and had accompanied Tingley on his carrier to Baria. Roger Tingley had earlier acquired three M60 machine guns with spares from the Americans for the cost of three pairs of GP boots and six cartons of Victoria Bitter beer. These weapons were dispersed among the troop and had been intended for use as night sentry weapons, as they had more flexible aiming capabilities than the fully mounted .50 cal. machine gun and could sustain 500 rounds without a belt change. Tingley had kept his troop's M60 on board the carrier and Ian Bates had earlier joined together three full belts of ammunition and stored them in a ration tin, much to the amusement of other troop members who did not imagine that they would ever be used.

At 9.35 am it was reported that five Australians and two US soldiers had been wounded and that Callsign 33 was transporting them to the main road out of Baria for evacuation. While this was happening

Tingley urgently dispatched Callsign 31Bravo to collect Barry Pitt, who had been placed in the culvert with the M60 machine gun to protect his and 31 Section's withdrawal route. By this time Tingley and 31 Section were to the north of Sector HQ, where they were targeted by enemy sniper fire on several occasions. However, the section continued to attack the enemy force, and as Tingley's carrier lifted over a pile of rubble it was hit with an RPG. The attack on his troop leader was reported at 10 am by John Murphy on Callsign 31. Ian Bates recalls that as he drove his carrier down the street the RPG round hit the vehicle, which slewed the carrier to its right, sending it crashing into a building and rendering him unconscious. The RPG round entered the front right-hand side of the vehicle and blew the back of the driver's seat off its mountings before smashing into the radios in the back of the carrier. Ian Bates had received serious wounds to his back while the radio operator, Roger Bicheno, was dazed. A New Zealand artillery foward observer radio operator who had accompanied the troop to Baria was also wounded. The explosion had blown Tingley out of his carrier, and he found himself hanging from a piece of guttering on the house that the carrier had smashed into when the RPG round hit. From his elevated position Tingley observed the RPG team in the process of reloading their RPG launcher in order to fire another round at the carrier, prompting him to drop to the ground. Meanwhile, having regained consciousness, Ian Bates saw Tingley, now on the ground, screaming at him, which he understood as an instruction for him to get out of the carrier. In actual fact Tingley had been trying to get him to reverse out of the building. Tingley reboarded the carrier and as Bates reversed out of the rubble of the building he depressed the .50 cal. machine gun to its maximum and opened fire, killing the two members of the RPG team that had hit his carrier.

Despite his wounds and in a great deal of pain, Ian Bates continued to drive the vehicle after it had been extricated from the building, although by this time it was operating on only three cylinders. After travelling only a short distance the carrier started to seize up. The APCs had managed to make it to the main intersection in Baria when the damaged carrier's engine died, and it was decided to stop and allow the other APCs to form a defensive position. However, when the crew dismounted from the damaged vehicle Ian Bates collapsed as a result of his wounds. He was placed on board John Fogarty's Callsign 33 and along with the wounded New Zealand forward observer's radio operator transported to the road at the Dat Do end of town, where they were to be taken to the 36 Evac Hospital at Vung Tau. The damaged APC with Roger Bicheno and the New Zealand foward observer, Captain Duncan Martin, whose hair had suddenly turned grey, eventually accompanied the vehicle to the main entrance to Baria, where it was used to protect the southeastern and western approaches to the town. Meanwhile Tingley walked to Sector HQ, where the broken-down Callsign 31Alpha was located. The vehicle was being used as a static block to protect three sides of Sector HQ from the northwestern corner. On reaching Callsign 31Alpha, Tingley used that vehicle's radio to contact Callsign 32Alpha, and advised the crew commander that he would take over command of his vehicle in order to regain control of his troop, which was under the temporary command of Sergeant John Murphy. It was fortunate that John Murphy, whom many regarded as the best troop sergeant in the Squadron at that time, had been with the Squadron since April 1967 and had acquired considerable command experience.

Tingley then became aware that the ARVN forces were firing at a nearby orphanage. The crew commander on Callsign 31Alpha had also identified many women and children in the orphanage, and when his and Tingley's requests for the ARVN to cease fire went unheeded Tingley threatened that he would order Callsigns 30Alpha (whose guns were still operable) and 31Alpha to open fire on the ARVN's position. This had the desired effect and allowed Tingley to ascertain that the ARVN had reported sniper fire coming from a tree inside the orphanage compound. After acquiring another rifle, Tingley climbed into a ditch and crawled along it to where he was able to observe the sniper's position before firing at the sniper and killing him. The nuns inside the orphanage quickly gathered all the children together inside their building before making their way to Callsign 31Alpha. While this was occurring the unit commander's diaries note that Sergeant John Murphy on board his Callsign 31 estimated at 10.53 am at least a battalion-sized Viet Cong force in the Baria area that appeared to be operating in small groups of 10–12 men.

Attempts to extract the aid workers from the American compound were stalling as the surrounding low walls were peppered by enemy fire. The enemy threw hand grenades over the walls and fired their RPGs into the surrounding roofs and trees for their shrapnel effect. The problem was overcome when it was decided to drive one of the APCs at the surrounding wall and knock it down. The three occupants of the compound scrambled aboard the APC to be rescued from an attacking force of at least Viet Cong platoon strength.

While Tingley remained at Sector HQ and 31 Section had deployed to the US compound, 33 Section had moved to the administration and logistics compound, where a large number of US and ARVN troops had been wounded. On arrival the section commenced evacuating the wounded. At 11.05 am John Murphy reported that he had been requested to secure the Vung Tau to Nui Dat road on the northern approaches to Baria. At 11.51 am Murphy reported that the section at the administration and logistics compound had loaded 17 ARVN troops and two Australians from 3 Platoon that had been wounded, and that he had tasked Callsign 32 to evacuate them to the arranged dustoff point. A dustoff flight was requested to meet 32 Section, which had started the task of transporting the wounded to a point on the 'main road' to Vung Tau for evacuation. As the section moved to the dustoff point Callsign 32Bravo was attacked by RPGs, with one round striking one of the roadwheels. Despite the damage caused by the rocket the crew continued to drive the vehicle and engage the enemy, killing one of the RPG team members that had fired at their vehicle.

It should be noted at this point that, as casualties among the Australian, Vietnamese and American forces mounted during the day, 3 Troop was charged with the evacuation of the wounded to the dustoff point established on the Vung Tau road. Despite the extreme danger, the troop successfully evacuated 28 men while under fire.

At 11.30 am Senior US Adviser Colonel Austin requested the Australians' assistance to rescue a CIA operative named Mr Johnson, still trapped in one of the houses in the US compound. The house was situated near the main Route 2/Route 15 intersection on the eastern approach to the main precinct of Baria. An earlier request to rescue Mr Johnson had been turned down because of heavy enemy fire in the area, which was being directed from prepared positions. However, it was revealed that the operative had in his possession a quantity of sensitive documents that required destruction before they could be captured by the enemy. Callsigns 32Alpha and 32Bravo had thus returned to Sector HQ to pick up Tingley so that he could resume control of the troop. While Tingley had originally intended to take over Callsign 32Alpha, he in fact took over Callsign 32Bravo and departed from Sector HQ at 11.31 am. He was accompanied by 2 Platoon, A Company 3 RAR and an 'ARVN' guide provided by Sector HQ. The guide proved uncooperative and initially led the two carriers in a circle. After they had driven past the same house twice, Tingley told Sector HQ that he was returning to their location as he suspected the guide to be a Viet Cong 'plant'. The guide, on hearing that he was being returned, became very agitated, which prompted Tingley to instruct the radio operator to shoot the guide if he moved on the trip back to Sector HQ.

The two carriers eventually set off again for their destination, and on the way to the US advisers' compound called at the province's reconnaissance units' house. Here they collected another CIA operative, Mr Heity, and an Australian AATTV member, Warrant Officer Tony Parrello, who were to assist with the destruction of the material held by the CIA operative in the US compound.

The two carriers reached the house in which the CIA operative was harboured without incident and the two Americans and Australian AATTV member set about destroying various documents. Meanwhile the CIA operative's pregnant mistress, four *nung* mercenaries and some boxes of documents were loaded on board Callsign 32Bravo. Callsign 32Alpha had been deployed to cover the main Route 15/Route 2 intersection near the compound, while the infantry platoon was deployed around the compound and to cover the intersection. A short time after 32Alpha was deployed Tingley noted that the carrier was in an exposed position in the middle of the intersection, and he instructed it to move to a more secure position. Before the carrier could move the enemy fired an RPG round which struck the front of the vehicle and penetrated the vehicle's engine, wounding the driver, Trooper Derek Conroy, and Crew Commander Corporal John 'Shorty' Miller as well as some of the infantry. The Viet Cong RPG team then started to reload their weapon.

Realising what was happening Tingley instructed all those now on board his carrier, including the two CIA operatives, Tony Parrello and the *nung* mercenaries, to dismount. After all refused he instructed his driver, John Fox, to drive 32Bravo between the enemy and the disabled carrier in order to engage the enemy with his machine guns. As Fox drove the APC forward, Tingley fired his gun at the RPG team that had fired at Callsign 32Alpha and killed them. In the meantime another RPG team, which was located in the school ground opposite the intersection, was preparing to fire its weapons. As Tingley leaned to his left to get another belt of ammunition for his gun an RPG round struck Tony Parrello in the chest, killing him, the CIA operatives, the mistress and the four *nung* mercenaries. Tingley was again blown out of the carrier and onto the road, where he lay wounded and in a dazed condition. As soon as he regained consciousness he became fully alert, and set about assessing the situation that confronted him. The crew of 32Alpha and one of the infantry sections were still at the intersection and exposed to enemy fire, so he ordered a withdrawal from their position using fire to move back into the US compound.

On reaching the compound, platoon medic John Davis administered first aid to the wounded, including Tingley, who was given morphine for the pain from his wounds. Tingley decided that the mobility status of the carriers should be determined, and that Davis should check those that had been killed and remained on board the two carriers. So, together with Davis and two other infantrymen, Tingley ran through the enemy crossfire to the two carriers while the rest of the platoon provided counterfire. The scene of the dead in the back of Callsign 32Bravo was devastating, but Tingley assessed that, while 32Alpha would need to be towed, 32Bravo could be driven. Given their location at the intersection it was important that the damaged APCs be recovered before dark. On his return to the compound, Tingley (despite the pain and morphine) talked to and comforted the three wounded crewmen. Derek Conroy was in considerable pain, while Shorty Miller and John Fox were stunned, but all three were in good spirits and described by Tingley as 'good men'.

To gain an appreciation of their surroundings, Tingley decided to take a tour of the house and its grounds. He had noted the large communications system in the house and an ample supply of whisky. As he moved about the perimeter of the compound two of the infantrymen mentioned to him that they had seen a 'pipe' occasionally being pushed out of the window of a building across the street. Realising that the 3 RAR had only just arrived in country and that they had not recognised the 'pipe' as an RPG launcher, Tingley told the two infantrymen to shoot at it the next time it appeared at the window. The infantrymen were successful in removing this threat, much to Tingley's relief.

While Tingley and the others remained in the US advisers' house, the other APCs from the troop and the Company HQ had returned to the province's reconnaissance unit's house to provide support and flank protection. As the afternoon wore on the US advisers' compound continued to be engaged by sniper and sporadic RPG fire. Tingley had spoken to the infantry platoon commander, who was the ground commander, on several occasions about extracting the damaged carriers, but he was unwilling at that time to move from their location in the compound. At approximately 4 pm an attempt to recover the vehicles was made by a company from the 52nd ARVN Ranger Battalion. The enemy's position and situation were advised to the ARVN unit's commanding officer and his American adviser before they launched their assault. The ARVN reported, however, that the enemy's defence was too strong, and they were unable to secure the area to allow recovery of the damaged APCs.

While the action at the compound was taking place Sergeant John Murphy had again assumed command of the troop. At 3.20 pm Murphy was advised by the Squadron's second in command that in view of the dangerous and continuing situation that confronted the troop they were to remain in Baria for the night. At 4.30 pm Tingley was beginning to feel extremely anxious about recovering the APCs and was able to make contact with Sector HQ and the commander of A Company 3 RAR via the infantry platoon's radio. Tingley's request not to leave the APCs in their position after dark met with an unenthusiastic reponse, so he set about devising his own plan. Derek Conroy remained in considerable pain, but Shorty Miller and John Fox were ready to help their troop leader extract the two carriers. Tingley's plan involved bringing the remaining carriers in the troop to the US advisers' compound and using fire and movement to secure the two damaged carriers at their location. Cobra gunships were to be used to cover both sides of the street while a towline was attached to Callsign 32Alpha. Although Callsign 32Bravo had sustained damage, it was thought to be still capable of being driven to allow recovery.

When Tingley submitted his plan to the platoon commander at the compound shortly before 5 pm and it was relayed to the company commander he again met with a negative response. But Tingley forced the issue, and informed the platoon commander that the cavalry would be leaving the compound and recovering its vehicles at 5 pm. His insistence finally won through and at 5 pm he was advised by the commander A Company that his plan had been accepted.

A short time later the remaining carriers from the troop, with 3 Platoon and Company HQ on board, had made their way towards the US advisers' compound to await the air strike and move to their night position. At 5.30 pm the Cobra gunships arrived and commenced hovering 800 metres north of the intersection. From this position they were able to view the situation and fire their mini-guns down both sides of the road on which the carriers were standing. The recovery of the two APCs commenced with 33 Section firing their machine guns down the side of the damaged carriers. The infantrymen and the wounded moved into a ditch on the side of the road and made their way back to the waiting carriers. Tingley and the infantry platoon commander had popped red smoke grenades so that the helicopters could identify their position before they also commenced putting down suppression fire on either side of the carriers.

As the gunships started firing their mini-guns Sergeant John Murphy reversed his APC some 70 metres towards the intersection, where he was exposed to enemy fire. Murphy dismounted from his vehicle and, under fire and unarmed, ran forward and attached a towline to Callsign 32Alpha. The rounds from the gunships' mini-guns were landing 20 metres from the APCs recovery area. The enemy had made the nearby movie theatre at Baria their staging post and command centre, and a substantial amount of fire was coming from that building. 'Red' Webb on 33Bravo used his weaponry to punch a hole in the upper front wall of the theatre to give John Murphy covering fire as he attempted to reverse away from the intersection with 32Alpha under tow. However, as Murphy's carrier began to reverse the towline snapped, and Murphy was forced to dismount from his vehicle and under fire re-attach the towline.

Callsign 32Bravo was the last vehicle to be recovered, as it could be driven. However, as John Fox and Roger Tingley climbed in through the back door to get to their respective compartments they were forced to climb over body parts that had not yet been recovered following the RPG attack earlier in the afternoon. John Fox had been particularly distressed at the sight of the bodies and having to climb over them to escape from the carrier; having to do it again was equally distressing. Callsign 33 fired down both sides of the vehicle as it drove away from the intersection and towards the other carriers, which proceeded to move towards the central water tower in Baria.

With the infantry on foot, the party moved to the bridge over the Song Dinh river which was adjacent to the water tower and about 100 metres from the town square. Meanwhile a section from the troop was dispatched to pick up a platoon of A Company 3 RAR infantry that had been left at the ammunition compound to assist with its defences. On arrival at the bridge one of the disabled APCs was placed so as to block the bridge while the other APCs and the infantry were deployed in an all-round defensive position. At 5.45 pm Company HQ requested a dustoff flight for Roger Tingley, Derek Conroy and the other wounded that had been evacuated to the water tower. However, he was told that the RAAF helicopters were still receiving fire from the enemy, and the area where it was intended to evacuate the wounded was not sufficiently secure to allow them to land. This situation continued until 9.15 that evening when a pilot with 161 Recce Flight offered to assist and flew his smaller Sioux helicopter to Baria. The pilot landed near the town's water tower, which had been marked with ignited petrol tins, and commenced to evacuate the wounded and fly them one at a time to a US dustoff helicopter about 1 kilometre away. Once Roger Tingley had been evacuated the Squadron's second in command requested that John Murphy take command of the troop until he could be relieved.

At 10 pm Murphy reported that they were located on the eastern side of the bridge and open to sniper fire. One of the disabled vehicles had been placed so that it blocked the bridge, and the members of the troop were placed on 50% 'stand-to' while they waited in their night defensive position for the enemy to attack. The enemy continued to fire RPGs at the top of the surrounding houses for shrapnel effect on the APCs throughout the night. Supporting the Australians that evening was the 161 Battery (RNZA), which fired over 500 illumination rounds, enabling the Ready Reaction Force to detect any enemy activity in the area to the west of their location. The fighting in Baria went on into the early hours of the next morning, when the Viet Cong ceased to be a significant fighting force. The enemy had 40 of its troops confirmed as killed in action; the number of wounded was not known but believed to be considerable. Of the enemy killed, over 12 were directly attributed to the actions of the troop. The troop had four of its members wounded, of whom three were evacuated and one elected to remain on duty. Two of the vehicles were immobilised from the RPG rounds that had scored direct hits; three others had received minor damage but could still be driven. A Company 3 RAR had 12 of its members wounded, and the artillery's foward observer's radio operator was wounded.

To add to the woes of the wounded members of the troop evacuated to Vung Tau, the enemy decided to mortar the Australian logistical and support base that evening. The patients of the Australian Field Hospital, which included those members of the troop who had been wounded, were all told to get under their beds as the mortar rounds started exploding. Ian Bates, still only semi-conscious from an operation earlier that day, was unable to get out of his bed, and so medical staff lifted him onto the floor and threw a pile of mattresses over him for protection.

At first light at Baria the infantrymen from A Company spread out to cover the whole block surrounding the area in which the APCs had been harboured for the evening. Sporadic contact with the enemy continued to the east of where the Australians were located and an ARVN post remained constantly under enemy fire. A sniper continued to fire on the Australians, fortunately without result, and normal civilian activity was able to be resumed for short periods around mid-morning. At 3 pm, B Company 3 RAR arrived in Baria to escort the battle-scarred Ready Reaction Force back to Nui Dat. The three disabled carriers were once again rigged for towing and attached to the serviceable carriers, then slowly driven to Nui Dat via Route 2, arriving back at the base at 4.30 pm.

Rick Wells, the driver of Callsign 33, whose section was commanded by Sergeant John Fogarty, stated that because there were only nine carriers available, individual carriers were required to carry out tasks in Baria rather than the normal procedure of operating in sections. He stated that the troop was sent to Baria to 'do what you can', with no specific orders given or any appreciation of what the troop was being committed to. He was left with the feeling that the Task Force was prepared to sacrifice the troop in this instance, as the confusion created by the enemy and the ferocity of their attack on Baria had taken the Australian Command completely by surprise. Between 20 and 30 RPG rounds were fired directly at the APCs, with six actually striking the vehicles. It was perhaps good luck that no-one from the troop was killed, as the enemy's aim was said to be good, but most rounds passed over the vehicles at head height. Of the six that did hit the APCs, four caused damage to the vehicle, one was a scrape and another was a 'dud'.

One of the memories of that day that remains with Rick Wells relates to WO Clarrie Rule, who was one of the Armoured Corps AATTV members based at Baria. When a refrigeration system in one of the American PX stores in Baria had its electrical supply cut off as a result of the fighting, a large supply of ice cream for the US military personnel had started to melt. Rule, who was quite a personality, showed Corps loyalty late in the afternoon by chasing the carriers around Baria, distributing two gallon tubs of melting ice cream to the troop members. Rick was astonished to hear a banging on the back door of his carrier and to see a large container of ice cream thrown in.

Many members of the troop had only a couple of days to go before they were due to return to Australia at the end of their tour of duty, but the men of 3 Troop had accounted for themselves with bravery and distinction in this action. The men from A Company 3 RAR had only recently arrived in the country, and this was the first major action in which they were involved. Accordingly, the leadership displayed by the cavalry's troop leader, 2nd Lieutenant Roger Tingley, was exceptional, many believing he deserved Australia's highest military honour. Perhaps the most disappointing issue for the members of the troop was that Tingley's tour of duty ended when he was evacuated from Baria, and they never had the chance to say farewell to their leader. For his efforts and leadership, Tingley was awarded the Military Cross. The citation for his award, reads:

> On 1st February 1968 as commander of 3 Troop A Squadron 3rd Cavalry Regiment, Second Lieutenant Tingley assisted in the defence of Sector Headquarters in Baria, Phuoc Tuy Province. His Troop was in contact from approximately 0845 hours until 1910 hours, during which time they evacuated 28 casualties as well as providing support to the infantry company and assisting in the defence of the Sector Headquarters.
>
> While under sniper fire Second Lieutenant Tingley killed three snipers. Later when his vehicle was struck by a rocket he continued to fire his machine gun and killed the enemy who engaged him. He changed vehicles and when another carrier near him was hit by a rocket he brought his own vehicle between it and the enemy. He engaged the enemy but was hit. He was wounded and thrown from his vehicle.

Sergeant John Murphy's efforts during the action—especially his ability to take command when his troop leader's vehicle was damaged and later when he was wounded—were also recognised. From his hospital bed Roger Tingley had recommended that his troop sergeant receive the Military Medal, but it was decided to award him Mentioned in Dispatches. The citation for his award reads:

> On 1 February 1968 as a member of 3 Troop A Squadron 3rd Cavalry Regiment, Sergeant Murphy assisted in the defence of Sector Headquarters in Baria, Phuoc Tuy Province.
>
> Twice during the battle Sergeant Murphy assumed command of 3 Troop, firstly when his Commander's vehicle was knocked out and secondly when his commander was later wounded. On both occasions the troop was under fire and in difficulties. Nevertheless, with great professional skill and judgement, he continued the action, organised the evacuation of Australian and American casualties, and also the recovery of a damaged armoured personnel carrier. His coolness under fire and his personal courage when he dismounted to connect tow ropes to a disabled carrier steadied and encouraged his troop and contributed to the success in this action.

It is considered appropriate that the final words in relation to this action be contributed by the Commanding Officer, A Company 3 RAR, Major B.W. Howard, who compiled the after-action report. In the 'special comments' section of the report, Howard wrote the following:[2]

> This report was written from an Infantry point of view. However, the APC Troop played a vital role in the success of the action. A Company would like to record three points concerning 3 Troop A Squadron 3rd Cavalry Regiment.
>
> a. The personal courage of 2nd Lieutenant Tingley.
> b. The professional ability of Sergeant Murphy.
> c. The excellent performance of No 3 Troop and the cooperation given to A Company throughout the whole action.

While 3 Troop spent an uncomfortable night at Baria, back at Nui Dat on 2 February at 3.50 am the Task Force was placed on Red Alert, as it was believed the enemy was probing the Task Force's perimeter defences. At 4.15 am movement was detected on the wire outside the Squadron's perimeter. The M108 howitzers from 6 Troop were dispatched to the perimeter wires where they fired on an undetermined enemy force with unknown results. The next day 3 Troop, who had spent the night guarding the bridge at Baria, reported at 8.30 am that they believed they had accounted for at least 20 Viet Cong who had been killed in the course of action the previous day, albeit only 10 attributed directly to them. They also believed that a significant number of the enemy who had attacked Baria were from the 274 Regiment.

At the village of Trang Bom, near FSB Anderson in Bien Hoa province, trouble was again brewing. 2 Troop, which had departed

Trang Bom on 31 January 1968 after removing the Viet Cong troops who had taken over the village, reported that it had been retaken by enemy forces. The report stated that an engineer mini-team was taking fire from the northeastern side of the village, indicating that the enemy had returned to the village. It was thus decided that 2 Troop and D Company 2 RAR should again deploy to the village and drive off the occupying enemy force. Once they had determined that the local population had left the village, the troop attacked. The enemy suffered numerous casualties during this action without loss to 2 Troop or the infantry. At 10.05 am the troop undertook a clearing patrol and reported locating the bodies of 11 enemy troops killed in the encounter. 2 Troop continued a thorough search of the village and at 12.08 pm reported that the villagers were being allowed to return to their homes.[3]

On 3 February, 1 and 2 Troops continued to operate from FSB Anderson in Bien Hoa province. It was during this time that a carrier from 22 Section of 2 Troop was involved in a traffic accident while undertaking an escort task back to Nui Dat. One of the APCs was transporting troops from D&E Platoon and accidentally hit a wood truck. The infantrymen riding on top of the carrier were thrown off, killing one of the platoon and injuring several others. The vehicle's crew commander was knocked unconscious and two dustoff flights were required to evacuate the dead and wounded. Back at the Task Force base 3 Troop had returned to Nui Dat after the recapture of Baria. The respite was short-lived, as it was required to accompany B Company 3 RAR to Long Dien where the enemy had attempted to take over the village. In a fierce fire fight, troops from 3 RAR killed nine Viet Cong and lost three of their own men. 3 Troop moved back to Nui Dat on 4 February before again accompanying 3 RAR to Hoa Long, which was cordoned off for a thorough search of the suspected enemy stronghold.

In Bien Hoa province at FSB Anderson there had been substantial enemy activity. On the night of 6 February three Viet Cong troops walked into the perimeter wire outside 2 Troop's area. They were engaged and two of the enemy were killed in the exchange. On 14 February 1 Troop, under the command of 2nd Lieutenant K.H. McAndrew, moved to FSB Anderson with a company from 3 RAR; at midnight on 17 February the enemy attacked the base. Ron Oxer, one of the troop, recalls that other members of the troop had been playing cards with some American gunners from the 155 mm artillery battery located close to the troop's APCs. Someone was heard to jokingly remark that 'it was a fine night for a mortar attack'. No sooner had he finished his sentence than the sound of the enemy's mortar primaries could be heard, closely followed by the explosions in the base. Initially, .60 mm and .82 mm mortar shells and RPG rocket attacks were launched on the fire support base. The unit log shows that one of the APCs was hit by a mortar round, as a result of which attack three members of the troop were wounded—Sergeant J.T.W. Connell, Trooper P.R. Droop and Trooper A.F. Eilola, all of whom were subsequently taken to the 24th Evac Hospital at Long Binh. The Squadron's commanding officer, who visited the three men at Long Binh, reported that they had all been wounded by the first salvo of exceptionally accurate mortar fire. All had small fragment wounds, received while they tried to close their vehicle's doors and hatches.

The mortar and rocket attack was followed by an all-out assault from two companies of North Vietnamese regular forces, who raced across part of the unprotected knoll close to the area defended by the Australians. The enemy pressed onto the coiled barbed wire defences, surrounding the base in two waves. The first wave blasted the wire defences with grenades but was met by the Australian's claymore mine defences. The second wave was much heavier and succeeded in making their way through the defences, where the US guns were being seriously threatened by the enemy. However, as had happened several times since the Squadron had been in South Vietnam, the .50 cal. machine guns of 1 Troop opened fire. The heavy machine guns of the APCs had a devastating effect on the enemy, who immediately turned and retreated.

It was obvious that the main target of the enemy attack was the US 155 mm guns, so McAndrew dispatched a section from 1 Troop with the specific task of defending them when the enemy again attacked. The next attack came about an hour later. The placement of the APCs near the 155 mm guns had substantially stiffened the perimeter defences; they were located in a position to specifically catch the main elements of the attacking force. The attack lacked the ferocity of the earlier ones and the enemy were dispatched once the .50 cal. machine guns opened fire. By this time a flare ship had arrived which lit the scene, allowing the APCs to direct their fire on the attackers even more accurately. They were assisted by the arrival of helicopter gunships and 'Puff the Magic Dragon', a DC3 aircraft loaded with mini-gun cannons. Another concerted attack on the base was made two nights later, on 19 February, then again on 28 February. On both these occasions the two troops from the Squadron who took part in defending the base played integral roles in repelling the enemy's attacks, thus denying the enemy a strategic advantage. By the end of the month FSB Anderson had served its strategic purpose and was to be closed down.

Back at Task Force HQ in Nui Dat, Squadron HQ, 2 and 3 Troops and the M108 howitzers from 6 Troop were dispatched on Operation

CLAYTON on the southern outskirts of Baria on 20 February. The aim of the operation was to secure the area surrounding the provincial capital following the enemy's attempts to take over the town at the beginning of the month. As it was to be Major Murphy's last operation, he states that he persuaded Task Force HQ to allow the M108 howitzers to fire into the Dinh Co area to distract the enemy from the operation's main objective. He thought the M108s should do something offensive after so much base defence work. Earlier in the month, on 15 and 16 February, elements from the Squadron assisted 7 RAR on a similar operation called OAKLEIGH, which involved a cordon-and-search of Hoa Long village following the events at Baria earlier in the month. At the end of February, 3 Troop remained at Baria while 2 Troop returned to Nui Dat and redeployed with A Company 7 RAR in an operation to the southeast of Hoa Long. Squadron HQ and 6 Troop had deployed to the north of the province, where they conducted patrols around Ap Suoi Nghe.

On 25 February the command of the Squadron by Major G.J. Murphy ended and he was replaced by Major J.D. Keldie. Murphy had made a significant contribution to the Australian Task Force's efforts by effectively structuring the Squadron in a manner that ensured maximum operational efficiency and support for other units.[4] For his efforts, Major Gordon Murphy received the award of Mentioned in Dispatches. The citation for his award reads:

> Major Murphy led his Squadron during 12 months of operations in Vietnam. During this period his unit took part in all Task Force operations; carrying infantry into battle, fighting as armoured vehicles, providing alternative communications, escorting convoys and casualty evacuation under fire.
>
> At all times Major Murphy's planning, co-ordination and supervision were of the highest order. On many occasions he exercised his command responsibilities in the face of enemy fire without regard for his own safety. His aggressive attitude and sound tactics made his unit a most effective force, and one to be very seriously reasoned with by the enemy.
>
> Major Murphy's unit was continuously in operations in the whole or in part, for the whole of his tour. His command involved long and arduous hours in the field and continuous planning for future operations; a task which he did with drive and enthusiasm.

Operation PINAROO

On 1 March 1968 the Squadron was again called on to send one of its troops with accompanying infantry from 3 RAR to Baria, where an enemy force had made an assault on the installations within the town's precinct. This task was given to 3 Troop, which included a section led by Sergeant John Fogarty (Callsign 33). During the course of the action to clear the enemy, the vehicles in his section came under attack from an RCL team on the southeastern outskirts of Baria at Tam Phuoc. Two RCL 57 mm rounds were fired at and hit Fogarty's vehicle, penetrating the armoured skin and exploding among the substantial ammunition supplies. The ammunition was stored under the passenger seats and when the RCL round hit they were occupied by the infantrymen from 3 RAR. Fogarty's driver, Trooper Paul Atkinson, was blown out of the carrier by the force of the blast and was seriously wounded, while the operator, Gary (Snowy) Croyden, escaped relatively unscathed. Despite the explosions set off by the live ammunition within the carrier, Fogarty stayed on board the vehicle until all personnel had been evacuated. The other members of the section could do little but keep a safe distance with their heads down as live rounds exploded and whistled past their vehicles. The carrier was totally destroyed, with hundreds of exploded and unexploded rounds from the APC strewn about the area where it had been hit.

While the Squadron's deployment around Baria continued, Squadron HQ and 2 Troop moved up to FSB Anderson to provide 1 Troop with support in escorting the vehicles returning to Nui Dat following the closure of that fire support base. The next day 3 Troop was deployed on Operation PINAROO, where it was planned to make another move into the Long Hai hills area. The operation was scheduled to commence on 2 March, and the Squadron was tasked to accompany C Squadron 1st Armoured Regiment together with 2 and 3 RAR in what the Task Force commanders hoped would be a significant strike against the local D445 VC Battalion's home base. The enemy had long used the rugged terrain of the Long Hai hills as a supply and staging area for its troops. 3 Troop would commence the Squadron's role in this operation, even though it had initially been tasked to move 2 RAR to Long Dien on 2 March before returning to Baria. However, after the infantry had been delivered and the troop were returning to Baria they were ambushed by an unsighted and unknown enemy force. The troop exchanged fire with the enemy but results were unable to be established; there were no casualties among the members of the troop.

Operation PINAROO was carried out under trying conditions, with the threat from both anti-tank and anti-personnel mines proliferating the area a constant hazard to the Australian troops. It was intended that 1 and 2 Troops would also deploy on Operation PINAROO on 8 March. To facilitate this move the Squadron's commanding officer, Major John 'Blue' Keldie, accompanied by his second in command, Captain Anthony

The wreck of Callsign 33 which was hit by two RCL rounds at Tam Phuoc on the southern outskirts of Baria on 1 March 1968. (3rd Cavalry Regiment (Vietnam) Association)

Lanarch-Jones, acquired the use of a helicopter the day before the two troops moved into the area and made a reconnaissance over the area in which the APCs would be operating. While 3 and 6 Troops remained in Baria as a protection force, 1 and 2 Troops commenced their deployment on Operation PINAROO on the morning of 8 March. As the two troops moved into the area of operation, 2 Troop was engaged by the enemy on the southern side of Hoi My village at 10.30 am. Fire was returned, but results of the contact could not be determined. A search of the area after the contact did, however, uncover a small rice cache.

The next day at 9.20 am the enemy again attacked 2 Troop, approximately 500 metres west of the previous contact. Initially, the enemy fired one RPG2 round at the troop with no casualties or damage to the vehicles reported; 10 minutes later another RPG round was fired at the troop's 22 Section from a distance of 200 metres. One of the APCs in the section received a direct hit from an RPG7, which caused substantial damage and wounded Crew Commander Corporal Pat Eaton and a

Vietnamese interpreter named Duc. The driver, Graeme Bowen, escaped relatively unscathed although shaken by the attack. Realising what had happened, Corporal E.J. 'Blue' Collins on Callsign 21Alpha immediately got driver Bob Tronk to move their APC in front of the stricken vehicle. He then engaged the enemy with his machine guns to afford the wounded crew protection while they were evacuated. Rex Warren, who was also a member of the troop, ran forward and connected a towline to the vehicle so it could be extracted from the enemy's line of fire. The crew members were successfully extracted from the seriously damaged carrier and evacuated from the site.

It was later discovered that the troop had come across a Viet Cong anti-armour training facility. The facility contained blackboards showing different profiles of an M113 APC. The RPG rounds that had been fired at the troop were part of their training exercise for the day, and were concrete evidence that the enemy were specifically targeting the Australian armoured vehicles. Bruce Richards recalls seeing the Viet Cong trainee fire the second RPG7 round at the troop. At the time he assumed that the distance over which the missile had to travel would be too great to allow any degree of accuracy. However, when the round hit the carrier and he was also showered with shrapnel he quickly gained an appreciation for the more powerful RPG7.

The following day, 10 March, 2 Troop located four enemy bunkers approximately 1.5 kilometres northwest of Phuoc Hai (as they continued their patrols in the area). An M16 mine, some detonators and a quantity of rice were recovered from the complex. Four days later a carrier from 2 Troop's 21 Section detonated an M16 mine near where the RPG attack on 22 Section had occurred on 10 March. One of the vehicle's crew commanders, Ed Levy, was reported as wounded by shrapnel. On 19 March, 1 Troop was operating about 3 kilometres due west of Phuoc Hai when one of the carriers detonated a booby trap. One of the crew members was slightly wounded by the explosion, which caused only light damage to the vehicle. After three weeks of deployment in the Long Hai area of the province, 1 and 2 Troops returned to Nui Dat on 30 March and were replaced by 3 Troop to support the Squadron's ongoing deployment in support of the two infantry battalions on Operation PINAROO.[5]

Following the Squadron's involvement in Operation PINAROO, 3 Troop was recalled to the Task Force base on 11 April 1968, where together with 2 and 6 Troops, it received orders for Operation COOKTOWN ORCHARD VI. This was to be a reconnaissance-in-force type of operation into the Long Green area in the southeast corner

Callsign 32A of A Squadron moving through dense bush in the Long Green area during Operation COOKTOWN ORCHARD VI in April 1968. Driver Trooper Gillard (pictured right) was later killed in August 1968 when the APC ran over a mine. (Australian War Memorial, negative number P01777.003)

of the province, and would also involve C Squadron 1st Armoured Regiment and 2 RAR. The next afternoon at 3.15, as 6 Troop deployed into the area of operation and was moving to the western side of Phuoc Hai, one of the M108 howitzers detonated an anti-mine which wounded three members of the crew. The remainder of the operation was a relatively quiet event as there were no other contacts by the Squadron during this time.

5

Coral and Balmoral, 1968

While the Viet Cong's Tet activity in Phuoc Tuy province was centred around the provincial capital of Baria and surrounding areas, the enemy's high command Tet activities were primarily directed at the nation's capital, Saigon. It was intended that the enemy infiltrate and take over strategic locations in the capital, thus causing maximum damage to the Saigon government's reputation and its allies. To facilitate the defence of Saigon, the Australian Task Force had been requested to move north and away from its designated area within Phuoc Tuy. The main focus of the Task Force was to assist in the defence of the strategically important military bases of Bien Hoa and Long Binh. The Squadron's initial role in this process was to escort the numerous road convoys between the Task Force's area in Phuoc Tuy province and the new area on the Bien Hoa/Binh Duong provincial border that had been designated for defence by the Australians. Additionally, the Squadron had been charged with assisting the infantry in securing areas from which the enemy intended firing its rockets at Saigon.

The enemy were now scheduling another 'mini-Tet' throughout South Vietnam for the month of May 1968 and were planning to attack government and military installations across the country. The North Vietnamese government had agreed to attend Paris peace talks with the Americans, but continued with a secret agenda to inflict as much damage as possible on the Saigon government while the peace talks were in progress. Based on intelligence reports that the enemy were preposing a mini-Tet, the Australian Task force was again requested to move north, away from its Task Force area in Phuoc Tuy province.

A part of the Task Force had been in Bien Hoa province since early 1968, where it had continued with the task of assisting in the defence of the large logistics base at Long Binh and the giant US Airforce base at Bien Hoa. As well as assisting with the defence of FSB Anderson during January and February, the Squadron had undertaken considerable convoy escort duties by arranging and controlling the convoys between Nui Dat and Bien Hoa. Additionally, they had carried out reconnaissance and patrol actions, including patrolling the approach routes to Saigon along which enemy engineers continued to transport large quantities of explosives, destined for use against the capital in their latest offensive. However, unlike previous deployments into the southern regions of Bien Hoa, the deployment the Squadron was about to embark on would see it operating far to the north of its previous areas of operation.

Operation TOAN THANG commenced in mid-April 1968 and was ultimately to involve the Australian Task Force in developing three fire support bases, known as Coogee, Coral and Balmoral, in Bien Hoa province over the ensuing six weeks. 1 Troop was the first contingent from the Squadron to be deployed on Operation TOAN THANG and departed Nui Dat on 21 April with the task of securing a landing zone at FSB Thorton on the Bien Hoa/Long Khanh provincial border some 70 kilometres north of the Task Force base. The following day 3 Troop departed Nui Dat to assist 1 Troop on the operation. By the end of the month, 1 Troop was still deployed on Operation TOAN THANG and had moved to an area near the Bien Hoa/Long Khanh provincial border, approximately 5 kilometres southeast of the now deserted FSB Anderson. 2 Troop was assisting with land-clearing operations on the eastern side of the Long Hai hills, while 3 Troop was stationed at FSB Clowes, 2 kilometres west of the southern outskirts of Hoa Long village. Squadron HQ remained at the Task Force base pending the deployment of the rest of the Squadron on Operation TOAN THANG.

The new area to which the Australian Task Force had been assigned sat astride the borders of Binh Duong and Bien Hoa provinces. This area of operations was known as SURFERS and lay approximately 30 kilometres northeast of Saigon. Intelligence reports were indicating that, as expected, large numbers of Viet Cong and NVA regulars had been observed moving down approach routes to Saigon in force to carry out an assault on the capital. To counter this move, two battalions from the Australian Task Force accompanied by the 102 and 161 Field Batteries from 12 Field Regiment were required to develop two fire support

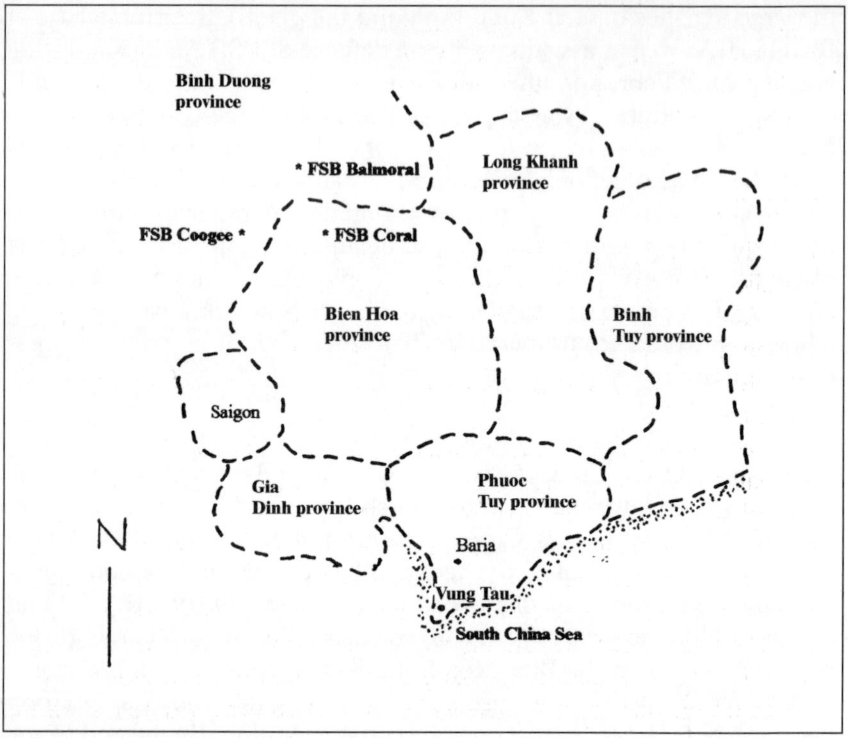

FSBs Coral and Balmoral

bases, known as Coogee (3 RAR) and Coral (1 RAR), which sat astride Route 16 in the operations area. The Australians were to intercept enemy forces moving from the south and southeast towards Saigon. To the west of the Australians' position would be the US 3rd Brigade from the 1st Division; to the east, 2nd Battalion 506th Airborne Regiment of 3rd Brigade 101st Airborne Division; and to the north, 1st Battalion ARVN 48 Regiment, 5th Division.

Intelligence reports had indicated that within AO SURFERS the enemy units deployed included: 141 Regt (strength, 975 men), 165 Regt (694 men), 274 Regt (720 men), 275 Regt (strength unknown), Dong Nai Regt (between 800 and 900 men). Also, operating within the vicinity were three Viet Cong local force units, with a strength of approximately 500 men, and a further 900 troops undertaking logistical and support roles. The Australians had been warned that, unlike previous operations they had undertaken in Phuoc Tuy province where the focus was on searching for the enemy, in this operation they could expect the enemy to come looking for them! Bruce Richards, Troop Leader of 2 Troop, quickly realised that whereas previously the Squadron had largely been involved in guerilla-based warfare, in the coming weeks his men would be faced with a conventional war scenario.

FSB Coral

Initially, FSB Coral was secured by 3 RAR on 12 May, when that battalion was flown in by helicopter; this was to be followed a short time later by 1 RAR. However, delays meant that 1 RAR was not landed until later that same afternoon, which gave them barely enough time to construct their defensive positions and establish perimeters. That night the enemy took full advantage of the confusion that had resulted through the delayed arrival and attacked Coral in strength. A small element from Support Troop's mortar carriers was said to have moved to FSB Coogee on 12 May, where they acted as the base's protection force pending the arrival of 3 RAR. These were the only elements from the Squadron within AO SURFERS at that time. The base was initially attacked in the early hours of 13 May by mortar and rockets, then about 400 enemy troops rushed the wire surrounding the base. They succeeded in breaking through the defensive positions and overrunning the mortar platoon from 1 RAR, causing the abandonment of one of the 102 battery gun pits. The engagement lasted until about 8 o'clock the next morning, when 'Puff the Magic Dragon' (a DC3 equipped with mini-guns) and helicopter gunships were used to fend off the attackers. The Australians had paid a heavy price for the inadequately prepared defences of the fire support base, with nine of the defenders killed and a further 28 wounded.

It was evident that the enemy would be back in force, and to counter the next invasion the Squadron was to be called up to the vulnerable fire support bases to give their defensive fire power some 'punch'. At dawn on 13 May, 2 Troop deployed from Long Binh where the men had spent the evening enjoying the hospitality of their American hosts. The troop had been scrambled in response to the need to get the APCs' fire power to the bases as quickly as possible. Bruce Richards recalls being in radio contact with John Crossman, who was the Squadron's liaison officer, and told to 'get to Coral ASAP' because further attacks were expected on the base. Travelling with the troop was a battery of 155 mm guns to bolster the base's defences. The trip to Coral was not without danger, as the approaches to the base had been mined, and as the troop neared Coral elements from the enemy's previous night's activity around the base were sighted. Despite a few hangovers among its members, 2 Troop arrived at Coral at approximately 9 am.

When the troop arrived at Coral it was informed that it would be accompanying D Company 3 RAR to FSB Coogee, where it was to act as Ready Reaction Force in the event of another attack on the base. Initially, Bruce Richards moved in a northwesterly direction, although FSB Coogee was located almost directly west of Coral. After travelling about 2 kilometres, Richards turned his troop to the southwest. As the troop approached the base it was contacted by a large enemy force. The carriers immediately opened fire on the enemy, but this was quickly stopped when an anxious commander from some of the 3 RAR troops already in Coogee somewhat hesitantly enquired over the radio net whether the troop was firing its .50 cal. machine guns. It transpired that the overshoots from the heavy-calibre machine guns were landing in Coogee and that some of the rounds had cut the battalion's RSM webbing to shreds. On arrival at Coogee the troop settled in, and started undertaking reconnaissance patrols of the area.

Up to this time 'Blue' Keldie had deployed his Squadron HQ in Binh Duong and Bien Hoa provinces to the south of FSB Coral, which was located some 8 kilometres north of the town of Tan Uyen. Before moving into Coral he took the opportunity to carry out reconnaissance over the area in which the Squadron would be deployed. Keldie and his Squadron HQ had been tasked to escort six 6000-gallon fuel tankers from Bear Cat via Saigon to Binh Co, where another American cavalry unit would take over the escort duties. The number of enemy troops now proliferating in the area made these duties extremely dangerous and Keldie's troop encountered two ambushes while undertaking this escort task. However, the APCs were able to race through each ambush site, using their speed and machine gun suppression fire to deliver the convoy to the hand-over point before moving into FSB Coral.

Bruce Richards had moved to Coral and then on to Coogee early in the morning, and Keldie's Squadron HQ 1 Troop, commanded by Captain Geoff Auhl, arrived at FSB Coral later that same morning. Other elements from the Squadron, including some sections from 3 Troop and Support Troop, would follow later. Meanwhile, those troops that had not been deployed to AO SURFERS, which included the remaining elements from 3 Troop and Support Troop, remained at the Task Force base at Nui Dat as Ready Reaction Force. During this time those remaining at the base undertook numerous patrols with the men of the SAS's 2 Squadron to maintain the Task Force's area security while the rest of the Task Force was absent.

When the Squadron arrived at Coral they immediately began patrolling the area around the fire support base as a security measure. However, further development of the base meant that even more resources were being sent to support the troops already stationed at FSBs Coral and Coogee. Their most immediate focus thus changed from patrolling and reconnaissance to undertaking further escort duties. The next two days were spent rushing back and forth, escorting both Australian and US vehicles entering and leaving the two bases. Planning and controlling these movements was undertaken by the Squadron HQ, and proved extremely demanding. During this time one particularly large convoy, consisting of 130 vehicles containing stores and equipment necessary to sustain the troops at FSB's Coral and Coogee, had to be brought forward under the protection of the Squadron APCs, requiring substantial planning by Keldie and his men.

Apart from the difficulties the crews of the APCs experienced when travelling long distances in their escort tasks, many of the roads on which the APCs were travelling suffered from a large concentration of enemy troops occupying the surrounding area. Route 15 through Bien Hoa province, over which many of the convoys traversed, was closed due to enemy pressure. On one occasion, when the local Viet Cong cadre along Route 15 attempted to ambush 1 Troop, the latter simply raced through the ambush site at full speed, not allowing the enemy the time to deploy their weapons against the speeding APCs.

During the time 2 Troop operated out of FSB Coogee, a carrier in Corporal 'Blue' Collins' 21 Section detonated an anti-tank mine which wounded the vehicle's crew commander. It was normal procedure that each section within the troop and Squadron be accompanied by an engineering mini-team, but on this occasion there were no engineers present. Collins organised a dustoff flight for the evacuation of the wounded crew member, but as the area needed to be swept for mines before the helicopter flight could land, Collins set about assembling the mine detection equipment on board his carrier and proceeded to sweep and clear the dustoff helicopter's landing area. As he swept the area surrounding the mine crater he located another large anti-tank mine. The location of this mine was marked and he continued to sweep the area to clear a landing zone for the dustoff helicopter. Once the wounded crew member was evacuated, the unexploded anti-tank mine was destroyed by engineers using explosives.

It was during one of the escort tasks that the Squadron's LAD radio mechanic, Jerry Schellhorn, arrived at FSB Coral. Jerry recalls arriving at the base and being confronted with a large tarpaulin, under which the Australian dead from the attack on the night of 12/13 May had been placed pending their evacuation. The dead soldiers' GP boots, the only things visible under the tarpaulin, were a poignant sight to the new arrivals, and highlighted the serious situation confronting the defenders of the base. On arrival Jerry was attached to Squadron HQ by SSM Ivan Maher; his main duties apart from repairing the Squadron's radios were to spend what he described as endless hours on radio picket in the Squadron's armoured command vehicle (ACV), Callsign Zero Charlie. He remembers that many senior officers from Task Force command would spend a lot of time either in or around the ACV. As a 'digger' he decided to alienate himself. Along with the LAD's vehicle mechanic, 'Digger' O'Hearn, and one of the Squadron's Q Store personnel, he decided to dig a trench about 50 metres from the ACV and place their hoochies over the top. Digging a deep trench was difficult because of the heat and humidity, and they felt they could always dig deeper later on. Initially, they thought they would live in their shallow trench for the duration of their time at Coral, but events would shortly change their plans.

The extent of enemy troops operating in the area was brought home to Keldie when one of his troops returned from an escort task. The troop sighted an entire company of NVA regulars crossing the road in a confident manner, unconcerned by the Australian APCs. The enemy troops quickly crossed the road before disappearing into 2-metre-high grass, from which they could not be seen by the crew members once the APCs had reached their crossing point. The situation was reported to Keldie, who arranged for assault helicopters from the Bien Hoa airforce base to be deployed to the area where they would be able to sight the enemy troops from above and attack them.

On completion of the convoy tasks at 3 o'clock on the afternoon of 15 May, the elements from the Squadron moved back into FSB Coral in force. Keldie was charged by Task Force Commander Brigadier R.I. Hughes with the task of defence commander of the fire support base. Keldie was to ensure that the defensive layout of Coral would prevent penetration by the enemy and to coordinate the various units and troops within the FSB area. In total, Keldie had 35 APCs from the Squadron now in AO SURFERS. The carriers at FSB Coral comprised vehicles from 1 Troop, elements of 3 Troop, Squadron HQ and carriers from Support Troop, including the mortar carriers. 2 Troop remained stationed at FSB Coogee, where it provided security for that base if necessary as Ready Reaction Force. As well, the ACV would be used by Keldie to coordinate and control the defence of the base. In the three hours before nightfall, the carriers were dispersed around the perimeter of the base, which measured some 400 metres wide by 700 metres long.

Squadron HQ was located in the centre of the base so that Keldie could coordinate the defensive effort during the night from the ACV. Captain Geoff Auhl's 1 Troop was located on the eastern perimeter, and would become the counter-penetration force if called on. The other carriers were dispersed around the base in defensive positions on the western perimeter. Later that afternoon, the troop commanders and section leaders made a reconnaissance of the base by walking and observing likely vulnerable points in case they were required to drive around the base at night. Meanwhile, at FSB Coogee, Bruce Richards' 2 Troop, which was the Ready Reaction Force, was placed on one minute's notice to move to Coral in the event that the base was threatened and likely to be overrun by the enemy.

With the APCs now in FSB Coral the defences of the base were far more robust and better prepared for an enemy assault than during the previous attack on 13 May, and on this basis they settled down for the night, with some nervous anticipation. As expected, the enemy commenced their attack on Coral in the early morning of 16 May, at about 2.30 am. It had rained that evening and conditions were humid, prompting crews to leave hatches open to circulate air in the back of the carriers. The enemy's attack on the base began with a heavy mortar bombardment, accompanied by constant RPG fire. The ACV in which Keldie had set up base had six antennas, and had been specifically targeted by the enemy mortar crews as an obvious command vehicle. As the mortars rained down and RPGs crashed through the rubber trees in the base, the crews of the APCs immediately 'stood to', with their engines running and the vehicles' hatches hurriedly closed. At this time the carriers were fitted with either 1 cm steel MG shields or an AAI Model 74C turret, which was being trialled for possible addition to all carriers in the Squadron. While it was said that the M113A1 could withstand exploding mortar fire against its sides, it was necessary for crews to place all hatches in the closed-down position on the vehicle during an attack, to avoid both a direct hit and any shrapnel thrown up by the blasts. As the mortars landed and exploded, the APCs were shaken violently and several carriers received damage to external fittings, with items such as jerry cans being torn from their external mountings.

A group of engineers located near the 3 Troop carriers on the western perimeter sought safety by scrambling through the back hatch of one of the carriers when the bombardment commenced. Their stay was quickly curtailed after one salvo violently rocked the APC. This persuaded them to retreat to the perceived safety of their trenches. In the middle of the base, where Squadron HQ had been targeted by the enemy's mortars, Jerry Schellhorn was awoken by the sound of screaming mortars and suddenly realised that his trench was in no way deep enough. However, he says that 'when our side started retaliating . . . the incoming fire reduced markedly', so he rolled over on his back to view the 'fireworks', which included exploding RPG rounds in the trees and green tracer rounds.

The heavy mortar and RPG attack lasted about half an hour before the enemy moved forward in assault formation. The attacking force approached the carriers of 1 Troop, which were interspersed between the various elements of 1 RAR and formed a defensive position on the right-hand side of the base. Fierce fighting erupted, with the APCs and infantry repelling attacks by the enemy. An air strike was called in to break up one attack as the enemy troops attempted to penetrate the defensive perimeter. When the enemy did succeed in taking over a portion of the base, defended by a platoon from 1 RAR, an artillery barrage was called in to dislodge them from their position. The fighting continued throughout the early morning, with continuous mortar and rocket attacks by the enemy.

During some respite from these attacks, a number of the APCs were required to leave their defensive perimeter positions and move around the base, collecting the dead and wounded. They also began resupplying the now hard-pressed companies of 1 RAR with ammunition and boosting the defences of weakened positions. The Americans had a 40 mm duster anti-aircraft gun on the southeast sector of the base, and when a section from 1 Troop became pinned down with enemy fire the leader of 11 Section cooperated with the US gunners by spotting targets with his .50 cal. MG tracer rounds and then allowing the operators of the 40 mm duster to fire their heavier weapon at the offending targets. On another occasion, when the duster had a stoppage and ceased firing, 'Blue' Keldie never missed a beat, calmly and politely inviting the Americans to join in the Squadron's firing efforts as soon as the stoppage had been cleared.

Despite being under heavy attack, Keldie became aware that his APC crews were having difficulty moving about the base in the darkness. He decided the best option for directing his APCs was for him to stand halfway out of the ACV and act as a reference point. From this position he could communicate directions to the crew commanders as they drove around the base. The sight of Keldie, his body silhouette illuminated by the close flashes of exploding bombs as he waved his hands while directing traffic, was inspirational. On one occasion an RPG hit the ACV and penetrated the generator mounted on the front, transmitting severe electrical shocks to the troops working in the vehicle. On another occasion a mortar round hit the top of the ACV, but fortunately exploded on the vehicle's armoured skin without penetrating the hull.

The APCs with only steel MG guards found it difficult to move about the base: the limited protection afforded by the shields left the crew commanders partially exposed to small arms fire and shrapnel from exploding mortar and RPG rounds. Given that the night was pitch black, the crews acquitted themselves well under such difficult circumstances. The APCs and the men that crewed them had proven effective in both their defensive role and moving about the base while under constant fire. In a fine display of leadership, despite the intensity of the attacks, Sergeant John Fogarty on board Callsign 33 distinguished himself and was a calming influence on those around him. On numerous occasions he would expose himself to direct enemy fire in order to determine the direction of their fire and to locate their position precisely. As section leader he also showed concern for the other members of his section, and even under heavy fire would leave the protection afforded by his APC to personally check on their welfare.

The final enemy attack occurred at approximately 6.05 am, with a battalion-sized attack on the southwestern boundary of the base; this in turn was repelled. Despite the size of the attack, Keldie had already planned to send his APCs to pursue the enemy as they moved away from their form-up positions for the assaults. This task was given to 1 Troop, which moved off shortly after dawn and proceeded through the broken trees and uprooted stumps that now surrounded the base. Jerry Schellhorn recalls the carriers from 1 Troop rolling past his position as they went in pursuit of the enemy. There were enemy bodies scattered about and after the troop had travelled a short distance it came under attack from the enemy in the wooded area around the base. The troop immediately returned fire to the right of their position. A 'possum' light army spotter plane, flying above and observing the action below, reported a bunker system to the troop's left flank. As they moved towards the enemy position, accompanied by infantry, they were confronted by several enemy troops. It then became necessary for the APC crew members to resort to personal weapons, because the .50 cal. MG rounds being fired were overshooting and disrupting the flight paths of the helicopters that were now starting to arrive at the base. By this time Jerry Schellhorn was in the ACV; he states that 'Blue' Keldie was annoyed that the crew commanders on board the carriers had been prevented from using their .50 cal. machine guns, as the enemy had been using .50 cal. weapons on the aircraft coming into the base. Keldie thought his APCs should have been able to retaliate against the enemy with their heavy machine guns.

Several skirmishes ensued as the enemy were pursued. John Flood, crew commander of 13Bravo, recalls his section rolling through a stand of light rubber trees when he suddenly saw an AK47 rifle pointed at him. The weapon was held by an NVA soldier who did not fire, allowing John to draw his own 9 mm pistol and point it at the NVA soldier, not realising at the time that there was a piece of cleaning cloth still in the barrel which had been left there to facilitate snap weapons inspections. The NVA was taken prisoner and loaded onto the back of the carrier where he was fed and given a cigarette before accompanying the troop as it continued its sweep of the area. The troop eventually returned to FSB Coral with weapons, prisoners and enemy bodies that had been loaded in the back and on the lowered trim vane on the front of the carriers. Jerry Schellhorn on radio picket remembers Gus Ballantine requesting a large amount of disinfectant most persuasively, for the stench from the dead that had been carried on board.

The loss inflicted on the enemy was severe, with 34 bodies recovered and buried. The final enemy casualty count was impossible to estimate, as there were signs that the enemy had dragged away large numbers of their dead. (This was a predetermined strategy to prevent the Australians from calculating the precise losses they had inflicted: the enemy thus sought to deny valuable information that would have given a boost to the Australians' morale and indirectly supported the efforts of the defence of the fire support base.) As a result of this action the Australian defenders lost five killed and another 19 wounded.

The previous night's attack on Coral had taught Jerry Schellhorn two valuable lessons. The first was that he and his two mates should dig their trenches a lot deeper. Second, they should move their position closer to the ACV: despite the 'brass' hanging about, they felt that if the enemy launched another mortar attack on the base they could seek shelter either in or under the large armoured vehicle. The decision to move closer to the ACV was largely motivated by the sight of their Land Rover, which was now riddled with bullet and shrapnel holes.

The contribution made to the defence of FSB Coral by the Squadron was enormous, with its fire power an important factor in repelling the continued enemy attacks on the base. Their radio net also played a vital role in the quick passage of information and orders. As well, it was required to evacuate the wounded and resupply the infantry while their positions and the base generally were being hard-pressed by the enemy's constant fire. When the attack finally broke off, 1 Troop pursued and harried the retreating enemy so closely that it was forced to leave behind the wounded and large numbers of weapons. Acting

Task Force Commander Colonel D.B. Dunstan summed up the contribution made by the Squadron when he stated that 'without the support of the armoured carriers the whole garrison might have been over-run and lost'. Such was the intensity and ferocity of the enemy's attacks.

For his efforts Major J.D. Keldie was awarded the Military Cross. The citation for his award reads:[1]

> During May 1968, the Task Force was deployed to intercept strong enemy forces advancing towards Saigon. In its offensive operations from its Fire Support Base Coral and Balmoral, the Task Force continually encountered heavy and determined enemy opposition. In all these operations Major Keldie's Squadron contributed to a marked degree to the successes the Task Force gained in inflicting severe losses on the enemy.
>
> In the early hours of darkness on 15 May 1968 the enemy attacked Fire Support Base Coral with three Battalions over a period of four hours, before being repulsed by the defenders. Throughout this attack Major Keldie manoeuvred his Squadron to reinforce threatened sections, personally organised and directed his armoured personnel carriers in the resupply of troops becoming short of ammunition and in the evacuation of casualties from the forward defences. Throughout the attacks he remained in an exposed position under heavy mortar and rocket fire in order to command his troops and direct them.

The complexion of future Australian deployment strategies changed when a decision was made to bring the tanks of C Squadron 1st Armoured Regiment from Nui Dat to AO SURFERS. Three troops of tanks arrived at FSB Coral on 23 May, which was now occupied by 3 Troop, 3rd Cavalry Regiment.

In the interim, on 21 May, one of the carriers from Bruce Richards' 2 Troop suffered serious damage when it hit a command-detonated anti-tank mine as it crossed the Ba Pho river. Corporal Allan Powell, one of the armourers from the LAD that had accompanied the troop, was standing on an ammunition box when the mine detonated. He was thrown high in the air from the blast and sustained serious wounds. A dustoff flight was organised to evacuate him. The carrier was taken back to FSB Coral where a replacement was eventually organised to join the troop.

On that same evening Sergeant Jock Douglas' APC, Callsign 22, which was stationed at FSB Coogee, caught fire and exploded. The cause of the fire was never discovered although Zeke Brooks, whose own carrier (Callsign 23) was nearby, put the cause of the incident down to ageing ammunition that had been aboard the carrier for at least 12 months without being replaced. It was thought that a pin from a grenade or a flare had either rusted or worked its way loose, setting off large explosions as ammunition rounds and grenades detonated. Several crews tried to help put out the flames, but the explosions became so intense that the carrier was abandoned and left to burn itself out. Geoff Murray, who was Zeke Brooks' driver, recalls the chaotic situation with grenades and .50 cal. ammunition exploding. He took the wise option by electing to stay in his carrier until all the ammunition had been expended. The vehicle's driver, Roger Mika, recalls his crew commander Sergeant Jock Douglas standing on top of the vehicle behind the cargo hatch trying to remove a box of grenades behind the driver's hatch with a long pole. Before he could get the steel box containing the grenades out the entire box exploded, throwing him from the vehicle. The cargo hatch was blown off and the force of the blast dropped the rear ramp. Jock Douglas, who had only recently arrived in South Vietnam, having replaced Sergeant 'Nooka' Stewart as Section Commander, was seriously wounded in the blast and was evacuated from the fire support base.

FSB Balmoral

A decision was made by the acting Task Force commander Colonel D.B. Dunstan to relocate 3 RAR from Coogee to a new fire support base some 7 kilometres to the north. This was to be known as FSB Balmoral and had been set up specifically to lure the enemy so that they could again be engaged in a large-scale battle. Bruce Richards used the analogy of 'setting a piece of cheese in a mouse trap'.

The move to Balmoral was made on 24 May, and the APCs from Bruce Richards' 2 Troop accompanied Battalion HQ and other elements. Initially, one of the companies from 3 RAR would walk to the new base and secure the area while other elements of the battalion would either be flown in by helicopter or arrive with the APCs. Geoff Murray from 2 Troop recalls that en route from Coogee to Balmoral the troop came across a new Lambretta motor scooter. Why it had been left in the vicinity is unknown, although it had most likely been abandoned by enemy forces involved in the attacks on Coral on the previous days. The motor scooter was loaded into the back of Geoff's carrier, and on arrival at Balmoral was transferred to a helicopter and shipped back to Nui Dat. When 2 Troop eventually returned to Nui Dat it had already been seconded and put to use by other members of the Squadron, who were using it as an alternative means of transport.

FSB Balmoral was located in low scrub surrounded by open spaces of dried swamps, normally under water during the wet season. The surrounding area was slightly undulating and littered with large craters caused by US bombers in an earlier action. The base's position provided relatively clear firing lines for the APCs' machine guns and the tanks from the 1st Armoured Regiment that would shortly be moving into the base to assist with its defences. The main threat would come from an area of jungle close to the fire support base on the northeast and northwest sectors.

Once the battalion had been established at FSB Balmoral, the commanding officer of 3 RAR requested that the two mortar carriers from 81 Section deploy with a section from 2 Troop on a fast run around the surrounding area, discharging mortar rounds from various locations to confuse the enemy. If contact was made with the enemy they were to break contact and return immediately to the base. The mortar carriers raced out of the base with the accompanying section from 2 Troop, but before travelling any great distance the leading APC dislodged a red ant's nest with one of its antennas, showering the first three carriers with the enraged insects. The APCs came to an immediate halt and crews and passengers jumped out of the carriers, stripping off their clothes. The other two carriers were brought forward to protect the flanks of the now deserted APCs while crews and passengers composed themselves and the ants were cleaned out. One can only imagine the enemy's reaction had they been observing the Australians stripping off their clothes in the middle of this hostile area.

While this unusual activity was taking place the defences of the fire support base were being established by its inhabitants in anticipation of an enemy attack. On 25 May, the tanks from 2 Troop C Squadron 1 Armoured Regiment arrived at Balmoral, accompanied by a further company of infantry from 3 RAR. After consultation with 2 Troop's leader, Bruce Richards, the tanks were positioned on the northern side of the base, protecting the northeast and northwest approaches. Richards had already interspersed his carriers among the infantry platoons so as to protect the northeastern, northwestern and southern approaches to the base. The APCs also sited the gate to the southwest of the base and overlooked an area of low scrub that encroached to within 40 metres of the base's perimeter. Barbed-wire entanglements had been placed around the area's defensive perimeter and held in place by star pickets, making access to the defended positions reasonably difficult. The carriers had to have dirt bunds constructed around them for protection, something Ken Frazer, operator on 20Bravo, and his driver Bob Tronk remember well, having had to undertake the work by hand in the hot afternoon sun. At that stage the infantry had no command post, so Bruce Richards positioned his carrier in order that the infantry commanders could avail themselves of reasonably secure communications.

At about 2 am on 26 May 1968 the pickets on the APCs reported hearing the sound of bugles followed by tracer rounds and shots. At 3.30 am the enemy started firing their mortars and RPG rounds at the base. When the mortar attack started Ken Frazer recalls that his crew commander and troop officer, Lieutenant W.G. Reddrop, had been consulting Bruce Richards in Callsign 20Alpha, which was positioned next to his. When the first mortar exploded he dived out of Richards' carrier and ran to his own, where he found the back door locked. By this time mortar shells were exploding all around the carriers and the crew commander started banging on the door trying to get the attention of Frazer and Tronk. Although apprehensive, Ken Frazer did open the door just as a mortar round landed nearby, which blew the troop officer into the back of the carrier. Both crew members were lucky to sustain only minor shrapnel wounds. After what seemed an eternity, the accurate and sustained mortar attack ceased and the enemy commenced an assault on the western approaches to the base. The APCs that were interspersed with A Company 3 RAR went into action immediately and repulsed the attack with their machine guns and the claymore mines that had been placed on the defensive perimeter of the base. The assault from the west was not sustained and the carriers on the eastern side of the base were now reporting fire from the northern and northeastern sectors of Balmoral.

A troop of tanks had been positioned on the northeastern sector to cover any attack from the jungle encroaching the base. This proved to be a good strategy, as the enemy attacked in force from this position. The initial attack on the APCs on the western side of the base was a diversionary tactic, designed to draw attention away from the main attack intended from the north. When the attack on the northeastern boundary came, large numbers of enemy troops started moving quite confidently towards the wired perimeter. Bruce Richards states that when the assault force was about 30 metres from the wire, Mick Butler's two tanks each fired one round of canister from their main armaments and his APCs then opened up with their .50 cal. machine guns. The canister ammunition contained ball-bearing-type pellets, comparable to giant shotgun rounds. These two blasts had a devastating effect on the enemy, who could do nothing but go to ground. Their positions were raked with the continual thumping sound of the APCs' .50 cal. machine guns and the blasts from the tanks' guns. The assault on Balmoral from the northeast was synchronised with another mortar and RPG attack on

FSB Coral. The guns firing from Coral to support Balmoral were required to divert their attention and also fire suppression missions at their own attackers. Air strikes were called to help suppress the enemy attacks on Balmoral during the course of the battle. The assaults on FSB Balmoral ended at 5.30 am when the enemy started to withdraw and, given the unexpected mauling they had received at the hands of the APCs and the tanks, to reconsider their options for further assaults.

The next morning the tanks based at Coral accompanied by infantry made a move against the enemy positions surrounding the base. A number of enemy bunker systems in the vicinity of Coral were successfully destroyed and the enemy's ability to make further concerted attacks on that base severely hampered. Back at Balmoral the Australians dug in, in anticipation of a further attempt by the enemy to overrun the base. A bulldozer was moved in and the bunds that had previously been dug by the crew members were constructed even higher to give protection to the APCs, which up to that point had been exposed to the mortar and RPG rounds landing and exploding in the base. The APCs equipped with the AAI model 74C turrets were placed in the most strategic positions to allow crews protection in their picket and observation duties. The crewmen in the carriers with the steel MG shields remained vulnerable to exploding bomb fragments and small arms fire.

While the defences of the base were being developed, the mortar carriers continued to leave the security of the base and race about the countryside, firing salvoes of .81 mm bombs into the jungle. This was to keep the enemy 'on edge' and not allow them to relax as they awaited the opportunity to mount another assault on Balmoral. The next attack on FSB Balmoral came at 2.30 am on 28 May. Reports had been coming in since 1.30 that morning that the enemy could be heard moving about outside the wire. Task Force HQ at FSB Coral had contacted the Balmoral headquarters, warning that they had detected substantial enemy movements and that they should prepare for an attack. The assault began with another mortar and RPG bombardment. A simultaneous attack had again been mounted against Coral to keep the artillery at that base occupied while the main assault was mounted against Balmoral.

As with the previous attack on the morning of 26 May, the enemy assaulted the southern approaches to the base. Bangalore torpedoes were used to blow the gate which the APCs and tanks had been using. The APCs from 2 Troop went into action immediately with their machine guns and fought off the attackers after about 10 minutes of sustained assault. The enemy had previously mounted claymore mines in trees just outside the base's perimeter which they also fired down on the base's defenders. During this attack Bruce Richards maintains that the enemy did reach the inner perimeter of the defences and that he saw enemy assault troops with AK47 rifles inside the base's wire. The focus then shifted to the northern side of the base, with a heavy mortar and RPG bombardment. This attack was followed by continued waves of troops from the infiltration groups of the enemy. As in the attack on 26 May, the APCs facing the eastern and western sides assisted with the defence, as the points of the attacks continued to be directed from the north and northeast of the base. During the ongoing assaults on the northern sector by the enemy, air strikes and artillery supported the APCs and tanks which continued to repel the enemy with .50 cal. machine gun fire and canister rounds as they assaulted the barbed wire defensive perimeter.

The enemy broke off the assaults on FSB Balmoral at approximately 6 am, and two tanks, after blowing away the barbed wire defences with their guns, moved out into the open spaces to make a reconnaissance of the area. Several enemy troops that had been unable to make it back to their jungle hides had sheltered in the large bomb craters surrounding the base, making it difficult for the tank crews to detect them. The APCs, accompanied by elements from the infantry, were dispatched there and several prisoners were taken. Geoff Murray and his crew commander, who had driven out to help with the location of prisoners, also took the opportunity to dump some rubbish that they had been carrying around in a sandbag tied to the back of their carrier. Unsuspecting, they drove over a bomb crater and started emptying the contents of the garbage bag, when a wounded NVA soldier suddenly jumped up and surrendered. Geoff states that not having his weapon on hand made the situation somewhat precarious, although the NVA had probably endured enough by this stage and having a pile of garbage poured on top of him was beyond his endurance. As well as the wounded there were large numbers of dead enemy soldiers to be collected and buried. Several of these were found in the bomb craters that littered the area. Many of the craters were half-filled with water, which made retrieval of the bodies difficult.

Back at FSB Coral on 29 May, 1 Troop, with C Company 1 RAR on board, moved south on a reconnaissance mission to locate the headquarters of the 7th NVA Division, but finding nothing it returned to the base. The following morning 1 Troop, with C Company 1 RAR again on board, moved out to search to the east of FSB Coral. After travelling about 5 kilometres the infantry dismounted on the edge of a heavy jungle area and continued on foot. It was about 8.30 am and the infantry had travelled only a short distance when they met with heavy small arms and mortar fire from a hostile bunker system in the jungle. C Company became pinned down and a decision was made to have them extracted. Captain Geoff Auhl ordered his APCs into the jungle, but it soon became obvious that they were too light to push through the huge trees and the heavy jungle surrounding the area where the infantry was positioned. The centurion tanks at FSB Coral were in the midst of a much-needed and overdue service; despite this, two tanks from 1 Troop C Squadron 1st Armoured Regiment were sent to assist. On arrival at the point where 1 Troop 3rd Cavalry Regiment was waiting, the tanks would lead the push into C Company's position with the APCs following to give protection to their flanks and rear.

The tanks pushed through the dense jungle, reaching the first infantry section at about 10.30 am. Two wounded Australians were loaded onto one of the APCs and the tanks continued the assault, now firing canister rounds from their main armaments to clear the scrub so that they could pick out the enemy bunkers. The tanks created havoc once they were among the bunker system, allowing the wounded infantrymen to be evacuated in an APC while the rest of the company made their way back to the remainder of the APCs. Unsighted, an enemy RPG team managed to get close enough to fire a round at the APC that was evacuating the wounded. The round hit the carrier on the side and smashed through the vehicle's armoured skin, but the point where the rocket entered the APC's hull was directly in line with five full water jerry cans stored in the right-hand sponson. The effect was largely neutralised by the water, which took the full force of the explosion. The explosion did cause the vehicle's tail gate to drop and the occupants staggered out concussed and deafened, but neither the crew nor the wounded passengers being evacuated were reported as suffering any further serious injury from the blast.

In the meantime Major 'Blue' Keldie, who was still at Coral, had mustered another composite troop of APCs and, together with the assault pioneers and a platoon from A Company 1 RAR, raced to the area where C Company had entered the jungle. Geoff Auhl and his troop, who were still assisting the tanks and the infantry at the site of the action, reported at 11.15 am that the tanks were withdrawing. Dustoff flights were organised to evacuate the wounded at a landing zone near where the infantry had initially entered the jungle. Once the wounded had been evacuated the APCs, with C Company on board, and the tanks that had taken a battering, returned to the relative safety of FSB Coral.

On 1 June Squadron HQ was still at Coral, and 2 Troop had deployed with A Company 3 RAR and 2 Troop C Squadron 1st Armoured Regiment and patrolled north of FSB Balmoral, where they continued to suppress any enemy attempts to mount further attacks on the base. Similarly, 1 Troop had joined 1 Troop C Squadron 1st Armoured Regiment and continued patrolling to the east of Coral, again to suppress any enemy deployment against the base. 3 Troop had returned to Nui Dat where it continued its defence of the base, but by this time operations in AO SURFERS were beginning to wind down and the whole Task Force was preparing to return to Nui Dat. The next day at Coral, 1 Troop and the tanks from 1 Troop C Squadron 1st Armoured Regiment were again deployed to the area near where C Company 1 RAR had run into trouble on 30 May. The area was reported to be devastated by the havoc created by the two tanks three days previously and there was no evidence that the enemy had returned to their previous stronghold. In the course of this patrol five enemy bodies were recovered, two enemy were taken POW, and one AK47 and one AK50 were recovered.

Return to Nui Dat

FSB Balmoral was finally abandoned on 5 June 1968, and 2 Troop moved to FSB Coral to assist with the return of the Task Force to its base at Nui Dat, which was scheduled for 6 June. 3 Troop had earlier moved from the Task Force base in Phuoc Tuy province to Coral, where it would also assist with escorting vehicles on the long journey back to Nui Dat. The Squadron reverted to the long hours of convoy escorts for the 300 vehicles returning to Nui Dat and Vung Tau. Despite the reduction in enemy activity in AO SURFERS, many of the roads the APCs were to traverse as the convoys returned to Phuoc Tuy province were still considered dangerous, with continued enemy ambushes a real prospect. The convoy escorts started moving from Coral early on the morning of 6 June, a task that was to see the Squadron fully deployed so that the entire fire support base could be abandoned by the end of the day. At 10.40 am, and as the Squadron commenced its convoy protection tasks, Callsign 11Bravo from 1 Troop detonated a large anti-tank mine between Tan Uyen and FSB Coral. The mine caused extensive damage to the carrier and Crew Commander Brian Plunkett was wounded in the attack, while his driver Brian Neve escaped injury.

The withdrawal from Coral was staggered, with 3 Troop departing the base for the final time at 1.30 pm, 1 Troop at 3.30 pm and 2 Troop at 4 pm together with Squadron HQ, which were the last elements of the Squadron to leave. During the day the Squadron's APCs had been charged with collecting all the surplus ammunition within Coral, as the tropical climate had been particularly harsh on exposed ordinance. Large piles of artillery, mortar and small arms ammunition were collected and dumped in a large bomb crater, where they were wired with plastic explosives and detonated by the engineers. The final act before Squadron HQ departed was supervising the destruction of the base's main command post, which was also blown up by the engineers using explosives. The last of the APCs left just after 4 pm, driving out of the now-abandoned base and characteristically heading cross country for their return journey to the south. Because of the late hour in departing the base, Squadron HQ, 1 and 2 Troops travelled only as far as the large US base at Bear Cat, arriving at 6.30 pm. For many members of the Squadron it was the first night of relative comfort after many weeks of harsh living conditions, and most of the crews availed themselves of the Americans' hospitality. The final part of the journey commenced early the next morning, with the whole Squadron back at Nui Dat the next day. Thus concluded the Squadron's role in what was a vital part in the defence of South Vietnam's capital city.

The wreck of a US APC that hit an anti-tank mine in AO Surfers, close to where FSB Coral was located. (3/4 Cavalry Regiment Museum)

The role undertaken by the Squadron had been critical to the Task Force's deployment in operations conducted in the SURFERS area, and without question prevented the enemy from overrunning the bases which the Australians had defended. This was especially so during the second attack on Coral on 16 May, as the defenders had barely kept the enemy at bay during the first attack on that base on 12 and 13 May. Without the cavalry defending the base on the morning of 16 May and given the strength of the attack by the enemy, it is highly probable that the base would have been overrun. This possibility was acknowledged by the acting Task Force commander. The importance of the overall Australian effort needs to be viewed in a strategic context. Had the Viet Cong and the NVA successfully overrun one of the bases defended by the Australians it would have presented the enemy with a substantial bargaining chip at the Paris peace conference, which was being held while the battles for Coral and Balmoral were being fought.

With the introduction of the tanks of the 1st Armoured Regiment and the use of ACVs in fire support bases now established, the use of armour was widely being acknowledged for its contribution to the Task Force's efforts. From an operational perspective it was also acknowledged that the tanks, supported by the APCs, had proven so devastating that the enemy decided to avoid the three Australian fire support bases that had been established, and eventually withdrew from the area.

Losses inflicted on the enemy during these battles include 267 confirmed killed in action, plus a possible further 60 whose bodies had been evacuated from the battlefields by their own troops. Additionally, substantial supplies of weapons were recovered. Casualties suffered by the Australians included the loss of 25 of their troops killed in action during the whole of the time in the SURFERS operation area.[2]

6

Task Force defence and support, 1968

A substantial portion of the Squadron was made up of National Servicemen who had undergone training at Armoured Centre, Puckapunyal, with their Regular Army counterparts to attain army trade qualifications as driver/signallers. On completion of the 10-week course, they were posted to the 3rd Cavalry Regiment's squadron in residence at Holsworthy for possible posting to South Vietnam. Some were later selected to return to Armoured Centre to undertake crew commanders' courses for replacement of troops in Vietnam. Prior to posting to South Vietnam all troops (without exception) were required to undertake a tough three-week course at the Jungle Warfare Training Centre at Canungra in southeast Queensland. Once a member had completed his course at Canungra he was granted the status of FE (Forward Everywhere), qualifying him for a posting in South Vietnam, where he would replace a member of the Squadron who had completed his tour of duty.

The program to eventually equip all APCs in the Australian Army with the T50 turret had begun in August 1968, with a brief that those carriers destined for service in Vietnam be given priority. This program continued through 1969, and by November that year the Squadron had 40 of its vehicles fitted with the turrets. The T50 turret was made from steel armour plate, with vision plates for use when the turret hatch was closed down. It was capable of taking twin .30 cal. machine guns, or one .30 and one .50 cal. machine gun. Some difficulties were experienced with the turret initially, the major problem being the inadequate space afforded to the crew commander and the difficulty this presented in operating the vehicle's armaments.

It was initially accepted that once a vehicle had completed 16 000 kilometres it became an operational and maintenance liability, beyond the repair capability of the LAD. The distance travelled by vehicles was later extended to 24 000 kilometres before being deemed beyond repair by the LAD. These vehicles were returned to Australia, where a complete overhaul at a base workshop was undertaken before it was returned for service in Vietnam. In many instances vehicles undertook more than one 'tour of duty' once the overhaul had been completed.[1]

The men arriving for the first time soon discovered that life in the Squadron and the way it operated on a day-to day basis was substantially different from what they had been used to. The Squadron's area of responsibility in Nui Dat consisted of a reasonably large site overlooking Route 2, from which arcs of fire were defined and governed by machine gun bunkers located within an earthen wall about 2 metres high. When the carriers of the various troops were in Nui Dat they were located behind this earthen embankment in troop numerical order. Complex barbed wire entanglements enhanced the Squadron's defensive positions and extended out past the embankment. Interspersed in the barbed wire were claymore mines. In each machine gun bunker was a .30 cal. machine gun and a radio that was linked to the Squadron's command post. The machine gun bunkers were all manned during the night between 'stand-to' at 6 pm and 'stand-down' at 6 am.

When the unit's position was first established, living conditions were very basic. But once the Task Force was established in Nui Dat, tents were erected with sandbags lining the exterior walls for added protection. In mid-1968 a decision was made that in view of the prolonged nature of the war more permanent accommodation should be constructed. Accordingly, cement slabs were laid by members of the Squadron on which corrugated iron huts were erected. As well as the accommodation huts the unit's lines consisted of an orderly room, OR mess and separate sergeants' and officers' messes. Immediately across the road from the cavalry lines were the LAD workshop and the unit's Q store. In time, various other comforts were added to the unit's facilities, including shower blocks. With a degree of ingenuity, an OR canteen was constructed to include a bar made from bamboo, a pool table made out of used wooden ammunition boxes, and an outdoor cinema was added to the Squadron's facilities.

It was important for morale that the men be afforded a degree of comfort when they returned to their unit lines in Nui Dat, given that when the troops deployed they were invariably away from the Task Force base for long periods at a time. It was not unusual for a member of the squadron to be away from Nui Dat anywhere between a fortnight and two months. During their time of deployment the crew would spend all their time in their carrier. Apart from travelling long distances during the day and standing picket behind the guns at night, all cooking,

The OR boozer in the Squadron's lines at Nui Dat. (3rd Cavalry Regiment (Vietnam) Association)

sleeping and general living was carried out in the back of the carrier. The smell of diesel from the fuel tanks and being surrounded by boxes of ammunition made life within the confined spaces of the APC certainly different, and at times difficult. The short time spent in Nui Dat meant being able to relax and eat mess-cooked meals—a welcome change from the ration packs consumed by members deployed for long periods of time. At night, and depending on availability, beer could be bought and consumed in the messes. Again depending on availability, movies were often shown to the men.

The time spent in Nui Dat was generally only a brief visit for major servicing tasks, or for mustering the troops of the Squadron prior to redeployment to a new area of operation. On return to the base, and before any other task was undertaken, the crews refuelled and topped up the APCs water supplies, replenishing necessary ammunition and rations in case the carriers needed to deploy at short notice.

Maintenance of the APCs was a never-ending task and had to be performed every day the vehicle was deployed. The crews would generally perform the heavy work such as changing tracks and roadwheels, while the RAEME mechanics undertook the more technical tasks such as engine replacements, gun and radio repairs and any welding. The carriers had a number of different systems requiring oils and lubricants which had to be constantly checked and monitored by the crews, as did the wear condition of the roadwheels and tracks. This work was not readily appreciated by the infantry and others, who failed to understand the complexity of maintaining an APC in the field. A crew might have spent the entire afternoon in the heat replacing a set of tracks that had come off the rear idler wheel—a frequent occurrence. They would then be compelled to spend long night hours in the turret or behind the gun shield sharing a picket between two or three crew members in an ambush site. These were fighting vehicles, weighing in excess of 11 tons, and maintained through hot, heavy and energy-sapping work in order to keep them operational.

The amount of water carried by the APCs was a contentious point among the troops who operated with the Squadron, who were required to restrict and ration their own water supplies. The unit's policy was that each carrier would take five plastic jerry cans of water at the front of the right-hand sponson as an emergency supply for the vehicle's engine only. Another three jerry cans of water were strapped on top of the battery housing at the back right-hand corner of the carrier for the crew's use. The sight of APC crew members using a handbasin full of water to undertake their ablutions, while others were restricted to meagre water supplies carried in water bottles, was at times a source of envy and resentment.

Once a troop was deployed, members settled into a routine that continued for the whole period of their deployment away from Nui Dat. This consisted of carrying out the tasks they had been assigned, usually within a set area of operation. A mini-team consisting of two mine-clearance engineers was usually assigned to each section in the troop, which gave a complement of between eight or nine personnel. When the troop stopped for any length of time it would form up in a circular 'wagon train' defensive formation as in the wild west, with each vehicle in the troop having its guns facing outwards. If one of the sections was operating independently of the troop, they would form a 'fishtail' by tightly parking the three vehicles in a three-point star formation, with each vehicle's guns facing outwards. The common theme in these formations was that pickets were always posted behind the guns on one vehicle in each section once the APCs had formed their defensive position. The pickets usually operated for two-hour periods, with each member of the section, irrespective of rank, taking his turn behind the guns.

At night the sections were assigned to ambushing sites or to fire support bases to boost their defensive fire power in the event of an enemy assault. When assigned to an ambush position, it was usual for members of the section to have a meal late in the afternoon before

Members of A Squadron test a protective chain link screen designed to lessen the effects of enemy rockets by detonating the missile before the carrier could be damaged. Bien Hoa province, July 1968. (Australian War Memorial, negative number ERR/68/0647/VN)

driving to the site of the ambush just before darkness set in. These sites were usually located to target known enemy trails. On arrival the section would form a 'fishtail', with two vehicles covering the right and left approaches to the ambush site and the third covering the rear of the site. Claymore mines in series of six were then set out along the trail for maximum effect once the enemy had entered the killing zone. Additionally, claymore mines were set to encircle the whole section. Early-warning devices were set further down the trail to alert the section to any approach to the ambush site. The trim vanes were placed outwards to combat the effects of RPGs directed at the front of the vehicles. Pickets were then posted on one of the carriers facing the trail and the one covering the rear. These would change every two hours. The rest of the crews would sling hammocks in the back of the carriers and try to sleep while awaiting their turn behind the guns. The essence of the techniques employed was stealth. On reaching a site, the engines were left running for five minutes to give the impression to anyone in the vicinity that the vehicles were still moving. Each engine would then be turned off one by one, distorting the sound and leaving any listener with the impression that the section had moved off. Once the engines had been turned off, absolute silence among the crews was imposed for the rest of the night.

In the event of an ambush being activated, the bank of claymores would be detonated first and the area sprayed with machine gun fire. The contact would be reported back immediately to the Squadron's command post in Nui Dat for logging as well as alerting other members of the troop. This reporting mechanism was used when any member of the Squadron initiated a contact with the enemy. As well as alerting Squadron HQ, the Task Force HQ was put on notice should additional support be required by the troop or section in contact. Conversely, if any crew members were wounded during a contact or on hitting a mine, a radio message would be sent requesting a dustoff flight to evacuate the wounded. It was said that within three minutes of the word 'dustoff' being reported from anywhere in Phuoc Tuy province, a helicopter at Nui Dat would already have started its engines in preparation to fly out and collect the wounded.

The climate in South Vietnam is extremely hot and humid, interspersed with monsoonal rainstorms in the afternoon during the 'wet' season. Invariably, crew members would be soaked to the skin if the carriers were being driven when the storm struck. It was normal for crews to sleep in damp and mud-covered clothing, as very few carried spare clothing while deployed. During the 'dry' season roads and tracks turned to dust, which made its way into the pores of the skin and infiltrated everything within the carriers. A large bag of 'one size fits all' jungle greens was sent out every couple of weeks when it became necessary to resupply the troop with stores, giving the crews a couple of hours in relatively clean clothes before they were once again covered in mud or dust. Despite these harsh conditions, morale among the members generally remained high.

Invariably, when a troop or section was deployed it would be to either assist in an actual combat role or undertake a task that required a considerable degree of care and skill. Every time an APC drove down a dirt road, track or crossing there was a chance that it had been mined with anti-tank devices. This factor is evidenced by the high casualty rate suffered by crew members on APCs. Were it not for the degree of training and skill attained by the crews, this figure would have been substantially higher.

Mid-1968

The whole Squadron was back in Nui Dat on 8 June 1968, where it prepared to meet the Australian Prime Minister, Mr Harold Holt, who was visiting the Task Force base. On its return to Phuoc Tuy province, the Squadron resumed its previous role in supporting the Task Force as both an armoured personnel and cavalry unit until the end of the month.

On 30 June 1 and 3 Troops again moved to Long Binh in Bien Hoa province for Operation TOAN THANG while Squadron HQ and 2 Troop remained at the Task Force base and undertook land-clearing operations on the eastern side of the Long Hai hills. On 1 July the two troops at Long Binh again deployed, with 1 Troop moving to FSB Concord and 3 Troop to FSB Kiama in Bien Hoa province.

On 15 July 3 Troop, which had returned from Bien Hoa, moved to a new area of operation called SALMON on the eastern side of the Long Hai peninsula, where it was deployed in support of 1 RAR on Operation ALBANY. As part of the deployment one of the sections from the troop moved into an area some 5.5 kilometres northeast of Phuoc Hai village, where one of the carriers 'threw' a track. The area in which the section was operating was said to be heavily mined, and the infantry on board were instructed not to leave the vehicle while the crew reattached the track. As soon as the track was reattached the section moved forward in heavy jungle. They were then caught in an ambush and engaged by the enemy with AK47 fire and command-detonated mines. The APC on which Corporal Ken Turnham and Craftsman Doug Borlace, an LAD mechanic, were crewmen was hit with a command-detonated mine from the rear. The mine killed Doug Borlace, who was sitting on the back of the vehicle, and wounded his crew commander and three other passengers. Despite continued small arms fire the section's leader, Sergeant John Fogarty, successfully evacuated the dead and wounded from the carrier and then extracted his section from the area.

For this action and for two previous occasions at Baria and FSB Coral, Sergeant Fogarty received the award of Mentioned in Dispatches. The citation for his award reads[2]:

Sergeant Gus Ballantine on picket duty on board Callsign 31 near the beach below Phuoc Hai. (3rd Cavalry Regiment (Vietnam) Association)

> On all occasions when he has been in contact with the enemy he has displayed above average ability to overcome hazardous situations.
>
> On 1 March 1968 when his Troop was employed to assist clearing an enemy force from Baria, Sergeant Fogarty's armoured personnel carrier was hit by an enemy rocket and caught fire. The ammunition in the carrier commenced to explode but Sergeant Fogarty remained inside the vehicle until he was sure that all troops on board had escaped.
>
> In the period May to June 1968 Sergeant Fogarty was at Fire Support Base Coral when it sustained numerous heavy mortar and rocket attacks. During these attacks Sergeant Fogarty displayed exceptional coolness under fire when he repeatedly exposed himself to check the safety of his own Troop and to determine the direction of the enemy attacks.
>
> In July 1968, on operations, a vehicle in his section was mined causing one fatality and several other casualties. Although the area was being swept by enemy fire Sergeant Fogarty successfully extracted the casualties and his section from the area.

On the same day, Squadron HQ had moved to Long Binh to support 1 Troop, which was operating with 4 RAR out of FSB Concord, and

2 Troop, which had moved to FSB Kiama. The following day the Squadron deployed 6 RAR along Route 15 at the foot of the southern end of the Nui Dinh hills. Four patrols from the SAS's 2 Squadron had been inserted by APCs earlier in the afternoon. The SAS Squadron's Commanding Officer, Major John Murphy, had devised a method when operating with the APCs whereby the driver would lower the rear ramp while the carrier was moving. The driver would continue at a slow pace to the drop-off point, where the SAS troops would step off the vehicle's lowered ramp and 'melt' into the surrounding jungle. This disguised their departure from the vehicle and allowed them to move away undetected.

Three days later, on 19 July 1968, as Squadron HQ were assisting to move the Task Force to a new area of operations around the northern part of the Long Hai hills near Tam Phuoc they came under attack from enemy mortars. Several rounds exploded near the carriers, although there were no casualties reported among the troop. On 23 July 3 Troop had moved to the northern sector of the province, where one of its carriers detonated an M16 mine near the village of Ngai Giao. Again there were no casualties. The following day, 2 Troop's 23 Section was engaged by an unknown enemy force near FSB Kiama. The section returned fire, which resulted in one of the Viet Cong attackers being killed and an RPG launcher and two rounds recovered.

After almost a month away from the Task Force base Squadron HQ, 1 and 3 Troops returned to Nui Dat for redeployment. On 30 July 3 Troop was deployed on Operation KIMBERLY near Route 15 on the province's western border with Bien Hoa province. At 2.10 pm, while deploying 1 RAR on the provincial border some 5 kilometres east of Route 15, 33 Section was engaged by six enemy troops. Fire was returned, but results of the engagement could not be determined as the enemy quickly left the area after the attack. After conducting a search of the area, the troop returned to FSB Gladstone 2 kilometres south of Phu My for the evening. At the end of the month Squadron HQ and 1 Troop remained at Nui Dat, where they were joined by 2 Troop returning from its deployment in Bien Hoa province.[3]

A further act of courage was displayed by a member of the Squadron in August 1968. 2 Troop's 21 Section, of which Corporal E.J. 'Blue' Collins was a member, had been tasked to escort and protect a bull-dozer with two engineers on board near Phu My in the northwest of Phuoc Tuy province. Extensive land-clearing operations were being undertaken in this area in preparation for a major push against the enemy forces operating in that sector. As the bulldozer moved along it detonated a large anti-tank mine, wounding the two engineers. Corporal Collins immediately secured the area and attended to the engineers (having already arranged a dustoff flight). 'Blue' Collins recalls with some amusement that after both engineers had been blown from the vehicle the bulldozer, still in gear, continued to trundle on despite the massive blast it had sustained. Some members of the section were forced to chase after the dozer and disengage the gears to prevent it from exploding other mines in the area.

For his actions here and on two previous occasions on Operations PINAROO and TOAN THANG, Corporal Collins received the award of Mentioned in Dispatches. The citation for the award reads:[4]

> On operation Pinaroo in March 1968, a vehicle in Corporal Collins' section was damaged by rocket fire and the crew wounded. Corporal Collins immediately brought his own vehicle forward to an exposed position to engage the enemy and provide covering fire whilst the injured crewman was rescued.
>
> On Operation Toan Thang in May 1968, a vehicle in Corporal Collins' section detonated an anti-tank mine and the crew commander was wounded. There were no engineers present so Corporal Collins operated the mine detector to clear the area for the medical evacuation helicopter. His prompt action, personal courage, initiative and leadership enabled the evacuation of the casualty.
>
> During a land clearing operation in August 1968, Corporal Collins was escorting a bulldozer which detonated an anti-tank mine wounding two engineers. Corporal Collins immediately secured the area and personally supervised the evacuation of the wounded.
>
> Corporal Collins has consistently shown that he is a cool, quick thinking NCO who has shown above average qualities of initiative, courage and leadership. His actions whilst in contact with enemy have been inspirational to other members of his Troop.

Attack at Baria

After the Task Force returned from Operation TOAN THANG at the end of June 1968 the APCs from the Squadron were to be deployed with tanks and B Company 1 RAR along a stretch of Route 15 to the west and northwest of Baria. The strategy surrounding this move by the Australians was to cut off a well-used enemy supply route leading from the Rung Sat waterway zone to the eastern parts of the province. A series of operations to support this strategy were being planned by the

Task Force and were to be carried out over a period of several months, commencing in August 1968. During this time the Squadron was to play an integral role in forcing the enemy to abandon the vital supply routes that previously dissected Route 2 to the east. The aim was to force the enemy to move towards the jungles of Long Khanh province to the north of the Task Force's area. During the early period of this deployment Operation ULLADULLA was undertaken, and the tanks of 1st Armoured Regiment engaged and sank seven barges from the river line that encroached on the area of operation.

However, things began badly with the commencement of Operation PLATYPUS on 2 August. 3 Troop had been deployed early that morning with D Company 1 RAR and had been tasked to move the infantry along the timbered edge of a firetrail in the Hat Dich area of Bien Hoa province. Timber from the cleared firetrail had been pushed into the jungle on the side, hindering the progress of the APCs. At one stage the jungle became so heavy the leading carrier was forced to use an enemy trail to negotiate a path around the timber debris. As Callsign 32Alpha turned onto the track it detonated an anti-tank mine, which flung the APC vertically into the air, rolling it over so that the tracks and remaining roadwheels were in the air and the front faced the way it had just come. The driver, Trooper Robert Gillard, was killed instantly while his crew commander, Corporal Jock Thompson, was blown out of the turret, landing some 30 metres from his vehicle, and was seriously wounded. An infantryman from D Company 1 RAR who had been riding on top of the carrier was killed and four of his comrades wounded. The extent of Jock's wounds was not realised until several days after his evacuation, when it was discovered that a large piece of shrapnel had embedded itself in his spine. The mine, estimated at approximately 50 pounds of explosive, blew a large hole in the bottom of the vehicle's hull behind the driver's seat. Damage to the vehicle was extensive and it needed to be dragged upright before the body of Bob Gillard could be removed and the APC recovered.

The move by the Australian Task Force into the Hat Dich area was nevertheless starting to threaten the enemy's traditional supply routes. The Viet Cong reacted strongly to this inconvenience, and intelligence reports indicated that the enemy might again attempt an all-out attack on the provincial capital of Baria. To counter this threat the Task Force moved 3 Troop as well as 3 Troop from C Squadron 1 Armoured Regiment and a company of infantry to Baria, where they set up camp in the sports stadium on 8 August. The intelligence reports proved accurate when enemy attacked the Long Dien Regional Forces' post in the early morning of 12 August. A Section from 3 Troop and a troop of tanks were dispatched to the village to assist, but on arrival at

8.30 am they found the enemy had already left the village after heavy attacks on the Regional Force's base. The cavalry troop, together with C Company 1 RAR, thus redeployed to the Dinh Co region of the Long Hai hills. Although intelligence reports suggested that the enemy had retreated to the protection afforded by the hills, a search found no real evidence that the enemy force was in the immediate area, and 3 Troop returned to Baria.

Intelligence reports continued to indicate that the enemy were about to mount another substantial attack on Baria. The Squadron's US counterparts, the 11th Armoured Cavalry Base at Black Horse in the southern region of Long Khanh, had received a heavy mortar attack lasting more than three hours on 15 August, and it was believed the NVA 274 Regiment was stationed at Thua Tich and was poised to move to the south on the provincial capital. To maintain security of Long Dien and Baria, 3 Troop initially assisted the Regional Forces by providing a cordon around Long Dien village as they carried out a search of the former Viet Cong stronghold. However, the search proved fruitless, and the troop returned to its temporary base at the sports stadium.

Finally, the enemy again attacked in force on 22 August. The Regional Forces at Hoa Long reported an attack at 1 am followed by another attack on Dat Do at 1.50 am. The enemy, as predicted, also attacked Long Dien in force at 2.45 am, so 3 Troop, with B Company 1 RAR on board, deployed with tanks from 3 Troop 1st Armoured Regiment on the morning of 22 August to assist the ARVN forces. On reaching the southern outskirts of Long Dien at about 10.30 am, the column was engaged by the enemy aiming RPG rounds and small arms fire at the Australian relief force. To counter the RPG attacks, two of the tanks took the lead in line-ahead formation as the column prepared to enter the town. Meanwhile, the infantry had disembarked from the 3 Troop carriers in order to follow the armoured vehicles. The Australians then moved off to drive the Viet Cong attackers from the town, and the remainder of the day was spent in action as the armoured vehicles and infantry engaged the enemy in house-to-house fighting and the township was cleared of the enemy.

In the fierce fighting B Company 1 RAR suffered several casualties, but the ferocity of the fire fights prevented the infantry from evacuating their wounded, who were located near the village square. Eventually, one of the infantry commanders asked Lance Corporal Peter Purcell to take his APC forward and collect the wounded. This was a dangerous task, with the enemy still very active and an RPG attack on his vehicle highly probable. As his vehicle moved forward it was engaged by the enemy with RPG rounds and small arms fire, which he countered with his machine guns. To collect all the wounded Australians the crew of the

APC were required to make several stops in order to load them onto the carrier. John Flood recalls Peter Purcell asking his driver to reverse the vehicle so that it could return to the arranged evacuation point. However, as the driver, who could not see to his rear, started to reverse he unexpectedly crashed into a small Citroën ambulance being used by the Viet Cong to evacuate their wounded. This 'traffic accident' in the midst of combat turned out to be a fortuitous event, as the Citroën was extensively damaged and the occupants crushed in their vehicle. One of the hapless passengers in the vehicle happened to be the local Viet Cong cadre leader, who was seriously injured in the accident. The enemy was thus immediately denied the leadership of one of the commanders who had been directing troops in the action at Long Dien.

By late afternoon many of the enemy, now without adequate command, attempted to escape southwards across rice paddy fields towards the Long Hai hills, which would have afforded them protection from any pursuing force. However, the tanks had anticipated this move, and engaged the enemy when they attempted to run across the open ground. A light fire team consisting of Australian Bushranger gunships was also requested so that the remaining enemy could be 'cleaned up'.

While the town had been largely cleared of the Viet Cong, isolated pockets of enemy still remained, although the lateness of the day prevented any further action by the Australians. The following morning, 3 Troop with D Company 1 RAR on board moved back into Long Dien and commenced a search of the battle area. Nine graves containing 11 enemy bodies were located. The villagers reported that the remaining elements of the Viet Cong attackers, who had been identified as C1, C2 and C4 of the local D445 Battalion, had left the previous evening and had taken a large number of their dead and wounded with them.

For his action in taking his vehicle forward under enemy fire to collect the wounded infantrymen, Lance Corporal P.F.J. Purcell received the award of Mentioned in Dispatches. The citation reads:[5]

> In August 1968, during street fighting in Long Dien in Phuoc Tuy province, several soldiers of 1st Battalion The Royal Australian Regiment were wounded. Lance Corporal Purcell was asked by the infantry to collect the wounded in his carrier. While moving forward his vehicle was engaged by rocket and small arms fire. Lance Corporal Purcell returned fire and in spite of enemy ground fire he continued to move his vehicle forward and make several halts to collect all the wounded infantrymen. He then turned his vehicle about and withdrew through the enemy fire to take the wounded to safety. His coolness and personal courage in advancing in the face of enemy fire to rescue the wounded were of great reassurance to the infantry he was supporting.

Support operations, September 1968

At the beginning of September 1968, Squadron HQ was at Nui Dat while 1 Troop was the Task Force's Ready Reaction Force. 2 Troop commenced 'road runner' operations with elements from 1 RAR along Route 15 to support Operation TUMUT on 2 September. The troop was initially based at FSB Cook approximately 10 kilometres west of Baria. The troop's role in this deployment was meant to be escort duties for US truck convoys moving along Route 15. However, the US truck drivers, wishing to cover their journey as quickly as possible to avoid enemy contact, invariably drove their trucks at speeds that surpassed the Australian APCs' capabilities. The troop would almost always end up at the rear of the fast-disappearing heavily laden trucks; it was eventually decided that, rather than moving along the road with the trucks, the APCs would move along the route stopping infrequently in the villages and clearing culverts and other likely enemy ambush sites.

While 2 Troop concentrated on the security of Route 15, 3 Troop had been deployed to support land-clearing operations with 4 RAR in the WARBURTON area of operation. FSB Hokinui was established midway between the Task Force base and Route 15 to support this operation.

Given the enemy's reaction to the Task Force's move to cut off their supply routes to the west and their subsequent attacks on Long Dien on 22 August it was decided to base a permanent ready reaction force in Baria. This force would take over the task undertaken by 3 Troop in the previous month. The role was handed to 81 Section, who based themselves midway between Baria and Long Dien to cover any further attacks. 82 Section, the other independent section, remained in Nui Dat to support Squadron HQ.

On 8 September 2 Troop was deployed on a particularly large 'road runner' operation. The troop's task was to escort, between Baria and Long Binh, two large convoys of US vehicles, consisting of over 140 vehicles and stretching over 16 kilometres. The length of the convoy on the road and the possibility of an enemy ambush, made speed of the essence, and it was critical that no stoppages occur during the journey. One section of APCs took to the middle of the road at the head of the convoy and at full speed set off along Route 15, with the convoy of trucks following. Large volumes of civilian traffic along the route had been backed up on either side of the road while the convoy sped past. The APCs at full speed made an awesome sight, and anyone brave or foolish enough to be there had the option of either moving to the side or being crushed by the APCs as they hurtled straight down the centre of the road

On 15 September, Major L.G. O'Donnell, who had been operations staff officer at the Australian Forces' Headquarters in Saigon, replaced Major J.D. Keldie as Commanding Officer A Squadron 3rd Cavalry Regiment. O'Donnell would later be joined by his second in command, Captain John Grey. At this time, as well as covering any enemy offensive around Long Dien and Baria, the Squadron supported 1 and 3 RAR as they moved into the Hat Dich jungles to the west of Nui Dat and 4 RAR into the WARBURTON area of operation, also to the west of the Task Force base.

The Squadron was also engaged in a variety of tasks to support the Task Force. Extensive land-clearing operations continued throughout Phuoc Tuy and surrounding provinces, as did the necessary tasks of road clearance and convoy escorts. The commander's diary notes that the Squadron continued to escort the many large US convoys from the port of Vung Tau to the giant US bases at Long Binh and Bien Hoa via Route 15. The Australian responsibility for these convoys extended from Baria to Tham Thien some 30 kilometres to the north, where another escort of troops from Thailand would take over. Additionally, the Squadron was required to participate in operations being undertaken by the Task Force as fire support bases were set up along Route 15. Many convoy escorts were undertaken as the artillery units moved into numerous FSBs developed along this route to support the Australian infantry units. At the end of the month 3 Troop, together with 82 Section, moved to FSB Hokinui to replace 2 Troop, who had been there since the beginning of the month. During this exchange the mini-team accompanying the troop located a large anti-tank mine (which was subsequently destroyed) on the track leading from Route 15 to FSB Hokinui.[6]

Operations STIRRUP CUP and HUNTING HOUND

In October 1968 the Squadron participated in two major operations. The first was Operation STIRRUP CUP and was commanded by Major Laurie O'Donnell, the Squadron's newly appointed OC, who also had under his command V Company of the Royal New Zealand Infantry Regiment. This operation involved searching the area around Tham Thien in Bien Hoa province and east of Route 15, and commenced on 3 October with the deployment of Squadron HQ, 1 Troop, 2 Troop's 21 Section and 81 Section. As the carriers swept in an east-to-west manoeuvre they came into contact with four enemy troops about 2 kilometres east of Tham Thien. One of the enemy was killed; an AK47 rifle was recovered and a large cache of over 500 bags of rice was discovered and distributed among the local population. The success of this operation was largely attributed to ARVN intelligence sources, whose agents had proven extremely valuable in uncovering other substantial enemy activity in the area.

1 Troop and 82 Section were deployed on 8 October to a new area of operation called Cougar centred on the village of Thai Thien to support 3 RAR. At 12.37 pm, as 1 Troop moved to the east of Route 15 approximately 1.5 kilometres from Thai Thien, it was ambushed by a large enemy force. The result of this contact was that two of the 3 RAR infantrymen accompanying the troop were killed and another six reported as wounded. In a later search of the area 28-pound bags of rice were located. As the deployment continued further large caches of rice were uncovered, which indicated the accuracy of previous ARVN intelligence sources, and that the area contained a number of the enemy's important logistics bases. The following day at 3.15 pm 1 Troop were again engaged by the enemy close to the same area. One of the enemy force was killed and another large cache of rice recovered, bringing the total amount to 233 bags. Over the next three days a further 2500 pounds of rice was recovered in searches covering an area up to 2 kilometres north from their previous area of operation. Following the successful conclusion of their part in the operation 1 Troop and 82 Section returned to Nui Dat on 12 October.

While 1 Troop and 82 Section were uncovering the large rice caches in Bien Hoa province the other Troops of the Squadron continued to provide security along Route 15. There were numerous convoys continuing to travel this route and the task of providing convoy escorts had to be shared around. Numerous other tasks were carried out by the Squadron in response to Task Force needs and were a reflection of the extremely busy nature of the members of the Squadron. The second major operation scheduled for October was Operation HUNTING HOUND to be carried out between 16 and 17 October and focused on the eastern sector of the province. The Squadron's role in this operation involved the clearing of Route 23 as far as Xuyen Moc so that the various regional ARVN forces could be brought permanently within Phuoc Tuy province's regional command structure.

At the conclusion of Operation HUNTING HOUND, 3 Troop and 81 Section were tasked to lift A Company 1 RAR on 21 October to establish FSB Wilton. This new base was to be established some 9 kilometres west of Binh Gia in order that a new area of operation to the northeast of the Task Force base could be opened up. 3 Troop, under the command of Captain B.C. Kollias, was then deployed to the Xa Bang area on Route 2 to assist in Operation DIAMOND PIN. This was intended to be another reconnaissance-in-force operation in which

3 Troop would be joined by the tank squadron and infantry. The northern parts of Phuoc Tuy province were again searched for enemy activity and their camps were destroyed.

AO EVERGLADES

A series of operations was being planned by the Task Force which was to see most of the troops in the Squadron diverted from the base at Nui Dat for prolonged periods in AO EVERGLADES. This area, which bordered the Song Thi Vai river and Rung Sat swamp, was a major supply and infiltration route for the enemy as they moved into camps in the dense jungles surrounding the Hat Dich district. FSB Nelson was established near the village of Phu My and it was from this base that the Squadron operated, carrying infantry patrols around the northwestern corner of the province.

The first of these operations was Operation HARVEST, which was conducted between 25 October and 2 November. This deployment saw the Squadron again near Tham Thien in the Hat Dich region working with 3 RAR to clear both sides of Route 15. On 30 October Squadron HQ, 1 and 2 Troops and 82 Section were deployed in operations in the vicinity of FSB Nelson. In the middle of the afternoon 2 Troop located a large enemy bunker system on the western side of Route 15 approximately 2 kilometres north of Thai Thien in Bien Hoa province. In what was to become a regular task for the Squadron in the coming months, 1 Troop and C Company 3 RAR moved to the west of FSB Nelson on 31 October and set up a series of ambush sites for the evening. The first night of this strategic operation proved non-eventful, with no contact with the enemy reported, although this would shortly change.

The strategy of ambushing the area was predicated on reports of there being heavy enemy concentrations along Route 15, a fact borne out by an action by Support Troop two days previously, on the morning of 29 October. Support Troop had been tasked to clear Route 15 which by this time had become a vital link with the country's capital, Saigon. This was carried out every day along the busy road before the numerous convoys started their runs between Vung Tau and Long Binh. At 8 am the troop encountered a roadblock near FSB Nelson on the northern side of Phu My, which they successfully cleared before resuming their run south. However, approximately 5 kilometres south of Phu My the troop was ambushed by an enemy force, who fired two command-detonated mines at the APCs. This attack was followed up with concentrated AK47 rifle fire by the enemy force. The troop immediately returned fire and, although results could not be determined as the enemy retreated, this did support the intelligence that there were large numbers of enemy forces in the area.[7]

At the beginning of November Squadron HQ was based at FSB Nelson with 1 Troop, which continued its deployment with 3 RAR in the EVERGLADES area of operations. 2 Troop was back at the Task Force base as Ready Reaction Force while 3 Troop continued to be deployed with C Squadron 1st Armoured Regiment in the northern sector of Phuoc Tuy province to the west of Route 2 as part of TANGO FORCE supporting 1 RAR. Support Troop continued in its role of providing security for Route 15.

On 3 November a major 'follow-up' operation to support the successful outcomes from Operation HUNTING HOUND saw the local ARVN forces integrated within the Regional Command structure. To demonstrate the Regional Command's continuing commitment to the ARVN, Operation CAPITAL was scheduled for participation by the Squadron. This was to be a major cavalry operation in the Thua Tich area north of Xuyen Moc, and one in which considerable planning was required.

The Squadron was charged with planning the movement and protection of a large convoy as it travelled to the north along Route 23 and then along the secondary Route 328 leading to FSB Lion at Thua Tich, where the operation would be undertaken. Squadron HQ, 1 and 2 Troops were to be deployed on a considerable number of reconnaissance patrols through the surrounding jungles to ensure the safe delivery of the convoy. This was a pure cavalry operation, with infantry on board the carriers during the reconnaissance tasks. On 9 November 3 Troop joined the operation along secondary Route 330. While moving approximately 2.5 kilometres north of Thua Tich, one of the carriers from the troop detonated an anti-tank mine. One member of the crew was reported wounded and the damage caused to the carrier was described as moderate. The individual troops later redeployed to other areas of operation, while Squadron HQ stayed at FSB Lion for the remainder of the month. While at FSB Lion, Squadron HQ was charged with coordinating the local defence as well as the defence of the main Task Force base at Nui Dat.

About this time the Squadron was given responsibility for the town of Xuyen Moc as part of the Australian pacification program, which meant that the Squadron would soon be deployed more extensively in this area. Pacification programs had been initiated throughout the province to capitalise on the enemy's failure to undertake any substantial Tet Offensive activities and the now reduced Viet Cong presence in the province. A meeting was held on 13 November between the members of the Xuyen Moc Pacification Program Committee to set out their role. The committee comprised the following members: Captain Le Van Duc, Chairman and District Chief; Major L.G O'Donnell, OC A Squadron 3rd Cavalry Regt; Captain J.C. Grey, Second in Command A Squadron 3rd Cavalry Regt; 2nd Lieutenant J. Crossman, Intelligence/Liaison Officer A Squadron 3rd Cavalry Regt. The aims of the program were as follows:

1. When intelligence sources reveal likely enemy threats to Xuyen Moc, an operational plan is to be prepared and submitted.
2. Plan the construction of defensive work to protect the civilian population of Xuyen Moc.
3. Prepare requests for civil aid and allocate priorities.

Meanwhile, on 21 November, over in AO EVERGLADES, 83 Section from Support Troop had been deployed along the banks of the Long Tau channel. At 8.22 that morning the enemy attacked the section with a command-detonated mine, but fortunately none of the members was wounded or any carriers damaged.

On 27 November FSB Lion was closed down and the Squadron was called on to escort the convoy of vehicles as they returned to the Task Force base at Nui Dat. By the end of November the vehicles from the Squadron had travelled a total of 49 700 kilometres, an average of 904 kilometres that month for each of the 55 APCs now attached to the Squadron.[8]

Armoured contact reports

It is at this point in the unit's history that Australian Armour began to report many of the contacts they had initiated with the enemy to the command structure in Australia. In the past armoured contacts were reported by the infantry units under which they were commanded, but the infantry reporting officers often overlooked Armour's involvement in many of the contacts, attributing the results of the contact to the company or platoon to which the unit was attached. When armoured contacts were extracted from the infantry-initiated reports, little information could be gained on the performance of the armoured units.[9]

The contact reports now being initiated by the two armoured squadrons gave the armoured command structure in Australia a more accurate picture of how they were performing in Vietnam. Perhaps more importantly, the contact reports relating to anti-tank mine and RPG attacks provided valuable technical data on how the structure of the vehicles might be improved to preserve the lives of crew members. This was an important development, as it eventually led to improvements to the hull design and modification to the M113A1 APC. It had become apparent that certain points in the M113A1 hull needed reinforcing, and these reports were the catalyst for the eventual addition of belly armour to all the Squadron's vehicles.

From a historical point of view, the armoured contact reports provide an account of the daily enemy contacts initiated by the Squadron and the damage inflicted on the vehicles by the enemy. What the reports did not show is the other vital activities carried out by the Squadron on a daily basis, such as the convoy, reconnaissance and fire support base protection tasks. These were tasks critical to the Task Force's overall operations (as previously stated, too numerous to be documented in this history).

7

1969

In early December 1968 the Task Force moved its full strategic focus to the western sector of Phuoc Tuy and the southeastern sector of Bien Hoa into an area known as Hat Dich. There the Squadron would participate in Operation GOODWOOD from 3 December 1968 to 16 February 1969. The operation would require a considerable degree of expertise in ambushing techniques—especially so along Route 15, where the enemy had been using the nearby Song Thi Vai waterway to ferry supplies and troops in from the Mekong Delta.

To facilitate the move to Hat Dich, on 3 December the Squadron escorted a large 1 ATF convoy to FSB Julia in Bien Hoa province which was established midway between the villages of Thai Thien and Tham Thien. Once the Task Force HQ was established at FSB Julia the Squadron moved off to clear a trail to another fire support base, called FSB Dyke, that was to be established later in the day some 6 kilometres east of FSB Julia. The Squadron then deployed elements from 1 RAR to FSB Dyke before returning to FSB Julia.

While the rest of the Squadron remained to support the Task Force at the two fire support bases, 1 Troop returned to Nui Dat that evening where they were tasked as the Ready Reaction Force. Meanwhile, Support Troop continued its role in providing security to Route 15 from Baria to the Phuoc Tuy and Bien Hoa border.

On 10 December 1 Troop was deployed with D&E Platoon in a reconnaissance-in-force operation. At 2.55 pm Callsign 13Alpha was reported as having detonated an anti-tank mine approximately 3 kilometres to the southeast of FSB Julia in Bien Hoa province. Both the

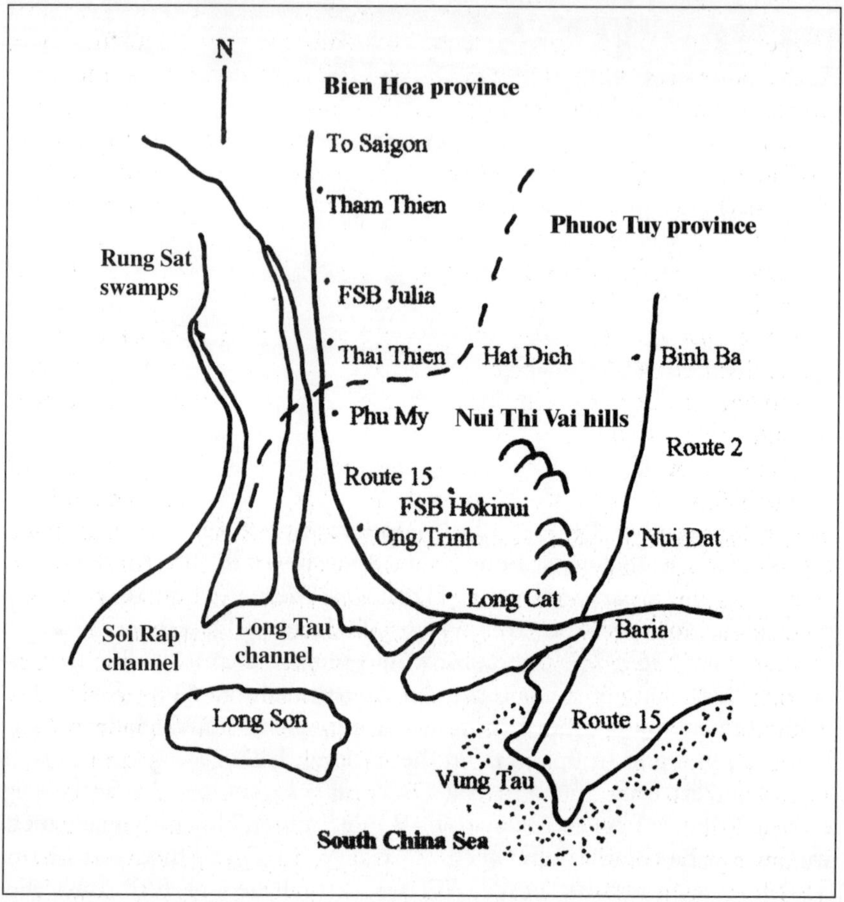

Hat Dich area of operations

driver, Trooper D.G. Pirie, and the crew commander, Lance Corporal L.D. Taylor, were wounded and evacuated from the site. The vehicle was reported as being heavily damaged. The mine was thought to have been manufactured from a 105 mm artillery shell and the strike point was between the second and third torsion bars. The second and third suspension stations collapsed, causing the torsion bars to break through the vehicle's floor. The floor and belly of the vehicle were lifted 45 centimetres around a 30-centimetre diameter hole. The transfer case and transmission were ripped off and there was a large hole in the vehicle's engine housing. The crew commander's basket and components of the T50 turret were seriously damaged. Both crew members were extremely lucky to escape with their lives.

The following day 2 Troop was tasked to escort a convoy to FSB Digger's Rest. At 9.55 am the troop was ambushed by an enemy force, in the same area where the carrier from 1 Troop had hit the mine the previous day. The enemy aimed RPGs and small arms fire at the carriers from 2 Troop which resulted in one crew member being wounded. The troop returned fire but the enemy, who remained in a concealed position, could not be identified and the outcome of the troop's counterambush measures was unable to be determined.

On 12 December 3 Troop was deployed with 9 RAR, who was operating in the Courtney rubber plantation in Phuoc Tuy province near the village of Cam My, when Callsign 33 detonated an anti-tank mine. Section Leader Sergeant Bill Schofield was wounded but elected to remain on duty. Only minor damage was sustained by the APC and it could still be driven after the incident.

The following day, as 2 Troop was escorting a convoy from FSB Digger's Rest along Route 15 through the village of Tham Thien in Bien Hoa province, it encountered an enemy roadblock. An Australian mine clearance engineer and a US adviser who were travelling with the troop were wounded when a booby trap attached to the roadblock was detonated as they attempted to clear the obstruction from the road.

On 14 December the Squadron was provided with intelligence reports indicating a substantial enemy concentration approximately 3 kilometres west of Tam Phuoc village in Bien Hoa. Squadron HQ, 1 and 2 Troops lifted B Company 4 RAR and D&E Platoon and started to move to the area. At 5 pm 23 Section engaged a party of enemy troops, which resulted in one of the Viet Cong forces being killed. Following this contact Squadron HQ and the two troops moved back to FSB Julia, with 2 Troop again deploying the next day with C Squadron 1st Armoured Regiment in a reconnaissance-in-force operation to the west of FSB Julia.

The Regiment's records indicate that around this time the Squadron started to ambush extensively in the area of operations in which the APCs were operating. The unit commander's narrative starts by noting the ambush positions of various sites in which the troops and section had been deployed for their night activities. Rather than harbouring in fire support bases it would appear that a strategic decision had been made to deploy the APCs in a more proactive role.

By this time 1 Troop had again been redeployed to the western sector of the province. On 18 December, as the troop moved along a remote track about 2 kilometres southeast of FSB Julia in Bien Hoa province, one of the carriers detonated a large anti-tank mine of undetermined explosive power. The strike point of the mine was under the second right-hand roadwheel, which caused the vehicle's body to crack up to 120 centimetres along the weld from the second roadwheel station. The rear shock absorber was destroyed and the engine mounting damaged. The sill in the engine housing at the strike point was warped, with an 8 × 30-centimetre dent. There were no casualties reported.

Two days later, on 20 December, 1 Troop was deployed with 4 RAR for a reconnaissance-in-force operation approximately 5 kilometres south of FSB Julia in Bien Hoa province adjacent to Route 15. When in close proximity to FSB Doody at 9.44 am, Callsign 12Alpha detonated an anti-tank pressure mine. The mine was estimated to be between 20 and 40 pounds of explosive, with the strike point directed at the inside front-right roadwheel which was subsequently blown off together with the two roadwheels on the left-hand side of the carrier. The blast also caused the driver's seat to be torn away, and damage to be sustained to the hull, engine and T50 turret traversing mechanism. Five personnel, including driver Trooper Ray Howard and the engineer, were wounded and subsequently evacuated from the site.

On 22 December elements from 2 Troop had been placed in an ambush site on a track about 2.5 kilometres west of Route 15 and to the northeast of Phu My village in Phuoc Tuy province. That evening at 11.58 the ambush was sprung: six enemy were killed, one was taken prisoner, and 13 oxcarts were destroyed.

Earlier that same day a carrier from 3 Troop, which was supporting 9 RAR to the north of Ngai Giao, detonated an anti-tank mine, sustaining moderate damage. No casualties were reported.

The following day 22 Section from 2 Troop was deployed in the area approximately 7 kilometres east of Tam Phuoc in Bien Hoa province when they sighted two enemy troops moving to the east. The section fired on the enemy but were unable to confirm whether their fire was successful, as the enemy fled into dense undergrowth.

On 24 December Squadron HQ and 2 Troop moved from FSB Julia to FSB Redhat 2 on the western Bien Hoa border on Route 320. On the return journey, as the troop neared the junction of Routes 15 and 320, a 155 mm artillery shell/anti-tank mine was located and later destroyed.

As the year drew to a close the whole of the Squadron was back at FSB Julia in Bien Hoa, where Operation GOODWOOD was taking place. The manoeuvre was to occur prior to the Task Force moving once again to the Long Binh and Bien Hoa bases in preparation for the expected Tet

Offensive early in the new year. Because of the strategic importance of the Hat Dich area to the enemy it was necessary to continually revisit the area and disrupt their activities so that supply lines were constantly cut.

Christmas Day was enjoyed by both the 3rd Cavalry Regiment and 1st Armoured Regiment, who held a joint Christmas lunch under the surrounding rubber trees at FSB Julia. Unfortunately, shortly after lunch the enemy fired a RPG round at a US vehicle travelling along Route 15. A number of tanks and APCs with members of D&E Platoon were scrambled to investigate the disturbance. As the armoured vehicles passed the wrecked US jeep a spotter aircraft appeared overhead and directed the APCs to movement in dense scrub. The area was engaged with machine gun fire and members of D&E Platoon made a sweep of the area, reporting numerous tracks leading from the area.

The other ranks had earlier in the day been served their Christmas lunch by the officers and sergeants from both squadrons. Ken Frazer, who was a member of 2 Troop (Callsign 20Bravo), remembers that the Squadron's cooks were sent out from Nui Dat and that Christmas dinner consisted of layers of prawns spread across three trestle tables. Although each man was to receive a ration of three cans of beer, more beer mysteriously appeared for those still thirsty. But the enemy's attack on the US vehicle had somewhat disrupted the conviviality of the occasion.

The next three days proved relatively quiet. However, on 28 December, 13 Section from 1 Troop was placed in an ambush site about 2 kilometres to the southwest of FSB Julia near one of the tributaries of the Rung Sat waterways. At 5.20 pm the ambush was activated, with one Viet Cong soldier killed, one sampan sunk and 80 pounds of rice recovered.

On 31 December Squadron HQ and 1 Troop conducted a clearing operation from FSB Julia northwards for approximately 10 kilometres. 2 Troop remained at FSB Julia before moving out to their ambush positions that night. 22 Section, who were in a site approximately 1.5 kilometres south of FSB Julia, sprang an ambush against a party of Viet Cong at 8.20 pm. The enemy withdrew to the east after the ambush was activated, and results could not be determined. On the same day 3 Troop concluded its deployment with 9 RAR in the northern sector of Phuoc Tuy province and returned to Nui Dat. Support Troop continued its task of providing security for Route 15. During the month the Squadron had travelled a total of 57 107 kilometres, with an average of 848 kilometres per vehicle.[1]

Enter 1969

The expected Tet Offensive around Long Binh and Bien Hoa in early 1969 would eventuate as a series of minor disturbances; nothing compared to the events of the previous year. The enemy had been so badly mauled at FSBs Coral and Balmoral that they appeared demoralised and not inclined to undertake any serious attacks on the government or US bases that were defended by Australian troops. However, despite the enemy's lack of motivation to attack major SVN and US installations in force, they continued with their guerrilla activities by extensively mining the roads and tracks in the areas in which the Squadron was operating.The first six weeks of 1969 would prove to be an extremely busy time for the Squadron.

On New Year's Day 1969, 1 Troop deployed to secure a landing zone for 1 RAR, which was to move into FSB Chestnut on the outskirts of Thai Thien village in the southern sector of Bien Hoa province. 2 Troop, which had been deployed at FSB Julia on Route 15, returned to Nui Dat to become the Task Force's Ready Reaction Force; however, during its return journey 22 Section encountered an enemy party moving to the east, which was fired on with the APCs' machine guns. The enemy fled and the result of the attack by the section could not be determined, although a wallet containing some documents was recovered in a search of the area.

3 Troop replaced 2 Troop at FSB Julia while Support Troop continued its task of route security between Baria and FSB Doody on the Bien Hoa border. On 2 January 3 Troop was deployed on a reconnaissance-in-force mission about 2 kilometres to the east of Thai Thien village and Route 15 in Bien Hoa province. During this deployment a recently vacated Viet Cong camp was located and two substantial food caches destroyed. Additionally, an 8-inch artillery shell and 105 mm shell rigged as a command-detonated mine were located and destroyed. While continuing its deployment on 3 January, 3 Troop was again assigned to a reconnaissance-in-force mission approximately 3.5 kilometres south of FSB Julia in Bien Hoa province. As the troop moved through the area a 20 pound anti-tank mine was located and destroyed. Several small enemy camps were located and these were also destroyed. On 5 January 1 Troop from the Squadron together with 1 Troop, 1st Armoured Regiment, were deployed on a reconnaissance-in-force mission approximately 2 kilometres west of Tam Phuoc village in Bien Hoa province. Two enemy camps were located and 15 structures and bunkers subsequently destroyed.

Soon after 3 Troop was deployed in a night ambush 3 kilometres west of Phu My village in Phuoc Tuy province adjacent to Route 15, on the edge of the Rung Sat swamp. The ambush was activated that evening and resulted in a 35-foot motorised junk and a sampan being sunk. Three Viet Cong troops were also killed. The following day, 7 January 1969, an APC from 3 Troop detonated an M26 grenade on a trail about 3 kilometres west of FSB Julia in Bien Hoa. No damage was reported to the vehicle, nor any injuries sustained.

On 8 January elements from 3 Troop were deployed on a reconnaissance-in-force operation approximately 6 kilometres due north of FSB Julia in Bien Hoa province and 5 kilometres west of Route 15. Here a section from the troop located a freshly evacuated enemy camp and at 10.55 am came into contact with five enemy troops near the village of Long Son at the southern end of the Rung Sat waterway. One Viet Cong was killed and an AK47 rifle and documents recovered. Trooper Frank McAnally suffered fragmentation wounds as a result of the action. On the same day 1 Troop, which had also been deployed in a reconnaissance-in-force operation 2 kilometres west of Thai Thien, located and destroyed two small enemy camps.

The following evening at 5.50 pm an APC from 1 Troop detonated a mine as they set off to the night ambush positions. The attack occurred approximately 1.5 kilometres west of Phu My village in Phuoc Tuy province. The mine had been manufactured from a 105 mm artillery shell, and light damage was sustained by the vehicle. The driver, Trooper Stewart Leak, was wounded in the attack and evacuated. The APC was repaired at the site before the troop returned to FSB Julia.

On 11 January 31 Section from 3 Troop was placed in an ambush on the outskirts of Thai Thien in Bien Hoa province. At 7.30 pm the ambush was activated and one Viet Cong captured. The following day at 7.30 am an APC from 31 Section detonated a mine about 2 kilometres west of Thai Thien village in Bien Hoa. The mine did not damage the vehicle, nor were any casualties reported. At approximately 4.30 pm, 12 Section from 1 Troop captured one Viet Cong soldier and two sampans in one of the tributaries of the northern extremities of the Rung Sat swamp. At 11.17 pm, 32 Section from 3 Troop activated an ambush close to FSB Chestnut. Two enemy were contacted but withdrew before results could be determined.

On 13 January 1 RAR moved to establish FSB Margaret about 1 kilometre east of Tam Phuoc in Bien Hoa province. To secure the area 3 Troop was deployed with D Company 1 RAR and some Swift patrol boats from the US Navy, and were tasked to clear a creek running into the Rung Sat swamp. But the terrain in which the APCs were deployed was extremely 'boggy' and totally unsuitable for M113A1 operations, and one carrier almost sank in the mud. The infantry were unloaded from the carriers before being picked up by the Swift patrol boats.

The following day Squadron HQ, elements from 1 and 3 Troops together with 4 Troop 1st Armoured Regiment conducted a reconnaissance-in-force operation in an area located between Routes 15 and 2 and known as AO SHERMAN. On moving to the area they located an enemy camp about 9 kilometres east of the Task Force base and close to FSB Nola, which had recently been established in the dense jungle to support operations in the area. At 1.10 pm a tank from 4 Troop 1 Armoured Regiment detonated an anti-tank mine and sustained light damage. A security force was left with the damaged tank pending its recovery while the rest of the troop returned to FSB Julia.

On 16 January at FSB Margaret in Bien Hoa province intelligence reports had been received relating to enemy activity to the east of the base. At 7.30 that morning 31 Section from 3 Troop and a troop of tanks were deployed from FSB Julia and tasked to accompany C Company 1 RAR in an easterly sweep of the area. No significant enemy positions or activities were revealed, and the section returned to FSB Julia later that day.

On 18 January during Operation GOODWOOD, the force of the enemy's guerilla activities was felt. A section of APCs from Squadron HQ had been deployed to resupply D Company 1 RAR, which was engaged in operations near the Bien Hoa/Phuoc Tuy border approximately 8 kilometres west of Thai Thien on Route 15. The section was commanded by Corporal Peter Malone, who was being accompanied on the task by the Squadron's Sergeant Major, Roy Hughes. There were also several passengers on board Callsign 9Echo when it hit a large anti-tank mine at 11.42 am. The mine was estimated at 50 pounds of explosive, and when it detonated it mortally wounded Corporal Malone. His driver, Trooper Les Bright, SSM Roy Hughes and several of the passengers were also seriously wounded. The mine's point of strike was directly under the crew commander's cupola, blasting out a piece of the vehicle's belly measuring 30 × 180 centimetres. A further 120 × 90 centimetre depression surrounded the point of strike. Several roadwheels and suspension arms were blown off, as were the machine gun shield and crew commander's cupola. The engine was completely shattered, and part of the transfer case hung through a hole in the floor.

The leading carrier in the section was commanded by Lance Corporal David Izatt, who had unknowingly avoided the mine. Unfortunately, Corporal Malone's vehicle was the next APC in the column, and his vehicle detonated the mine. David Izatt, who was relatively inexperienced, immediately organised his own crew and deployed the engineers on his vehicle to clear the area of further mines. He then calmly organised dustoff flights for the crew and the five passengers on the damaged APC. Once the wounded were cleared he proceeded to arrange recovery of the damaged vehicle.

For his swift action Lance Corporal D.J. Izatt received the award of Mentioned in Dispatches. The citation for his award reads:[2]

> On 18 January 1969 during operation Goodwood, Lance Corporal Izatt was the Crew Commander on the lead vehicle in an armoured personnel carrier section conducting a resupply mission for an infantry company. At approximately 1143 hours, the Section Commander's vehicle which was moving behind Corporal Izatt's vehicle, detonated a large anti-tank mine. The detonation severely damaged the armoured personnel carrier, fatally wounded the Crew Commander and seriously wounded the other five occupants of the vehicle.
>
> Corporal Izatt reacted immediately and organised his own crew and the attached engineer element to secure the area from possible enemy action and to check it for any further mines. He then calmly organised assistance to the wounded and their evacuation by air. All these events took place in a very rapid space of time. With this completed he then proceeded to organise the recovery of the damaged carrier.
>
> Corporal Izatt, by his presence of mind, reacted immediately to master a confusing situation. Despite his inexperience, his was an above average performance under adverse conditions and his personal conduct set an example for all.

The following day, 19 January 1969, 22 Section from 2 Troop under the command of Captain Thomas Arrowsmith, together with SAS troops, were placed in an ambush site approximately 5 kilometres east of FSB Chestnut in Bien Hoa province. They had been observing an enemy trail for several days. At 5.16 pm the ambush was activated against a large enemy force, which resulted in three enemy troops killed and another two wounded but able to escape. An RPG launcher and two rounds were recovered. In spite of their earlier losses, the enemy decided to regroup and wait for cover of night in order to counterattack. A couple of hours after the ambush had been initiated the enemy attacked the SAS ambush site and attempted to overrun their position. The APCs countered this attack by directing fire at the enemy, which allowed the SAS patrol to withdraw.

That same evening 33 Section of 3 Troop were placed in an ambush site close to FSB Chestnut. The ambush was activated at 8.23 pm against an estimated enemy force of 12 Viet Cong troops. One enemy was killed, three others were wounded and a rifle was recovered.

Earlier that day 1 Troop had returned to the base at Nui Dat, where they undertook the task of providing the Task Force's Ready Reaction Force. During this time, elements from the Squadron's 2 Troop were deployed in support of A Brigade of the ARVN Marine Regiment and the 52 ARVN Regiment, who had been deployed to AO MOORE about 20 kilometres north of the Australian Task Force's area of operation around FSB Julia.

On 26 January, 21 Section from 2 Troop were placed in an ambush position 2 kilometres south of Thai Thien, where at 8 am they took an enemy soldier prisoner.

On 28 January 4 RAR entered a new area of operation west of FSB Julia which required the Squadron to provide numerous delivery and extraction and route security tasks to FSB Dyke. That evening enemy movement was detected on the wire outside FSB Julia, which was followed by enemy fire on the positions of elements from 2 and 3 Troops. Loud screams were heard from the enemy's position on the wire, but in a later sweep of the area nothing was found. The following day 2 and 3 Troops continued to support 4 RAR in their new area of operation. 22 Section remained in an ambush position west of FSB Julia where they heard enemy movement, but because the enemy remained unsighted they could not be engaged. On 30 January, 32 Section of 3 Troop were supporting land-clearing operations when they located a 10 pound chicom pressure mine while clearing a track about 2 kilometres south of Thai Thien in Bien Hoa province. The mine was subsequently destroyed by the engineer's mini-team.

At the end of the month 2 Troop had returned to the Task Force base at Nui Dat where they replaced as Ready Reaction Force 1 Troop, which had undertaken numerous 'road runner' and escort tasks along Route 15. When 1 Troop deployed they commenced operations with 1 RAR, while 3 Troop supported elements operating from FSB Jenny. During the month the Squadron's vehicles had covered 52 528 kilometres which equated to 740 kilometres per vehicle.[3]

The demands of the previous month continued on into February. On the night of 1 February, 3 Troop was placed in an ambush on the edge of the waterway to the southwest of FSB Julia in Bien Hoa province. The ambush was activated at 2.08 am on 2 February, which resulted in two Viet Cong being killed and one sampan sunk. On 6 February, 12 Section from 1 Troop, together with elements from D&E Platoon and 3 Troop 1st Armoured Regiment, conducted a reconnaissance-in-force operation 4 kilometres west of Tam Phuoc in Bien Hoa province. 3 Troop 1st Armoured Regiment departed at the end of the day, leaving 12 Section and D&E Platoon in an ambush site some 5 kilometres to the west of the village of Tam Phuoc along the Soi Rap channel. That evening a sampan moving south to north was fired on when the ambush was activated. At the same time movement was detected on the western bank of the channel and was fired on, but results of the contact could not be ascertained. The following day 1 Troop and elements from D&E Platoon continued the reconnaissance-in-force operation to the west of Tam Phuoc village. At 8.30 am two Viet Cong were contacted, which resulted in two AK47 rifles being captured along with a quantity of supplies, including three bags of barley.

The results of the ambush by 22 Section on the evening of 19 January were thought to be greater than those originally reported, with the discovery of three graves approximately 1 kilometre west of FSB Chestnut on 9 February. The bodies were about three weeks old and the wounds sustained were attributed to the weapons used by 22 Section when the ambush was activated.

On 16 February elements from the Squadron together with D&E Platoon conducted another reconnaissance-in-force operation 4 kilometres east of FSB Julia in Bien Hoa province. At 12.20 pm two enemy were contacted and fired on, but the outcome of the APCs' fire could not be determined as the enemy retreated into heavy scrub.

During the period October 1968 to January 1969 the Squadron effected 10 successful ambushes in the Hat Dich area. The new ambushing techniques being employed were the brainchild of the Squadron's Intelligence Officer, 2nd Lieutenant John Crossman, and were designed specifically for the cavalry. During Operations HARVEST, CAPITAL and GOODWOOD, Crossman, who had been working closely with the US Army, was able to impart information to the troops within the Squadron, enabling them to successfully employ the techniques he had devised. Not only did Crossman devise and instigate these new ambushing techniques to ensure their operational suitability—he personally supervised their practical application by deploying with the troops as they moved into ambush sites.

For his efforts Crossman received the award of Mentioned in Dispatches. The citation for his award reads:

> He commenced his tour of duty as a troop officer and then later became the Squadron intelligence and liaison officer. An extremely dedicated and competent young officer he approached all his responsibilities in a most professional manner.
>
> As Squadron intelligence officer Second Lieutenant Crossman was very thorough in the performance of his duty and constantly sought ways and means to improve his knowledge. On several occasions he successfully devised new ambushing techniques for cavalry, which he personally put into practice.
>
> During Operations Harvest, Capital and Goodwood between October 1968 and January 1969, he deployed as a liaison officer with the United

> States Army units working to support the Australian Task Force. His exemplary conduct, bearing, cooperation and grasp of military affairs at all times enabled him to be held in the highest regard by the allied units to which he was attached.

During the previous six months the Squadron had incurred a large number of casualties as a result of anti-tank mines and booby traps, which had inflicted horrific wounds on members of the APC crews. Fifteen APCs had been severely damaged during this period. At the time, the carriers in the Squadron were covering distances of between 55 000 and 60 000 track kilometres each month. Based on these figures it was expected that one APC could expect to hit a mine every 20 000 kilometres that the Squadron travelled. The large kilometrage being travelled was mainly attributed to the weekly convoy escorts of up to 700 American vehicles travelling along Route 15. Initially, these escorts ran between Baria and Thai Tien, but the escorts were being extended to include the whole route between Vung Tau and Long Binh.

Corporal Bob Veall and Trooper Greg Aitken inspect a drive shaft blown from one of the Squadron's APCs after it detonated an anti-tank mine. (3/4 Cavalry Regiment Museum)

In an attempt to overcome the effects of mine blasts, sandbags filled with dirt were placed in the back of the carriers. However, as the dirt in the sandbags became compacted from the effects of rain and traffic within the vehicle no real benefit was achieved, and in some cases the concrete-like hardened sand bags compounded the wounds suffered by crews when their APCs hit a mine. As a reflection of the increased activities being undertaken by the Squadron in 1968/69, the number of casualties had risen dramatically over the previous year. Whereas at the end of 1967 the Squadron had suffered only 13 incidents in which men were killed, wounded or injured, this number had risen to 33 in 1968 and was to get worse.

As well as through the convoy escorts undertaken by the Squadron, kilometres were added through the support given by cavalry to various infantry operations. In one instance the Squadron, which had in February 1968 accompanied 3 RAR to put down the attempted takeover of Baria during the Tet Offensive, and later in that same year supported them at FSB Balmoral, cooperated with that battalion on no fewer than 18 operations out of a total of 26 conducted during their tour of duty in South Vietnam. It must also be remembered that there were two other battalions that were supported by the Squadron on comparable numbers of operations, making the unit the most mobile and busiest in the Task Force.

Bien Hoa province

On 17 February 1969 Squadron HQ, who had until that date been coordinating the defence of the Task Force base from FSB Julia, moved to a new area of operation known as AO MAJURA. This new area was deep inside Bien Hoa province and saw Squadron HQ relocate to FSB Kerry, from where it would continue its role of coordinating the defence of the base at Nui Dat. The Squadron also continued to allocate one of its troops as part of the Task Force's Ready Reaction Force. This meant that while the Squadron operated extensively throughout the surrounding districts and provinces, one troop from the Squadron was required to be able to respond to any actions that might compromise the security of the Task Force base area and surrounding townships. The Ready Reaction Force during the Tet period of February 1969 was the Squadron's 3 Troop led by Captain Ray DeVere, who had taken over the troop only a month earlier after being posted to the Squadron.

As part of their annual Phuoc Tuy provincial Tet Offensive program, the enemy again attacked the village of Long Dien to the south of the Task Force base on 18 February. The Squadron's 3 Troop was dispatched with B Company 9 RAR and succeeded in clearing the enemy from the village. DeVere attacked the enemy, driving the infiltrators from the village but not before encountering heavy fighting from the large enemy force. DeVere's 3 Troop was once again in action on the night of 22/23 February, when the enemy attacked the provincial capital of Baria. As Ready Reaction Force, the troop was dispatched to Baria to assist in repelling the enemy, who had attacked in force and attempted to take over the town as in the previous year. Again the troop was involved in heavy fighting as the enemy forces resisted the defensive efforts of the Australians.

While 3 Troop was active around Baria in Phuoc Tuy province, 1 and 2 Troops continued their deployment in Bien Hoa province supporting the 1/2 US Infantry Battalion. On 22 February at 12.50 pm elements from 2 Troop contacted approximately 20 enemy. One of the enemy troops was wounded and taken prisoner. Also captured was an AK47 rifle, a bangalore torpedo and two RPG rounds.

On 26 February there were two mine attacks involving carriers from 2 Troop. The troop had been redeployed to the eastern sector of Bien Hoa province where they were supporting 4 RAR. The first attack occurred early in the afternoon at 12.20 some 2 kilometres south of Trang Bom village. Only moderate damage was sustained by the carrier when a 20-pound mine was detonated under the front right-hand track. The right-hand track was broken and the front roadwheel was blown off. The support arm was bent and a 10-centimetre hole sustained by the hull adjacent to the front support arm. However, there was no damage to the engine and no injuries or wounds were reported.

The second attack occurred 20 minutes later, about 200 metres south of the previous attack. The carrier sustained heavy damage when it hit a 20 pound anti-tank mine under the front of the right track. The right-hand track was broken and the front roadwheel blown off. The support arm was bent, the shock absorber twisted and the torsion bar broken. A hole 15 centimetres in diameter was sustained adjacent to the support arm bearing, and both the final drive housing and drive sprocket were cracked. The belly warped 12 millimetres at the front half of the vehicle's hull, causing the engine to move from its mountings. The vehicle's crew commander, Corporal Bill Jackson, was reported as sustaining wounds as a result of the explosion.

At the end of the month Squadron HQ remained at FSB Kerry, where it continued to coordinate the defence of the Task Force base. 1 and 2 Troops remained in Bien Hoa province in AOs ARUNDA and BELCONNEN, where they continued to support both 4 and 9 RAR. 3 and Support Troops remained at Nui Dat as the Task Force's Ready

Reaction Force. They also continued to carry out numerous 'road runner' and escort tasks along Route 15. During the month the Squadron's vehicles had covered a total of 55 745 kilometres, which equated to an average of 888 kilometres per vehicle.[4]

The first two weeks of March proved uneventful. Operations continued in Bien Hoa province where the Squadron supported both 9 and 5 RAR, while 4 RAR had moved their area of operations and were now deploying from the Horseshoe in Phuoc Tuy province. On the morning of 16 March 1 Troop and B Company 2/52 Infantry Battalion (ARVN) conducted a reconnaissance-in-force operation approximately 2 kilometres south of Trang Bom village in Bien Hoa. After a brief fire fight at 9.30 am one enemy who had been wounded in the action was taken prisoner by the troop. The troop continued to sweep the area and at 11 am located a large enemy camp that they estimated to be of at least battalion strength. On 18 March at 7.19 am, 32 Section from 3 Troop was operating along Route 15 near Hoi Phuoc village in Phuoc Tuy province when one of the carriers from the section was attacked by an enemy force. Two RPG rounds were fired at the carrier, hitting it on the left-hand side about 120 centimetres from the front of the vehicle. The RPG round penetrated the side of the vehicle, leaving a 5-centimetre hole. The round then passed through the side engine panel before smashing into the engine, where it caused substantial damage. The driver, Trooper Robin Apps, was wounded and evacuated. After firing their rockets the enemy force, whose strength was not able to be determined, withdrew from the area, although it was reported that they were subsequently engaged by a light fire team.

On 27 March elements of the Squadron were tasked to escort a convoy of trucks and support the movement of 5 and 9 RAR as they moved into AOs MANUKA and REID respectively. As the convoy travelled along Route 15 well inside Bien Hoa province two trucks from the US Army struck mines. Seven Australians and one US serviceman were wounded. Meanwhile 1 Troop was supporting C Company 4 RAR in AO DRAYTON near the Courtney rubber plantation in the northern sector of Phuoc Tuy province. At 1.10 pm south of Cam My village the troop contacted five enemy troops, who immediately withdrew when fired on, making results of the contact indeterminable. On 30 March 2 Troop engaged and killed an armed person who had run off as the troop approached him. He was later identified as being a member of a local Viet Cong force.

At the end of the month Squadron HQ remained at FSB Kerry. 1 Troop was stationed at Nui Dat as Ready Reaction Force with

W Company 4 RAR. 2 and 3 Troops remained in Bien Hoa province, where they supported 5 and 9 RAR on operations. Support Troop continued to provide 'road runner' and escort duties along Route 15.[5]

BACK TO PHUOC TUY PROVINCE

The Task Force role in the operations in Bien Hoa province had begun to wind down and it was planned to move the Squadron back to Phuoc Tuy province in April. The bulk of the Task Force had been away from the province for almost 12 months and a series of operations was now required to re-establish the Australian presence there. The Squadron's 1 Troop led by Captain D.R. Lawrence and 2 Troop led by Captain T.H. Arrowsmith were committed to Operations STAFFORD and SURFSIDE in the Xuan Loc and Phu My districts, aimed primarily at clearing the Viet Cong from Long Khanh province and the northwest and western parts of Phuoc Tuy province. To facilitate this strategy Squadron HQ vacated FSB Kerry on 3 April and moved to FSB Jillian, which was located in Long Khanh province midway between Xuyen Loc and Trang Bom and about 3 kilometres south of Route 1.

On the same day reports were being received of enemy activity on the eastern side of the Binh Ba rubber plantation. 1 Troop with 2 Troop 1st Armoured Regiment and V Company 4 RAR were dispatched to investigate these reports. While no enemy were located, some bunkers were found and subsequently destroyed.

On 5 April 2 Troop was deployed to AO REID in Long Khanh province in an area approximately 10 kilometres northwest of the US base of Black Horse. The previous day had seen 2 and 3 Troops operating with D&E Platoon in a reconnaissance-in-force operation in the new AO REID. During the day elements of the two troops were involved in a number of actions. The day began when 2 Troop activated an ambush on a party of 12 enemy at 5.53 am. Results could not be determined, although it was estimated that casualties had been inflicted on the party. At 2.23 pm, as 2 Troop swept an area 4 kilometres south of FSB Jillian, they discovered an enormous bunker complex containing over 150 bunkers. Several ambush positions were allocated to the two troops for the evening to cover the bunker system discovered earlier in the day, which was thought to be a centralised staging point in view of the large enemy concentrations in the area. 22 Section was placed in an ambush position some 2.5 kilometres southeast of Jillian where two groups of enemy, each containing 20 troops, were fired on by the section. Six of the enemy forces were confirmed killed when the ambush was initiated, with another five enemy troops possibly killed (their bodies dragged away before confirmation could be sought).

The same day 3 Troop, which was operating a little further north and approximately 6 kilometres west of Xuan Loc, was fired on by a sniper. Fire was not returned as the sniper's position could not be determined. The next morning at 7.50 am a Viet Cong soldier, one of the party that was ambushed the previous morning by 2 Troop, surrendered at FSB Jillian. He had in his possession a PRC radio set.

At 1.50 pm on 8 April, elements of 3 Troop, which was operating in Long Khanh province about 10 kilometres west of the Courtney rubber plantation, contacted an unidentified and undetermined number of enemy forces. A fire fight ensued but results could not be determined. The following day other elements of 3 Troop had been deployed approximately 2 kilometres west of Thai Thien village in Bien Hoa province. At 10.20 pm the troop activated an ambush on a sampan. A sweep of the area the next day confirmed that two enemy troops had been killed, and there was the probability of another enemy soldier killed in the ambush. A carbine rifle was recovered, along with a quantity of drugs, clothing and documents.

On the morning of 12 April elements from the Squadron under the operational control of 9 RAR were travelling along a track approximately 4 kilometres southeast of Thai Thien on the Bien Hoa/Phuoc Tuy border when at 8.57 am an APC detonated a 15 pound anti-tank mine. The strike point of the mine was beneath the front of the left-hand track, which resulted in Crew Commander Corporal George Abdoo being wounded. The force of the explosion severed the track and buckled the front drive sprocket. The left-hand front support arm was destroyed and the engine sustained minor damage. The hull was not penetrated and the vehicle was rendered serviceable the following day.

On 13 April elements from 3 Troop had been deployed under the operational control of 4 RAR in AO MARULAN. At 7.34 am, as the troop was moving along a track 3 kilometres west of the village of Thai Thien in Bien Hoa province, one of their APCs detonated a 15 pound anti-tank mine. No injuries were sustained. The mine detonated under the front left-hand track, destroying the second and third roadwheels. The sponson sill was scored and the hull penetrated with a small hole. The vehicle was able to be repaired and rendered serviceable later that day. On 15 April Squadron HQ, which had been deployed continually on operations, finally returned to the Task Force base at Nui Dat after moving briefly from FSB Jillian to FSB Martine in the western sector of the province the previous day.

On 17 April 3 Troop had again been redeployed to the area where George Abdoo's carrier had detonated a mine on 12 April in Bien Hoa. That morning at 9.20, as the troop travelled along the same track, another one of the carriers from 33 Section detonated an anti-tank mine. Moderate damage was sustained by the vehicle, but none of the crew sustained serious wounds. The Squadron's LAD carrier was dispatched to render assistance, and it travelled along the same track that 33 Section had used one hour before. At 10.20 am, when the LAD vehicle was about 1 kilometre from the location of the damaged carrier, it detonated a smaller anti-tank mine. Only light damage was sustained by the LAD carrier and no serious wounds were reported.

On 19 April 1 Troop was deployed with 9 RAR and was operating approximately 7 kilometres southwest of Xuyen Moc near FSB Mardi in Phuoc Tuy province when Callsign 13B detonated an anti-tank mine. The mine had been manufactured from a 155 mm artillery shell and had a further explosive charge of between 10 and 20 pounds of chicom added to the device. The point of strike was under the front left-hand track, which blew the vehicle on its right-hand side against a tree. The driver, Trooper Terry O'Callaghan, was seriously wounded by the explosion and evacuated. Crew Commander Corporal Fred Newby and two other passengers also suffered wounds. The left-hand drive sprocket and housing were blown off as were the left hand shock absorber, support arm and the first and second roadwheel stations. The belly was warped and the access plate dislodged. The hull was cracked from the front final drive to the shock absorber mount at the rear of the vehicle. The driver's controls and instruments were destroyed. The turret gearbox seized and the machine gun mounting bolts sheared off. The engine access doors were blown off, the ramp twisted and the vehicle's radios were rendered unserviceable.

On the morning of 20 April, 11 Section from 1 Troop was operating on Route 23, supporting engineers who were repairing culverts along the road. At 8.50 am the section was about 5 kilometres south of Xuyen Moc in Phuoc Tuy province when one of the APCs detonated a claymore mine. Only light damage was caused to the carrier by the blast but one Australian was reported as being wounded. On the following day 3 Troop and a section of the mortar carriers from Support Troop were tasked to extract an SAS patrol and some ARVN troops from an area about 1 kilometre south of Thua Tich. The troop then moved east, where a party of enemy was sighted. Because the terrain was extremely rough it was decided to deploy the Support Troop mortars against the enemy, but the results of their bombardment of the enemy's position could not be determined. After the extraction of the ARVN and SAS troops, 3 Troop and the Mortar Section from Support Troop deployed with 5 RAR in the Xuyen Moc region.

On 23 April 3 Troop deployed to an area approximately 8 kilometres due south of Xuyen Moc. At 1.40 pm as the troop carried out a

Sergeants C. Haydock and P. Edwards inspecting damage to Callsign 13Bravo. (3/4 Cavalry Regiment Museum)

reconnaissance mission a cache of over 600 pounds of rice and other items was located. Little other activity was reported during the last week of April 1969, during which the Squadron supported both 4 and 5 RAR on operations as well as providing the endless escort along Route 15.[6]

The first week of May 1969 saw the Squadron performing myriad tasks to support the Task Force. While Squadron HQ remained at Nui Dat, different troops and sections revolved through the operation control of 4 and 5 RAR and the engineering teams of 1 Field Squadron as they continued their landing-clearing operations in the southern sector of the province.

On 3 May, as 1 Troop was moving D Company 5 RAR to the Nui Thi Vai region, it engaged one enemy soldier, with unknown results. Two days later the troop had deployed to the eastern sector of the province where they were operating approximately 8 kilometres east of Xuyen Moc along Route 23. An enemy party of between two and four persons was sighted half a kilometre to the north of Route 23 and was engaged with mortars and machine gun fire, with unknown results. The next reported mine attack against the Squadron's vehicles occurred at 8.15 am on 8 May, when Callsign 29Juliet from 2 Troop detonated an anti-tank mine of between 15 and 20 pounds of explosive as it travelled along Route 23 about 5 kilometres east of Xuyen Moc village. Only light damage was sustained by the vehicle and none of the crew were wounded. Later that evening 21 Section from 2 Troop and 3 Platoon W Company 4 RAR were placed in an ambush some 6 kilometres southeast of Xuyen Moc. Three enemy troops approached the ambush site but failed to enter the 'killing zone'. The ambush was activated but without result.

The following evening Support Troop's 83 Section had been placed in an ambush on the western edge of the Binh Ba rubber plantation. At 9.45 pm the section was surrounded by an enemy force estimated to consist of 20 personnel. This was reported to elements from 2 Troop, who were close by and had been accompanied by an infantry mortar unit at their night location. The mortar section put down a mortar barrage which allowed 83 Section to withdraw.

A CHANGE IN COMMAND

On 13 May, A Squadron 3rd Cavalry Regiment became B Squadron 3rd Cavalry Regiment when Major L.G. O'Donnell was replaced by Major R.E. Rooks. O'Donnell returned from Bien Hoa province in order to hand over command to Rooks. In fact, while O'Donnell was commanding officer of A Squadron 3rd Cavalry Regiment he was also charged with the responsibility of defence commander of the Task Force HQ each time it was deployed. Given his dual role during the nine months with the Squadron, he had been extremely busy. For his efforts Major L.G. O'Donnell received the award of Mentioned in Dispatches. The citation for his award reads:[7]

> Throughout nine months of continuous operations, Major O'Donnell maintained his squadron at a high standard of efficiency and participated in a wide range of successful operations. These varied from convoy escort and route clearance to ambushes and the insertion of Special Air Service Patrols.
>
> In addition to commanding his Squadron, Major O'Donnell had the added responsibility as defence commander for the Task Force headquarters when it was deployed. This involved much detailed and exacting work in the early stages of each deployment and was accomplished without prejudice to his other responsibilities.

> Major O'Donnell displayed unfailing energy, fine leadership and a highly professional ability. His command of A Squadron 3rd Cavalry Regiment throughout this period of intense activity was exemplary.

Rooks had as his second in command Captain John Grey, who would be replaced by Captain Doug Formby in October 1969 when his tour of duty had been completed. Under Major Rooks' command, the squadron now had 14 officers, 19 warrant officers/sergeants and 125 other ranks, totalling 158.

Two days after Rooks took control of the Squadron the enemy attacked sector elements at Dat Do. The Squadron deployed its Ready Reaction Force from Nui Dat at 9.40 that morning. The Ready Reaction Force, consisting of 1 Troop's Troop HQ and 11 Section, moved to assist re-establish control at Dat Do after the previous evening's activities. The troop remained at Dat Do for two days assisting 9 RAR with a cordon search of the town before returning to the Task Force base. On its return to Nui Dat it was again deployed as the Ready Reaction Force at 4 pm on 19 May to the south of the Task Force base after reports of enemy activity in that area.

While Dat Do was being cleared, No 2 Troop continued its deployment in the southeastern sector of the province known as AO SCORPION. On 17 May the troop located a training area consisting of benches and a bunker. Further investigation revealed a substantial rice garden and a cemetery consisting of eight graves less than six months old.

On 20 May, deep in Bien Hoa province, a carrier from the Squadron detonated an anti-tank mine with an estimated 25 pounds of chicom explosive. The point of strike was under the front left-hand roadwheel. The crew members were wounded and all suffered hearing damage from the explosion. The first left-hand roadwheel and suspension arm were blown off. A hole measuring 45 × 15 centimetres was sustained by the vehicle's side channel and its sponson was buckled and gouged.

On 22 May 2 Troop was operating in AO SCORPION on Route 328, 7 kilometres due south of Xuyen Moc and about 4 kilometres from the coast, when one of the carriers detonated an anti-tank mine with an estimated 30 pounds of chicom explosive. The strike point of the mine was under the vehicle's front left-hand track. The fourth suspension station was blown off, creating a 60-centimetre long hole behind the fourth and fifth stations. The floor of the hull was holed, with minor penetration in six other places. The sponson was also holed. The machine gun and the gun shield were blown off, the cargo hatch hinge and ramp door were broken. Crew Commander Corporal Rod

APCs from the Squadron moving through Dat Do, 1969. (3/4 Cavalry Regiment Museum)

Pullinger was seriously wounded as a result of the gun shield being blown off, and he was evacuated from the site.

The following day at 10.45 am, 2 Troop was operating on Route 23 some 8 kilometres east of Xuyen Moc when they came into contact with eight enemy troops. In the ensuing fire fight two enemy troops were wounded and a large quantity of documents were recovered. No casualties were sustained by members of the troop. On 25 May 2 Troop was again operating on Route 23 approximately 2 kilometres east of the incident of 23 May. The troop came into contact with a group of 20 enemy soldiers. A fire fight ensued, but results could not be determined as the enemy retreated. As with the contact two days previously no casualties were sustained by members of the troop.

2 Troop continued to operate along Route 23, and on 27 May an APC from the troop detonated an anti-tank mine close to the location

of the enemy contact of 25 May. The mine was estimated at 50 pounds of chicom explosive, causing heavy damage to the carrier. Both driver and crew commander were wounded, together with two of the passengers. The strike point of the mine was beneath the front left-hand track, which resulted in the final drive being blown off its housing. The sponson was ripped open, the driver's instrument panels torn off and the side channel between the first and second stations blown open. The driver of the vehicle, Trooper Donald Dann, suffered extensive fragmentation wounds. The two wounded crew members and the two passengers were evacuated.

AMBUSH AT THUA TICH

On 29 May Captain T.H. Arrowsmith's 2 Troop had shifted operations from AO SCORPION to AO FROG, where they deployed with D&E Platoon in a combined infantry/cavalry ambush site around the remains of the resettled village of Thua Tich on Route 328. As well as the three sections and Troop HQ the troop was accompanied by a section of mortar carriers from Support Troop and an APC recovery vehicle from the LAD. At 8.30 pm a D&E Platoon section leader reported that a large group of enemy had passed his position and were moving quickly north along Route 328 towards the APCs. He also reported that a number of the enemy party were carrying heavy packs.

At 8.32 pm the ambush was activated by Troop HQ with claymore mines and sustained machine gun fire on the leading elements after the three scouts were allowed to pass out of the killing ground. At the same time as the APCs engaged the enemy, D&E Platoon, which was located to the south of the troop, also engaged the enemy troops in their killing ground. At that stage there were estimated to be 50 enemy troops in the two killing grounds, but it was not known how many enemy were still to the south of the ambush site. On initiation of the ambush, 20 rounds of HE were fired and hit between the two ambush sites on the eastern side of Route 328, where it was expected that the enemy would withdraw. A series of hand-held flares were also fired to provide illumination. During this period sustained machine gun fire from the APCs was maintained for 10 minutes in an endeavour to engage any enemy that might withdraw to the east.

In the meantime the three enemy scouts who had been allowed through the killing ground had manoeuvred their way around to the northern side of the ambush site and commenced firing their AK47s at the troop. Approximately 50 rounds were fired with two rounds hitting the APC recovery vehicle, and some small shrapnel pieces hit the crew commander in the foot. These three enemy were engaged with machine gun fire and subsequently withdrew. Shortly after the firing had stopped the commander of D&E Platoon reported movement about 200 metres to his southeast. This was thought to have been the wounded enemy troops trying to withdraw.

At 9.30 pm the Task Force's liaison officer at Xuyen Moc reported that a 'spooky' gunship was available for support. Captain Arrowsmith called for this support and the gunship proceeded to fly around the area of contact for 45 minutes, putting mini-gunfire around the two ambush locations with particular attention to the east and south. This was to deter the enemy from regrouping and to cut off the most likely escape routes. Because of the isolation of the area in which the ambush had been set, Arrowsmith was prepared for a counter-assault by the enemy, who it was thought would return to the area with a counter-force to recover the dead and the substantial number of packs the enemy troops had been carrying. Compounding the danger for the Australians was the fact that they were out of range of the supporting artillery. At that stage no attempt had been made to recover the enemy's weapons or

Within an instant of emptying his M60 machine gun, Lance Corporal Len Ellcombe grabs his M16 rifle and returns the fire of a Viet Cong group who are attempting to ambush the APCs, Thua Tich, June 1969. (Australian War Memorial negative number BEL/69/0354A/UN)

packs. To ensure that the enemy were kept away from the area, the 'spooky' gunship returned to the site at 12.30 am on 30 May and proceeded to put down more prophylactic fire in the two areas attended to earlier that night. However, unlike the previous January, when Arrowsmith had been involved with the SAS ambush at Xuyen Moc, the expected counter-assault did not occur. An uncomfortable night was spent by the Australians as both the cavalry and infantry 'stood to' and waited. Again at 4 am on 30 May 18 rounds of 81 mm HE were fired at the eastern side of Thua Tich, clearing the area southeast of the position occupied by D&E Platoon, who were covering the entry/exit points to the ambush site.

Despite the enemy's reluctance to mount an immediate counter-assault the Australians were not out of trouble. At first light the Australian force undertook a sweep of the area. 22 Section moved from its location at 6.10 am to the main killing ground to support a sweep of the area, which commenced at 6.30 am and moved north to south. By this time the Squadron's second in command had flown out in a possum aircraft to observe and remain as support. Several trails used by the enemy to escape were located on the eastern side of the Thua Tich clearing, but these led to thick and overgrown vegetation and foliage. To clear these obstructions, machine gun fire from the carriers was directed at them to probe the area. Eleven enemy bodies were located, and three blood trails indicated a further three wounded. Six AK47, one AK50 and one RPG2 launcher, and a large quantity of ammunition for the weapons were recovered, as well as grenades, medical supplies and packs.

By midday the area had been swept and the troop started to move back to Xuyen Moc along Route 328. It was accompanied overhead by the Squadron's 2I/C in the possum aircraft and a light fire team to afford additional protection. However, at 1.52 pm, having travelled approximately 9 kilometres south from Thua Tich, the troop was ambushed by an enemy party consisting of four personnel who fired RPG7 rounds at the carriers. One of the rounds hit a carrier from 23 Section, but failed to explode as it had been fired at too close a range. The gunships from the light fire team and the troop returned fire with their machine guns and swept through the area, which was estimated to contain another 10 enemy troops. The result of this sweep was another five enemy killed and one RPG7 launcher, one RPG2 launcher and a 7.62 chicom pistol captured. A quantity of ammunition for the weapons was also recovered. Despite the magnitude of these two actions the troop did not sustain any serious casualties, and were able to return safely to Xuyen Moc for the evening.[8]

For this action and others, Captain Thomas Arrowsmith received the award of Mentioned in Dispatches. The citation for his award reads:[9]

> On 19 January 1969, Captain Arrowsmith was the commander of a combined Special Air Service, infantry and cavalry ambush which had been observing an enemy supply route for several days. At 1715 hours a successful ambush was initiated against an enemy party. Several hours later the enemy probed the ambush site and attempted to overrun the Special Air Service position. Captain Arrowsmith calmly deployed his troop and with skilful timing and fire control extracted the Special Air Service group to safety, without casualties.
>
> On 29 May 1969, Captain Arrowsmith was deployed in combined infantry and cavalry ambush sites on Route 326. At 2030 hours, points were initiated against a force of over fifty, resulting in substantial casualties to the enemy. Throughout the night Captain Arrowsmith calmly controlled his troops in the ambush site reassuring his force with his own confidence, although out of artillery range and expecting an enemy counter attack at any time. Next day, in returning to base down Route 328, he again came in contact with the enemy. In close country and whilst being fired upon by enemy rocket launchers, he skilfully manoeuvred his force completely routing the enemy without casualties to his troop.
>
> In these contacts with the enemy and in other such engagements, Captain Arrowsmith has displayed a standard of professionalism and personal courage, that has been an inspiration to troops serving under him and to the remainder of the squadron.

At the beginning of June 1969 Squadron HQ was at Nui Dat, while the troops remained on operations in AOs VINCENT and ALDGATE. These areas encompassed the province's eastern and northern sectors. Support Troop continued to provide route security on Route 15. On 2 June, 1 Troop was redeployed to AO SCORPION under the operational control of 5 RAR while the other elements of the Squadron remained under the operational control of 6 and 9 RAR.

8

Binh Ba, 1969

One of the most significant battles of the Vietnam War was fought by the 3rd Cavalry Regiment and the 1st Armoured Regiment on 6 June 1969 in the village of Binh Ba. Operation HAMMER largely featured Australian Armour, and the battle is recounted here in detail to highlight the value of cavalry and tanks when working together. Moreover, it demonstrated the tactics and strategies used by Armour when confronted with a larger enemy force.

Binh Ba and the Gallia rubber plantation were situated approximately 5 kilometres north of Nui Dat on Route 2. The area had been originally settled by the colonial French, who had established the rubber industry in that district. The village of Binh Ba was a collection of masonry buildings set out in street formation, and accommodated a population of about 2000. The cottages were occupied by the workers on the rubber plantation and in the adjacent Duc Trung factory complex, which processed the latex once it had been harvested. Unlike the more southern hamlets, such as Hoa Long and Long Dien where the Viet Cong had been extremely active, Binh Ba had never really captured the attention of the Task Force. This is largely because the southern hamlets were occupied by subsistent peasant farmers who worked the rice paddy fields for their existence, and their poverty had been easily exploited by the Viet Cong. By contrast, the people of Binh Ba relied on employment within the rubber industry and were able to acquire wages and live in a modest degree of comfort. The Viet Cong practised extortion on the Binh Ba population, rather than living among them. Accordingly, the Viet Cong did not receive the degree of support around Binh Ba that they did from the peasant farmers.

The North Vietnamese Army had decided to challenge the Australian Task Force when reports were received that 1 Company 1st Battalion of the 33rd Regiment had moved into Binh Ba on the night of 5 June 1969. The local population had been informed by the NVA that they had come to take over their town and that they would not be turned out. The Viet Cong had been evicted from the village in July 1966 by the Task Force. This latest move by the enemy was a direct provocation to the Task Force, which had no desire to see an enemy presence in the town. The area around Binh Ba had been searched some months earlier and the roads in the area were considered to be reasonably safe. The bold approach by the NVA presented the Task Force with a situation needing immediate intervention.

On 5 June 6 RAR was operating with two troops of tanks from the 1st Armoured Regiment in a jungle area near FSB Virginia some 15 kilometres northwest of Nui Dat. When one of the tanks broke down a replacement tank was dispatched at 8 am on 6 June, and was accompanied by the ARV. As the tank drew level with the southern outskirts of Binh Ba, the enemy fired an RPG which hit the tank's turret. The damage to the tank was substantial. Its turret could not be traversed and the operator was seriously wounded in the arm. Both the tank and ARV returned fire with their machine guns. The damaged tank drove on through the ambush while the ARV reversed out of the contact and returned to Nui Dat. The incident was reported to the Task Force HQ. The local ARVN forces were already investigating a previous incident, and reported that there was possibly an enemy platoon in Binh Ba. The Sector HQ at Baria asked the Australian Task Force to assist in dealing with the enemy.

The Ready Reaction Force at Nui Dat was commanded by the company commander of D Company 5 RAR, Major M.P. Blake, and was placed on standby for deployment to Binh Ba. The Ready Reaction Force consisted of: three APCs from 3 Troop B Squadron 3rd Cavalry Regiment, led by Captain R. DeVere; a composite troop consisting of four tanks from B Squadron 1st Armoured Regiment, led by 2nd Lieutenant B. Sullivan; and D Company 5th Battalion RAR led by Major Blake (not at full strength). Blake and DeVere were briefed at Task Force HQ and the column set off at 10 am in line-ahead along Route 2 for Binh Ba. DeVere briefed Sullivan by radio on the situation as they moved out. About half a kilometre from Binh Ba, the tank leading the column was fired on by a platoon-sized force from the left-hand side of the road. The tank returned fire but the armoured column did not stop. As the column approached a slight rise on the eastern side of the road leading to the village it went into a defensive formation. Information could not be readily ascertained on the situation within the village, and no definite plans to attack the enemy could be formulated at that stage. However, almost immediately the enemy opened fire, with 15 RPG rounds directed at the nearest tank. The firing of the rockets was interspersed with small arms fire from the house on the corner of the village. Reports from the ARVN were also being received that more enemy troops could be seen at the northern end of the village.

It was obvious that the infantry could not be offloaded in the prevailing circumstances, with Major Blake agreeing that an armoured assault would be the best option in dealing with the entrenched enemy. As the houses in Binh Ba were constructed of masonry walls with tiled roofs, before an assault could take place authorisation was required from Task Force HQ. There were two main issues that concerned the Ready Reaction Force. First, that all the civilians and ARVN troops in the villages had either left or been evacuated from Binh Ba. Second, it was likely that substantial damage to the houses in Binh Ba would occur once the tanks and APCs started firing their armaments. Clearance for the assault on the village was received at the same time confirmation was received that the villagers had all been cleared or evacuated, and that the local ARVN forces had withdrawn from the village. In reality and without the Australians' knowledge, many of the Binh Ba villagers had descended into the basements of their houses for protection.

Communication was to play an important part in the Australian Armour's operational tactics. DeVere had his radio sets tuned to the troop, Task Force and D Company 5 RAR nets. Troop Officer Lieutenant J. Ballance had his radio set to the troop, Squadron and US sector nets. The tanks were using their own net with a '29' set to communicate with the APCs. Ballance was receiving information from the US sector, which was constantly updated and was proving far more accurate than that being received from Task Force HQ.

Binh Ba was set out in a rectangular shape, with a frontage of some 350 metres adjacent to Route 2 and 700 metres to the west. It consisted of several streets with houses close together on both sides of the street. The plan of attack involved each tank being directed down four of the streets. Three APCs were to accompany each tank on the right and left flanks with another three APCs accompanying the two tanks in the centre. The remaining APCs, led by Ballance, covered the rear. Major Blake and his tactical headquarters were aboard DeVere's APC, which followed Sullivan's tank on the centre-left of the advance.

The tanks and APCs set off at 10.30 am and on Captain DeVere's orders started moving from east to west. As the Australian armoured force moved slowly forward they were immediately attacked with RPG and small arms fire from within the houses and their surrounds, which were partly hidden by trees and bushes. The attacks at this stage were not intense, so it was decided that the infantry platoon in the rear carriers would be dismounted and given the task of ensuring that each house was cleared and that no enemy remained once the armoured vehicles had passed. The rest of the infantry company remained on board the APCs and were able to listen to the battle as it unfolded on the carriers' radio loudspeakers. A couple of infantryman fortunate enough to be able to stand up through the cargo hatch assisted by using their rifles against snipers. Care was taken by the armoured vehicles not to outpace the infantry platoon at the rear, so as not to leave them stranded as they searched the 'cleared' houses.

The advance had moved about 250 metres into the village when a helicopter reported about 60 enemy troops moving to the northwest corner. The tank on the right-hand flank commanded by Lieutenant Ritchie immediately disengaged from the advance, as it is thought he had seen enemy movement. The tank commanded by Corporal Bennett which was moving down the next street across also disengaged, moving off at speed after Ritchie's tank and towards the reported enemy position. The APCs accompanying Ritchie's and Bennett's tanks on the right flank were not in communication with them, so they reported the departure of both tanks to DeVere. By this time the two disengaged tanks had moved about 100 metres to the northwest.

DeVere had no knowledge of what was happening on the right flank, and the message he received that 'both tanks have gone' from the APCs that had accompanied them added to the confusion. At that stage no orders had been given for the two tanks to disengage and outflank the enemy force. To add to the confusion the remaining APCs and tanks came under heavy enemy fire and had difficulty maintaining security. During the ensuing fire fight the APC commanders continued to give clear and brief reports over the net to DeVere as it became apparent that they were facing a force far in excess of company strength and in possession of heavy weapons.

It was at this stage that Bennett's tank, which had moved to the northwest, was hit by an RPG round, which damaged the turret's traversing mechanism. DeVere had received unconfirmed reports that Bennett's tank had been 'knocked out'. According to a subsequent report both tanks had broken through the enemy lines and were now stationary on the western outskirts of the town in open ground. From that position they were engaging the enemy and inflicting heavy casualties with their guns. Bennett's tank, which had been hit by the RPG, had suffered considerable damage; some of its crew members were wounded. The wounded crewmen were moved to the relative safety of Ritchie's tank but could not be evacuated from the battlefield because of the heavy fire.

Meanwhile, the remainder of the armoured vehicles, which had continued to advance with the infantry platoon bringing up the rear, had reached the village square—an open area located 400 metres east of where they had entered the village. Until this point, the armoured vehicles had been taking care to stay close to the houses from which the enemy were firing their RPGs. This was to nullify the effects of the RPG rounds, which needed to travel some distance before they became active. Once at the edge of the market square the enemy fire against the armoured vehicles became intense, with RPG and 12.7 mm machine gun fire being received from positions on three sides of the village square. DeVere estimated that they were confronted by an enemy force of at least company strength.

When DeVere reached the village square he had lost radio contact with the tank from which Lieutenant Sullivan was leading the advance. DeVere thus decided to take matters into his own hands: he dismounted from his own vehicle under heavy fire, ran forward and climbed onto Sullivan's tank so he could sort out the communication problems. On board Sullivan's tank he determined that the radio had been damaged and they agreed to continue using hand signals. As they crouched on the tank's turret and discussed the situation, an RPG round was fired at them. The round passed between both men, with its fin lightly slicing through Sullivan's back.

The most immediate problem confronting DeVere concerned the wounded tank crew members from Bennett's tank on the northwestern side of the town, who needed evacuation. An APC on the right of the advance was ordered to cover the evacuation of the wounded crew, while another tank (Bennier's) in the middle of the advance was ordered to move to the north to strengthen the right flank. In the meantime, Ballance was requested to organise a dustoff flight and to clear a landing zone for the helicopters on the eastern side of the village.

As soon as Bennier's tank attempted to move to the north to protect the right flank it was hit by three RPG rounds, the enemy stepping up fire in an attempt to assert their perceived command of the situation. Bennier's tank was in serious difficulty, and a group of APCs moved forward to protect it. The APCs and Sullivan's tanks commenced firing with all armaments, including the APCs' .50 cal. and .30 cal. machine guns, which kept the enemy at bay until Bennier's tank was secured. Then Sullivan's tank, which at that time appeared to be the only one operational, moved in and out of the houses, firing high-explosive and canister rounds from its gun at the enemy positions.

Given the magnitude of the conflict at the edge of the square it was decided to remount the infantry platoon, who until that stage had remained on foot so that the fire from the APCs and the remaining tank would not be restricted. DeVere also called in Bushranger helicopter gunships to cover the withdrawal of the two 'disengaged' tanks and the APCs protecting them on the right-hand side of the village. On arrival the helicopters reported that the area around Bennett's tanks, which had been 'knocked out' earlier in the morning, appeared to be now reasonably secure, and no enemy troops could be sighted. Based on this information DeVere directed the Bushrangers to assist with the assault on enemy positions in the centre of the village.

The APCs had perfect communications with the Bushranger gunships and were able to identify enemy targets with smoke grenades, which allowed the gunships to commence attacking the enemy positions with their mini-guns and rockets. Targets were engaged by the gunships with some of their rockets exploding only 50 metres away from the APCs. As the gunships dived in low over the village on their runs the APCs assisted with their machine guns, by firing them into the houses in which the enemy were located while firing at the helicopters. From one of the enemy positions a 12.7 mm machine gun crew fired at the APCs, hitting and damaging one of the carriers in the centre grouping. As the enemy machine gun crew attempted to withdraw to another position the operator on DeVere's APC, Corporal Peter Davis, opened fire, hitting the enemy with a blast from the carrier's .30 cal. machine guns.

The Australians had been in constant action for over two hours, and at 12 pm DeVere made a decision to break out of the village square where they had been held by the enemy's constant machine gun fire and RPG attacks. Fortunately, the heavy fire from both APCs and tanks had reduced the enemy's resistance. A plan was now put in place for the tanks and APCs to break out of the square to the south, and make their way around to the western side of the village to outflank and cut off the enemy. Several of the tank crew members had been wounded and almost all of their ammunition expended. Ballance had been able to facilitate the evacuation of the wounded by organising a landing zone at the eastern end of the village for dustoff flights.

Back at Nui Dat, B company 5 RAR had been put on warning and were preparing to move to assist the armoured troops in Binh Ba. Captain Tom Arrowsmith, who was now the Squadron's technical officer, had been charged with taking command of any of the remaining APCs in Nui Dat so that he could move B company to the battle area. Arrowsmith quickly organised a composite group of carriers and moved them to the outskirts of Binh Ba, where they took up blocking positions on the southern side of the village and cordoned off its eastern face. From the north of the province raced 4 Troop B Squadron 1st Armoured Regiment under the command of Lieutenant C. Sweeney, who had been deployed with 6 RAR on operations. Given the serious damage that the enemy had inflicted on Sullivan's troop, the relief by 4 Troop was essential to resolve the action. On arrival at Binh Ba, 4 Troop was directed to a form-up point on the western side of the plantation.

Once the breakout manoeuvre had been successfully completed, DeVere moved his troop to the western side of the village. However, as they approached the western side, which was covered in rubber trees and light scrub, DeVere received a report from the US sector radio net that enemy movement had been detected in the area. Realising that this area had not been cleared he ordered Sweeney's tank and the nearest APCs to open fire. His decision proved correct, because hidden from the Australians in the undergrowth was an enemy force of company-sized strength which was preparing to counterattack the village. The ensuing fire from the APCs and the tank inflicted heavy losses on the enemy force, with a casualty rate said to be in the order of 75%.

The leader of the Ready Reaction Force, Major Blake of D Company 5 RAR, now resumed control. The APCs, the tanks of 4 Troop and the dismounted infantrymen from D Company 5 RAR started to move east, back towards the centre of the village. The tanks of 4 Troop and DeVere's APCs were again in close support as they started to advance. Almost immediately heavy enemy machine gun fire halted the infantry advance. The tank's troop leader, Sergeant Browning, moved forward and with his main armament destroyed the machine gun post that was located in a house on the western side of the village. Once again the advance moved off with the infantry leading. As further machine gun posts in the houses were identified a tank would be brought forward and a hole knocked in the side of the building. The tanks and APCs would then cover the infantry with canister and machine gun fire as the infantry moved in to mop up any remaining defenders.

As the Australian force regained the village square they were once more met by heavy enemy fire. Blake returned to DeVere's vehicle to get better communications and be in a position to manoeuvre his troops on the ground. What they did not realise was that the village square was occupied by the enemy's Battalion Headquarters, from where their operations were being directed. Meanwhile, on the northern edge of the village, the infantry came under heavy attack from an enemy machine gun post. A tank was dispatched to assist the infantry and was immediately hit by several RPG rounds, forcing it to withdraw. The accuracy of the enemy anti-tank team would have meant the destruction of the tank had it remained in its location. Such was their concern that DeVere and Blake moved the APC over to the north to assess the situation, where they discovered that the enemy were in a well-concealed location, between a house and a wellhead. Before they could react, Corporal Peter Strudwick, without the support of any other carriers in the troop, raced his APC over open ground outside the village in order to outflank the enemy machine gun crew and RPG teams. From this open position he commenced firing his machine guns, killing the anti-tank RPG team. He continued to fire his weapon at the enemy machine gun post until the tank was once again brought forward and the enemy's machine gun crew dispatched.

About 10 minutes later Corporal Strudwick brought off a similar manoeuvre as the enemy continued to resist. By now, though, the infantry mopping-up force were moving a lot faster as they drove through the village towards the eastern boundary, where they met B Company who had been dispatched from Nui Dat to assist them. Another sweep was made through the village and further prisoners were taken as the enemy attempted to mingle with the villagers, who had hidden in basements under their houses as the battle raged above them. Several enemy troops were identified and handed over to the Australians by the villagers of Binh Ba.

The second sweep ceased at last light, with the village still not secured. DeVere's 3 Troop returned to Nui Dat without infantry for the evening, while the remaining troops remained to cordon off the village. Sergeants Bill Schofield, Jock Wilson and Noel Beare, whose composite sections had come down to Binh Ba with Captain Arrowsmith earlier that afternoon, were assigned to B Company 5 RAR and placed on 50% 'stand-to' for the evening. No major incidents were reported that evening, although Bill Schofield's section, which was placed in the rubber plantation on the southern side of the village, killed two enemy troops as they attempted to break out of the cordon.

Action in the Binh Ba and adjoining Duc Trung rubber factory continued over the following two days. On the morning of 7 June one of the APCs from the Squadron was fired on from the Duc Trung factory. A force of approximately 80 enemy troops was located in the complex but managed to escape before the infantry could assault their position. Meanwhile the infantry made another sweep through Binh Ba, with the APCs and tanks blocking the southeast corner of the village. More prisoners were taken and evacuated. At about 1 pm fighting again flared in Duc Trung, where an ARVN company was overrun by the enemy. The APCs and tanks were ordered to assault the enemy, who immediately withdrew to the northeast but were harassed by artillery and gunships.

The action finally concluded on the morning of 8 June when the Australian Civil Affairs unit arrived to resettle the Binh Ba villagers whose houses had been destroyed or severely damaged.

The losses inflicted on the enemy were horrific, and it is difficult to understand their openly challenging the Australian Task Force in that manner. Those enemy forces taking part were later identified as the 1 Company, 1st Battalion 33 NVA Regiment and their medical company. Elements of the Viet Cong's D440 Battalion, including their signal platoon, the Binh Ba and Ngai Giao guerilla squads and the Chau Duc district company, also took part in the siege. Final enemy losses were in excess of 100 confirmed killed, with many more bodies and wounded removed from the battlefield by their NVA and Viet Cong comrades.

Casualties for the Australians included one of the men from D Company 5 RAR, who was killed in action, and another 10 wounded. Of the wounded, six were tank crew members and two were from the APCs. The most telling testimony to the Australian Armour's effort was that the Australian Infantry were spared the heavy losses they might have sustained if unaccompanied by the APCs and tanks.

For their part the cavalry fought with tenacity, and their fire power was a significant contributory factor to the comprehensive defeat of the

APCs of B Squadron patrolling the road and adjoining banana plantation for any sign of the North Vietnam Army, Binh Ba, June 1969. (Australian War Memorial, negative number BEL/69/0386/UN)

large enemy force. But for the action of the APC crews, who on numerous occasions protected tanks that had sustained damage from the unrelenting rocket attacks, the losses to the tanks and their crews would have been substantially greater. The strategy of having the tanks and the APCs operate together proved effective in this house-to-house battle environment. The fire power that both armoured units contributed to the battle was the significant factor. The enemy could not sustain their efforts against the Australian armoured forces as they systematically destroyed each of the enemy's defensive positions.

In the past the Australian Task Force strategy had been to surround a village, put down a cordon and wait. Invariably, the enemy would escape under cover of darkness. Captain DeVere attributes the success of the Binh Ba operation to the fact that on this occasion the armoured force acted aggressively and decisively. The behaviour of his men was exceptional. Despite the fact that the APCs were facing heavy machine guns and RPGs the members of the troop remained calm and adhered to basic armoured operational procedures. For example, trim vanes were lowered to help counter the effects of RPGs, flak jackets were worn, and the correct stowage of ammunition and equipment meant that these items could be quickly retrieved. Most importantly, each section exercised control of their machine gun fire, with mutual support afforded among the crews and their vehicles. Finally, the communication within the troop was first-class, with radio reports being rapid, brief and always accurate.[1]

For his action in neutralising the enemy anti-tank and machine gun crews that afternoon, Corporal Peter Strudwick received the Military Medal. The citation for his award reads:[2]

> On 6 June 1969, Corporal Strudwick's Troop was deployed to the village of Binh Ba, where they came under heavy anti-tank and small arms fire during house to house fighting. The infantry on the right were pinned down by intense machine gun fire from a house. A tank which moved forward in support, was forced to withdraw because of accurate anti-tank fire.
>
> Corporal Strudwick immediately moved the armoured personnel carrier he was commanding into open ground to outflank the enemy anti-tank rocket position. Although his vehicle was without support from the remainder of the troop, he remained in an exposed position and directed accurate machine gun fire killing the anti-tank rocket crew. He remained in this position neutralising the enemy machine gun until such time as the tank moved forward and destroyed the machine gun position.
>
> Corporal Strudwick continued for the remainder of the operation to show outstanding bravery and initiative during similar incidents. On all occasions, he has displayed above average leadership against the enemy.

9

A shift in strategy, 1969–70

Despite the heavy action experienced by DeVere's troop on 6 June 1969, more was in store for 3 Troop as it continued its deployment as the Task Force's Ready Reaction Force on 7 June. In what appeared to be a diversionary attack, the Viet Cong's Chau Duc company occupied the northern part of the village of Hoa Long, which was only 3 kilometres south of Nui Dat. Hoa Long was notorious for its sympathetic attitude towards the Viet Cong, and in the past had been subject to numerous Task Force operations to secure the surrounding area.

The operation to clear the enemy was to be controlled by C Company 5 RAR. 3 Troop, under the command of Captain DeVere, while still recovering from the harrowing events of the previous day, might have expected a well-earned rest. However, the situation confronting the infantry again required the cavalry to take an integral role to oust the enemy from its position. Similarly, the tanks of the 1st Armoured Regiment, which had taken numerous casualties and sustained enormous damage to their vehicles the previous day, were called on to assist with the assault. This presented a problem because of the low number of serviceable tanks now left in Nui Dat. The two other troops of the tank squadron continued their deployment in the north of the province with 6 RAR, but a composite troop was quickly thrown together, to be led by Lieutenant D. Ritchie.

The enemy had dug themselves into a position containing 40 well-hidden and camouflaged weapon pits. The enemy's position was in heavy undergrowth on the northwest corner of Hoa Long, from where they could inflict maximum casualties on any assaulting force trying to relieve the village of their presence. C Company were driven to the starting point of the assault on the western approach to Hoa Long village by 3 Troop, where they dismounted. The tactics for the assault on the enemy positions were to be similar to those employed the previous day at Binh Ba. The tanks would lead the assault, with DeVere's APCs following to provide flank and rear protection for the tanks and following infantry. The tanks again led off the line of assault, moving to the western extremity of the village where the enemy were located. The tanks had travelled only a short distance when they came under heavy enemy small arms, RPG and machine gun fire. Unlike the previous day, when the tanks led the assault and the infantry remained in the carriers, the infantry had dismounted and were able to identify the camouflaged weapon pits for the armoured vehicles. Both the tanks and APCs used their heavier weapons as they swept through the enemy lines, firing at and destroying each defended position as it was located. The enemy again fought tenaciously, but were finally forced to retreat in the face of the Australian Armour, which kept advancing towards their positions despite heavy fire.

While the enemy had been driven from their position and suffered numerous casualties, not one Australian casualty was sustained. To prevent the enemy from returning, the assaulting force set up a defensive harbour on the ground that had been taken from the enemy that afternoon. As it was late, a thorough search of the area was delayed and scheduled for the following day. Next morning revealed the enemy's elusive nature: prisoners were taken after spending the night in a tunnel in the middle of the defensive harbour that had been established by the Australians the previous evening. The remainder of this enemy force was forced into open country and finally dispersed.

On 11 June 1969 at 10 am 1 Troop was operating in AO SCORPION along Route 23 approximately 9 kilometres east of Xuyen Moc when Callsign 12 detonated an anti-tank mine. The carrier was heavily damaged. The driver, Trooper Roger Lingard, and the crew commander, Sergeant Jim McQuade, crewman Lance Corporal Bob Kennedy as well as one of the US passengers were reported as being seriously wounded. The mine was estimated to be between 40 and 50 pounds of chicom explosive with the point of strike beneath the front left-hand roadwheel. The force of the explosion ripped off the front two left-hand suspension stations and penetrated the hull with a 60-centimetre hole adjacent to the driver's seat. The sponson seams were torn open with a 120-centimetre opening, and the left-hand floor channel penetrated with a 7.5-centimetre hole near the left-hand support arm housing. Both the floor of the hull and the fuel cell were buckled. The three wounded crewmen and their passengers were evacuated from the site.

Later that week, on 17 June 1969, 2 Troop was escorting a US convoy of trucks along Route 15. Approximately 2 kilometres south of the village of Phu My in the west of Phuoc Tuy province the convoy was attacked by the enemy with RPG fire. The APCs returned fire and were later joined by a light fire team; the results of the counterattack could not be determined, although an AK47 assault rifle was captured, indicating that the enemy had sustained casualties.

Resettlement of Thua Tich, mines, ambushes and elephants

In mid-June 1969 the district chief requested the cooperation of the Task Force in assisting to reopen the Thua Tich area to some of the local population for resettlement. The area had been cleared of the population many years before, and before the people could return it needed to be cleared of enemy forces. The Squadron, which had been patrolling in force and ambushing extensively in the area, was required to manoeuvre into heavy jungle areas adjacent to Thua Tich. It was during one of these patrols, on 21 June 1969, that one of the troops came across a cunningly concealed enemy garden that had been cut into the edge of a large clearing, making it virtually impossible to detect from the air. The APCs had run over the large variety of produce with their tracks, thus denying the enemy a vital source of sustenance. In the southern sector of the province 2 Troop had been operating out of FSB Thrust on the edge of the eastern Long Hai hills, approximately 4 kilometres due west of the village of Phuoc Hai in the southeast of the province. On 23 June Callsign 22Bravo detonated an anti-personnel mine, but no damage was reported to the carrier or the crew.

The Squadron suffered a substantial loss on 24 June when two of its members, Lance Corporal Keith Dewar and Trooper Robert Young, were killed. The carrier on which they were crew members was Callsign 22Alpha from 2 Troop, which had been involved in land-clearing operations in the Long Hai hills area. Like Callsign 22Bravo which had hit an anti-personnel mine the day before, it had been operating some 2 kilometres west of FSB Thrust in AO ALDGATE on the eastern side of the Long Hai hills. The attack occurred at 11.57 am and the size of the mine was estimated at between 60 and 80 pounds of chicom explosive. The point of strike was under the front centre of the vehicle which blew it upside down, resulting in the death of both crewmen. An area of the hull's floor, measuring 150 × 110 centimetres, was warped. Both final drives and the front three left-hand suspension arms were blown off, as were the tracks on both sides. The engine, differential, gearbox and driver's fittings and controls were all destroyed.

Later that day at 6.20 pm, as 2 Troop's HQ was escorting a convoy along Route 15, it was fired on with an RPG round approximately 8 kilometres west of Baria. The RPG missed the carriers, and in view of the late hour no action could be taken against the enemy force that had fired it. These harrowing events had prompted extra caution as members of the Squadron carried out their tasks. 1 Troop, which was deployed in the eastern sector of the province, located two large anti-tank mines as it deployed throughout AO SCORPION. The first mine was located on Route 23 some 8 kilometres east of Xuyen Moc at 1.30 that afternoon and had a strength of 40 pounds of explosive. The second mine was located at 4 pm on a little-used track about 5 kilometres west of Xuyen Moc and had a strength of 30 pounds of explosive. On 26 June in the Gallia rubber plantation, about 500 metres north of the village of Binh Ba, a carrier from 2 Troop detonated an anti-tank mine. The strength of the mine was unable to be determined, but damage to the vehicle was described as moderate. None of the crew sustained any serious wounds in the attack.

Australian gunners loading artillery into the back of an APC before moving into the west of Phuoc Tuy province, June 1970. (3/4 Cavalry Regiment Museum)

At the end of June Squadron HQ was located in Nui Dat, and 1 Troop and Support Troop's 82 Section remained deployed in AO SCORPION. 2 Troop was operating out of FSB Thrust in the Long Hai region and 3 Troop remained under the operational control of 5, 6 and 9 RAR. Support Troop had its 84 Section located at FSB Longreach, while 86 Section was deployed in AO TOM THUMB and was located at FSB Flinders in the province's northern sector.[1]

On 5 July at 11.15 am 2 Troop was operating on the western side of Route 2 and about 1 kilometre south of Courtney hill, where they were providing landing zone security for one of the infantry battalions. Contact was made with some 20 enemy troops, and in the ensuing fire fight one Viet Cong was killed and another three wounded. Four packs were recovered containing documents, medical supplies and ammunition. No casualties were sustained by the troop in this action. 1 Troop remained deployed in the west of the province and at 5.45 pm an

Vietnamese children watch a convoy of APCs transporting artillery to Phuoc Tuy province to assist 2nd Battalion in an operation, June 1970. (3/4 Cavalry Regiment Museum)

ambushing party consisting of 12 Section and 19Juliet were deployed in an ambush site approximately 6 kilometres southwest of Xuyen Moc near Route 23. An enemy party of about 20 personnel was contacted, although none of the enemy entered the ambush site. The enemy party was engaged with mortar fire, but results could not be determined. Sergeant Peter Bohrnsen, a member of the ambushing party, was reported as suffering slight wounds as a result of the action.

On the evening of 7 July 1 Troop and 82 Section were located on the southern outskirts of Xuyen Moc. That evening the enemy crawled to within 50 metres of the troop's location where they set out a series of claymore mines, which were directed at the APCs. At 5 am the next morning two mines were detonated, but no casualties were reported among members of the troop. A search of the area revealed another two unexploded claymore mines in the vicinity of the two detonated mines. On 11 July an APC from the Squadron detonated an anti-tank mine 1.5 kilometres south of Courtney hill. The mine caused heavy damage to the vehicle and seriously wounded the driver, Trooper Ray Rouhan. The strength of the mine was estimated at about 40 pounds of TNT/plastic explosive. The point of strike was inside the left-hand road-wheels, causing the track links to disintegrate. The floor of the hull was penetrated, tearing forwards and to the rear of the access plate. Both engine and transmission were severely damaged. The driver's compartment was heavily damaged, including the driver's seat, controls and engine access panels. The driver was evacuated from the site.

On 16 July 3 Troop was deployed to Baria along with other elements of the Task Force's Ready Reaction Force after reports were received of the enemy's intention to again try to enter Baria. The troop was placed on the northern approaches to the town where it remained until 18 July, when it was relieved by 2 Troop. That evening the enemy attacked FSB Clare near Tham Thien in Bien Hoa province, where Squadron HQ had been deployed. During the attack 15 mortar rounds were fired into the base, wounding seven South Vietnamese marines and three members of D&E Platoon. No casualties were reported among members of Squadron HQ as a result of this attack.

On 20 July 3 Troop, which had been deployed on Operation GARY OWEN in the eastern sector of the province, was placed in an ambush site 200 metres south of Route 23 near FSB Elaine. At 5.45 pm that evening they sighted and fired on one enemy, who then withdrew to the south. Earlier in the day, 84 Section, which had been deployed near the Binh Ba rubber plantation, located four bunkers that were well concealed with overhead protection. The following day 3 Troop was deployed with 5 RAR on Operation DISTANT TRUMPET in AO PANTHER in the northeastern sector of the province. At 6.45 pm

32 Section was placed in an ambush on Route 329 approximately 9 kilometres north of Xuyen Moc when they contacted four enemy, but the results of the engagement could not be determined. On 22 July at 9.45 am contact was made with one enemy soldier about 1 kilometre north of the night ambush site. He was fired on, subsequently wounded, and taken prisoner.

On 31 July work commenced to clear the minefield that had been laid between the Horseshoe feature and Phuoc Hai on the coast. This minefield had been planted by the Task Force some two years previously in an attempt to prevent enemy troop movement in the southern and more populated area of Phuoc Tuy province. Unfortunately, the enemy had been able to infiltrate the minefield and remove the mines almost at will, then used them to great effect on the Australian troops. Their removal was thus considered an essential preventive measure. An APC was fitted with a series of rollers on the right rear of the vehicle. The carrier then drove over the minefield, exploding the M16 anti-personnel mines using pressure. The explosions from the mines were not powerful enough to inflict damage on the M113A1.

The previous day 1 Troop had been deployed near the beach some 10 kilometres south of Xuyen Moc, as reports had been received that local Viet Cong forces were gathering en masse there. After a search of the area (nothing was located) the troop returned to Xuyen Moc to continue its pacification operations around the district.[2] Thus, at the beginning of August 1 Troop remained at Xuyen Moc. 2 Troop and 82 Section were in Bien Hoa province, east of Tham Thien. 3 Troop was in the northeastern sector near Thua Tich with Squadron HQ and 81 Section. 83 and 84 Sections continued to operate out of FSB Longreach.

On 5 August at 3 pm, 3 Troop located a Russian anti-tank mine in Binh Tuy province some 15 kilometres west of Xuyen Moc on Route 23. Later that evening Captain DeVere sited his 3 Troop in a series of ambushes on the coast near the Nui Tam Bo hills. 32 Section, 30Bravo, 39Juliet, 39Mike and Callsign 98 were placed in an ambush near the beach. At 10 pm an enemy party of some 25 personnel crossed the beach and entered the ambush. The ambush was sprung and in the ensuing fire fight 13 Viet Cong were killed, with a further four wounded and one taken prisoner. Also captured were four M1 rifles, one Garand rifle, one SKS rifle and 14 packs containing ammunition, food and medical supplies. No casualties were sustained by the troop.

Captain DeVere, who had joined the Squadron in January 1969, had proven an inspirational leader, and for this action and previous ones in which his troop was involved received the award of the Military Cross. The citation for his award reads:[3]

> Captain DeVere commanded a cavalry troop for ten months and has been in many actions against the enemy. In the month of February 1969 during the Tet offensive, his troop was deployed as part of the Task Force Ready Reaction Force. On 18 February, his troop took part in an attack to dislodge an enemy force from the village of Long Dien. On the night of 22/23 February his troop was involved in actions when the enemy attacked the Provincial Capital Baria. In both these actions Captain DeVere displayed a high standard of professionalism and personal courage.
>
> On 6 June 1969, Captain ReVere commanded a combined force consisting of a tank troop and his own troop, against a strong enemy force in the village of Binh Ba. In this action, he displayed complete calmness and control whilst under fire. His personal actions and orders significantly contributed to the defeat of the enemy. On 7 and 8 June 1969, his troop redeployed to the village of Long Dien where once again they performed creditably.
>
> On 24 August 1969, Captain DeVere sited his troop in ambush positions on the coast near the Nui Tam Bo hills. One of the ambush points was sprung against a party of twenty five of the enemy. The subsequent actions of his troop at night resulted in fifteen of the enemy being killed.
>
> On these and many other occasions Captain DeVere displayed above average leadership qualities. He moulded his troop into a proficient fighting force and his personal efforts and the excellent performance of his troop are a credit to him and a fine example to all.

Earlier in the evening, before the 3 Troop ambush, 1 Troop located an M16 mine near FSB Lance, 3 kilometres northeast of the Horseshoe. 3 Troop was still operating in the southeastern corner of the province, where elements of the troop had been placed in an ambush on 7 August. At 6.45 pm two enemy were contacted on the beach. One enemy soldier was wounded in the ensuing encounter and later taken prisoner of war. Two days later 1 Troop was deployed near the village of Phuoc Hai, and at 12.47 pm Callsign 11 detonated a small anti-tank mine estimated at approximately 10 pounds of chicom. Only minor damage was sustained by the vehicle, but Sergeant Geoffrey Mason was reported as suffering wounds as a result of the explosion. On 14 August elements from the Squadron (thought to be 86 Section) assisting with minefield clearance near Phuoc Hai, were involved in a mine incident. Trooper Patrick Burton was wounded, but rather than be evacuated he elected to remain on duty.[4]

As the year continued, the Task Force took on itself a concerted campaign to assist the South Vietnamese military and civilian population. In one instance in August, one of the troops from the Squadron located an extensive enemy garden complex about 10 kilometres north of the Task Force base. The total area under cultivation was approximately 6 hectares and consisted of corn, pumpkins, peanuts and several other vegetables. As the vegetables were starting to ripen the villagers from La Van and Vinh Tan were invited to harvest the crops for their own use. These villagers were Montagnard people—the aborigines of Vietnam, with a deep dislike for the Viet Cong—and had long resisted Viet Cong attempts to take over their villages. The Squadron assisted by providing eight 5-ton trucks for the villagers to load and transport the crops back to their villages. Protection was also provided by several APCs while the crops were being harvested, to ensure that the enemy did not interfere with the villagers as they worked.

At the beginning of September 1969 1 Troop and elements of Support Troop were under the operational control of 6 RAR in AO STUART, where land-clearing operations in the Long Green area in the south-eastern sector of the province were being carried out. 2 Troop was stationed at Nui Dat acting as Ready Reaction Force while 3 Troop had been deployed to FSB Mohawk in the southeast sector of Bien Hoa province. Support Troop's 83 and 84 Sections were under the operational control of the 1st Armoured Regiment in AO SABOT in the Binh Ba rubber plantation area, while 86 Section was under the operational control of 9 RAR in AO BURR in the Xuyen Moc area.

On 6 September 2 Troop was deployed to the Courtney rubber plantation some 3 kilometres south of Cam My village on the Phuoc Tuy/Long Khanh border. Here three enemy were engaged by the troop but they retreated and losses could not be determined. The next two weeks were relatively quiet before 2 Troop, the Ready Reaction Force, was deployed to the Binh Ba rubber plantation on 17 September in response to reports of enemy activity. The reports proved negative and the troop returned to Nui Dat. However, the following day the enemy attacked Callsign 29Mike and other elements from the troop with four RPG rounds approximately 4 kilometres north of Lang Phuoc on the eastern side of Route 15. Fire was returned and no casualties were reported among the crew. The enemy fled to the south and were pursued, but results of returned fire by the APCs could not be determined.

An unusual request for the Squadron's assistance was received on 19 September. 84 Section was called to the government post at Xa Bang on Route 2 when it was reported that an elephant had walked into a

APCs from the squadron protecting villagers as they harvest crops grown by the Viet Cong. The squadron had previously uncovered an extensive garden complex and invited the local villagers to harvest the crops. (3/4 Cavalry Regiment Museum)

minefield near the village. On arrival 84 Section discovered the bodies of two Viet Cong near the dead elephant's body, and it was assumed that they had been handling the elephant when it stepped on a mine.[5]

The busy squadron

The Task Force's two armoured squadrons were in demand, and this period proved to be one of the busiest experienced by the cavalry during its time in South Vietnam. The Squadron assisted the local military in various operations within the province, and protected the civilians while their crops were harvested. And its never-ending role of escorting convoys along Route 15 continued. One of the major tasks assigned to the Squadron by the Task Force during the last three months of 1969 was to act as protection for land-clearing operations in the Hat Dich area, bordering Phuoc Tuy and Bien Hoa provinces. 3 Troop took part in Operation BURHAM under the operational control of 9 RAR, during which time it was based at FSB Apache in AO STUART. Similarly, land-clearing operations were continuing in the Long Green area, and 1 Troop, deployed to assist in this task, was based at FSB Ben in AO MAX under the operational control of 5 RAR. These elements of the Squadron were to help the infantry clear the area as well as to protect the bulldozers from enemy attacks as the engineers continued their land-clearing work. 2 Troop remained as the Task Force's Ready Reaction Force at the start of October 1969.

The latter part of 1969 would prove a harrowing time for the Squadron, with three of its members killed in action through RPG and anti-tank mine attacks, but the first two weeks of October were relatively uneventful. 3 Troop concluded Operation BURHAM on 16 October and, after escorting the land-clearing team to Long Binh, returned to Nui Dat. However, on 17 October intelligence reports started to be received of enemy activity around the southern parts of the province. Elements from the Ready Reaction Force's 2 Troop were tasked to assist with a cordon-and-search operation of Dat Do on 18 October. The same day Callsign 20Bravo led another section to an area northeast of Baria following reports of enemy activity. The next day elements from 2 Troop fired on four Viet Cong as they moved into AO STUART some 3 kilometres east of Thai Thien for deployment under the operational control of 9 RAR. Results of the troop's fire on the four enemy personnel could not be determined.

On 20 October the 1 Troop's 11 Section, which was the Ready Reaction Force, was deployed to the beach approximately 3 kilometres east of Phuoc Hai after reports that a company from the local Viet Cong D445 Battalion was in the area. Nothing was reported as a result of this reaction, but 22 October was a very traumatic day for the Squadron, with two attacks on its vehicles in different sectors of the province. The first of these attacks occurred when 1 Troop's 13 Section was deployed with D Company 6 RAR in a joint ARVN/Australian operation near the coast on the eastern side of the Long Hai peninsula. The section was sweeping past an enemy bunker system when the carrier on which Trooper Bert Casey was a crew member was attacked by three enemy troops in an ambush. Two RPG rounds were fired at his carrier with one of the rounds hitting and penetrating the left-hand side of the turret, destroying the traverse gearbox and the vision blocks. Crew Commander Fred Venema was seriously wounded with blast and fragmentation wounds. The other RPG round hit the engine louvre covers and the driver's hatch. Bert Casey did not have time to react and was mortally wounded by the exploding fragments from the RPG round. One of the members of the mini-team, Sapper Anthony Lisle from 1 Field Squadron, was seriously wounded, and another member of the mini-team was wounded; all were evacuated from the site of the attack. Anthony Lisle died of his wounds on 12 November. A sweep of the area was subsequently carried out, but the enemy who had ambushed the section had withdrawn.

That same day 2 Troop's 22 Section was in an ambush near Phu My in the western sector of the province. The ambush was sprung when four enemy walked into the killing zone. The four were believed to be the lead elements of a much larger force. After activating the ambush a fire fight ensued. The enemy fired RPG rounds at the section commander's APC, one of which hit and seriously wounded Sergeant Jim Stones in the neck. He was evacuated from the site of the attack and was extremely lucky to escape with his life. As a result of the ambush one Viet Cong was killed and another wounded.

There was to be no let-up for the members of the Squadron. On 23 October there were two anti-tank mine attacks on the Squadron's APCs in different provinces. The first occurred on a track approximately half a kilometre to the western side of Route 2 between Cam My and Ngai Giao in Phuoc Tuy province. An APC detonated a 20 pound anti-tank mine with the strike point under the front of the right track; the first and second roadwheels were blown off, the right-hand sponson was dented and the weld cracked. The hull was warped, one track disintegrated and 10 track links were damaged. There were no serious casualties reported among the crew members. The second attack occurred to the east of Route 15 near Tham Thien in Bien Hoa province. The point of strike for the 20 pound anti-tank mine was directed at the forward left-hand side of the vehicle. The hull was penetrated and warped and the final drive-well weld was torn. The engine mounting cracked and the steering laterals sheared. In spite of the damage there were no serious casualties sustained by members of the crew.

The remainder of October was relatively quiet, the only other contact with the enemy occurring on 25 October when 12 Section from 1 Troop contacted and fired on five Viet Cong on the road near Thua Tich. Results of the section's fire on the enemy were not determined. At the end of the month 1 Troop was the Ready Reaction Force while 2 Troop remained deployed with 9 RAR in the western sector of the province on Operation KINGS CROSS. 3 Troop was preparing to join 6 RAR on Operation ROSS on the Phuoc Tuy/Binh Tuy border, where it was intended to target the Viet Cong's gardens in an attempt to deny the enemy local sources of sustenance. 83 and 84 Sections from Support Troop remained under the operational control of the 1st Armoured Regiment in the Binh Ba rubber plantation.[6]

November 1969 was to prove a very active month for the Squadron. On the morning of 2 November 2 Troop contacted a large Viet Cong force at 10.30 am approximately 1.5 kilometres west of Tham Thien in Bien Hoa province. The ensuing fire fight saw two enemy killed and another wounded. No casualties among members of the troop were reported. The next day the troop continued to sweep the area and another three bodies were located, bringing the total number of enemy killed in that contact to five. One AK47 rifle, one SKS rifle and a pistol were also recovered, along with eight packs and a quantity of medical supplies. A Viet Cong, *hoi chanh*, who surrendered later that day, advised that there had been eight of his colleagues killed in the fire fight the previous day, including a doctor.

On 5 November at 1.30 pm, 1 Troop reported that an unknown Viet Cong force had fired two RPG rounds at one of the bulldozers that the troop had been protecting as it was undertaking land-clearing operations in the Long Green area north of Phuoc Hai. An artillery fire mission was directed at the area to which the enemy had retreated. At 6.20 pm 23 Section contacted six local force Viet Cong about half a kilometre east of Thai Thien in Bien Hoa province. A sweep of the area the next morning failed to reveal any results of the previous night's contact. On 7 November 2 Troop contacted two enemy troops approximately 2.5 kilometres southeast of Thai Thien. The troop fired on the enemy which fled, but two packs were subsequently located.

Meanwhile, 3 Troop, which remained deployed in the eastern sector of the province searching for Viet Cong gardens, also had two contacts with the enemy on 6 November. Results in each incident were unable to be determined. The next morning at 8.55 as the troop continued to search for Viet Cong gardens an enemy force of undetermined numbers was contacted. The enemy withdrew to the west, with negative results reported. However, the search for enemy gardens was successful, and at

5 pm the troop came across a large cornfield measuring 300 × 100 metres on the Phuoc Tuy/Binh Tuy border. Trails leading from east to west were followed but apart from a couple of small caches of rice and implements nothing else was located. As a result of this discovery a possum aircraft was called in the next day to assist in the continuing search. A large rice field was then found some 3 kilometres west of the garden located the previous evening in Binh Tuy province. A Viet Cong at the site was engaged by the possum, which resulted in two secondary explosions. Further investigation revealed a large rice cache, consisting of over 500 pounds of rice drying on mats. A dustoff flight was required by the troop after a tree fell on Corporal Ken Wagner late in the afternoon. That same day 86 Section located an anti-tank mine consisting of a 105 mm artillery round and MIG mine detonator approximately 1.5 kilometres west of Ngai Giao. The mine was destroyed by the engineers from the mini-team attached to the section.

On 9 November at 12.40 am elements from 1 Troop, the Ready Reaction Force, were deployed to Long Dien in response to reported enemy activity. En route, Callsign 10Bravo encountered a booby trap on a tripwire. After dismantling the mine the Reaction Force went on to Long Dien, where everything was reported as being quiet. After staying the night the troop returned to Nui Dat the next morning at 6.50 pm. Later that morning Callsign 13 located a cache in a bunker system approximately 3 kilometres east of Phuoc Loi village. That afternoon 3 Troop, which remained deployed on the border of Phuoc Tuy and Binh Tuy provinces, reported locating a base camp to the east of Route 331 in Binh Tuy. A quantity of blood-stained clothing and Australian webbing was recovered from the site. The next morning at 7.50 as the troop continued to search the area it uncovered an unusual cache, which had been stored in a tree about a metre off the ground. The cache contained 300 pounds of rice and had been camouflaged under a sheet of brown plastic. On 11 November at 11 am 3 Troop located another 50-pound cache of rice close to the previous day's rice cache. Meanwhile Callsign 19Mike reported locating another bunker system and recovered a small quantity of ammunition, including an RPG round and a grenade, near the bunker system that Callsign 13 had discovered the previous day.

2 Troop returned to the Task Force base on 11 November and was replaced by 1 Troop in the western sector of the province under the operational control of 9 RAR. At 6.40 pm 12 Section contacted an enemy force of undetermined strength half a kilometre north of Tham Phuoc in Bien Hoa province. During the ensuing fire fight a number of RPG rounds and small arms were fired at the section. A subsequent sweep of the area found five blood trails although no further trace of the enemy force.

The following day at 8.15 am 1 Troop conducted a sweep of the area in which the contact had taken place. The blood trails leading from the site of the contact were discovered as well as a hole that had been dug to plant an anti-tank mine. At 10.40 am Callsign 10Alpha detonated an anti-tank mine on a track 2 kilometres west of Tham Phuoc in Bien Hoa province. The mine had an approximate strength of 20 pounds of chicom explosive, with the point of strike inside the rear left-hand roadwheel. The third and fifth roadwheel support arms were blown off and the idler assembly torn and bent. The hull was penetrated and the ramp door hinges were broken. The passenger seat mounting was torn off and the turret jammed as a result of the hull distortion. None of the crew was reported as having sustained serious wounds.

As land-clearing operations continued in the Long Green area, 86 Section, which was deployed to provide protection to the engineers undertaking the work, uncovered a rice cache consisting of three 16-litre drums of rice. The following day Callsign 86 reported that one of the dozers undertaking the land-clearing had hit a CS gas mine and three personnel had been affected. That same evening back at Nui Dat the Squadron was 'stood to' after the base received incoming fire from the enemy, but no casualties resulted. The next afternoon at 4.18, Callsign 86 reported detonating an M16 mine, but no casualties were sustained among members of the crew. At 9.15 pm Callsign 85Bravo on the eastern edge of Dat Do reported being under enemy mortar fire. No casualties were reported.

On 16 November at 10.20 am Lieutenant Craig Mitchell, who had been deployed with the Cat Lo patrol boats as the Squadron's liaison officer, reported that his patrol boat had attacked an enemy force in the Soi Rap channel some 5 kilometres northwest of Phu My. Five enemy were reported as being killed in the attack and a B40 rocket launcher was captured. That evening at 9.43 Callsign 10Alpha reported having engaged a spotlight 100 metres from their location about 1 kilometre west of FSB Julia in Bien Hoa province.

On 18 November 1 Troop continued its deployment in the western sector of the province, while 3 Troop completed its deployment in the eastern sector. 2 Troop's 23 Section was operating on the eastern side of Route 2, approximately 2 kilometres north of Ngai Giao. At 4 pm it was reported that Callsign 23Alpha had detonated an anti-tank mine with an estimated strength of 65 pounds of explosive. The point of strike was beneath the right-hand rear corner of the vehicle, with the blast destroying two suspension stations. The hull floor was penetrated with a 100 × 15-centimetre hole. The ramp was damaged, the cargo hatch hinges broken, the battery housing damaged and two sections of seats destroyed. Three of those on board were reported as having sustained wounds. Crew Commander Roger Locke sustained cuts to his face and neck and, together with two engineers from the mini-team, was evacuated from the site. The nature of the explosion led those investigating the attack to conclude that the mine was a shaped charge.

The following day, 19 November, 1 Troop from the Squadron and the 1st Armoured Regiment supported local ARVN forces in an assault on a bunker system 2 kilometres directly east of Route 15 near FSB Julia in Bien Hoa province. No casualties were sustained by members of the Squadron or 1st Armoured Regiment. However, four members of the 90-strong ARVN force were wounded in action. The enemy had four of their troops killed in action as a result of the assault by the Australian armoured force. At 9.56 am Callsign 84 had located two M16 mines 2 kilometres east of Hoi My. The mines had been placed above the ground and booby-trapped to target passengers travelling on an APC.

On 20 November, Callsign 20Alpha contacted two soldiers from the NVA 4 kilometres east of Ngai Giao at 7.15 pm. One of the NVA was killed and his AK47 rifle captured while the other withdrew to the southeast. At 1 am on 21 November elements from 2 Troop together with D&E Platoon, who had been deployed in the northern sector of the province, set an ambush approximately 7 kilometres south of Courtney hill and 2 kilometres west of Route 2. The ambush was activated against a substantial enemy force moving on a track to the west. A sweep of the area later that morning revealed that five enemy had been killed in the ambush. Two AK47 rifles, one chicom pistol and a quantity of documents and money were recovered. Subsequent intelligence reports indicated that four of those killed were high-ranking officers from the Viet Cong's MR7 staff. No casualties were sustained by members of the troop or the infantry.

On 23 November 83 Section reported that it had located an anti-tank mine on Route 2 near Ngai Giao. The mine consisted of a 105 mm shell with an additional 12 pounds of explosive and an electric pressure switch. One week later on 30 November 1969 a carrier from 1 Troop detonated a mine on a track leading off Route 15 some 2 kilometres southwest of FSB Julia in Bien Hoa province. The strength of the mine was approximately 40 pounds of explosive, with the point of strike under the inside right-hand front roadwheel. The first and second suspension stations and the final drive were destroyed. The sponsons were dented and the hull's floor plate was warped and penetrated in three locations. The engine mountings were damaged and overall damage to the carrier was classified as severe. The crew suffered only minor wounds; given the strength of the mine they were lucky not to have sustained more serious injuries.[7]

At the beginning of December 1969 1 Troop and 82 Section remained under the operational control of 5 RAR in AO LINTON in the eastern sector of the province. 2 Troop with Callsigns 9Bravo and 9Echo commenced Operation MARSDEN in AO GULLIVER under the operational control of 6 RAR in the northwestern sector, where they were joined at FSB Picton by 3 Troop on 3 December. Support Troops 81, 85 and 86 were deployed in both the Long Green area with the land-clearing teams and at FSB Discovery on Route 328 some 5 kilometres west of Xuyen Moc. On 5 December 3 Troop redeployed to AO GRACE in the southwestern sector of the province, where they came under the operational control of 5 RAR. The following evening Callsign 30Bravo initiated an ambush at 7.10 pm against three enemy troops in a sampan in the swamp approximately 1 kilometre to the west of FSB Julia in Bien Hoa. Two Viet Cong were reported as killed and a sampan was sunk. At 4 am on 7 December other elements from 3 Troop initiated an ambush against three enemy in a sampan about half a kilometre north of the contact point of the previous evening. Another two Viet Cong were reported as killed, one was wounded and the sampan sunk.

In the northeastern sector of the province during Operation MARSDEN on 8 December, 2 Troop was moving from FSB Picton to FSB Discovery. When the troop was approximately 2 kilometres to the north of Thua Tich and to the east of Route 328, Callsign 23Alpha, on which Corporal Roger Locke and Trooper Viv French were crew members, hit an anti-tank mine with an approximate strength of 30–60 pounds of explosive. The blast from the mine exploded another two mines that had been planted nearby. The point of strike of the primary mine was directly beneath the driver's compartment and the force severed the track and tore three roadwheels on the left-hand and one on the right-hand side from their mountings. A 125 × 60-centimetre hole was blown out under the driver's compartment, killing Viv French and one of the passengers. Roger Locke's crew commander's turret cage was severely buckled, seriously wounding him and another of the passengers. So destructive was the explosion that the trim vane, engine access door, cargo hatch and rear door were all blown off. But this was not the end of the action: when the dustoff helicopter on which the dead and wounded were to be evacuated attempted to land, it detonated another mine. The explosion rendered the helicopter inoperable and wounded another Australian soldier. The mine incidents were so horrendous that they delayed 2 Troop's progress, and the troop was forced to set up a defensive night location on the eastern outskirts of Thua Tich.

On 10 December at 11.20 am Callsign 84 reported hitting an M16 mine on a track approximately 5 kilometres southeast of Dat Do. No casualties were reported as a result of the explosion, but the full impact of the enemy's current mining activities was to be felt over the next couple of days. 14 December was another terrible day, with two mine incidents involving members of the Squadron. The first occurred when elements from 1 Troop moved to relieve 13 Section, which had been based at FSB Peggy in AO ASHGROVE in the northern sector of the province. As 13 Section was returning to Nui Dat along the road near Ngai Giao it drew near to an ARVN truck transporting troops. As the section neared the truck it detonated an anti-tank mine, which killed 13 ARVN soldiers and wounded another three. The truck was totally destroyed in the attack.

Another mine attack occurred at 3.45 that afternoon when Callsign 20Bravo hit an anti-tank mine about 1.5 kilometres south of the attack on the ARVN truck. On a rubber plantation access road leading off Route 2 about 1 kilometre to the west of Ngai Giao, the carrier containing Doug Voysey and 2nd Lieutenant Craig Mitchell, the troop's second in command, was negotiating the entry to a water course when the explosion occurred. The mine was estimated at between 30 and 40 pounds of explosive; the force created by the placement of the mine was so great that it overturned the carrier end over end, trapping Doug Voysey, who was still in the driver's compartment. Unfortunately, the upturned carrier had landed in the water course, and the driver's compartment began to fill with water. Despite frantic efforts by other members of the section and the engineers, they were unable to free the driver. Crew Commander Craig Mitchell and two of the passengers were wounded and evacuated from the site. The point of strike in this incident was the left rear of the carrier, with the idler wheel and the last two roadwheels and suspension arms blown off. The hull was penetrated, with a 100 × 30-centimetre hole being blown through the floor and the ramp and cargo hatches blown off.

These anti-tank mines and RPG attacks over the past three months had killed three drivers and some of their passengers, and the crew commanders and other passengers on each of the vehicles had been extremely fortunate to escape with their lives. The Squadron nevertheless continued the role with which it had been charged, and on 16 December 3 Troop commenced operations with elements of the SAS north of FSB Discovery. No other incidents of note occurred until 22 December, when 3 Troop reported locating a mine marker near the Nui Ti Vai mountains and 96 Section reported that one of the land-clearing bulldozers it was protecting hit a mine in the Long Green area. Neither incident was considered serious, and there were no casualties reported.

On 24 December 1969 the Squadron started returning to Nui Dat to observe the Christmas truce that had been called by both sides of the war. All the troops had returned to the Task Force base on Christmas Eve with the exception of 12 Section, which remained on the western side of the Courtney rubber plantation, and 21 and 81 Sections and Callsign 85Bravo which remained at FSB Picton in the northwestern sector of the province. No incidents were reported over the Christmas break, but on Boxing Day 12 Section, which was in the Courtney rubber plantation in lower Long Khanh province, located and destroyed a 30 pound chicom anti-tank mine with an attached electronic detonating system.

On 27 December 11 Section relieved 12 Section, which returned to Nui Dat for their Christmas break. At 1 pm 11 Section, which had set out on a patrol of the area they had taken over from 12 Section, located a booby trap approximately 6 kilometres south of Courtney hill. The device consisted of two chicom hand grenades tied together and set 130 centimetres above the ground with a tripwire leading off. On the morning of 29 December at 4 am 11 Section, which was located at FSB Peggy, detected movement on the wire surrounding the base. The area was engaged with machine gun fire, but a sweep of the area revealed nothing. Later in the day, as 1 Troop's HQ moved to FSB Peggy, an enemy force was sighted some 3 kilometres south of the base. The area was engaged with machine gun fire, with negative results. Following this contact the troop resumed its journey to FSB Peggy, and at 4.20 pm had moved about 500 metres from where the enemy had been engaged earlier that afternoon. At this point a tank from 1st Armoured Regiment, which was accompanying the APC Troop HQ to FSB Peggy, detonated an anti-tank mine which resulted in the tank 'brewing up'. While the tank suffered substantial damage, there were no serious casualties reported among the crew members.[8]

By the end of 1969 the Squadron's casualty rate had risen alarmingly. During the year, six of its members had lost their lives and a further 29 had been wounded or injured in combat. To reduce the number of deaths and wounds suffered by crew members, the decision was made to reinforce different sections of the vehicle's hull. First, the sponsons on the side of the vehicle, under which the tracks and roadwheels ran, were reinforced with an additional armoured skin in an effort to negate the effects of mine explosions when the tracks ran over a mine. Further enhancements were made to the vehicle's hull and in mid-1970 'belly armour' kits started being fitted to the APCs to absorb the initial shock of a mine exploding under the carrier. The 'belly armour' kit consisted of a 38 mm aluminium plate, which covered the whole underside of the carrier and was bolted onto the vehicle's hull. Bolting rather than welding was designed to allow the plate to absorb the shock of the exploding mine, which in turn would cause it to drop off the hull. Rather than the unprotected hull absorbing the whole blast, the major portion of the shock energy would be absorbed by the attached armour plating.[9]

THE NEW YEAR

New Year's Day 1970 saw the Squadron again fully deployed. 1 Troop remained at Nui Dat as Ready Reaction Force. 2 Troop moved to FSB Pat near Thua Tich, where it came under the operational control of 5 RAR. 3 Troop returned to FSB Peggy in the northern sector of the province. 86 and 85 Sections continued to support the land-clearing teams in Long Green, where they uncovered a bunker system 2.5 kilometres northeast of Phuoc Loi. On 2 January 86 Section reported locating another bunker system, almost 2 kilometres east of where they had located the bunker system the previous day. A quantity of claymore mines, bangalore torpedoes and M79 rounds were recovered from a cache in the bunkers. It was decided that the area required further investigation. Accordingly, on 4 January 86 Section escorted a platoon of infantry and three tanks as they moved to an area some 3 kilometres northeast of Phuoc Loi. The enemy fired 12 RPG rounds at the tanks as they advanced on the area, but neither party sustained any casualties, with the enemy immediately retreating after firing their weapons.

On 5 January 1 Troop replaced 2 Troop at FSB Pat in AO ROSSLYN at Thua Tich. Shortly after arrival, 1 Troop advised that it had contacted and fired on one Viet Cong on the southern outskirts of Thua Tich, but the results could not be determined. On leaving FSB Pat 2 Troop commenced a four-day independent operation with Regional Forces in an area southeast of Xuyen Moc. On the same day 84 Section orchestrated an artillery bombardment on the Long Hai hills, which resulted in a number of civilians in the free fire zone being apprehended. At 8.15 pm on 8 January 31 Section, which had earlier in the day replaced 32 section at FSB Peggy, was scrambled to assist an infantry platoon from A Company 8 RAR that had been in heavy contact with an enemy force about 1 kilometre north of the fire support base. The section stayed with the platoon during the night to provide them with protection. At first light the other APCs in the troop boarded the remainder of A Company 8 RAR and set off for the contact area. Numerous blood trails were located leading from the area, but no enemy bodies were located. After reporting the situation 3 Troop boarded A Company 8 RAR and returned to Nui Dat. The previous day during the joint independent operation conducted by 2 Troop and the Regional Forces in the Xuyen Moc area, one of the Regional Forces' soldiers stood on an anti-tank mine and died instantly, while two of his comrades were seriously wounded. On 11 January 1 Troop detained a *chieu hoi* near FSB Picton after taking possession of his AK47 and three magazines of ammunition.

MATILDA FORCE

The Task Force's two armoured squadrons had been continually fully deployed and their capabilities so appreciated by the Task Force command that it had been decided to undertake an independent armoured operation. This operation, codenamed MATILDA, commenced on 15 January 1970 and took place in a large area northeast of Nui Dat. A total of 44 armoured vehicles from the Australian Task Force's two armoured squadrons were involved in the operation. The Squadron provided 27 APCs which included 3 Troop and Support Troop's 82, 83, 84 and 86 Sections as well as Squadron HQ's vehicles, all under the command of Captain K.C. Ashman. Also participating were half of the tanks from A Squadron 1st Armoured Regiment and B Company 6 RAR. A large team of engineers was also required to undertake this operation. As the Australians were outside their artillery operating range, four mortar carriers from Support Troop were deployed as operational support. This operation by Australian Armour was said to be the biggest undertaken since World War II and was known as MATILDA FORCE. The operation was to highlight the mobility that could be attained by the tanks and APCs in covering and securing large tracts of land relatively quickly and efficiently.

The area of operation was quite large, covering three provinces with a border area of some 200 kilometres. It extended in a rectangle through Xuyen Moc and into Binh Tuy province, northeast along the coastal road through Ham Tan to the junction of Routes 28 and 1, west some 60 kilometres to the Binh Tuy/Long Khanh border using Route 1 and finally south through the May Tao mountains. This was a particularly difficult operation because a number of roads in the eastern sector of the operations area had not been used for a number of years, and all the bridges had been destroyed. The rivers all had steep banks, and it was an overgrown and thick jungle environment.

The APCs were able to traverse the country far more easily than the 50 ton centurion tanks, which had trouble with the river crossings. Even so, the APC in which the Squadron's commander was travelling smashed a final drive in the rough terrain. The initial move from Nui Dat to Ham Tam in Binh Tuy province, some 46 kilometres northeast of the base, had taken three and a half days to cover, a testament to the harsh country through which the vehicles were forced to travel. A resupply for the MATILDA FORCE had been arranged for 21 January, which was undertaken by 21 Section accompanied by the LAD's fitter vehicle. The LAD had included a replacement final drive as part of its inventory to effect the necessary repairs to the Squadron commander's vehicle from the ARV. The route taken for the resupply was long and indirect, and necessitated the APCs travelling along Route 15 to Long Binh, where they turned right and travelled to Xuan Loc along Route 1, then another 50 kilometres east along Route 1 to Binh Tuy province where the rendezvous site had been arranged for the following day, 22 January. Earlier that day at 2 pm three Viet Cong were contacted by MATILDA FORCE, which resulted in one enemy killed and one SKS rifle captured.

Despite the hardships endured, the operation did much for the morale of the Americans attached to the ARVN forces, as well as the local district officials and Regional Forces in the area. Parts of the operation area had never been visited by the Australians, and the show of force by such a large armoured contingent could not but impress these people. As the armoured troops moved south, a large deserted enemy camp was discovered in dense jungle. The camp was destroyed by a helicopter hovering above the huts, the crew dropping grenades on the structures below.

While Operation MATILDA continued, 1 Troop, which had remained deployed in the northeastern sector of the province, initiated an ambush against four enemy troops about 1 kilometre northwest of FSB Picton on 19 January, but results could not be determined. On 22 January Callsign 13Bravo detonated an anti-tank mine as it travelled along Route 329 approximately 12 kilometres northeast of Xuyen Moc. The carrier was being towed, and it was reported that both driver and crew commander had dismounted from the vehicle before the mine detonated. It was estimated that the mine was made up of about 40 pounds of explosive, with the strike point beneath the left front track. The final drive, the first two roadwheels on the left and the first two roadwheels on the right were blown off. The ramp, engine hatch and driver's hatch were blown off and the driver's compartment floor was twisted and penetrated. There was extensive damage to both the driver's and engine compartments. The crew were not on the vehicle when the mine was detonated, but the vehicle's crew commander was reported to be suffering the effects of the explosion.

The resupply of the MATILDA FORCE was effected on 22 January as arranged, with 21 Section then returning to Xuan Loc where it spent the evening. At 10.45 pm an ambush in Binh Tuy province was activated by 3 Troop when they contacted three local force Viet Cong. However, a subsequent sweep of the area produced no results. Three days later 22 Section together with W Company 6 RAR had been deployed on the eastern side of Route 2 approximately 5 kilometres due south of Cam My village. At 12.45 pm a platoon from W Company entered some bamboo where a party of 11 enemy troops were contacted. In the ensuing fire fight one Australian infantrymen was seriously wounded in the head, which necessitated Callsign 22 arranging a dustoff. It is interesting to note how quickly the wounded could be evacuated by the dustoff flights as shown by the commander's diary, which relates the following details:

> The Squadron's command post at Nui Dat advised Callsign 22 that after the contact was reported at 12.45 pm the Dustoff was placed on stand by at 12.47 pm. At 1.27 pm Callsign 22 reported to Nui Dat that the Dustoff evacuation had been completed. Losses to the enemy as a result of this contact were unable to be determined.

On 27 January at 12.54 pm 11 Section, which had been operating out of FSB Pat near Thua Tich under the operational control of 5 RAR, was called to assist two of its platoons which were in contact with a large enemy force approximately 2 kilometres southwest of FSB Discovery. Callsign 11 reported at 1.33 pm that contact with the enemy had been broken, but they had received both RPG and small arms fire as they had moved into the area of contact. A subsequent sweep of the area revealed that six of the enemy had been killed.[10]

At the start of February 1 Troop was under the operational control of 5 RAR on Operation BONDI 2 and remained based at FSB Pat at Thua Tich. 2 Troop was under the operational control of 6 RAR on Operation NAPIER at FSB Peggy between the Courtney rubber plantation and Ngai Giao. 3 Troop was the Ready Reaction Force based at Nui Dat while Support Troop's 86 and 85 Sections were at the Horseshoe. 84 Section had accompanied 17 Construction Squadron to FSB Dakota in the western section of the province, where they remained under that unit's operational control as they undertook land-clearing operations around Thai Thien.

On 5 February at 11.50 am 84 Section reported that it had located a cache containing 30 sandbags full of rice and a number of RPG rounds and rockets 500 metres north of Dakota. Another report was filed at 2 pm, stating that a further rice cache containing some 250 pounds of rice had been located 100 metres south of the earlier find. The US forces in the area decided to set up an ambush at the site of the last cache discovery for that evening. At 7.15 pm 84 Section reported that it was deploying to assist the US personnel who had activated the ambush and had taken casualties. After rendering assistance to the US troops, 84 Section returned to FSB Dakota for the evening.[11]

Since the havoc caused by Australian Armour at Binh Ba the previous year, the enemy were anxious to avoid contact with large armoured patrols and reluctant to stand and fight in defence of their bunker systems. In the early days of the Task Force the infantry had been engaged in clearing out enemy positions and bunker systems with the support of only artillery and aircraft. The success of the combined armoured/infantry forces at FSBs Coral and Balmoral and Binh Ba had caused a strategic change in the operational methods now being employed by the Australian Task Force. The infantry in major operations was given the role of initially reconnoitring the area in which it was suspected that the enemy bunker systems were located. The tanks, with APCs providing flank and rear protection, would assault the bunkers using their superior fire power. The infantry was also deployed in blocking positions from where they ambushed exit points as the enemy attempted to escape. The employment of this strategy and the dangers faced by the men who served with the Task Force's two Australian Armoured units is best illustrated in the next chapter.

10

The Long Hai hills, 1970

In February 1970 a decision had been made by the Australians to upgrade Route 44, which ran from Baria south down past the Long Hai hills before turning east along the coast and then north to Dat Do. The Long Hais were a series of hills running from the south near the coast some 20 kilometres to the north towards Route 326. It was thought that the Viet Cong's domination of the area could be undermined by providing a more accessible route to the markets for the local population. Additionally, the upgraded road would allow contact with larger areas of the population, and this would facilitate the pacification of the local communities by allowing the Australians to move into the area and build schools and hospitals. These facilities and services were already being provided by the Australians to other communities throughout the province.

To undertake the upgrading of Route 44 a quarry was required, and a site was selected on the western side of the northern set of the Long Hai hills, which was accessible to Route 44. The Long Hai hills area had long been a Viet Cong and NVA stronghold, and one which the Australian Task Force had long wanted to clear. The area was well defended by the enemy with mines that had been lifted from the ill-conceived Australian minefield between Dat Do and Phuoc Hai. Previous operations in the area had not gone well for the Australians. The most notable, Operation BRIBIE in 1966 to the east of the Long Hais and Operation PINAROO in early 1968, proved just how difficult it was to oust the enemy firmly entrenched there. Several other major operations had been conducted in the area, but the high rate of casualties sustained, especially from the M16 anti-personnel mines that had been pilfered by the enemy, had attracted a lot of negative publicity in the Australian press.

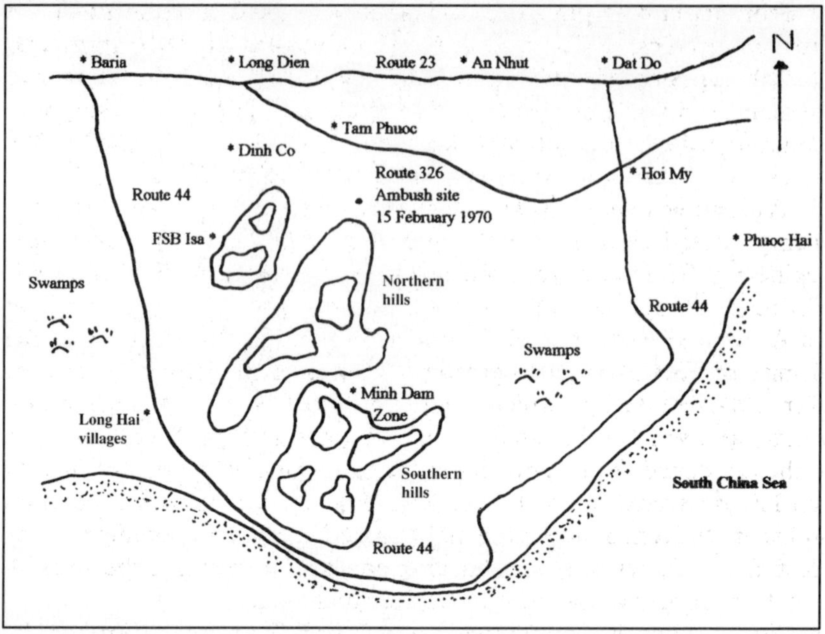

The Long Hai hills

The enemy had set up heavy defensive positions at the southern end of the hills to protect the Minh Dam 'secret zone', which they regarded as their own territory. Given the defensive structures they had created, the enemy felt it highly unlikely that the Australians would mount an attack and risk further high casualty rates. Various elements from the Squadron had been deployed to the Long Hai peninsula and had been operating in the area. In one particular incident, on the morning of 10 February on the eastern side of the hills near Phuoc Hai, Callsign 86 detonated two M16 mines with the point of strike at the rear of the vehicle. In the attack, which occurred at 9.30 am, Crew Commander Sergeant Ron McFayden and three others, including the two mini-team members who were riding on top of the vehicle, were wounded by shrapnel. Two ARVN soldiers deployed with the section were also wounded by the explosion. Damage sustained by the vehicle was minimal, with a few fragmentation marks visible on the rear of the vehicle.

At 6.30 that evening Callsign 29Juliet reported contact with nine enemy 2.5 kilometres south of Tam Phuoc in the northern Long Hai hills. No results from the contact were reported. Five minutes later Callsign 29Juliet reported that it had detonated an M16 mine, but no casualties had been sustained. A further mine attack occurred on

11 February at 4.45 pm about 2 kilometres to the east of the attack the previous evening. Callsign 20Bravo reported that an M16 mine and possibly a pound of TNT exploded under the left track at the rear of the vehicle while it was reversing. Five tracks and the track adjuster were damaged. One of the infantrymen from 8 RAR was wounded in the attack, but no casualties were sustained by the crew.

As soon as operations and work commenced at the quarry site, the enemy started sniping at the engineers. To afford protection to the engineers FSB Isa was set up near the quarry site. This base was initially manned by elements from C Company 8 RAR and 2 Troop 1st Armoured Regiment. Early on the evening of 15 February in the vicinity of FSB Isa, a platoon from C Company ambushed a force of over 100 Viet Cong, which counterattacked the platoon's position shortly afterwards. The tanks located at Isa were scrambled and came to the assistance of the hard-pressed infantrymen, who were starting to run low on ammunition. The tanks eventually recovered the situation and spent the remainder of the night parked between the enemy and the Australian infantry to prevent further attacks. The result of the ambush was 34 members of the local D445 Regiment killed.

Fearing that the enemy might attack FSB Isa in retaliation for the losses inflicted on their troops, the Task Force commander decided to deploy the Cavalry Squadron's 3 Troop, which was the Ready Reaction Force. The troop was placed on notice at 7.19 pm with orders to move immediately to FSB Isa to secure the base, in the absence of the tanks that were protecting the platoon from C Company which had initiated the ambush. The troop boarded the remainder of the platoons from C Company 8 RAR and set off for the Long Hais, arriving at 9.15 pm at Isa where they took over security of the base for the evening.

This ambush proved the catalyst for the Task Force commander, Brigadier S.P. Weir, to make a decision to resolve the situation surrounding the Long Hai hills area, which for so long had been a thorn in the side of the Australian forces and was preventing the upgrade of Route 44. Intelligence reports indicated that the entire D445 Battalion was in the Long Hai/Minh Dam 'secret zone', and that the opportunity was now available to deal a telling blow to enemy forces in the area. In addition to 3 Troop under the command of Captain Kenneth Ashman, which had moved to the Long Hais on the evening of 15 February, 1 Troop 1st Armoured Regiment had moved down to FSB Isa during the night. It was also decided to deploy B and D Company 8 RAR, who were to join C Company for Operation HAMMERSLEY.

On 16 February 1970 at 9 am 3 Troop deployed to the eastern side of the hills, where it began sweeping the area. At 1 am Major Rooks with his Squadron HQ and 1 Troop also deployed to the Long Hais under the operational control of 8 RAR. As Armour was going to play an integral role in this operation, the 1st Armoured Regiment's Commanding Officer Major Chipman also joined his cavalry counterpart at FSB Isa. To emphasise the ongoing dangers of mines in the area, both Callsigns 30Bravo and 32Bravo reported at 1.55 pm that they had detonated M16 mines on the eastern side of the northern hills approximately 4 kilometres to the northeast of Isa. That evening both troops deployed to various ambush sites on the eastern side of the hills. At 10.50 pm Callsign 11 reported it was in contact after it activated an ambush against a party of three enemy personnel moving along a track 2 kilometres northeast of FSB Isa. One Viet Cong was reported killed as a result of the ambush. No casualties were reported among the members of the section.

The plan of attack on the Long Hai hills involved an initial move towards the enemy-held valley on the eastern side of the southern group of hills. B Company 8 RAR would provide a blocking force, covering escape routes at the southern end of the hills. 3 Troop and elements from Support Troop, together with the tanks and C and D Company 8 RAR, would move in a southerly direction in a reconnaissance-in-force manoeuvre in order to have the enemy disclose their main defensive positions. Throughout the operation the infantry was instructed that it was to ride in the APCs in the closed-down position, as there were many booby traps set in the trees that could send showers of schrapnel downwards. Additionally, anti-personnel mines over the entire area made it too risky to allow the infantry to proceed on foot. Orders were given that the infantry were not to dismount from the carriers until the area had been cleared of mines. As usual, the tanks would lead the advance, with the APCs providing rear and flank protection.

Once again the tanks and APCs would be responsible for the outcome of the operation and could expect to undertake the major portion of the fighting when it occurred. At 8.30 am on 18 February 2 Troop deployed from Nui Dat to relieve 1 Troop on Operation HAMMERSLEY. Meanwhile C Company 8 RAR was loaded on board the carriers of 3 Troop, which was joined by 2 Troop B Squadron 1st Armoured Regiment under the command of Lieutenant J.H. Brennan, and then set off along the eastern side of the hills, moving towards the southern hills. On reaching the northern spur of the southern hills the tanks went into two-up formation, with one section of APCs following on either side to provide flank protection and the remaining APCs providing rear protection for the advancing formation. At 11.02 am, and after travelling about 4000 metres around the side of the hills, the leading tanks found themselves inside a bunker system, where three armed Viet Cong fired their weapons on the Australian forces. Fire was returned, and one prisoner (who was a member of an entertainment troop) was taken captive and handed over to the commanding officer of 8 RAR, who later persuaded him to point out the locations of the various minefields.

The APCs continued to push along the side of the hilly feature, where a deviation from the tanks was required to avoid an impassable water course. This brought elements from the troop out in a low scrubby area at the mouth of a deep valley. The members of the troop were now unwittingly in the enemy's Minh Dam 'secret zone', which for many years had been considered a no-go area for government forces in pursuit of the Viet Cong and NVA. The enemy reception of the troop was indicative of the regard in which the enemy held this area. It was 11.31 am when the Australian force entered the valley, and the APC troop was immediately hit with heavy enemy fire. The infantry on board the carriers were unable to dismount as anti-personnel mines virtually covered the area; so thick were the M16 mines that the infantry could hear the 'thump' of the explosions as the carriers ran over them. As the crew of Callsign 83Alpha, which was accompanying 3 Troop, moved forward to counter the enemy's fire it became suspended on a hidden tree stump, making it immovable. As the other two APCs in the section moved forward to lend assistance, the carrier crewed by Lance Corporal Barry Whiston and Trooper Hugh Carlyle was hit by two RPG rounds, causing it to burst into flames. At this stage the accompanying tanks were still attempting to cross the water course and were unable to lend assistance.

Meanwhile the APCs had become involved in a bitter fire fight with the enemy as they attempted to recover the .50 cal. machine gun from the burning carrier. Corporal Ron Macey, who had been travelling adjacent to Whiston and Carlyle's vehicle, instructed his driver to steer the APC to a position from which he could assist the crew and passengers in the now burning carrier. Ron Macey and Corporal B.K. Coe of C Company 8 RAR dismounted from their carrier and ran forward under heavy fire from nearby enemy bunkers, in an attempt to remove the crew and the five passengers from the rear of the vehicle. However, on reaching the vehicle they found that the rear door was jammed. Corporal Macey removed his 9 mm pistol and, using it as a lever, forced the door open. The enemy continued to fire on Coe and Macey during the rescue attempt. The two corporals eventually succeeded in removing the five passengers and their weapons from the back of the carrier, then carried and led them to a relatively safe position. The two wounded crew members remained in their badly damaged carrier awaiting rescue as the enemy directed fire at their position.

In the interim the tanks had located a crossing for the water course and were directed by Captain Ashman to move forward and assist the stricken APC. Once the passengers had been moved to a relatively safe position, Coe and Macey returned to the burning vehicle intent on removing the crew members, Whiston and Carlyle, who were still trapped there. They were accompanied by two crew members from one of the tanks, Corporal Gary Gott and Lance Corporal Peter Moore, who had dismounted from their vehicle with a towline to attach to the back of the burning APC. By this stage the enemy fire had intensified. The towline was attached to the vehicle, but disengaged when an attempt was made to tow the damaged carrier away. Realising what the Australians were trying to achieve, the enemy lobbed a satchel full of explosives into the carrier, which destroyed the APC and wounded some of those trying to rescue the trapped crew members. Both Barry Whiston and Hugh Carlyle were killed instantly. Ron Macey was wounded, as was Corporal D. Hocking, who was one of the 1 Field Squadron mini-team engineers. Callsigns 30Alpha and 83 were also reported as being damaged during the attack.

With Brennan's tanks leading and Ashman's APCs following, the armoured vehicles pressed on through the bunker system. Both the tanks and APCs proceeded with all hatches in the closed position because of the enemy mines planted in the trees. The enemy also fired their RPG rounds overhead so they exploded in the tree foliage, sending shrapnel bursts down towards the tanks and APCs. The enemy remained hidden in their bunkers until the Australians approached a line of anti-tank mines that had been identified by the Viet Cong prisoner captured earlier that day. The commanding officer of 8 RAR had taken the POW, a 16-year-old youth, up in his helicopter after he agreed to identify the various features of the Minh Dam defence lines. As soon as the armoured vehicles stopped at the anti-tank minefield the Viet Cong emerged from their bunkers and started firing RPG rounds at the Australians. This forced the tanks and the APCs to fight their way back through the bunker system, with the tanks using their massive fire power to overcome the hostile resistance of the Viet Cong defenders. Several tanks received direct hits from RPG rounds, but as they moved clear of the bunker system all were still in action and firing their guns.

Artillery, mortar and air strikes were directed at the bunker system once the tanks and APCs were clear of the area. The situation that confronted the two squadrons suggested that they were up against an enemy force of at least battalion strength. The fighting that had taken place had exhausted the entire ammunition supply of the tanks of 2 Troop's main armament and necessitated an emergency resupply of ammunition by helicopter. This was necessary so that they could again attack the bunkers to drive the enemy towards selected ambush sites surrounding the contact area. Meanwhile, plans were made to have

B and D Company 8 RAR loaded on board APCs from the Squadron's 2 Troop for deployment to the selected ambush sites once they had arrived at the area of operation. Tanks from 3 Troop 1st Armoured Regiment would accompany the APCs when they deployed to the ambush sites; these would be to the north and east of the Minh Dam area, where it was expected that the Viet Cong would attempt to withdraw. Artillery and air strikes would be used to block the southern and western routes.

The Viet Cong realised that they were being surrounded by the Australian forces, and started to fight their way out of their plight. 2 Troop had arrived in the area of operation having earlier replaced 1 Troop, who had returned to Nui Dat at 12.15 pm. As the APC from 2 Troop commenced deploying the infantry to the proposed ambush sites on the eastern side of the hills, it again ran into heavy enemy fire. One of the tanks accompanying the troop received a direct hit from an RPG round that penetrated the hull, wounding some of the crew members. At 1.25 pm 22 Section, led by Sergeant David Davies, was moving along a jungle trail close to the northern hills about 2 kilometres northeast of FSB Isa when it was attacked by an RPG team. Davies' APC received a direct hit from an RPG, which penetrated the hull, wounding driver Mick Elliott and the operator, Barry Pitt. David Davies was also wounded, but was able to remove his driver from his compartment and drive the vehicle back to a more secure area. The RPG entered the vehicle's hull on the left-hand side of the vehicle behind the driver's compartment and had damaged the vehicle's radios and electrical systems. Despite his wounds, Davies left his vehicle and ran to another from which he was able to direct counterfire against the enemy; as a result the enemy were forced to withdraw.

At 3.45 pm Callsign 21 reported that he and Sergeant David Sheppard's 23 Section were in contact with the enemy, having just deposited a platoon from B Company 8 RAR in an ambush site on the eastern side of the southern hills some 4.5 kilometres southeast of FSB Isa. It was reported that the section was receiving heavy small arms and RPG fire from a nearby enemy position and that an RPG round had ripped through Sheppard's carrier, Callsign 23, seriously wounding driver Phil Stent and blowing Sheppard out of the turret and onto the ground. The RPG round entered the left-hand side of the vehicle's hull behind the driver's compartment, leaving a 50-centimetre hole in the hull. Although suffering from a serious and painful neck injury, Sheppard immediately remounted his vehicle and organised the other APCs in his section into a defensive formation. The section commenced to pour machine gun fire into the enemy's position to protect the infantry platoon as they organised themselves.

2 Troop and B Company had been in heavy contact with the enemy during the course of the afternoon, and four of the APCs had been damaged in the fighting. D Company had proceeded to its allocated ambushing sites. To reach its ambushing sites, B Company was required to pass through D Company's location, a fact which at that stage was unknown to either B Company or 2 Troop. As the troop with B Company passed through D Company's position, movement was detected and the APCs immediately opened fire. But the movement was from D Company's position and the APCs had accidentally fired on their own infantry troops. The result was 10 Australian infantrymen from D Company's 11 Platoon were wounded. It had originally been planned that B Company would move to its ambushing location before D Company, to avoid having to move through each other's ambush site. Unfortunately, the staff at Task Force HQ controlling the movement of all the units had failed to alert the Squadron that they had changed the order and placed D Company in its ambushing position before B Company. Given the heavy action the troop had been involved in that afternoon, which had seriously delayed its movement, and the number of enemy forces in the area, it is understandable that a shoot-first-and-ask-questions-later policy had been adopted. A decision was made to absolve the troop of any blame in firing on its own troops.

While these problems were being sorted out, action to the south had continued. Because of the situation surrounding the Minh Dam area it was decided to make a further assault on the enemy's position. The tanks had been resupplied with ammunition as they again prepared to enter the main bunker system and clear it of any remaining enemy troops. As well, the carrier of Whiston and Carlyle was still at the site where it had been destroyed earlier that day, and the bodies of both crew members had not been recovered. Viet Cong had been reported at the wrecked carrier and were still attempting to strip the wrecked APC of its machine guns. Three troops of tanks again entered the Minh Dam bunker system and proceeded to destroy the bunkers with armoured piercing shells. They were accompanied by a tank dozer, which used its blades to recover the wrecked APC. As the tanks started withdrawing just on nightfall, one of the tank crew commanders noticed a .50 cal. machine gun lying on the ground that had been stripped by the enemy from Whiston and Carlyle's APC. He dismounted his tank and retrieved the gun, placing it on the engine deck before withdrawing from the area.

The remaining operative elements of 2 Troop adopted ambush positions on the northeastern side of the Long Hai hills some 5.5 kilometres east of FSB Isa. Similarly, the operative elements of 3 Troop adopted ambush sites some 500 metres west of 2 Troop's position. Squadron HQ returned to FSB Isa to participate in the planning for another armoured and infantry assault the next day. These plans were subsequently cancelled and instead a massive B52 bombing raid of the area was ordered, but the raid could not proceed for a least a further 24 hours as there was a statutory requirement for authorisation from the district and regional government authorities. 2 and 3 Troops thus deployed to the southern outskirts of Long Dien on 19 February and waited for the B52 raid. Meanwhile, Callsign 84 was dispatched from Nui Dat to recover the wreck of Callsign 83Alpha via Route 326. As authorisation for the B52 raid had not been received on 20 February, 2 and 3 Troops, while still under the operational control of 8 RAR, returned to Nui Dat while Squadron HQ remained at FSB Isa to facilitate planning for further action in the area following the B52 raid.

By the time authorisation for the B52 raid had finally been received from the government authorities, the whole of Phuoc Tuy province knew the details. The enemy, which had their own very effective intelligence unit, had details of the intended raid communicated to their own command. This intelligence had allowed the enemy force to withdraw from the intended B52 target area. The operational requirements for a B52 bombing raid was a safety clearance distance of 3000 metres, which meant the Australian forces were too thinly spread, and this allowed the Viet Cong to slip through the gaps in the widened circle surrounding the enemy's position. Nevertheless, the B52 raid on the Long Hais took place at 6 am on 21 February 1970, and 1, 2 and 3 Troops deployed from Nui Dat back to the area while this was occurring.

After the B52 bombing raid the Squadron loaded three companies from 8 RAR and with the tanks from the 1st Armoured Regiment again entered the bunker system in the Minh Dam area. While no direct resistance was encountered, large stocks of weapons and supplies were recovered. Over 200 bunkers were destroyed. However, the enemy had decided before vacating their position to make things as difficult as possible for the Australians. The whole area had been mined and booby traps set at every possible point, and the commander's diary notes that numerous M16 mines were detonated by the carriers as they drove about the area. In one incident, while an engineering team was waiting to set off a located booby trap, an M16 anti-personnel mine was detonated. A dustoff flight was called to evacuate the wounded, but during this process another mine was detonated, killing nine Australians and wounding another 16. No-one from the Squadron sustained injury or wounds and none of the carriers were seriously damaged.

The whole outcome of Operation HAMMERSLEY was viewed very seriously by Canberra in light of the casualties that had occurred. A signal was received from Australia by 1ATF command demanding an explanation as to the 'costly nature and value of this operation'. The APCs and the tanks which had borne the brunt of the assault were battered and, to their credit, given the magnitude of the fighting that had occurred, only one APC had been totally destroyed. The LAD did a tremendous job, especially with the tanks—keeping them operational in order that they could continue to take the fight to the enemy. From the Task Force's point of view there were two important outcomes of the operation: first the Viet Cong had been 'kicked out' of what they regarded as their own safe haven, which they never anticipated might be entered and attacked by the Australians; second it demonstrated to the local population that the enemy's perceived stranglehold on the southern parts of the province had been irreparably broken. From the Squadron's point of view it had again demonstrated that cooperation with the tanks from the 1st Armoured Regiment was the best option available to the Task Force in dealing with a large enemy force in well-camouflaged and heavily defended positions. Except for the armoured vehicles' taking the brunt of the enemy's fire in this particular operation, it is considered the infantry losses would have been far higher.

During this operation the Squadron had two members killed in action, four wounded in action and four vehicles extensively damaged. The 1st Armoured Regiment had two tanks damaged. The enemy had 20 troops killed and one taken prisoner.

For his action in rescuing the wounded infantrymen from the burning APC of Whiston and Carlyle, Corporal R.C. Macey received the award of the Military Medal. The citation for his award reads:

> On 18 February 1970, during operation Hammersley in the Long Hai Hills, Phuoc Tuy Province, a company of infantry mounted in armoured personnel carriers was engaged by heavy enemy anti-tank and small arms fire. One armoured personnel carrier was hit by two anti-tank rockets, severely damaging it and causing it to catch fire. Attempts by other armoured personnel carriers to recover it, failed because of heavy anti-tank fire. Two crew members and five soldiers were trapped in the crippled and burning vehicle.
>
> Corporal Macey and Lance Corporal Coe who were travelling in an adjacent armoured personnel carrier, saw the plight of the soldiers trapped in the burning carrier and despite heavy small arms and grenade fire from enemy bunkers, dismounted in full view of the enemy and ran to the disabled vehicle. Together they forced open the heavy rear door of the carrier and with complete disregard for their own safety, Corporal Macey and Lance Corporal Coe rescued the five trapped soldiers and their weapons. All five, two of whom were unable to move, were in a dazed and shocked condition and had to be carried or led to safety.

> Corporal Macey and Lance Corporal Coe again ran to the burning carrier, intending to rescue the two trapped crew members. In the face of increased enemy small arms fire being directed at the disabled vehicle, their task had become even more hazardous. As they reached the burning carrier, a satchel charge exploded making recovery of the crewman impossible.

For his action in organising his section after being wounded, Sergeant D.W. Sheppard received the award of Mentioned in Dispatches. The citation for his award reads:

> On 18 February 1970, Sergeant Sheppard's Cavalry section was given the task of deploying a platoon of infantry into the jungle edge at the base of the Long Hai Mountains. The platoon had just dismounted from the armoured personnel carriers when the force came under accurate enemy anti-tank rocket and small arms fire.
>
> Sergeant Sheppard's vehicle was hit and penetrated by one of the rockets, seriously wounding the driver and blowing Sergeant Sheppard out

Entertainer Lorrae Desmond congratulates Corporal Ron Macey on receiving the Military Medal. (3/4 Cavalry Regiment Museum)

> of the turret onto the ground. Although suffering from severe neck injuries, he immediately remounted his vehicle, organised his section into an all round defensive position and directed the fire of his section at the enemy.
>
> His calm and determined action enabled the infantry platoon to re-organise and prevented the enemy from following up their initial success.

For his action in organising counterfire against the enemy while wounded, Sergeant D.W. Davies received the award of Mentioned in Dispatches. The citation for his award reads:[1]

> On 18 February 1970, the Cavalry Section Sergeant Davies was commanding was moving on a jungle trail at the base of the Long Hai mountains when it made contact with the enemy. Sergeant Davies' armoured personnel carrier was hit and penetrated by an enemy anti-tank rocket. The driver was seriously wounded. Although Sergeant Davies received a serious wound to his foot and the enemy was still in the area, he removed the driver from the driver's seat and drove the damaged armoured personnel carrier out of the danger zone.
>
> Sergeant Davies discovered at this time that his radio was damaged. Without considering his own injuries he ran to another carrier and organised counter fire against the enemy. As a result of this fire, the enemy quickly withdrew.

11

Mine warfare, 1970

The Squadron continued to operate in the Long Hai hills area after the main action of the previous days, where both the tanks from 1st Armoured Regiment and the APCs from the Squadron were involved in several mine incidents. On 23 February 1970, Callsign 30Bravo detonated an M16 mine on the eastern side of the Long Hais. However, the most serious of these mine incidents occurred on 25 February when Captain Peter Murphy's APC, Callsign 20Alpha, which had been deployed in the northern hills of the Long Hai area, detonated a mine of undetermined explosive power. The strike point of the mine was beneath the front middle of the carrier, and caused the belly plate to buckle and lift 30 centimetres. The force of the explosion blew a hole 30 centimetres in diameter in the hull, resulting in the differential being destroyed and the engine and transmission sustaining substantial damage. The left-hand final drive was blown off as were several road-wheels, and the steering laterals were bent. The driver, Trooper John Graham, received serious wounds and was evacuated from the site of the attack while Peter Murphy, although slightly wounded, elected to remain on duty.[1]

At the beginning of March, 1 Troop, 82 and 84 Sections remained under the operational command of 8 RAR in the Long Hais. 2 Troop was in Nui Dat minus 23 Section, which was at FSB Wilton under the operational control of 6 RAR on Operation NAPIER. 3 Troop was the Squadron's Ready Reaction Force. During the first week of the month, 2 Troop undertook training with the newly arrived 7 RAR. On the evening of 7 March, while on operational training in the northeast section of the Binh Ba rubber plantation, elements from 2 Troop engaged lights and noise at approximately 40 metres with their machine

The Squadron's lines at Nui Dat, 1970. (Rick Lovett, courtesy 3/4 Cavalry Regiment Museum)

guns. A check of the area at first light the following morning failed to reveal any results.

On the same day, 1 Troop and elements from 2 Troop were requested to form a blocking position for 8 RAR, which had moved its operations to FSB Discovery west of Xuyen Moc. On 8 March D Company 8 RAR ran into a bunker system of the local D445 Battalion some 7 kilometres southwest of Xuyen Moc. Three members of D Company were killed and 1 Troop, which was located near the junction of Routes 23 and 328, was asked to deploy to the area and intercept the Viet Cong forces as they attempted to withdraw. Unfortunately, by the time the troop arrived at the site of the earlier action and took up a blocking position, the enemy had already withdrawn. At 9 pm on 13 March the commander's diary notes that 23 Section was in contact with an enemy force near FSB Wilton some 4 kilometres east of Binh Gia. The diary writer must have had a sense of humour, as he notes that four pigs were killed in action. (It should be noted that the wild pigs that roamed the jungle were notorious for falsely initiating ambushes.)

Three days later, on 16 March, 86 Section was operating with the land-clearing team in the Long Hais and was deployed approximately 2 kilometres east of FSB Isa. At 8.35 am that morning Callsign 86Alpha detonated an anti-tank mine. This was a 30 pound pressure mine which caused moderate damage to the carrier. The point of strike was beneath the centre-right roadwheel. The track was broken and three right-hand support arms were damaged. The hull was penetrated with two holes in the sponsons. Driver Paul Ferris and one of the engineers from the mini-team were reported as having sustained serious wounds, and were evacuated from the site. The following day, 2 Troop, which was conducting an independent operation in the extreme eastern sector of the province some 15 kilometres east of Xuyen Moc, uncovered a cache. Callsign 20Bravo reported recovering the cache, which contained an AK47 rifle, a quantity of ammunition, a supply of anti-personnel mines and clothing.

In and around the Courtney rubber plantation

Another mine attack occurred a week later, on 23 March in the Courtney rubber plantation in Long Khanh province approximately 2 kilometres due north of Courtney hill. The strength of the mine was estimated at between 40 and 46 pounds of explosive. The point of strike was beneath the centre right-hand roadwheel, which caused the APC to turn on its side. The second support arm was blown off and the third axle stub blown out. The third and fifth roadwheels were blown off and a 100-centimetre dent was sustained by the belly plate. The hull was penetrated by the explosion, as were the sponsons in two places by secondary fragments. Two members of the crew, Trooper J. Dunhill-martin and Trooper Phillip Kadow, were reported as having suffered deafness, bruising and lacerations.

On the evening of 30 March at 6.15, 33 Section was 'reacted' to aid D Company 6 RAR in the southeast corner of Courtney rubber plantation some 4 kilometres southeast of Courtney hill. Contact was made with 15 enemy troops, and during the ensuing fire fight five Viet Cong were killed and a large number of drag marks subsequently detected. No casualties were reported by the Australian force.

At the end of the month 12 Section from 1 Troop remained under the operational command of 7 RAR on Operation FINCHAFFEN east of Ngai Giao, and 13 Section had deployed with Regional Forces in the Long Hais and was based at Dat Do. 2 Troop remained at Nui Dat as Ready Reaction Force, and 3 Troop were under the operational command of 6 RAR on Operation TOWNSVILLE in the Courtney rubber plantation. Support Troop's 85 and 86 Sections were based at the Horseshoe, where they assisted with the continuing land-clearing operations in that area.[2]

On 2 April at 1.40 pm 13 Section, on deployment with Regional Forces, was required to arrange a dustoff for the Regional Forces after one of their members stepped on an M16 mine near Route 44 on the southern tip of the Long Hai peninsula. The section remained under the operational command of the Regional Forces until 4 April, when they returned to Nui Dat. Meanwhile, 8 RAR had been deployed in the area surrounding the notorious Viet Cong-supported village of Hoa Long, where they set up a series of ambushes on the western side of Route 2. At 8.42 pm on 11 April an ambush was activated by 9 Platoon of C Company on a large enemy force. The Viet Cong immediately counterattacked, and the platoon called for the assistance of the Cavalry Squadron. The Squadron's Ready Reaction Force that evening (10Alpha, 11 Section and 33 Section) was scrambled and raced to the area some 3 kilometres to the southwest of the Task Force base. The arrival of the APCs put paid to the Viet Cong's attacks on the platoon's position and the enemy quickly withdrew. Callsigns 9Echo and 29Juliet were subsequently deployed to a location approximately 1 kilometre west of where the ambush had been initiated, and three of the wounded enemy were taken prisoner and returned to Nui Dat for treatment. 11 Section remained in the area to ensure the enemy stayed away, returning to Nui Dat at 7.20 pm the following evening.

On 14 April 11 Section, which remained deployed as Ready Reaction Force, was sent to FSB Isa on the western side of the Long Hai hills to meet a patrol from the SAS's 1 Squadron, which had been flown down from Nui Dat in an initial move for a disguised insertion. The task assigned to the APCs was to pick up the patrol and in a disguised move transport them back to Baria and then along Route 15 towards Vung Tau. Approximately 3 kilometres on the southern side of Baria, the APCs rendezvoused with recce boats and the patrol was again transferred for insertion to its task. Earlier that same day other elements from 1 Troop under the command of 10Bravo were deployed near a track on the eastern side of Route 2 approximately 5 kilometres south of Courtney hill after reports of enemy activity. In a subsequent sweep of the area contact was made with a party of five enemy troops. During the ensuing fire fight two Viet Cong were killed and another, who had been wounded, was taken prisoner. During the engagement a company of US infantry arrived unannounced at the site of the contact, much to the surprise of the Australians.

In April 1970, the command of B Squadron 3rd Cavalry Regiment held by Major R.E. Rooks was handed over to Major H.J. Coates. For his efforts in leading the squadron during a very active period of the war,

Major Rooks received the award of Mentioned in Dispatches. The citation for his award reads:[3]

> Major Rooks throughout his twelve month command of B Squadron 3rd cavalry Regiment on operations in South Vietnam, exercised command of his unit with a great deal of commonsense and understanding. His fine tactical sense and thorough appreciation of the use of his Armoured Personnel Carriers enabled him to give sound advice to the Task Force Commander and firm confident guidance to his troops.
>
> During his tour of duty the enemy intensified his use of mines causing more frequent and serious damage to the Armoured Personnel Carriers and increasing the casualties to crewmen of the squadron. Despite this, Major Rooks' inspired leadership was such that the Squadron was not daunted from any task and continued to operate at a high peak of efficiency.
>
> The efficiency of the Squadron and the high regard in which it is held by the infantry Battalions reflect great credit on Major Rooks' ability.

On 20 April 3 Troop was deployed at 5.30 in the morning with 8 RAR on Operation NUDGEE, which was centred on FSB Bond at the junction of Routes 23 and 328. At 9.02 am the carrier, crewed by Corporal Cameron Mitchell and Trooper Michael Tognolini, was in the process of ferrying a section of infantry to a new area of operation in the eastern sector of the province. The infantry had boarded the carrier at FSB Bond and proceeded to travel along Route 328 in a move to the eastern sector of the area of operation. Approximately 4 kilometres to the southwest of Xuyen Moc village the last APC in the section detonated a large anti-tank mine, which caused extensive damage to the vehicle. Michael Tognolini was seriously wounded and had to be surgically removed from the driver's compartment before he could be evacuated. His wounds were so severe that he died later that day at 1 Australian Field Hospital in Vung Tau. Crew Commander Cameron Mitchell was seriously wounded, as were 10 of the passengers from 8 RAR. The size of the mine was estimated at between 40 and 50 pounds of explosive and blew the carrier into the air, so that it ended up resting on its rear end. The strike point was the middle of the vehicle's hull, which penetrated the hull with a hole 100 × 35 centimetres, and split sections of the hull's welds. The engine access door and upper half of the engine compartment's armour were blown off. The engine and transmission were blown apart, the engine ending upside down in its compartment. The crew commander's turret basket was badly bent, and it is said that had all the passengers not been sitting on top of the vehicle the death rate would have been much higher. All the wounded were evacuated from the site.

3 Troop and Fitters vehicle in a defensive formation on the beach east of the Long Hai hills. (3rd Cavalry Regiment (Vietnam) Association)

The newly arrived 7 RAR commenced one of its operations, codenamed CONCRETE 1, on 21 April, which initially required the reopening and further development of FSB Discovery some 5 kilometres west of Xuyen Moc. 1 and 2 Troops assisted in re-establishing the base with a number of troop transport tasks before moving off to ambush surrounding areas while the defences of the base were developed. On 26 April, 11 Section from 1 Troop was deployed to insert a platoon from 7 RAR near the beach on the eastern side of the Long Hai peninsula for an ambush. As the section was returning to the Horseshoe from its task near Phuoc Hai village, Callsign 11 detonated an anti-tank mine. The strength of the mine was reported as being between 65 and 70 pounds of explosive, with the point of strike between the two rear roadwheel stations. Both ramp and cargo hatches were blown off and the roof of the vehicle was split open. The vehicle's belly was split, the floor lifted 130 centimetres, and the engine access panel was blown in. The force of the blast threw the vehicle end over end. Both driver and crew commander were seriously wounded, with the crew commander thrown from the vehicle. An infantry officer, who had gone with the section to make a reconnaissance of another possible ambush site and was riding on top of the APC, was killed. Trooper David Kirkpatrick, Trooper Ian Campbell, Sergeant Geoffrey Mason and Sergeant Robert

Cooper were wounded in the attack and blown from the vehicle. The wounded crewmen and dead officer were evacuated.

At the end of April, 1 Troop and Squadron HQ continued with Operation MONTAGE in the Courtney rubber plantation. 2 Troop's 21 Section was deployed east of Binh Gia, 22 Section was under the operational control of 1 Field Squadron in mine-clearing operations at Lo Gom, while 23 Section was at FSB Louise. 3 Troop was based at Nui Dat where it acted as Ready Reaction Force, 86 Section was based at FSB South Dakota on land-clearing operations, and 84 Section had deployed with 7 RAR on Operation CONCRETE.[4]

The early days of the newly arrived Squadron Commanding Officer, Major John Coates, saw the Squadron operating with the three infantry battalions in a number of reconnaissance-in-force operations. The ambushing techniques that had been devised by the Cavalry were now being used throughout the Task Force. In fact, the APCs of the Squadron had become highly favoured for this type of work. Once an infantry unit had been dropped off at an ambush site, the APCs would move off to another site and lay an ambush just on dark. This had a twofold effect: first, the members of the Squadron became highly proficient and experienced in this type of work; second, they remained relatively close to the infantry's position in case they got into trouble and required urgent assistance. Additionally, the Squadron continued to deploy numerous SAS patrols throughout the provinces in which the Task Force were deployed. The working relationship and understanding of operational and tactical issues of SAS and Squadron members had become inextricably linked, with both units adopting a high regard for each other's work and cooperative spirit.

On 1 May at 6.25 am Callsign 13 reported contact with a party of two enemy near Route 2, 2 kilometres south of Courtney hill, but results could not be determined. That evening at 8.10 pm elements from 3 Troop were reacted to assist the infantry, which was in contact with an enemy force east of Hoa Long. After deploying to the area of contact the APCs assisted the infantry in fighting off an enemy force consisting of at least 10 personnel. At 9.42 pm Callsign 31 reported that the crew commander of Callsign 32Alpha (believed to be Corporal C.R. Blackett) had received shrapnel wounds to his arm and was being returned to 8 Field Ambulance in Nui Dat for attention. The following evening at 6.32 Callsign 20Bravo, which had been deployed with 22 Section 3 kilometres to the east of Binh Gia, detected a large enemy concentration to its west and requested an urgent artillery fire mission from the the 105 mm guns at FSB Le Loi. After artillery bombardment of the area further movement was observed, although no contact was made with the enemy.

In early May, 8 RAR deployed on Operation NUDGEE in the eastern sector of the province, and on 3 May the Squadron was called to an ambush initiated by the assault Pioneer Platoon from A Company 8 RAR, southwest of the town of Dat Do. The platoon had activated the ambush at 8 pm but the Viet Cong had counterattacked their position for the next half hour. At 9 am 3 Troop, which was the Ready Reaction Force based at the Horseshoe, was called on to assist the infantry and raced to the area of contact. Shortly after the arrival of the APCs the enemy decided to break contact and at 9.30 pm withdrew from the area, allowing the troop to extract the infantry platoon from its position.

On 4 May at 6.30 am Callsign 22 reported being in contact on the southwest outskirts of Dat Do. Callsign 22 had arrived 30 minutes after the infantry had initiated a contact, and reported that the enemy had fired small arms and RPGs. Later that evening 1 Troop, which remained deployed on Operation MONTAGE in the Courtney rubber plantation and was operating about 2 kilometres south of Courtney hill, reported that Callsign 11Bravo had detonated an anti-tank mine at 7.55 am. The mine was believed to have a strength of 40 pounds of explosive and had been manufactured from a 155 mm artillery shell. The point of strike was beneath the driver's seat; the mine blew a 50-centimetre hole in the belly plate and penetrated the box frame for 45 centimetres. The transmission was destroyed, the left-hand final drives were damaged and the first and second roadwheel stations blown off. The fragments from the blast seriously wounded both crew members and a passenger. The driver, Trooper William Calder, was reported as being wounded in the back and suffering internal injuries. Crew Commander Corporal James Cranston was wounded in the feet and neck, while the passenger sustained body wounds. The wounded were evacuated from the site of attack and the carrier, which was extensively damaged, was taken back to Nui Dat.

Four days later, on 8 May, 3 Troop's 31 Section, which constituted part of the Ready Reaction Force, had been deployed in an area adjacent to Route 15 near the village of Thai Thien in Bien Hoa province. At 8.13 that morning Callsign 31 reported that 31Alpha had detonated a 155 mm artillery shell that had been booby-trapped as an anti-tank mine. The strength of the mine was estimated at approximately 30 pounds of explosive, with the strike point beneath the centre right-hand roadwheel. The explosion blew off the second and third roadwheels and severed the track. The box frame was penetrated over

35 centimetres, a 100-centimetre bulge was inflicted in the belly plate and a 130 centimetre bulge damaged the sponsons. A dustoff flight was requested for the wounded crew members and the vehicle required recovery back to Nui Dat.

On 11 May, 81 Section was deployed with 1 Troop as they continued Operation MONTAGE in the Courtney rubber plantation area. At 12.35 pm, while the troop was moving west on a road beneath the southern side of Courtney hill, Callsign 81 detonated an anti-tank mine. The mine had an estimated explosive strength of 30 pounds, with its point of strike beneath the front left-hand roadwheel. The first and second roadwheels were blown off, and the suspension arms and drive sprocket were damaged. The box frame was penetrated in two places, as was the hull. Crew Commander Corporal Michael Webb, driver Trooper Ian Ebzery and radio operator Trooper Alan Campbell were all seriously affected by the blast. Two passengers were also reported as being wounded by fragmentations. All were evacuated from the site and the vehicle was recovered back to Nui Dat.

Meanwhile, in the eastern sector of the province 2 Troop continued to support 7 RAR with Operation CONCRETE 2, which involved a series of ambushes along Routes 23 and 44. On the evening of 11 May, 2 Troop had been asked by the infantry to take up a large wagon-wheel formation in a rice paddy southwest of Phuoc Hai. It had been suggested that the enemy would see the silhouette of the APCs against the predicted clear night sky and divert their route around the APCs, which it was hoped would redirect them to a series of infantry ambushes that had been strategically sited to catch the enemy as they moved to avoid the troop. As anticipated, at 10.30 pm the troop engaged a party of 13 Viet Cong carrying packs. The troop members were fired on by the APCs as they moved around the troop's formation but were successful in avoiding the various infantry ambush sites. They were able to watch the enemy's movements through both their normal and night-vision binoculars and, when it became obvious that the enemy would escape, an artillery barrage from a nearby fire support base was directed at their location. A sweep of the area the next morning revealed nothing, although a *hoi chanh* who subsequently rallied claimed that he had been wounded by the APCs' machine gun fire in this contact.

At 6.30 am on 13 May, as 31 Section was returning to Nui Dat from Long Dien, it discovered the bodies of two young men who had been shot between the eyes at close range. Information regarding this matter was sought from Sector Headquarters in Baria, who indicated that the two victims had been murdered by the Viet Cong as they were both listed as police informers. On 14 May at 7.17 pm 11 Section was called to an infantry contact 1 kilometre southwest of Hoa Long. When the section arrived they secured the area for the infantry, then proceeded to undertake the task of collecting the bodies of seven dead Viet Cong troops whom the infantry had killed. The following evening 11 Section was again scrambled to the Tam Phuoc/An Nhut area where the infantry was in contact. The enemy had departed, but a sweep of the area by the section saw the recovery of one of the enemy's packs.

On 20 May Callsign 33 reported that it was in contact with a sampan containing three Viet Cong on the Long Tau channel, 1.5 kilometres from FSB South Dakota in the western sector of the province. It was reported that the enemy had pulled into the bank of the river where they commenced loading the contents of a cache on board. The sampan was hit several times by fire from the section's machine guns but managed to escape from the view of the APCs. A search of the area the following morning revealed nothing.

On 21 May 2 Troop continued its deployment on Operation CONCRETE 2 when 1 Platoon from A Company 7 RAR, accompanied by elements from the troop and a troop of tanks, moved to the north of Dat Do to search for a D445 camp. The force was being guided by a *hoi chanh* and at 1.30 pm 1 Platoon ran into a heavily defended enemy bunker system north of Dat Do. One infantryman was killed and several others were wounded in the initial contact, when the enemy fired RPGs as the infantrymen advanced on the bunkers. Given the intensity of the fire from the enemy's position and the danger of further anti-tank rocket attacks, evacuation of the wounded infantrymen was proving difficult. The possibility of an immediate dustoff flight could not be considered because of the extreme danger posed by the amount of enemy fire being directed at the Australians—in particular at one of the sections that had been pinned down and was unable to move.

At 1.35 pm Callsign 23Alpha reported the seriousness of the situation, but in spite of the danger the vehicle's crew commander, Corporal Jeffrey Swan, decided to manoeuvre his carrier forward where it became exposed to direct enemy fire. He did this in order to evacuate the wounded. The enemy in the meantime had sighted Callsign 20Bravo and fired a salvo of RPGs, with one of the rounds striking the APC's trim vane and wounding the driver, Trooper Robert Heggie. Crew Commander Second Lieutenant Graeme Smith was extremely lucky to escape injury when an accompanying burst from an enemy AK47 shot off his sunglasses. The RPG made a 20-centimetre hole in the trim vane before passing through the engine access door and damaging the camshaft. Despite the danger of further RPG attacks, Jeffrey Swan's crew were able to successfully board one group of the wounded and remove them from the site of the battle, before returning for the other wounded members of the infantry platoon.

Inside view of an APC after it was hit by a rocket. (3/4 Cavalry Regiment Museum)

Troop Leader Captain Peter Murphy, who at the time of contact was stationed at the Horseshoe, had been alerted to the plight of the platoon and scrambled a relief force consisting of some other APCs from his troop. 3 Platoon A Company 7 RAR were allocated to accompany the

APCs, which set off for the contact area immediately the infantrymen were boarded. On arrival Murphy arranged for Bushranger gunships to assault the bunker system using rockets and mini-guns to break up the enemy's position. The bunker system was secured at 4 pm, but by that time one of the Australians had been killed and 13 others wounded, including three members of the troop. The enemy suffered five killed and another three were taken prisoner.

For his action in removing the wounded infantrymen under fire, Corporal J.J. Swan received the award of Mentioned in Dispatches. The citation for his award reads:

> On the afternoon of 21 May 1970, Corporal Swan was commanding an armoured personnel carrier in a combined infantry and armoured force, when contact was made with the enemy in a strongly held bunker system.
>
> In the first few minutes of the contact one soldier was killed and twelve wounded. One of the infantry sections, in a dangerously exposed position and under continuous enemy fire from both anti-tank rockets and small arms fire was unable to evacuate its wounded.
>
> With deliberate disregard for his own safety, Corporal Swan manoeuvred his armoured personnel carrier into the area of enemy fire so that the casualties could be removed from the danger of small arms fire. Although his carrier was struck by an anti-tank rocket, he removed one group of the wounded to a safe area before returning for the remainder.

At 9.45 am the next day 82 Section joined 2 Troop in a sweep of the area in which the contact had occurred. A cache containing 100 pounds of rice was located and, as the troop moved to investigate a small group of women who had moved into the area, they received small arms fire. A further sweep of the area failed to reveal any enemy forces.

The remainder of the month was relatively quiet, with only two incidents reported. The first occurred at 12.16 am on 27 May when 22 Section, which was located near FSB Brigitte, reported contact with two enemy. A sweep of the area the following morning revealed two fresh trails. The second incident occurred at 10.15 pm on 29 May near FSB Isa, when 31 Section was scrambled to assist the infantry who were in contact with an enemy force. The section spent the night with the infantrymen to provide security and conducted a sweep the following morning, recovering an M16 and AK47 rifle together with a pack.

At the end of the month 1 Troop and 81 Section were under the operational control of 2 RAR on Operation CAPRICORN in the Courtney rubber plantation. 2 Troop, 82 and 86 Sections were under the operational control of 7 RAR on Operation CONCRETE 2 and were based at the Horseshoe. 3 Troop and 83 Section were on R&C at Vung Tau, and on their return were also to deploy with 7 RAR on Operation CONCRETE 2. Callsigns 85Alpha and 85Bravo were under the operational control of 1 Field Squadron on mine-clearing operations in Long Green at FSBs Elizabeth and Brigid respectively. Callsigns 84 and 9Golf were located at the Horseshoe on land-clearing operations, where they were visited by the Squadron's O/C.[5]

At 6.05 pm on 1 June 1970, Callsign 29Juliet reported that Callsign 22Alpha had detonated either an M16 or a small pressure mine, and that one of the vehicle's tracks had been blown off. As the attack had occurred only 1 kilometre northeast of FSB Brigid on the eastern side of the Long Hais it was decided to tow the damaged vehicle back to FSB Brigid, where the crew could spend the evening carrying out repairs. No crew were reported as casualties as a result of the attack.

On 4 June Callsign 11 reported locating an enemy installation at 11.22 am. The installation, which was unoccupied, was said to be in very good condition and consisted of a number of bunkers. At 7.08 pm 13 Section was called on to assist an infantry contact near the Long Tan rubber plantation. However, on their arrival the enemy had already departed, and they were not involved in any action. Still later that evening at 9.17, 22 Section activated an ambush on the coast near FSB Brigid against five enemy troops between their position and the beach. A sweep of the area found no results regarding the contact.

On 6 June at 4.14 am, Callsign 30Bravo reported having activated an ambush, approximately 200 metres west of Route 15 near Phu My, against two enemy. Later that morning three women were apprehended near a Regional Forces' post, as they were breaking the curfew. One of the women had been wounded and admitted that this had occurred in the 30Bravo ambush. She was subsequently evacuated to the Baria hospital for treatment.

In the Squadron's continuing role of responsibility for Xuyen Moc, 1 Troop, together with 81 and 86 Sections, commenced a reconnaissance-in-force operation with the 612 Regional Force Company on 12 June. The operation was conducted about 20 kilometres to the east of Xuyen Moc in Binh Tuy province and saw the APCs undertake numerous resupply tasks as well as uncover several bunker systems, albeit unoccupied. During this operation the troop and independent sections were visited by the Squadron OC, his second in command, the SSM and WO2 Hudson who, because of the distance, flew out to the area of operation in a helicopter.

THE CUNG CHUNG JOINT OFFENSIVE

In mid-June 1970 the Task Force was scheduled to participate in a series of operations called CUNG CHUNG (togetherness). The first of these was to be the largest combined Australian/South Vietnamese offensive operation ever undertaken. The Squadron joined the Task Force in this operation with the aim of denying the Viet Cong access to the towns and villages that sat astride Routes 23 and 44. The Squadron's role in this operation, as well as assisting with troop movements, was to set up nightly ambushing sites in conjunction with the other infantry units.

Two days after the commencement of this operation, on 14 June, 21 Section from 2 Troop was deployed on the southern side of the Long Hai peninsula on the western outskirts of Phuoc Hai. At 3.02 pm Callsign 21Alpha detonated an anti-tank mine estimated at a strength of 100 pounds of explosive. The APC was severely damaged and Crew Commander Corporal Ray Piper required his leg to be amputated below the knee. The driver, Trooper Roy Davies, sustained serious wounds from the blast. Both crewmen also received fragmentation wounds, severe lacerations and second-degree burns. An engineer from the mini-team sitting on top of the vehicle was killed and one of the passengers was wounded. The vehicle sustained considerable damage, with a 120 × 100-centimetre hole blasted in the floor.

To demonstrate just how dangerous the enemy's mining activities were, on 14 June Callsign 84 reported that it had located an area that appeared to be the site of a Viet Cong mine-laying accident. From the human body parts and pieces of equipment, including a live M16 mine lying on the ground, it was deduced that three or four enemy sappers had accidentally blown up two of their comrades and wounded themselves as they attempted to lay a mine inside Binh Tuy province.

The climatic conditions in the province were almost as harsh as the weaponry being used, and an incident demonstrating this occurred on 16 June when Callsigns 20Bravo, 22 and 22Bravo were in an ambush southwest of Lo Voi on Route 44. At 8 pm the sky became very dark and there was a great deal of lightning, with one large bolt arcing across the radio antennas on 22Bravo. An infantryman who was leaning against the carrier was hit by the lightning as it grounded through his body, killing him instantly. Damage to the vehicle was minor, although the two radio antennas were destroyed, as was one of the radio sets.

The following day Callsign 84, whose section was on land-clearing operations in the Long Hais, reported at 3.50 pm that one of the bulldozers operating near one of the section's carriers had detonated a 40 pound mine, which had wounded the dozer operator and caused extensive damage to his machine. Meanwhile, in the western sector of the province Callsign 83 reported having witnessed a cow detonate an unspecified mine on one of the firestone trails. It is interesting to note that on that day there were nine separate mine contacts in Phuoc Tuy province in the 24-hour reporting period. The enemy's mining activities were extensive throughout the province, as they appreciated the damage that this type of weapon could inflict on the Australian Task Force's troops and equipment. At 5 pm on 18 June in the northern sector of the province, and on a track leading off Route 2 about 3 kilometres south of Courtney hill, Callsign 11Alpha detonated an explosive device of unknown size or description. The explosion did not penetrate the hull, although some damage was reported to the engine and transmission. No casualties were sustained by members of the crew, and the vehicle was scheduled for recovery by the LAD back to Nui Dat the following morning.

On 19 June 1970, Vietnamese Army Day, the district chief of Xuyen Moc held a gala day as part of the anniversary. As a result of the civic and military aid that had been provided to the town the Squadron was invited to provide two volleyball teams to participate in the Xuyen Moc games. As well as the volleyball competition, this provided the Squadron's OC with an opportunity to determine the results of questioning seven Viet Cong suspects that had been arrested two nights previously. The suspects were captured following a contact between the district chief's bodyguards and the remnants of the Xuyen Moc guerrillas several kilometres northeast of Xuyen Moc. They were later discovered to be carrying a quantity of important documents. Major Coates learnt that under questioning the suspects had provided valuable information on the Viet Cong's activities around Xuyen Moc, and investigation of the information gleaned from the prisoners continued.

At 3 pm that afternoon 84 Section, which was under the operational command of 2 Troop A Squadron 1st Armoured Regiment, was scrambled to the southern Long Hai hills to provide fire support and extract the 577 Regional Forces Company, which was in contact with an enemy force of unknown size. This task was eventually achieved but not before the Regional Forces' troops had sustained two of their members killed and another 20 wounded. That evening 84 and 85 Sections returned to Nui Dat from their land-clearing operations, as the bulldozers that had been carrying out this work had all been destroyed by mine explosions in the Long Hai region.

With the South Vietnamese national elections scheduled shortly, it was the enemy's intention to use every means possible to disrupt the electoral process. To assist the district chief, various sections from the Squadron were deployed at Xuyen Moc over the ensuing week to ensure that the elections ran smoothly and without interference from the Viet Cong. Additionally, Second Lieutenant Graeme Smith from the Squadron was appointed as the Task Force's Liaison Officer at Xuyen Moc. Earlier in the month SAS patrols had identified elements from C3 and C4 of the D445 Battalion, which had moved into an area south of Xuyen Moc. D440 Battalion was reported to be in the same area and, in preparation for a deployment with 8 RAR at the Horseshoe, 23 Section had returned to Nui Dat where a move was to be made against the D440 Local Force Battalion.

The last mine attack against the Squadron's vehicles for the month occurred on 29 June at 6.15 pm. 33 Section was in the process of moving to its ambush position for the evening some 2 kilometres south of Courtney hill when Callsign 33 detonated an M14 anti-personnel mine. No damage was sustained by the vehicle and there were no casualties among the crew.

At the end of the month all elements from the Squadron were involved with Operation CUNG CHUNG under the operational control of 7 and 8 RAR. 1 and 3 Troops, together with 81 and 83 Sections, were operating in AO MULLET in the northern sector of the province. 2 Troop and 82 Section were located at the Horseshoe, 84 and 85 Sections were at FSBs Matthew and Kylie while Squadron HQ was at FSB Le Loi.[6]

By this time almost all the carriers in the Squadron had been fitted with T50 turrets. The Alpha and Bravo carriers were mounted with twin .30 cal. machine guns, while the section leader's vehicle was mounted with one .30 cal. and one .50 cal. machine gun. Additionally, a .30 cal. machine gun with a pistol grip and trigger on a pintle mount had been fitted to the top of the turret on all carriers. This revised armament arrangement allowed the crew commander much more flexibility, and overcame some of the constraints that the relatively small T50 turret imposed when the machine guns were being operated. The carriers of the independent sections that had been fitted out as the original mortar carriers had been retired from this task and made into a fully operational APC section. While three carriers in one of the independent sections still maintained the mortar base plates in the back of the carriers, like their counterparts in other sections they were now being deployed in both APC and cavalry roles.

In early July 1970 1 Troop was redeployed to the northern sector of the province and was operating in AO CAMEL to support 8 RAR on Operation QUARTERMILE. At 8.42 pm on 2 July 11 Section had been placed in an ambush adjacent to a track 3 kilometres west of Route 2 and midway between Ngai Giao and the Courtney rubber plantation. The ambush was activated against a large enemy party which was heard digging some 40 metres from the section's position. The enemy's position was initially engaged with claymore mines, followed by .50 and .30 cal. machine gun fire and M79 grenades. The enemy immediately counterattacked and returned fire on the section's position with machine guns, hand grenades and RPGs. The section requested that mortar illumination flares be fired from FSB Kylie to the west, which was followed by artillery illumination from FSB Le Loi to the south as the enemy continued to attack its position. A short time later a possum aircraft appeared overhead and proceeded to drop more flares, and the artillery from FSB Lois commenced firing HE rounds into the area 400 metres west-southwest of the contact site. Due to persistent enemy movement at the ambush site each time an HE round landed, two Shadow aircraft were called into the area. The artillery continued to fire their HE rounds at the enemy's position for the remainder of the night, eventually stopping at 5 am the following morning when contact with the enemy was broken. At first light the section undertook a limited sweep but was inhibited by the density of the jungle. Later in the morning 31 Section delivered a platoon from 8 RAR which carried out a more detailed sweep, out to 1000 metres around the original contact site.

It was felt that, because of the type of weapons used by the enemy and the persistent attempts they had made in counterattacking 11 Section, they were troops from the enemy's K8 heavy weapons company of D440 Local Force Battalion. The section had been in its ambush site for several days and it was observed that while many of the other cavalry and infantry units in the area had often moved their locations after insertion into their initial ambush positions, 11 Section had remained in its original position to activate the ambush. Meanwhile, 1 Troop HQ vehicles, which had also remained in their original ambush position for three days, engaged an apparent enemy force at 9.40 that morning. The apparent enemy force turned out to be C Company 8 RAR, which had been directed by their Battalion HQ to move into the vicinity of the old FSB Pat. However, 8 RAR Battalion HQ had failed to notify the company of the proximity of the cavalry ambush, and had also failed to notify Squadron HQ of C Company's move. This engagement resulted in three of the men from 8 RAR being wounded by the APCs' machine guns.

On 3 July at 8.15 pm 12 Section activated another ambush 3 kilometres southwest of Courtney hill. A party of three Viet Cong walked into the ambush, where they were engaged with claymore mines. One of the party was seen to fall twice after the area was engaged with machine gun fire and was taken prisoner, as his wounds had prevented any escape. At 4.30 pm on 4 July, 11 Section engaged eight enemy troops about 2 kilometres north of where the ambush had been initiated by 12 Section the previous evening. The enemy were moving to the south and were engaged with the APC's machine guns from a range of 150 metres. This prompted the enemy to immediately withdraw to the east where they were chased by the section into thick jungle, at which point the APCs broke off and returned to the original point of contact, where three enemy bodies were recovered. One chicom 7.62 mm pistol, three packs, some chicom explosives and a quantity of documents were also recovered. Earlier in the day one of the carriers from the troop had detonated a 10 pound anti-tank mine on a track 400 metres off Route 2 and about 3 kilometres south of Courtney hill. Damage to the APC was slight and none of the crew sustained serious wounds.

It was subsequently revealed that an NVA prisoner captured by B Company 8 RAR two days later had been a member of the group until just prior to the contact with 11 Section. He identified one of the dead enemy soldiers as a member of K54, the medical company of 274 Regiment. The documents captured included an instruction from the commander of 274 Regiment that all medical subunits were to use their RPGs only in the defence of hospital installations and to use booby-trapped 105 mm rounds for base defence.

Back at the Horseshoe, 3 Troop had been deployed with a company of infantry from the ARVN 18 Division for a 24-hour period of operational training, which was to conclude with an ambush to the east of the Horseshoe that night.

On 6 July, 1 Troop was travelling along a track on the western side of Route 2 some 5 kilometres south of Courtney hill when Callsign 19Juliet detonated an anti-tank mine with a strength of approximately 15 pounds of explosive. Although the carrier sustained only light damage and was capable of being driven, six of those on board including crew members Sergeant John Anstey and Trooper Keith Mitchell were reported as being wounded by the explosion and were evacuated to 1 Field Hospital at Vung Tau. Shortly after completion of the dustoff the engineers from the mini-team located a booby-trapped 105 mm artillery round, which was destroyed at the site. As 19Juliet did not have a crew but was capable of being driven, Corporal Chalk and Trooper Brady were deployed to FSB Kylie as the vehicle's new crew.

The next week saw 1 Troop uncover a number of bunker systems in the northern sector of the province, which were all destroyed. On the morning of 11 July the troop located the body of a Viet Cong soldier near the area of 11 Section's contact on 2/3 July, and his death was attributed to that section's action. On 13 July 1 Troop and 81 Section ended their deployment with 8 RAR and returned to Nui Dat for much-needed CES checks and non-tech inspections prior to redeploying. They were replaced by 3 Troop in AO CAMEL in the western sector of the province, where they deployed with 2 RAR on Operation NATHAN. While in Nui Dat, 1 Troop re-enacted the accidental shooting of the 8 RAR troops for the investigating officer, but no blame was apportioned to the cavalry for these events.

No other substantial activity occurred until 26 July, when 3 Troop was deployed approximately 5 kilometres east of Thai Thien in Bien Hoa province to support a company of Regional Forces during Operation NATHAN. Early that morning 33 Section, which had occupied an ambush position near Thai Thien since the previous evening, initiated the ambush when three NVA soldiers walked along a track where the APCs were sited. In the ensuing fire fight two of the enemy troops were killed while the remaining enemy soldier, although wounded, retreated into the surrounding scrub and escaped. One AK47 rifle and two packs were recovered. The enemy were subsequently identified as being members of the NVA's D67 Engineer Battalion, and had most likely been engaged in planting mines in the Squadron's area of operation.

On 27 July the OC of the Squadron accompanied Major Terry Walker, the OC of the Regiment's A Squadron in Australia, to Xuyen Moc to visit the district chief. Walker was scheduled to replace John Coates early in the new year and had travelled to the province on a familiarisation tour prior to taking up his command.

Three days later at 6 pm 84 Section had deployed on a task to insert one of the many SAS patrols that the Squadron undertook. This patrol required the APCs to transport the SAS's collapsible boats in order that they could commence an operation against the Long Son island. The SAS patrol was inserted near Phuoc Hoa adjacent to Route 15 just on dusk, and the section immediately moved off to provide security for the patrol as it made its way into the Long Tau channel of the Rung Sat waterway. This was fortunate for the pilot of a US Cobra gunship flying close by, as his helicopter experienced engine failure and was forced to land near the section's position. The section stayed with the gunship and the pilot providing protection until a recovery team arrived the following day.

On 31 July a tragic, accidental death occurred when Trooper David Doyle was struck by a helicopter blade. David Doyle was attached to 32 Section which was based at FSB Sharon, where it was under the operational control of the land-clearing team on Operation CRUMPET. At 7.50 that morning Doyle, who was the driver of

Callsign 32, had reversed his vehicle close to a helicopter in order to offload some equipment. Not appreciating just how close he was to the helicopter, he got out of his compartment and walked along the top of the carrier, where he was struck by one of the rotating blades and killed instantly. The OC conducted an immediate investigation and stressed to all officers the needlessness of such accidents.

At the end of July 1 Troop and 81 Section were under the operational control of 8 RAR on Operation DECADE. 2 Troop and 82 Section were under the operational control of 7 RAR on Operation PETRIE. 3 Troop minus 32 Section was under the operational control of 2 RAR on Operation NATHAN. 32 and 85 Sections remained under the operational control of the land-clearing team at FSB Sharon.[7]

3 Troop continued to operate in the western sector of the province, branching out from Route 15. Spasmodic contacts continued to be made with the enemy and on 5 August the troop fired on an enemy force of undetermined size. The enemy retreated when the troop opened fire, but results of the contact could not be determined. On 6 August one of the

A memorial service for Trooper David Doyle was attended by members of the Squadron after he was accidentally killed on 31 July 1970. (3/4 Calvary Regiment Museum)

sections from 3 Troop was tasked to evacuate a number of the members of a platoon from 2 RAR that had been wounded in a contact with the enemy. The contact occurred late in the afternoon some 1500 metres west of FSB Gail, which was located midway between Phu My and Ong Trinh on Route 15, and the section charged with the evacuation was required to retrieve the wounded later that night when the area had been secured. Earlier that afternoon 1 Troop had deployed to the Phuoc Tuy/Binh Tuy border, where they were to commence an operation with the Xuyen Moc district chief the next day.

At 3.30 pm on 10 August, 86 Section, which was deployed on the eastern side of the Long Hai peninsula approximately 3 kilometres south of the village of Phuoc Hai, detonated an M79 booby trap. Damage to the APC was slight but one of the engineers was reported as sustaining a wound to his lower leg. A subsequent search of the immediate area revealed another two M79 anti-personnel mines.

The continuation of Operation CUNG CHUNG saw 8 RAR again operating around Hoa Long village. On the evening of 11 August 8 Platoon from C Company had been placed in an ambush site half a kilometre to the west of the village. At 9 pm a large group of Viet Cong was observed entering the village, but it was decided to delay the ambush and catch the enemy as they departed the area. The situation was reported to Task Force HQ and 1 Troop was placed on warning to move to Hoa Long and assist the infantry should the ambush be activated. The ambush was activated at 3.15 am against an enemy force of 60 troops, and elements from 1 Troop who were the Squadron's Ready Reaction Force raced to the area as the Viet Cong split into two groups and counter-attacked the platoon. The enemy retreated when the APCs arrived and, after resupplying the infantry with ammunition, the APCs began to pursue the attackers by sweeping the area. Directed by a possum flare ship, Corporal Webb on Callsign 81 engaged a group of six Viet Cong in a clump of bushes to the south of Hoa Long. A short burst from his .50 cal. machine gun killed one of the enemy, which prompted the remaining five to surrender immediately. At the conclusion of the contact the enemy group were identified as belonging to the Chau Duc district and C41 Concentrate D Company. In total 19 enemy troops were killed, six were captured, and one *hoi chanh* later rallied. In addition, an assortment of weapons, 550 pounds of rice, 200 pounds of other foodstuffs, and documents were recovered. Trooper Daniel Healy received minor shrapnel wounds during the course of this action. The troop stayed with the infantry platoon until 7.30 that morning before returning to Nui Dat.

The next week remained relatively quiet, the only 'excitement' occurring when Callsign 23Bravo 'drowned' while 2 Troop were operating with 7 RAR along the beach some 7 kilometres northeast of Phuoc Hai. Callsign 23Bravo was following the other vehicles in 23 section across an estuary and became stuck on a sandbar where the fast-rising tide trapped it. The weapons and radios were recovered, and elements from 7 RAR provided security for the carrier as arrangements were made for its recovery. At 9 o'clock the next morning Troop Leader Captain Peter Murphy had arranged for the 1st Armoured Regiment's recovery tank to help drag the APC out of the water, but it was unable to get sufficiently close to the ocean shore to be of any assistance. It was then decided that the much lighter APCs would stand a better chance, and the other APCs in the troop then connected towlines and were able to extract the stricken carrier from its watery grave.

Major Coates' command of the squadron had become quite diverse. The APCs were now being deployed in a wide variety of operations and work. As individual troops and even sections were being allocated to the operational control of infantry and other subunits, manpower was becoming a major issue. Finding adequate numbers of Squadron personnel to service the growing demands of the other units had become a serious problem due to the lack of reinforcements. This situation had become so critical that a section from 1 Troop had to be temporarily 'grounded' in order to provide enough crew members to the other troops of the Squadron for them to undertake the forthcoming Operation MASSEY-HARRIS in the Binh Chau area. Coates expected the current manning situation to continue for some time—at least until more reinforcements arrived from Australia's A Squadron to boost B Squadron's numbers.

Operation MASSEY-HARRIS

In late August and early September the armoured operation code-named MASSEY-HARRIS was undertaken in AO SUSAN, which extended from the South China Sea northwards 20 kilometres and 10 kilometres west towards the Phuoc Tuy/Binh Tuy border. The force for this operation consisted of B Squadron 3rd Cavalry Regiment, a troop of tanks from C Squadron 1st Armoured Regiment, a large contingent of combat engineers from 1st Field Regiment RAE and the Task Force's Defence and Employment Platoon. An interesting addition to B Squadron was the US Marines naval gunfire team, which consisted of USS *Buck*, USS *Lloyd Thomas* and HMAS *Hobart*, whose guns were deployed to support the operation. This operation, in the eastern boundary area of Phuoc Tuy and Binh Tuy provinces, was under the command of 1 Troop HQ, initially led by Captain W.J. Parker and later by the Squadron's second in command, Captain R.K. Hill MC. Its aim was to demonstrate to the enemy that the area was still under the control of the Australian Task Force. In particular, the force was to eradicate large and flourishing enemy agricultural plots and gardens. The area in which the operation was to take place had originally come under the control of the Task Force in 1967 during Operation PORTSEA, but had since been infiltrated by the enemy who used the area as a substantial food bowl.

The operation, scheduled to commence on 28 August, had to be postponed for 20 hours after the three tanks that were to deploy to AO SUSAN and join 1 Troop became bogged just north of the Long Hais. Because of manpower shortages within the Squadron, 1 Troop comprised only 10 vehicles. The two carriers from 81 Section, which were mortar carriers, had to be seconded into the troop in order that three sections could be deployed.

On 29 August the operation began badly when Callsign 13Alpha reversed onto a large anti-tank mine, estimated to be at least 30 pounds of explosives. The APC was flung into the air and landed on the fuel tank of a nearby centurion tank. A Vietnamese scout who was sitting on the tank was killed. The vehicle's crew and eight members from D&E Platoon were wounded. The damage to the vehicle was extensive, but the 'belly armour' that had been fitted to the vehicle was effective and saved the lives of those on board. In fact, this was the first carrier from the Squadron fitted with 'belly armour' to detonate an anti-tank mine of a reasonable size, and this had certainly demonstrated its value.

The mine exploded at the rear of the carrier, penetrating the fuel cell sponson and blowing off the left-hand suspension units. The blast also caused the belly armour to 'drop off', but the floor of the vehicle was not penetrated. Crew Commander Corporal David Chalk and driver Trooper Brian Slocum, who suffered wounds, were subsequently evacuated to 1 Australian Field Hospital at Vung Tau, along with the wounded members of D&E Platoon. Operation MASSEY-HARRIS proved very successful, with the enemy's influence in the area again being seriously diminished.[8]

The operation continued until 20 September, and the after-action report notes the following losses were sustained by the enemy:

- two Viet Cong killed;
- one M1 carbine captured;
- one Garand rifle captured;
- one ARVN deserter arrested;
- one draft dodger (suspected) arrested.

The following enemy equipment that was captured included:

- approximately 17 hectares of rice and vegetables destroyed;
- approximately 10 fishing nets;
- two 1000 pound aerial bombs;
- 10 blast grenades;
- 10 pounds of chicom explosives;
- a quantity of medical supplies;
- a quantity of garden tools.

Losses inflicted on the Australians included:

- one APC extensively damaged;
- one Bushman scout killed;
- 10 wounded.

The crops discovered were destroyed by the engineers, who set fire to them. To facilitate the destruction of these crops, large quantities of petrol had to be transported by the APCs which could fit only three 44 gallon drums in the back of the carrier at any time; this was time-consuming and a task more suited to the TCVs (tarp-covered vehicles), had they been able to traverse the terrain.

The shortage of manpower in the Squadron also continued to create major problems. 11 Section, which had spent a long time in the field, was overdue for R&C. Eventually, a compromise was reached and the section was given one day's break in lieu of R&C while still deployed on the operation. Captain W.J. Parker, who initially led the troop on the operation, was due to return to Australia and was replaced on the operation by Captain R.K. Hill on 16 September to allow him to prepare for his RTA (return to Australia) procedures. Bob Hill, who had led the first Australian contingent of APCs in South Vietnam with the 4th/19th PWLH, had returned to the war the previous week as the Squadron's second in command, replacing Captain Doug Formby who had completed his tour of duty.

An increase in enemy mine attacks

The enemy were planting even larger anti-tank mines, and these hazards became a major concern for members of the Squadron. The enemy's knowledge and skill in mine warfare had become well developed over the years that the Australians had been in Phuoc Tuy province. They were now extraordinarily proficient in laying these anti-tank mines, which forced the Squadron to be extremely cautious when its APCs were travelling through the country. A road or track that might have been traversed a number of times by the APCs was a likely target for mining by the enemy. Having observed the movements and frequency of the APCs, the enemy would set and camouflage the mines when or where they felt the Australians were least likely to expect a detonation.

Invariably the enemy would leave warning signs in mined areas for their own forces, but detecting these signs placed a heavy burden on APC crews. To share the burden, mini-teams consisting of two engineering sappers from 1 Field Squadron were attached to each section. The sappers were specifically trained in mine detection and removal. The head of the team would sit on the driver's hatch of the leading vehicle observing the road ahead, while his number two remained on the last carrier in the section in the event that his leader was involved in a mine attack, in which case he would be required to take over. The task undertaken by these sappers was extremely dangerous and demanding, but was important in reducing the casualty rates of APC crew members. These teams travelled thousands of kilometres, usually at high speed, constantly watching for the telltale signs of mines and the accompanying warning signals. They were highly regarded by members of the Squadron, and to all intents and purposes were part of the crew. When deployed, they shared the pickets

Callsign 20A waiting recovery after detonating an anti-tank mine. The explosion blew off the engine inspection hatch as well as the tracks and several road wheels. (3rd Cavalry Regiment (Vietnam) Association)

at night and chores during the day with other crew members. In the previous 18 months, some 40 carriers had sustained mine damage, with the crews and the engineering mini-teams both risking death or serious wounds from the mine explosions.

To illustrate the constant danger of mine attacks on APC crews and mini-teams, on 19 September a carrier from 2 Troop, operating about 3 kilometres east of Dat Do village, detonated an M16 anti-personnel mine. The following day Major John Coates' carrier detonated an M16 approximately 1 kilometre north of Phuoc Hai village in the eastern sector of the province. Damage to both carriers was minimal and no casualties were reported. A more serious incident occurred on 28 September, and best serves to illustrate just how valuable the mini-teams were to the Squadron. At 8.45 that morning 86 Section was travelling along Route 2, and was some 5 kilometres south of Courtney hill when one of the mini-team members on board the leading APC visually detected an anti-tank mine in the middle of the road. The mine consisted of two RPG7 rounds affixed to the top of 30 pounds of chicom, which created a shaped pressure charge and had been placed in a puddle in the road by the enemy some time the previous evening. The mine was destroyed at the site by the engineers before the section continued its journey.

On 30 September at 2.05 pm 84 Section was scrambled to assist V Company 2 RAR, which had been in contact with two enemy approximately 1.5 kilometres southwest of Courtney hill. One of the enemy had been killed and the section was requested to assist in following up the one who had escaped, but this proved unsuccessful. At the end of the month 1 Troop (minus 11 Section) and 81 Section were deployed with 2 RAR on Operation CUNG CHUNG 3. 11 Section was under the operational control of 17 Construction Squadron on land-clearing operations. 2 Troop and 82 Section were deployed with 8 RAR on Operation CUNG CHUNG 3. 31 Section and 30Bravo were operating along Route 44 with the 302 Regional Forces Battalion while the other members of the troop constituted the Ready Reaction Force.[9]

At 12.15 pm on 6 October, 84 Section and elements from B Company 2 RAR reacted to information from local Regional Forces concerning the presence of 30 Viet Cong southwest of Courtney hill. A sweep of the area by the infantry produced one *hoi chanh*, one SKS rifle and one Garand rifle. The *hoi chanh* was later handed over to the national police for interrogation. The next day at 9 pm the Regional Forces deployed with 31 Section and Callsign 30Bravo. The four APCs were located some 500 metres from the Regional Forces along

Route 44, who reported receiving enemy small arms fire. As Callsign 30Bravo and 31 Section reacted to the attack on the South Vietnamese forces they also received small arms fire, which was immediately returned by the APCs' machine guns. There were no casualties reported on either side as a result of this action.

At 12.20 am on 10 October, 3 Troop with 83 and 86 Sections reacted to an ambush by 8 RAR 3 kilometres west of the Task Force base. The infantry had killed four enemy and wounded another, and the APCs were used to provide security for the infantry and sweep the area for further enemy troops. On 23 October, at the direction of HQ 1ATF, 3 Troop deployed along Route 15 in preparation for President Thieu's visit to Vung Tau, which had been scheduled for the following day. That evening the troop set up ambush sites around Thai Thien before resuming patrols the following day to provide security for the President.

At the end of October 1 Troop and 81 Section were in support of 7 RAR on Operation CUNG CHUNG after relieving 2 Troop, who had returned to Nui Dat. 3 Troop were in the western sector around Thai Thien supporting 2 RAR. Callsigns 83, 39Mike and 85Alpha were at FSB Scobie in support of the 2/35 US Artillery Battery, while 86 Section and Callsign 85 were under the operational control of 1 Field Squadron on mine-clearing operations around FSB Garth. Compared to the previous month, October had proven relatively quiet, although the Squadron remained busy with its various deployments in support of Task Force operations.[10]

Ready Reaction Force

One of the continuing tasks of the Squadron was supporting the Task Force's Ready Reaction Force. Here the APCs were charged with dealing with any emergency situation that might arise. This generally involved provincial government posts suddenly attacked by enemy forces or Australian Task Force ambushes that had 'gone wrong', which required either extraction or assisted fire power. This role was regarded very seriously by the troops. The Squadron had its own siren, which when activated would see members assigned to the Ready Reaction Force racing from their huts, in specially issued flying suits (for easy dress), down to where the carriers were parked. The Squadron had prided itself on its ability to have its APCs outside the gates of Nui Dat within three minutes of the warning siren being activated. The APC's engines would be started as soon as the driver was in his compartment, and the crew commander would activate the radios and load the guns as the carriers reversed away from the high earthen wall where the carriers were parked. The troop, in tactical operational order, would

Kids from Baria Orphanage boarding the APCs for novelty rides around the base, November 1970. (3/4 Cavalry Regiment Museum)

then race at full speed out of the Squadron's lines, turning into the road that would take them out of the main gates at Nui Dat. While this was happening crew commanders would be making frantic radio net checks with other APCs in the section and troop. Troop and section leaders would be receiving instructions over their radios from the Squadron's command post. There was perhaps no more inspiring or reassuring sight than a troop of carriers, in line-ahead formation, racing at full speed out of the gates of Nui Dat and onto Route 2 in response to a call for assistance. A good example of a reaction by the Squadron's Ready Reaction Force occurred on 29 November.

On 27, 28 and 29 November, 3 Troop had contacted and engaged large enemy parties in heavy country to the west of Route 328. On the evening of 27 November at 6.15 pm, 31 Section observed a number of lights and substantial movement 8 kilometres west of Ngai Giao which were subsequently engaged with machine gun fire. A daylight sweep of the area revealed nothing, as the area was surrounded by heavy jungle. At 11 pm the following evening 31 Section, which had moved its location some 500 metres west of its previous night's location, again engaged an enemy force with machine guns, with unknown results. At 9.35 pm on 29 November a large enemy force, comprising mostly the local D445 Battalion's C2, C3 and C4 accompanied by the D440 Battalion's K8 heavy weapons company attacked the 386 Regional Forces company compound near Xuyen Moc. Twenty mortar rounds were fired into the subsection headquarters and the subsection compound before the enemy attacked. Five Regional Forces troops were killed including the company commander. The enemy had captured 39 M16 rifles, 10 .45 cal. pistols, an M60 machine gun and a large quantity of stores and ammunition. The seriousness of the attack necessitated the scrambling of the Ready Reaction Force based at the Horseshoe. Major Coates took command of the Ready Reaction Force, which comprised his own Squadron HQ, 33 and 83 Sections, elements from 2 Troop and 98Alpha as well as a troop of tanks from 1st Armoured Regiment. They were accompanied by 10 Platoon C Company 7 RAR, which was loaded aboard the APCs.

Coates had been briefed in a telephone conversation by Task Force HQ before the Reaction Force left at great speed. Route 23, between the Horseshoe and Xuyen Moc, had not been cleared of mines, which made for an extremely dangerous journey. However, the APCs covered the 20 kilometres and arrived on the outskirts of Xuyen Moc in under an hour. The troops from the enemy's D445 and D440 Battalions had been in heavy contact with the local government forces, but the sight of the leading elements of the APCs and tanks as they passed through Nui Nhon caused the enemy to break off contact immediately and retreat to the south and west. This decision by the enemy once they realised that the Ready Reaction Force was nearby is significant, as it was known that the enemy were monitoring the Xuyen Moc Sector HQ's radio net prior to and during the assault; it explains their not remaining to fight.

On arrival at Sector HQ the Reaction Force organised for the evacuation of the military and civilian wounded, which was followed by a sweep of the area that failed to produce any further enemy activity. Most of the APCs and tanks remained at Xuyen Moc until 10 am the following day before returning to the Horseshoe. One section of APCs was left at the town for security.[11]

At the beginning of December 1970 1 Troop, 81 and 85 Sections were operating out of FSB Cook under the operational control of 2 RAR and 161 Battery. 2 Troop (minus 23 Section which was providing security for Xuyen Moc) and 82 Section were located at the Horseshoe and FSB Brigid under the operational control of 7 RAR. 3 Troop was on a Squadron operation which involved conducting a series of ambushes in the Thua Tich area (minus 33 Section, which was the Task Force's Ready Reaction Force).

On 4 December at 5.45 pm, 84 Section was moving to an ambush site for the evening on the eastern side of the Courtney rubber plantation, about 3 kilometres south of Courtney hill. As the section travelled along a road leading off Route 2, Callsign 84 detonated a 20-pound anti-tank mine. The point of strike was beneath the crew commander's turret, which caused a 5-centimetre penetration of the belly armour and substantial damage to the vehicle's transmission; the vehicle was recovered to Nui Dat. Fortunately, there were no casualties sustained by the crew members.

Meanwhile, 3 Troop continued its ambushing operations in the eastern sector of the province, with 32 Section placed in an ambush approximately 10 kilometres east of Xuyen Moc on the night of 12 December. At 5.30 am on 13 December the trip flares in the killing ground were ignited, whereupon the claymore mines were immediately detonated and the section's machine guns fired at the killing ground. Later further movement was heard and an immediate sweep of the area was undertaken, but nothing of significance was located.

On 15 December a company from 2 RAR was in contact with the enemy some 2 kilometres south of Courtney hill. One of the platoons from the company had two of their members wounded and the continuing attacks by the enemy on their position made it difficult for them to be evacuated. At 8.30 pm that evening the Squadron received an urgent request to evacuate the two wounded platoon members. A section of carriers was dispatched to the platoon's location, and when the APCs appeared the enemy broke off contact and retreated.

At 8.45 am on 19 December, 86 Section located a 10 pound explosive charge just below the surface on Route 2 near the southern edge of the Courtney rubber plantation. The section had noted with interest that a group of houses near the road that were normally occupied were locked up and there was no sign of the inhabitants. The charge was subsequently destroyed by the mini-team that had accompanied 86 Section.

11 Section, which was operating with 7 RAR, located a large enemy complex approximately 4 kilometres southwest of Xuyen Moc close to Route 23 on 22 December. The complex consisted of an area 50 × 10 metres and contained storage bays, fighting pits and a tunnel 18 metres long. The system was subsequently destroyed by the troops from 7 RAR accompanying the section. At 4.20 that same afternoon 3 Troop HQ was in the process of inserting an SAS patrol in the far northeastern corner of the province. As the section moved towards the drop-off point they engaged three enemy troops. The engagement saw two of the enemy wounded and an AK47 rifle and a quantity of explosive captured. At the conclusion of the incident the troop again moved off and successfully inserted the SAS patrol into its AO. At 5.15 pm Callsign 31Alpha detonated an anti-tank mine on a track leading east from Route 2 into the Courtney rubber plantation. The attack took place about 2 kilometres southeast of Courtney hill as the section was headed for its night ambush position. The mine was estimated at approximately 30 pounds of chicom explosive. No casualties were sustained by the crew members and there was little apparent damage to the carrier, which was later recovered to Nui Dat for RAEME assessment.

On 23 December 11 Section located another tunnel and storage area some 100 metres from the complex they had located the previous day. The 30-metre long tunnel had a storage area and had been used as recently as four days previously. The elements from 7 RAR with whom the section had been operating destroyed the complex. Meanwhile, 1 Troop HQ located some footprints when they moved to the boundary of the province's northeastern border. The footprints were less then six hours' old and were headed in a westerly direction. Immediate follow-up did not produce any results, but the number of footprints in the area confirmed that the enemy were moving en masse into the province. At 10.15 that evening 86 Section observed three lights, 2 kilometres from their position and moving south of their ambush position. The lights maintained their position until 12.15 am but were not engaged because of the distance and intervening vegetation. On Christmas Day at 12.10 am 86 Section engaged one enemy soldier, who approached their ambush position from the south and then withdrew to the west. A sweep of the area the next morning failed to produce anything of significance.

On 30 December, troops from B Company 7 RAR were engaged in Operation CUNG CHUNG Phase 3 in the Phuoc Bu area. A section from 2 Troop had been dispatched to meet 6 Platoon and return the platoon to the Horseshoe after it had completed searching an area near the Song Hoa river adjacent to Route 326. The section, led by Sergeant Grant Kemble, arrived at the arranged rendezvous point mid-morning and awaited the arrival of the platoon. However, at 11.15 am, 6 Platoon, which was still about 1 kilometre east of the rendezvous point, walked into an enemy bunker system where it was engaged by a company-sized enemy force who appeared from their concealed positions. Four members of the platoon were wounded, one mortally, and the rest of the platoon experienced continued heavy enemy fire with no hope of an immediate dustoff flight. When Kemble learnt of the platoon's plight and their inability to evacuate the wounded he immediately took his section towards the contact area. The major problem confronting Kemble was the requirement to navigate his APCs through heavy jungle to the hard-pressed Australians. Once in the vicinity of the enemy bunkers Kemble instructed his section members to direct their machine guns at the enemy's position. The sustained machine gun fire from the APCs forced the enemy to withdraw, and the pressure on the Australian infantrymen was finally relieved. Kemble then proceeded to load the wounded infantrymen onto the carriers and drive them to a nearby landing zone, where they were evacuated on a dustoff flight.

Meanwhile, the other carriers in the troop who were stationed at the Horseshoe were scrambled to the area with 4 Platoon B Company 7 RAR on board. On arrival 6 Platoon was also loaded on board the carriers and the troop moved about 1.5 kilometres to the south to cut off the enemy's expected withdrawal route. On arrival the infantry was unloaded and the troop set off to put in place a series of ambushes; however, the enemy had moved north, instead of to the south as expected.

For his action in relieving the pressure on the infantry platoon, Sergeant G.M. Kemble received the award of Mentioned in Dispatches. The citation for his award reads:

> On 30 December 1970, Sergeant Kemble was commanding a section of APCs in support of a rifle platoon operating in the Phuoc Bu area when the rifle platoon came heavily engaged with an enemy company group in a bunker system. Sergeant Kemble, who was some distance from the contact area, quickly assessed the situation and without hesitation led his section through thick and close country to the contact area where he immediately came into action. His prompt action forced the enemy to withdraw from the right flank of the contact area and greatly relieved the pressure on the rifle platoon. He then picked up the four badly wounded, moved to the nearest clearing and secured the area so that a helicopter could evacuate the wounded.

One of the Squadron's finest exponents of the ambushing techniques originally developed by John Crossman was Sergeant Ed Levy, who had joined B Squadron in September 1970. Levy was a member of 1 Troop and the section leader of 11 Section, and had come to South Vietnam for a second tour of duty. Ed Levy's section had been deployed some 5 kilometres to the northeast of where the contact had occurred with 6 Platoon earlier that morning, and to the southeast of Xuyen Moc. At 5 pm that evening Levy had sited his section for a night ambush in thick scrub adjacent to a track that led to the northern end of a clearing. Elements from 7 RAR were also posted to the ambush site to provide flank protection for the APCs. A total of 32 claymore mines had been sited along 40 metres of the track, which was to constitute the 'killing zone' of the ambush. At 4 am on 31 December a large enemy force approached the ambush site. The enemy's forward scout leading the Viet Cong column was allowed to pass through the ambush before it was activated by detonating the claymore mines. The blast from the mines initially killed a substantial number of the enemy before the APCs' machine guns were put into action. Despite horrendous losses the enemy counterattacked, directing their attacks at both flanks of the ambush; for the next three hours the section fired on the Viet Cong as they attempted both to avenge their comrades and to remove their bodies from the scene of the battle.

A Pilatus Porter aircraft was dispatched to the area and continued to drop flares until dawn to illuminate the area. By this time another section from the troop with a platoon from 7 RAR had been dispatched to help sweep the area. The result of this ambush was 21 enemy confirmed killed. There were many blood trails leading from the site, indicating that many more enemy troops had been either killed or wounded and had been removed from the ambush site. More importantly, although not immediately obvious, the ambush had seen a substantial portion of the local D445 Battalion command structure killed, including the battalion's second in command, the political officer, two platoon second in commands and two section commanders. It was also believed that the commanding officer of C2 D445, the platoon commander and three section commanders of the Recce Platoon C5 D445 had been killed. This explained the enemy's reluctance to retreat after the detonation of the claymore mines—such a loss to their command structure would demand every effort to keep this information from the Australian forces.

As dawn broke on the new year, 29 packs were recovered as well as an enormous amount of weapons and supplies. Follow-up and pursuit of the wounded and the remainder of the enemy force was denied because a 24-hour truce had previously been called by both sides of the war to celebrate New Year. Operations in the area concluded when 1 Troop and engineers from 1st Field Regiment returned to and destroyed the bunker system encountered by 6 Platoon B Company 7 RAR on 30 December.

At the conclusion of his tour of duty 2 Troop's leader, Captain Peter Murphy, received the award of Mentioned in Dispatches. It is worth mentioning that on arrival in South Vietnam the commander of 7 RAR had made personal representation to the Squadron that Captain Murphy be allocated to his battalion on a permanent basis to support its operations. Murphy had trained with 7 RAR on exercises in Australia before the battalion's departure for active duty in South Vietnam, and had impressed their somewhat demanding commander with his ability and willingness to support the battalion. Until that stage it had been regimental policy that the troops of the Squadron be rotated among the infantry and that no troop be permanently allocated to a particular battalion. However, on this occasion, and because Murphy had built up a strong working relationship with 7 RAR, the protocol was broken and 2 Troop was placed on an almost permanent deployment with that battalion. During its time with the battalion, 2 Troop conducted numerous operations in support of 7 RAR, and on all occasions when his troop was in action Peter Murphy displayed outstanding leadership qualities. The citation for Captain P.J. Murphy's award reads:[12]

> For most of 1970, Captain Murphy and his Troop of armoured personnel carriers have supported 7th Battalion, The Royal Australian Regiment on operations. Throughout the period Captain Murphy has set a high example of personal bravery coupled with excellent judgement and quick decision. On one occasion when commanding his troop in the field, his own armoured personnel carrier detonated an enemy mine, which badly damaged the carrier, causing several casualties and threw Captain Murphy bodily around the vehicle. He then continued with coolness and fortitude to command his troop from another vehicle.
>
> He has personally led many patrols and ambushes into enemy base areas resulting in contact and casualties to the enemy. His troop has performed with outstanding success due largely to the leadership and example of Captain Murphy.

During the year ended 31 December 1970, the Squadron had again suffered an extremely high rate of casualties. Four of its members had been killed. A further 34 had been wounded or injured. The casualty count was three more than the previous year. The number of vehicles hitting mines, however, had increased substantially. The addition of belly armour to the APCs was proving effective in countering the mine strategy adopted by the enemy, and had saved the lives of many members of the Squadron. However, the enemy were now using more destructive anti-tank mines. In many instances the amount of explosive being used by the enemy was increased to between 60 and 80 pounds in an effort to counter the effects of the belly armour that had been fitted to the carriers.[13]

12

Australia withdraws, 1971

In early 1971 the Australian government had decided to wind down its involvement in the Vietnam War. This decision was predicated on the 'assumption' that at the end of 1970 large numbers of the enemy had left Phuoc Tuy province and the pacification program was working. It was felt that the Australians had done what they initially set out to achieve and that security of the province could shortly be returned to the government. However, the dilemma facing the enemy was that the local population would interpret their prolonged absence from the province as a loss of face, and the government's position would be considerably enhanced. Rather than risk such a scenario the enemy began to move back into Phuoc Tuy province and carry the fight to the Australians. The Australian government had hoped for a smooth exit by the Task Force, but the enemy was determined that this would not be the case. One of the three infantry battalions had earlier been withdrawn from South Vietnam and not replaced. This meant that even more responsibility would be placed on the Squadron to support the Task Force.

At the commencement of the new year 1 Troop and 81 Section were under the operational control of 7 RAR, operating out of the Horseshoe and FSB Brigid. 2 Troop was the Ready Reaction Force and 22 Section had that day been reacted from Nui Dat to assist 7 RAR, which was in contact some 9 kilometres east of Xuyen Moc adjacent to Route 23. 3 Troop and 86 Section were under the operational control of 2 RAR at FSB Garth, 1 Field Squadron at NDP Lorraine and with the Xuyen Moc district chief. 83 and 85 Sections were under the operational control of 161 Field Battery at Thua Tich.

In the eastern sector of the province the local Viet Cong forces remained active. On 5 January, 12 Section from 1 Troop located a bunker system 1 kilometre east of Phuoc Loi on the western side of Long Green. Five Viet Cong were captured as they stepped out of their bunker and were surprised to see the APC section waiting with their guns trained on them. Also captured was one M16 rifle, a submachine gun, medical supplies and ammunition. Those captured were members of the Phuoc Loi Viet Cong unit and included the Secretary of the Phuoc Loi Party chapter.

Early on the evening of 7 January, 1 Troop's 11 Section had positioned itself in an ambush site 1 kilometre northwest of the Horseshoe base. That evening a party of approximately 20 enemy troops approached the ambush site, and although it was only a relatively short time after curfew it was decided to challenge them. The enemy immediately commenced cocking their weapons, which prompted the section's leader, Sergeant Ed Levy, to activate the ambush. Three enemy were killed, including the Secretary of the Hoa Long Viet Cong chapter and the Commander of the Chau Duc Viet Cong's Women's Association. One of the enemy was also captured and taken prisoner.

On 8 January Major T.F.H. Walker assumed command of the Squadron from Major H.J. Coates. The designation of the squadron also changed, from B to A Squadron. Major Coates had led the Squadron during a particularly difficult year for the Regiment, and was awarded a Member of the British Empire. The citation for his award reads:[1]

> He arrived in South Vietnam on 27 May 1970 as Commanding Officer B Squadron 3rd Cavalry Regiment.
>
> From the outset Major Coates displayed drive and aggressive characteristics of a sound cavalry commander. Through his assessment of the capacity of each of the sub units under his command he was able to deploy the correct force to meet the particular requirements of a given task.
>
> On 29 November 1970, in the village of Xuyen Moc, Phuoc Tuy province Vietnam, when a Vietnamese post was over-run by the enemy, Major Coates was appointed to the command of a relief force to stabilise the situation. His swift reaction and determined leadership on this occasion was an inspiration to the whole force in the corps area of operation.
>
> Major Coates was appointed the principal Operations Officer of Headquarters 1st Australian Task Force on 4 January 1971. In this position, Major Coates used his professional ability and operational experience to readily assess a situation providing sound staff direction and support of the units deployed on operations.

The establishment of A Squadron in January 1971 was as follows: officers, 14; warrant officers/sergeants, 22; other ranks, 127. The Squadron's second in command was Captain R.K. Hill MC (later to be replaced by Captain G. Ayre) and the Squadron's SSM was WO2 L.A Bailey. 1 Troop was commanded by Captain R.M. Earle, 2 Troop was led by Lieutenant C.E. Stephens and 3 Troop by Captain R.B. Wade.

THE NEW BROOM

When Major Terry Walker assumed command of the Squadron he had serious reservations as to the grouping and tasking of the vehicles. At that time deployment of the Squadron had been based mainly on section-sized groups, either under the operational command or in direct support of other units. Also, the tasking of the sections had been handled by the Squadron's second in command in his capacity as operations officer, and that system tended to bypass Troop HQ level. This meant that both troop and squadron commanders were not being given sufficient opportunity to exercise their command function. Terry Walker disagreed with this system, attributing it to the past successes of the Squadron undertaking a wide variety of tasks and becoming seriously overtasked. Accordingly, he set about regrouping the Squadron's vehicles in the following manner:

Squadron HQ	—Three APCs and one ACV
Under Command	—Task Force HQ five ACVs
	—LAD three M113A1 fitters' vehicles
1 Troop	—Troop HQ four APCs
	—Three sections each containing three APCs
2 Troop	—Troop HQ four APCs
	—Three sections each containing three APCs
3 Troop	—Troop HQ four APCs
	—Three sections each containing three APCs
81 Section	—One APC
	—Two M125A1 mortar carriers
82 Section	—One APC
	—Two M125A1 mortar carriers
83 Section	—One APC
	—Two M125A1 mortar carriers
84 Section	—Three APCs

In summary, the following types of vehicles were now under the Squadron's command: 48 M113A1 APCs, six M125A1 mortars, three M113A fitters and six M577A1 ACVs. By regrouping the Squadron's vehicles, four 'independent sections' were created which would become available for deployment on section-sized tasks, thereby releasing the three full troops to be used more beneficially as complete subunits. With this strategy Walker believed that the Squadron could more realistically deal with the enemy's threat. It would also allow commanders to exercise their initiative and tactical ability with benefits to themselves, the Squadron and eventually the Corps. With the imminent arrival of 4 RAR it was anticipated that 1 Troop would deploy with 4 RAR in the northern sector of the province and the lower sector of Long Khanh. 3 Troop would deploy with 3 RAR in the eastern sector of the province, with 2 Troop assisting both troops and acting as Ready Reaction Force. The independent sections would be allocated section-sized tasks, allowing the three full troops to act as full subunits.

Walker was also requested to provide a report on the M113 family of vehicles and their perceived worth in this theatre of war. He reported that the M113 had performed well, but the Squadron and the LAD continued to experiment and modify certain aspects of the vehicles. The most popular configuration for the T50 turret was the .50 cal. machine gun mounted in the turret with a pintle-mounted .30 cal. machine gun on the front of the turret. The Squadron's 2I/C's vehicle was being used to trial a pintle-mounted .50 cal. machine gun, despite fears that the weight distribution over a greater area might cause damage to the turret. At the time the report was submitted, approximately 60% of the vehicles had had new fuel cells mounted, which formed an integral part of the hull. The older type of cells had tended to crack along the length of the welds as the result of constant vibration. Servicing of the vehicles was generally being kept up to date on a mileage rather than time basis. The LAD were able to complete three or four 'D' services in a day, thus enabling a section to be absent from operational tasks only for a maximum of two days.

At the beginning of the new year the Task Force's TAOR was confined to the geographical borders of Phuoc Tuy province, and at the same time the areas of operation allotted to the territorial forces of ARVN were extended. The Vietnamese would now have responsibility for the western strip of the province astride Route 15 and the southern portion of the province below Hoa Long and east in a line between the Horseshoe and Phuoc Hai. Manpower problems were still being encountered as the reinforcement system of replacements coming from the Squadron in Australia was proving deficient. It had been recommended that, at some time in the future, replacement by sub-units would be more advantageous than the present 'trickle' system.

The main threat to the Squadron's vehicles and the crews was now being recognised as mine warfare rather than RPGs and small arms fire. This had resulted in many of the 'line' troops wearing flak jackets (and sitting on them) for protection. Additionally, many crew members had decided to discard their traditional black berets and earphones and to wear the much more cumbersome helmet that had internally mounted radio communication devices but afforded a greater degree of protection.

Business as usual

While the Task Force's TAOR had been compressed, demands on the Squadron did not diminish. At 6.50 am 9 January 1971 Callsign 22Bravo, which was under the operational command of 2 RAR at FSB Garth, detonated an anti-tank mine. None of the crew members was reported as sustaining wounds, and damage to the vehicle was minimal. On 17 January the Squadron's 2I/C, Captain R.K. Hill, led a composite troop on an independent operation to the extreme northeast of the Task Force's TAOR into the May Tao/Nui Be region. The operation comprised two missions: the first was to insert an SAS patrol, and the second was to destroy a bunker system and make a reconnaissance of the area. During the move to the area, Callsign 33Alpha detonated a 30 pound anti-tank chicom mine as it moved along Route 329 north of Xuyen Moc. It was reported that the driver, Jeff Townsend, received serious shrapnel wounds to his jaw and ankle, while the crew commander, Brien Plunkett, was also wounded in the attack. An engineer sitting on the driver's compartment hatch was blown off and, although injured and dazed, went to the aid of the crew before sweeping the immediate area for mines to allow other members of the section to assist with the evacuation of the wounded crew members. The belly armour was blown off, but its addition to the carriers had again demonstrated its value in lessening wounds and injuries sustained by crew. About an hour after the mine incident, a bushman scout stepped on another mine, which killed him and wounded one of the crewmen on a nearby APC and six other infantrymen from D&E Platoon, who were sitting on top of the vehicle.

It is interesting to note that a *hoi chanh* had recently revealed that C4 of D445 had been ordered to ambush armoured vehicles using Routes 329 and 331 in the extreme northeastern portion of the province. The enemy planned to allow the APCs to drive through the ambush point, then to place mines and await the vehicles on the return journey, which may have taken several days. In view of this intelligence Major Walker had told Hill that he was to exercise extreme caution while moving along these roads, to the extent that he was to walk his mini-teams when withdrawing from the area. In fact, Task Force HQ was so concerned about the enemy's intention to ambush and that D445 were reported to be in large numbers in the surrounding area that if Hill's troop suffered any more casualties they would be immediately withdrawn from the area without completing their second task. Fortunately, the troop was able to undertake its tasks and withdraw safely from the area.

On 19 January one of the sections from 2 Troop sighted three enemy troops carrying three bags of rice about 1.5 kilometres south of Courtney hill. The enemy was observed entering a hut located nearby, but rather than attack it was decided that the incident should be reported and logged as a possible ambush site. In the early evening of 22 January C Company 2 RAR activated an ambush on an enemy force near where the carriers from the Squadron had observed the enemy transporting the rice. At 6.45 pm a section from 2 Troop was requested to cut off the enemy as they retreated south. The section moved approximately 2 kilometres south of Courtney hill, where they contacted the retreating enemy force. The contact saw two enemy killed and one wounded.

There was one further mine attack on one of the Squadron's vehicles during the month; however, although similar to the incident on 9 January, it proved much less damaging than the attack on 33Alpha. The addition of belly armour was largely credited with the less damaging effects that mine explosions were having on APCs, although the effect of a mine with an explosive power in excess of 30 pounds of explosive had yet to be tested on vehicles with belly armour.[2]

At the beginning of February 1971, 1 Troop was stationed at the Horseshoe under the operational control of 7 RAR. 2 Troop (minus 22 Section) was under the operational control of C Company 2 RAR and was operating out of FSB Garth in the northern sector of the province, while 22 Section was under the operational control of the Duc Than district chief. 3 Troop (minus 31 Section), 81, 82 and 83 Sections were all based at Nui Dat, where they made up the Ready Reaction Force, while 31 Section was under the operational control of 161 Field Battery based at FSB Lynx.

Early in February 1 Troop and elements from 3 Troop were deployed to support 7 RAR as they carried out operations around the three fire support bases in the eastern sector of the province, which comprised the Horseshoe, and FSBs Brigid and Isa. Meanwhile 2 Troop continued to support 2 RAR around the Courtney rubber plantation and at 10.50 am on 13 February the troop's 22 Section was moving along a road in the plantation approximately 2 kilometres southeast of Courtney hill when Callsign 22Alpha detonated an anti-tank mine. The mine, consisting of about 20 pounds of chicom explosive attached to an RPG round, sheared off the belly armour and blew off one of the steering laterals in the driver's compartment. The driver was reported as being slightly wounded but damage to the vehicle was, in the circumstances, not considered excessive.

Six days later, on 19 February, 31 Section was moving through the Courtney rubber plantation approximately 1 kilometre south of the attack on Callsign 22Alpha the previous week when Callsign 31Alpha detonated an anti-tank mine. The mine was estimated to be a 30 pound pressure-type chicom mine, and damage to the vehicle was reported as extensive. The two crew members were reported as sustaining wounds and were evacuated from the site.[3]

At the beginning of March, 1 Troop was under the operational control of newly arrived 3 RAR in AO KIM. 2 Troop were under the operational control of A Battery 12 Field Regiment and 1 Field Squadron, with 21 Section at FSB Marge, 22 Section at NDP Dani and 23 Section at FSB Gwenda. 3 Troop and 84 Section were under the operational control of 2 RAR at FSB Garth, while 81, 82 and 83 Sections supported 3 RAR at FSB Marge.

On 1 March at 12.20 pm, 31 Section was moving through the Courtney rubber plantation some 100 metres west of the 19 February mine attack on Callsign 22Alpha when Callsign 31Alpha again detonated an anti-tank mine. This was a pressure-type mine, consisting of 30 pounds of chicom, which had been buried by the enemy on a track running through the rubber trees. The crew of Robert Abbott and Danny Handley were reported as sustaining minor wounds. The APC, which was new, having replaced the vehicle damaged in the mine attack the previous month, sustained what was described as moderate damage, with the front right-hand final drive, two sets of roadwheels and the right-hand track completely blown off.

Three weeks later, at 11.52 on the morning of 21 March, 86 Section was travelling on Route 328 about 1 kilometre north of Thua Tich when Callsign 86 detonated an anti-tank mine. The mine was described as consisting of an RPG3 round with a CBU. The vehicle was reported as being extensively damaged, with the explosion blowing off the right-hand track and the first two roadwheels. The crew of Dallas Burrage and Fred Fedorowytsch were lucky to escape serious injury. Earlier in the week and in line with the Task Force's strategy of handing over more responsibility to the government forces, 2 Troop accompanied the 302 Regional Forces' Battalion in an operation between 15 and 19 March. This operation saw the troop accompany South Vietnamese forces as they moved into the Long Hai hills in pursuit of elements of the enemy's D445 Battalion.

Another mine attack occurred on one of the Squadron's vehicles at 9.05 am on 26 March. 1 Troop was operating in the northwestern sector of the province some 9 kilometres north of Thua Tich in support of 3 RAR when Callsign 10Bravo detonated an anti-tank mine. This was a pressure-type mine with an explosive strength of approximately

40 pounds of chicom explosive. The crew commander, troop officer Dave Pakes and driver John Lieshman were reported as sustaining slight wounds but elected to remain on duty. The vehicle suffered substantial damage—with the left-hand final drive, two roadwheels and the track blown off—and had to be recovered back to Nui Dat.[4]

At the beginning of April 1 Troop and 3 Troop remained under the operational control of 3 RAR in AO DEBORAH in the northeastern sector of the province. 2 Troop (minus 23 Section, which was under the operational control of 17 Construction Squadron at Nui Nhon) was in the Task Force base's 'recce' area. The four vehicles in Squadron HQ constituted the Ready Reaction Force.

Mine attacks on the Squadron's vehicles continued, and on 2 April at 12.02 pm Callsign 29Mike detonated an anti-tank mine on the southern outskirts of Thua Tich. The mine was a pressure-type device with an estimated strength of 40 pounds of chicom explosive. Crew Commander, Corporal James Fletcher and driver Trooper Leslie Oldmeadow were both wounded as a result of the explosion, and were evacuated from the site. The vehicle was reported as being extensively damaged. That evening 3 RAR reported that it had been in contact with elements of the local Viet Cong D445 Battalion approximately 4 kilometres north of Xuyen Moc. At 7 am the following morning one of the independent sections was deployed to support 3 RAR by first inserting an SAS patrol about 1.5 kilometres northeast of Thua Tich. The section then moved off to a nearby site with the aim of ambushing the withdrawing enemy forces from D445 as they headed for the shelter of the May Tao hills. However, the elusive enemy prevailed and were successful in avoiding the ambush by APCs.

On 4 April at 9.05 am Callsign 98Bravo, one of the LAD fitters' vehicles, had travelled some 2 kilometres along Route 328 after turning off Route 23 when it detonated a pressure-type anti-tank mine with an estimated explosive strength of between 60 and 80 pounds of chicom; the vehicle was reported as sustaining extensive damage. Driver Craftsman Gary Davis was wounded and evacuated from the site.

The Squadron continued to perform a wide variety of tasks for the remainder of the month in support of various Task Force units within the newly defined TAOR. The last mine attack on the Squadron's vehicles for the month occurred at 4.55 on the afternoon of 23 April. Callsign 29Juliet, which was under the operational control of 2 RAR, was travelling along a road in the Courtney rubber plantation some 2 kilometres east of Route 2 and 3.5 kilometres southeast of Courtney hill when it detonated an anti-tank mine. The mine was a tilt-switch device comprising two RPG7 rounds. There were no casualties among the members of the crew and the vehicle was reported as being only slightly damaged.[5]

At the beginning of May, 1 Troop's 12 Section deployed on ambushing and reconnaissance tasks in the north of the province while the rest of the troop was under the operational control of 1 Field Squadron in AO DEBORAH based at NDP Susan in the eastern sector of the province. 2 Troop was in the north under the operational control of 2 RAR in AO LISA while 3 Troop was under the operational control of 3 RAR in AO DEBORAH in the eastern sector of the province. 82 Section was tasked to perform engineer escorts along Route 2 during the day and by night to revert to the operational control of the Duc Than district chief. 84 Section was under the operational control of C Battery 5/42 US Artillery at FSB Friendship in AO DUC THAN while 86 Section was under the operational control of 17 Construction Company at Nui Nhon at NDP Susan.

On 3 May Callsign 21Alpha detonated an anti-tank mine of undetermined strength. The mine caused moderate damage to the carrier, but the crew escaped serious injury. An engineer from the mini-team sitting on the driver's hatch was not so lucky, and sustained a broken leg. Five days later, on 8 May at 9.45 am, 13 Section contacted one enemy soldier approximately 6 kilometres east of Dat Do close to Route 23. The Viet Cong was fired on and killed and his M1 rifle captured. The remainder of the month was relatively quiet until 24 May, when Callsign 13Alpha detonated an anti-tank mine. 13 Section had been deployed about 9 kilometres west of the Courtney rubber plantation in the southern sector of Long Khanh province when the section's leading APC detonated a pressure-type mine with an estimated strength of 15 pounds of chicom explosive. Crew Commander Corporal Neville Cheetham and a mini-team member, Sapper Weston, were wounded in the attack and evacuated from the site. A sweep of the area by the other mini-team member located another 15-pound mine in the immediate vicinity of the first mine. Callsign 13Alpha was able to be recovered under its own power.[6]

With a view to adding to the Australian Army's range of armoured vehicles it was decided to trial a variation of the M113A1, and in mid-1971 a fire support vehicle had been developed and shipped to South Vietnam for tests.[7] The FSV consisted of the basic M113 hull and a Saladin turret mounted on the deck with a 76 mm gun as the vehicle's main armament. The addition of the 76 mm gun was probably influenced by the success the centurion tanks had encountered in the defence of FSB Balmoral in 1968. While still possessing a thin hull armour it was thought the FSV would provide greater fire power in defending FSBs than that currently provided by the M113A1 with

Preparing the newly arrived FSVs for operational duty in the LAD yard at Nui Dat, May 1971. (3rd Cavalry Regiment (Vietnam) Association)

machine gun capabilities only. It was envisaged that if the FSV was surrounded by an earthen barrier with only the gun and turret exposed it would receive adequate protection from an RPG round and would be capable of dispensing heavy fire on an attacking force.

The FSV, compared with the centurion tank, was limited in the tasks it could undertake. For example, it would never replace the tanks in assault tasks as its light armoured skin could not sustain a hit by an RPG round. It was felt, however, that placing these vehicles in fire support bases would free the tanks of the 1st Armoured Regiment of the task of FSB protection which they had undertaken since arriving in the province in 1968. This in turn would allow the tanks to take a more proactive role in supporting the Cavalry Squadron and infantry battalions in Task Force operations.

Lieutenant Ross McCormack had, on 29 May, been transferred from 3 Troop to command the FSVs in Support Troop, as it was to be known. Additionally, WO2 Leo Bonser arrived to instruct and co-ordinate training on the FSVs. The majority of the men who crewed these vehicles were seconded from the 2nd Cavalry Regiment because they had been trained in the operation of the Saladin turret and the 76 mm gun. The eight FSVs being trialled were organised into two sections, designated 41 and 42 Sections. Their operational employment mirrored that of the other independent sections of the Squadron, albeit in a different role. Snow Marshall, who served with the FSVs, recalls that the rounds used for the guns were primarily anti-personnel ammunition consisting of Hesh, Splintex and phosphorus. This ammunition was smaller than that used by the tanks of the 1st Armoured Regiment but fitted the vehicles' charter of FSB defence.

CHANGE OF PACE: OPERATION OVERLORD

The first five months of the year had proven relatively quiet, with most of the Squadron's action related to mine attacks on its vehicles. However, the members of the Squadron would soon be revising any misconceptions they might have had in relation to the enemy's ability to attack them. In the later part of May, intelligence reports revealed that large numbers of NVA forces were entering the province to the north and establishing camps and bunker systems to the east of the Courtney rubber plantation, bordering Long Khanh and Phuoc Tuy provinces. The Squadron had been engaged in numerous intelligence-based reconnaissance patrols to determine the size of the enemy force and direction in which it was moving. It was subsequently determined that a large force consisting of the NVA, 3rd Battalion 33 Regiment and elements of the local D445 Battalion had established a substantial base in southeastern Long Khanh province. A decision was made to deploy the whole Task Force in an operation codenamed OVERLORD commencing on 5 June. The Task Force's plan was to use the Squadron together with 4 RAR in blocking positions to the south and the 2nd Battalion 8th US Cavalry to the east. 3 RAR would be the searching force, moving in a southeasterly direction. Two days earlier, on 3/4 June, 1 Troop had deployed with the newly arrived 4 RAR approximately 5 kilometres northwest of Nui Dat on a two-day 'shakedown' operation called BOWHANI JUNCTION.

On the evening of 4 June the whole Squadron had returned to Nui Dat prior to its deployment in force on Operation OVERLORD, which was scheduled to commence early the next morning. A detachment consisting of Administration Troop, the majority of the LAD and elements of Squadron HQ were the only members of the Squadron that would remain at the base.

Operation OVERLORD proved to be one of the biggest operations ever undertaken by the Task Force. The Squadron was charged with initially transporting various infantry units along Route 2 and then some 8 kilometres to the east of the Courtney rubber plantation. This move started at 3.30 am on 5 June. Once the infantry had been deposited at their start-off points, the troops of the Squadron moved off

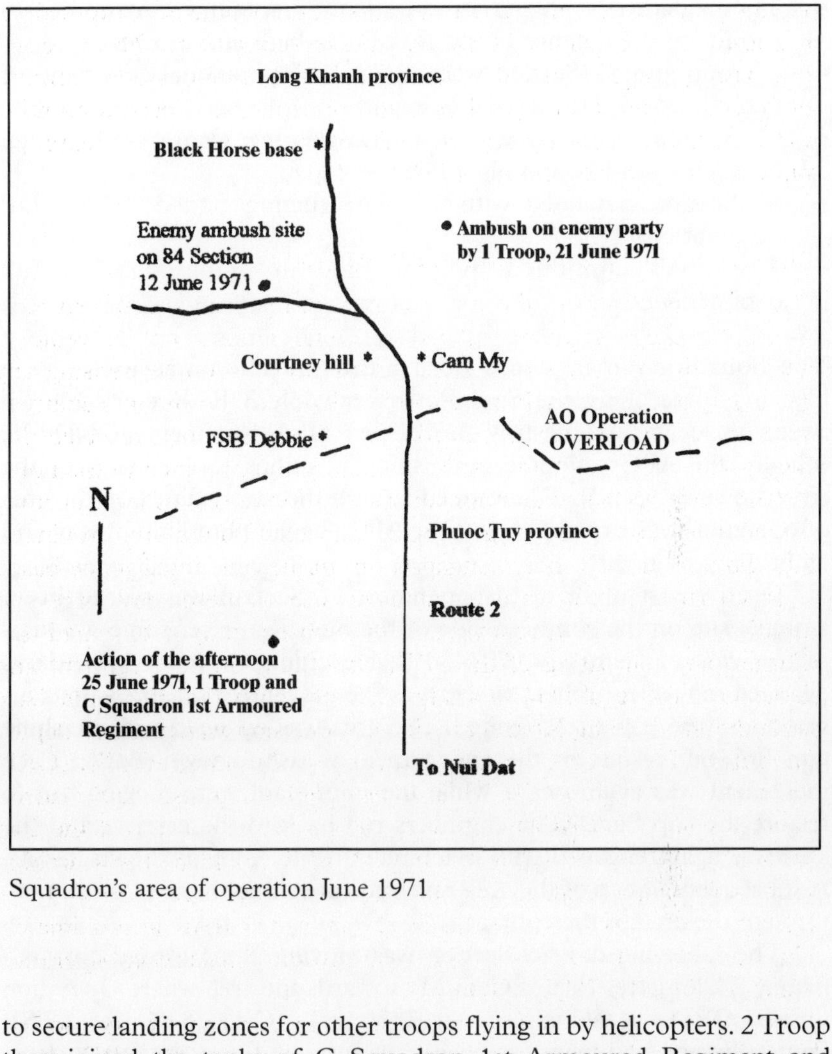

Squadron's area of operation June 1971

to secure landing zones for other troops flying in by helicopters. 2 Troop then joined the tanks of C Squadron 1st Armoured Regiment and elements of D Company 3 RAR to clear an area of land running 3000 metres to the northwest of Cam Tien. The other troops moved to the south of the operations area to adopt blocking ambush positions.

Grouping and deployments of the Squadron for this operation were as follows:

- Elements of Squadron HQ, 1 Troop, 3 Troop and 84 Section were to block along the Suoi Ran river.
- Elements of Squadron HQ, 86 Section were located on Courtney hill with the 1 ATF command.

- The Squadron's second in command, Captain G. Ayre, was to command the defence of the Task Force base at Nui Dat.
- 2 Troop and 82 Section were under the operational command of C Squadron 1 Armoured Regiment.
- 81 Section remained with the land-clearing team at NDP Jane between Cam My and Ngai Giao.
- 83 Section remained with 17 Construction Squadron at NDP Susan at Nui Nhon.
- The FSVs continued their training in preparation for full deployment.

The Squadron's main focus during this operation was to act as a blocking force along the Suoi Ran river while 3 RAR carried out a sweep to locate and destroy the 3/33rd NVA Regiment and D445. Initially, the APCs adopted ambushing positions to the south of the river; however, as 3 RAR advanced in a southeasterly direction the area of operation was expanded, and the APCs began patrolling by day and ambushing by night.

On the first night of the operation 11 Section was placed in an ambush site on the southern side of the Suoi Ran river some 4.5 kilometres east of Cam My. At 6.50 that evening Corporal Jeff Adams detected movement to the east, just as the movement sensors were activated and the trip flares ignited. The area was engaged with machine gun fire, but results of the engagement were unknown. At 7.10 pm movement was again heard while the mini-team were moving out to restore the trip flares. The engineers ran back to the carriers and the area was again engaged with machine gun fire, with unknown results. A subsequent sweep of the area revealed substantial signs of movement through the area of the contact.

The following day 86 Section was moving along a road approximately 2 kilometres east of Cam My towards the area where Operation OVERLORD was taking place. At 12.30 am, as Callsign 86 neared FSB Pamela, which had been established to support the operation, it detonated an anti-tank mine. The mine consisted of a 50 pound shaped charge of chicom explosive, and had only just been placed by the enemy to catch one of the Squadron's vehicles that had been using the road during the operation. It was subsequently discovered that the enemy had been quite aggressive and planted several anti-tank mines around the base when they had determined the strength and number of armoured vehicles deployed in the area. The explosion from the mine penetrated the left rear of Callsign 86's hull, twisted the ramp and blew off the driver's hatch. The extent of the wounds sustained by the crew was not reported, although the commander's diary noted that this was the fourth time that Crew Commander Lieutenant Craig Mitchell's vehicle had been involved in enemy mine attacks.

On 7 June, B Company 3 RAR engaged a large enemy force in heavy jungle; after air strikes and an artillery bombardment of the area the tanks of C Squadron 1st Armoured Regiment were called up to assist the infantry in the bunker system. 2 Troop delivered the reserve troops from D Company 3 RAR to the location of 3 and 5 Troops of the 1st Armoured Regiment where they dismounted and, accompanied by C Company 3 RAR and the tanks, made contact with the hard-pressed B company. 2 Troop subsequently joined the tanks and loaded the infantry's packs in the back of the carriers as they advanced through the bunker system. On reaching B Company the wounded were loaded aboard the carriers and evacuated.

That evening at 10.10 pm Corporal Jeff Adams' 11 Section, which was still in the ambush site it had occupied two nights previously, again detected movement in front of its position. The area was engaged with machine gun fire, but results could not be determined. The following morning, 8 June, 2 Troop returned to the bunker system that had been assaulted the previous day, where it was given the responsibility of securing the area to facilitate the destruction of the various structures by the engineers from 1 Field Squadron. At 10.26 pm Sergeant John Pass'

Centurion tanks from the 1st Armoured Regiment worked alongside the APCs during Operation OVERLORD in June 1971. (Australian War Memorial, negative number FOD/71/0304/VN)

33 Section detected movement from their ambush position, which was located approximately 400 metres east of FSB Pamela. The area was engaged with machine gun fire, but results could not be determined.

On 9 June at 6.15 am Callsign 39Juliet was in the process of withdrawing from its ambush position to the east of Cam My when it detonated an anti-tank mine. The mine consisted of two RPG rounds on the surface of the ground with the point of strike at the rear of the vehicle. No damage was sustained by the vehicle and the crew of Corporal Gary Conway and Trooper Les Moyle were reported as uninjured. The following evening 32 Section and Callsign 30Alpha were placed in an ambush on the northern side of the Suoi Ran river some 4.5 kilometres east of Cam My. At 11.35 pm the ambush was activated and the area engaged with machine gun fire, but results were unable to be determined. A sweep at first light revealed numerous footprints leading from the area.

The two infantry battalions taking part in Operation OVERLORD were subsequently withdrawn and redeployed to other areas. The Squadron, however, remained in Long Khanh province to carry out reconnaissance patrols and continue ambushing trails being used by the retreating 3/33rd Regiment, D445 and other elements. On 11 June at 5.12 pm, 12 Section had moved to its night ambushing position approximately 2 kilometres north of Cam My. As the section leader, Sergeant Bob Veall, made his reconnaissance of the area on foot he was confronted by two Viet Cong soldiers. The enemy were engaged by the crews on the APC with machine gun fire, which prompted them to make an immediate withdrawal. Results of the contact were unknown.

The next day was to prove one of the most harrowing during the unit's service in South Vietnam. At 10.25 am on 12 June, 84 Section, led by Corporal Kim Brumfield, had been patrolling along a track some 3 kilometres west of Courtney hill. The driver on leading carrier Callsign 84Alpha, Peter Holden, stopped when he saw an artillery illumination canister that had been placed on the track, and decided the matter required investigation. The enemy had in fact placed the illumination canister on the track as a decoy, and opened fire on the section with small arms and RPG fire. One of the RPG rounds hit a box of claymore mines on the last vehicle in the section, Callsign 84Bravo, as it passed through the ambush site, causing them to detonate with catastrophic results. Both the crew commander, Corporal Ken Boardman, and driver, Corporal John McCarthy, were killed instantly, as were five members of D&E Platoon; of three other wounded, one later died of his wounds. John McCarthy, although an NCO and nearing the end of his tour of duty, had been driving the carrier as there was a shortage of drivers in the Squadron at that time.

A creek line followed the road where the ambush had been effected by the enemy, and the enemy force retreated into the thick jungle surrounding the water course. It was thought that the enemy ambushing party consisted of elements of the enemy's 274 Regiment that had previously slipped through ambush cordons set for Operation OVERLORD. At 10.55 am Squadron HQ, 1 and 3 Troop converged in force at the ambush site and started patrolling the area, waiting for the enemy to emerge from the jungle creek line. In the meantime a light fire team was called in to support the dustoff flight as it took out the dead and wounded. At the same time B Company 4 RAR had been flown in and the Squadron was placed under their operational control.

The enemy again attacked at 3.20 pm that afternoon when another ambush was initiated against 3 Troop, which had moved off to make a reconnaissance to the southwest of where the enemy ambush had been initiated. After the troop had moved about 400 metres Callsign 31Alpha was hit by an RPG round, which penetrated the hull and wounded Crew Commander Corporal Len Cadzow and driver Trooper Danny Handley. On realising the severity of his crew commander's wounds, Danny Handley left his compartment and moved his crew commander from the line of enemy fire. He then set about restoring the machine guns to an operational state and immediately engaged the enemy, who were attempting to assault and capture the carrier. Corporal Cadzow's wounds were so severe that Handley had once again to render first aid before returning to the machine guns.

The enemy in the meantime had fired another five RPGs at the troop, which wounded Corporal Angus MacEwan, the crew commander of Callsign 31Bravo, and hit one of the other vehicles in the troop. The enemy also fired a claymore mine at Callsign 31 but without inflicting casualties. The troop was halted by enemy fire, with Corporal Cadzow's vehicle receiving at least 16 rounds of small arms fire and Corporal MacEwan another six rounds. The cavalry's attempts to recover were severely hampered by the number of aircraft that had converged on the area and were firing into the creek line. This necessitated the APC crews continually throwing smoke to mark their position for the pilots. The Squadron's radio net had been virtually monopolised by the pilots of the aircraft, who were told by Task Force HQ to use the net without consulting the Squadron.

1 Troop, which had moved to a flank ready to block the enemy's withdrawal and go to the assistance of 3 Troop, was ordered by the commander of B Company 4 RAR to withdraw because he had decided that he wanted to move his troops through the area. Meanwhile, 3 Troop Leader Captain Barry Wade, on board Callsign 30Alpha and 32 Section, had moved to a clearing to the southeast of the contact area.

As Sergeant Jim Warr's APC, Callsign 32, moved across the clearing it was hit with three bursts of small arms fire. The APCs engaged the area with their machine guns and then called in gunships to suppress the area before contact was broken off. Major Walker, whose Squadron HQ was accompanying B Company HQ, believed that the enemy were in the process of setting up another ambush against the APCs when they were engaged by 32 Section.

The enemy remained hidden in the heavy jungle surrounding the creek line running through the rubber trees, making it difficult for the Squadron to engage them and the bamboo making the .30 cal. machine guns largely ineffectual. The extent of damage that the Squadron had received to its vehicles and the number of dead and wounded crewmen dictated the best option of clearing the enemy—to attack the creek line with an air strike. The Squadron was withdrawn 300 metres, with the APCs from 1 and 3 Troops guarding either side of the creek in case the enemy appeared once the air strike had begun. Cobra gunships first assaulted the creek line with rockets and mini-gunfire before a team of Phantom jets arrived and dropped napalm on the area. By this stage it was late in the afternoon and nothing more could be achieved, and so the Squadron dispersed and set up ambushing sites in the area surrounding the Courtney rubber plantation. Squadron HQ, 1 and 3 Troops remained with B Company 4 RAR in the area until 14 June, when Squadron HQ and 1 Troop returned to Nui Dat with 3 Troop remaining under the operational command of 4 RAR.

It is interesting to note Major Terry Walker's comments following this engagement with the enemy. He first observes that the aircraft that converged on the area in the afternoon should have been held off while contact by the APCs was in progress and the direction and withdrawal of the enemy were being detected. It would have assisted considerably had an aircraft been made available to the Squadron to allow its 2I/C to accompany the other aircraft in order to control their movement and fire. The amount of time the APCs were in contact with the aircraft meant they were continually required to throw smoke, which eroded much time and effectively allowed the enemy to break contact. He also states that this was initially a cavalry battle, and he should have insisted to the B Company infantry commander that he be allowed to pursue the battle to the creek line before he took over. Finally, he admits that the Squadron had met an aggressive enemy in the first large contact for some time, who had stopped the Squadron 'cold'. While he does not think the enemy got out of the battle unscathed, they certainly got the better of the cavalry that day.

For his efforts and the manner in which he conducted himself when his crew commander was wounded, Trooper Dan Handley initially received the award of Mentioned in Dispatches. This award was later reviewed under the 'End of War List' and upgraded, and he received the award of the Medal of Gallantry on 7 April 2000. This award is equivalent to the Military Medal. The citation for the award of Mentioned in Dispatches reads:[8]

> On 12 June 1971, the troop in which Trooper Handley was serving reacted to a contact with the enemy. On deployment, his troop came under fire from several areas and the armoured personnel carrier which Trooper Handley was driving was struck by anti-tank projectiles, badly wounding the crew commander and jamming the turret. Trooper Handley was wounded in this engagement.
>
> On realising that his crew commander was wounded, Trooper Handley left his position, removed the crew commander from the turret, placed him on the side of the vehicle away from enemy fire and rendered first aid. He then returned to the turret and engaged the enemy with machine gun fire. Trooper Handley left the turret to render additional first aid and then again continued to engage the enemy until his vehicle was recovered. Trooper Handley and his crew commander were subsequently evacuated.

Following Operation OVERLORD the Squadron returned to what had virtually become the normal grouping and deployment, with one troop deployed with each of the two battalions and the other troop as Ready Reaction Force. The independent sections resumed their various escort and protection tasks. Generally, the Squadron continued to operate extensively in the northern part of the Phuoc Tuy and southern parts of Long Khanh provinces as well as in the Xuyen Moc area.

On the evening of 21 June, 1 Troop, which was led by Captain Rodney Earle, set up a series of ambush sites on the southern edge of the Courtney rubber plantation approximately 2 kilometres southeast of the Black Horse base in Long Khanh province. At 10.10 pm one of the sites occupied by 11 Section and 19Juliet under the command of Sergeant Ed Levy activated the ambush against a large enemy force. The enemy approached the ambush site from the west and were engaged by the picket at about 10 metres from the ambush site. The claymore mines were detonated and the area then engaged with machine gun fire, which was followed by an immediate sweep of the area. However, when the enemy counterattacked with hand grenades the sweep was stopped and the area surrounding the ambush site secured.

In the meantime the troop leader, Rodney Earle, and Sergeant Bob Veall's 12 Section broke from their nearby ambush site and again began to sweep the area. At 2.30 the following morning as 12 Section continued to sweep the area, Callsign 12Alpha heard movement at about 25 metres and engaged the area with machine gun fire. As the sweep of the area to the west continued a wounded enemy soldier was located and another surrendered as a prisoner of war. It should be noted that it had become Squadron policy to have all APCs in service in South Vietnam fitted with powerful helicopter spotlights, which aided the crews of the vehicles as they moved about in the darkness that night. The troop remained in action until 4 am the next morning. The final enemy casualty count was 12 NVA killed in action, another two wounded and two more taken prisoner. Two AK47s, four K54s, one AK50 rifle, three bags of documents and 22 packs were also recovered. There were no casualties to the troop. Intelligence reports subsequently revealed that the enemy force that had been ambushed was a 'taxation' group, which had been travelling throughout the area extorting money from the local population.

For this action and the previous ambushes initiated during the previous months of his tour of duty in Vietnam, Sergeant E.S. Levy was awarded the Distinguished Conduct Medal. The citation for his award reads:[9]

> Early on the morning of 31 December 1970, a large enemy group entered an ambush area south east of Xuyen Moc. The ambush was initiated by Sergeant Levy at precisely the right moment and for the next three hours he calmly and resolutely directed the fire of his section of three armoured personnel carriers. The fire from his small force was so effective that 21 enemy were killed and subsequent intelligence showed that many more were wounded.
>
> On the evening of 7 January 1971, Sergeant Levy was commanding his section in an ambush position near the Horseshoe feature. When an enemy group approached his position, Sergeant Levy initiated the ambush which resulted in three enemy killed and one prisoner captured.
>
> At 2210 hours on 21 June 1971, Sergeant Levy was commanding his section in an ambush position in southern Long Khanh province when an enemy group approached from the west. Contact was initiated on Sergeant Levy's order and continued until 0400 hours the following morning resulting in twelve enemy killed and three prisoners captured.
>
> On all occasions Sergeant Levy's calmness, resolution and sound judgement enabled his section to inflict heavy casualties on the enemy.

11 Section was again in action two nights later, on 23 June. At 7.20 that evening 11 Section, together with Callsign 10Bravo, moved to their ambush position some 2 kilometres southwest of Courtney hill. As the section moved through the long grass Callsign 11Alpha saw two people

at about 600 metres moving towards the west. As the section moved to investigate they sighted another 10 people in black, with weapons, running to the west. After a warning shot was fired the party was engaged, whereupon the enemy split into groups and fled in different directions. The .50 cal. machine gun proved very effective in the tall grass on this occasion, as a later search revealed one of the enemy killed and another two wounded and taken prisoner. A dustoff flight was subsequently called to take the wounded enemy soldiers to hospital, and during the evacuation the section was again engaged by the enemy with small arms fire. One round hit the ammunition belt on the .30 cal. machine gun flex mounting on Callsign 11Alpha, while another smashed the vehicle's tail light.

THE LAST MAJOR CONFLICT

The last major action in which the Squadron and the 1st Armoured Regiment fought occurred on the afternoon of 25 June 1971. V Company 4 RAR had been deployed on Operation HERMIT PARK and had been operating in an area to the west of Route 2, approximately 5 kilometres south of Courtney hill. The area in which V Company had been operating consisted of extremely thick jungle interspersed with bamboo thickets, some of the harshest country encountered by the Australians during their time in South Vietnam. Surrounding the immediate area were swampy grounds fed by bordering creeks. At mid-morning on 25 June, V Company came into contact with what was reported to be an enemy heavy machine gun company and took casualties. The infantrymen had been forced to withdraw in the face of heavy machine gun and RPG fire.

An armoured force consisting of 1 Troop from the Squadron and 3 and 5 Troops from the 1st Armoured Regiment were assembled on the northern edge of the jungle area. The force was under the command of the 1st Armoured Regiment's OC, Major Peter Bourke, with orders to assault the enemy's position. Supporting the armoured assaulting force were the guns from 104th Field Battery located at FSB Debbie, which had been established on the southern side of Courtney hill. An air strike was also called before the armoured vehicles proceeded to move towards the enemy's position.

The action commenced with US Cobra gunships firing rockets at the enemy's positions, followed by diving runs with their mini-guns. The enemy had constructed a large bunker system and the success of the air strike was hard to gauge, given the density of the jungle covering their position. The armoured force set out at approximately 1.30 pm with the tanks leading and two sections of APCs following on either side to provide rear and flank protection. I recall that the force had barely travelled 100 metres when it came under machine gun, small arms and RPG fire from the enemy, who had left their bunkers to meet the advancing Australian armour. An RPG smashed into one of the leading tanks as it attempted to move through a heavy clump of bamboo, wounding both crew commander and radio operator. The tank's machine gun was destroyed and the radios put out of action. The other two tanks in the troop that went to the damaged tank's aid also met with a barrage of RPG rounds.

In the meantime the enemy attempted to make their way down the side of the advancing armoured column and were headed towards the landing zone, where the wounded were to be evacuated. The APCs protecting the flanks of the tanks opened up with their machine guns in an attempt to contain the enemy's attempts to reach the landing zone. The tanks continued to fire their guns at a furious rate, while the enemy on a wide front continued firing their RPGs and machine guns at the tanks as they slowly moved forward. A short time later a tank leading the advance received a direct hit to its gun muzzle and another to the running gear, which wounded members of the crew. When the gunner on the now badly damaged tank attempted to fire his gun, the round ripped 20 centimetres off the end of the barrel. The battle continued fiercely, and the tanks began to run low on ammunition. In spite of this, Corporal Peter Turner on board Callsign 12Bravo drove his vehicle up to the side of both the damaged tanks and removed the wounded crew members while under fire. Corporal Geoffrey Ingram, on realising that the tanks were short of crew members because the wounded were in the process of being evacuated, volunteered to act as an operator on one of the tanks. Even as Rodney Earle gave Geoff Ingram quick basic instructions on the operation of the tank's guns they were peppered with enemy small arms fire.

Meanwhile, the enemy were attempting to overrun the position where the dustoff flights to evacuate the wounded tank crews were scheduled to land. This assault was successfully repulsed and 12 Section proceeded to evacuate the wounded from their vehicles and transport them back to the landing zone. On the return journey, the APCs were loaded with ammunition for delivery to the tanks—an extremely dangerous task given their light-skinned armour and the enemy RPG teams covering the area. The density of the jungle made it impossible to see the enemy from their hidden positions. Fortunately, the ammunition resupply was successfully completed without incident and the tanks were able to continue firing their main armaments.

The battle continued until late in the afternoon, when a decision was made to fall back to the landing zone. The two tanks that had been knocked out earlier were towed out of the jungle. A defensive harbour of all the armoured vehicles was set up around the landing zone on the edge of the jungle just as darkness was beginning to fall. There was concern that the enemy would attempt to counterattack the armoured vehicles that evening, so the guns of the 104 Field Battery at FSB Debbie and other bases were given fire missions at targets surrounding the armoured vehicles. The fire missions were logged as being 'danger—close distance', firing on and around the Squadron position in order to keep the enemy at bay during the night. So close were the shells landing to the Australian armoured vehicles' position that I recall dirt from the landing shells being thrown up and hitting the sides of the tanks and APCs.

3 Troop and Squadron HQ had supported C Company 4 RAR when they assaulted a suspected Chau Duc Company bunker system east of where 1 Troop was in action. On 25 June at 11.42 am the enemy had aimed RPGs and small arms fire at the APCs but no casualties were sustained among the members of the troop. Squadron HQ was to have been used as a blocking force on the Chau Duc bunker system, but in view of the substantial action 1 Troop had become involved in it was decided that the Squadron HQ carriers would be released at last light to enable Commanding Officer Terry Walker to better organise support and maintenance for the scattered elements of the Squadron. The morning had also seen 2 Troop in action: elements from 2 Troop had, at 1.45 am, activated an ambush against an unknown enemy force with claymore and machine gun fire 5 kilometres north of Thua Tich. Results of the ambush could not be determined.

The following morning the APCs and tanks were lined up in the formations they had adopted the previous day with the intention of returning to the enemy's position and continuing the assault. However, on reaching the enemy bunker systems it was determined that the enemy had withdrawn. The bodies of a number of enemy troops were located and the bunker system destroyed before the armoured force withdrew.

Activity for the remainder of the month remained low, although given the number of contacts in which the Squadron had been involved it was evident that the enemy were moving back into the province in force. At the end of the month 1 Troop remained under the operational command of 4 RAR in AO BIRDSVILLE in the north, 2 Troop was under the operational command of 3 RAR in AO GLENELG in the east of the province, while 3 Troop was at Nui Dat acting as Ready Reaction Force. The independent sections were charged with the protection of the engineers on construction along Routes 2 and 328 and artillery protective tasks at FSBs Debbie, Mary, Dianne, Lynette and Susan. Since the return of the Squadron from Operation OVERLORD it had resumed and undertaken numerous protective tasks. Despite the effective performance by the Squadron, Major Walker complained that he and his Squadron command continued to be denied the opportunity to exercise operational control or tactical influence. Walker and Squadron HQ, much to their frustration, spent long periods of time involved in the administration and maintenance tasks at Nui Dat.[10]

On the evening of 6 July, 21 Section led by Sergeant Jeff Tuntin were placed in an ambush site approximately 10 kilometres northeast of Xuyen Moc, where they were to ambush a track 200 metres off Route 329. The next day at 12.45 am three enemy approached the section's ambush point from the north and were engaged with claymore mines and machine gun fire. Because of the remoteness of the area in which the ambush had been sited, artillery also engaged the area. A sweep of the area failed to determine the results of this engagement.

During a subsequent sweep of the area of the ambush initiated by 11 Section on 21 June Bob Veall's 12 Section located the body of a female Viet Cong on 13 July. The body, which appeared to have been run over by an APC, was considered to be that of one of the party that had been ambushed by 11 Section and missed in the original sweep of the area. On 22 July 12 Section had another contact, when at 9.55 pm voices were heard approaching the location where the section had set up its evening ambush site some 11 kilometres due west of Cam My in southern Long Khanh province. The area was engaged with claymore mines and machine gun fire, but results were unable to be determined.

Two nights later, on 24 July, 11 Section was placed in an ambush position approximately 400 metres south of the 12 Section ambush site of 22 July. At 8.30 pm, movement and voices were heard to the south of the ambush site and the area was engaged by detonating the claymore mines that had been established along the killing zone, although results could not be determined. Ten minutes later, over in the eastern sector of the province, 33 Section led by John Pass engaged two enemy troops from its ambush site near Route 328, 4.5 kilometres due east of Xuyen Moc. It was later determined that the two enemy were the leading elements of a larger force which was following, and so the area was engaged with mortar fire as the enemy force retreated to the north.

The crew of Callsign 10Bravo had a lucky escape on 25 July when the troop rendezvoused in an area to the west of the Black Horse base in Long Khanh province to take on supplies. As the troop moved out of its position 10Bravo detonated an anti-tank mine, which caused only minor damage to the vehicle. However, the hole in the ground left by the explosion revealed an enormous amount of chicom explosive that was wrapped in plastic. Fortunately for the crew of Trooper Paul Shearman and 2nd Lieutenant Phil Lawrence, the explosive had been dampened and only a small portion of the chicom explosive had ignited when the mine detonated. A subsequent check of the 'mine map' revealed that the troop had rendezvoused close to the notorious Route 320, where anti-tank mines proliferated and several wrecked hulls of APCs from the US 11th Cavalry littered the area. The troop had unwittingly 'parked' in a minefield and were lucky to have moved out of the area without casualty.

On 28 July the majority of the Squadron's vehicles were deployed on Operation IRON FOX, where they were tasked to act as a blocking force in support of 4 RAR in the northern sector of the province. The deployment proved to be a relatively static task with three simple moves taking place during the entire operation. One of the early tasks assigned to the Squadron was to secure a landing zone so that 4 RAR HQ and a section of guns could fly in under the cover of darkness. Unfortunately, 2 Troop, which had been assigned this task, was required to move in total darkness without the aid of its lights and was incorrectly positioned. The movement was delayed while 2 Troop was repositioned in order to secure the landing zone.[11]

Two interesting observations outlining issues that had affected the Squadron were made in relation to Operation IRON FOX. The first concerned the lack of information that was being passed from Task Force HQ to Squadron HQ. The primary explanation given was that the Squadron did not possess secure means for the passage of information by radio. This meant that either the Task Force HQ had to provide the Squadron with secure means or the Task Force's Command Post staff would have to comply with the Squadron's means of security by encoding all transmissions. The second issue identified concerned the delay caused to the 4 RAR HQs' 'fly-in' due to the misplacement of 2 Troop, which was tasked to provide LZ security. This problem could easily have been overcome had the Squadron been given the use of a helicopter and an officer dispatched to identify the correct position of the LZ rather than leaving the APCs to navigate in the darkness, a near-impossible task over such a large area. The Squadron's request for the assignment of aircraft to assist them on operations continued to fall on deaf ears within Task Force command, although this was the norm in the US Cavalry units and for Australian battalion commanders, who had their own aircraft.

At the beginning of August the Squadron's deployment saw 1 Troop under the operational control of 4 RAR and 2 Troop under the operational control of 3 RAR. 3 Troop was the Ready Reaction Force, while the independent sections continued their task of providing route security and FSB protection. Throughout the month the Squadron continued to be heavily committed but again through the system of detaching elements under the operational control of other units, with the resultant exclusion of Squadron HQ from the command and control function. Terry Walker argued that, while there was value in infantry battalions having a troop under 'Opcon' for various phases of an operation, it should not be regarded as the norm (as it had become), and staff should have been more flexible in changing groupings.

THE FINAL MONTHS

On the evening of 18 August 1971, word reached the Task Force that the Australian government had announced it would be withdrawing the Task Force from South Vietnam, and it was anticipated that the majority of the Australian troops in South Vietnam would be home by Christmas that year. I well recall the moment the announcement was made, as I had been dispatched on an evening clearing patrol outside the wire of FSB Centenary just on dusk. The section in the patrol had travelled about 100 metres from the base and had 'cut' its engines for the evening stand-to, when silence was observed for about 10 minutes. Shortly after the engines had been shut off, wild cheering could be heard emanating from FSB Centenary, which alarmed the patrol as it was highly unusual behaviour and breached the security of the base. It was not until the patrol returned to the base that it learnt the news that the war would shortly be over for its members.

The following day, 19 August, 2 Troop was deployed to the west of Route 2 about 1 kilometre southeast of the Black Horse base in Long Khanh province when one of the carriers from the troop detonated an anti-tank mine. This was a pressure-type chicom mine with an estimated exposive strength of 35 pounds of explosive. Only light damage was sustained by the vehicle and none of the crew were reported as sustaining casualties. On 22 August elements from 2 Troop were in an ambush site some 4 kilometres south of Courtney hill and adjacent to Route 2. At 10.30 pm the ambush was activated when north-to-south movement was detected, but a search of the area the next day failed to reveal any results.

Despite the government's announcement that the Task Force would be withdrawn, this was not the end of the Squadron's involvement in the war. It was decided that a covering force comprising a troop from the Squadron and a company from 4 RAR would remain until all the Australian troops had been withdrawn. Lieutenant C.E. Stephens would replace Captain Rodney Earle as Troop Leader, 1 Troop, which would remain in South Vietnam during the Task Force's withdrawal phase.

As at the end of August 1971, the Squadron establishment had grown to 169 members, which was made up of 15 officers, 22 warrant officers/sergeants, and 132 other ranks. The remainder of August was spent reorganising the personnel within the three troops and independent sections as decisions were made on who would remain in South Vietnam to oversee the withdrawal and who would be returning to Australia. Generally, those who had been in the country the shortest time were selected to remain in South Vietnam, while the remaining members of the Squadron would be returning to Australia and/or the Squadron's new base at Townsville in Queensland, where the Regiment was to be relocated.

While these administrative matters were attended to, the Squadron continued its deployments. At the beginning of September the disposition of the Squadron saw Squadron HQ and the independent sections on protection tasks at FSBs Tanunda, Robin and Centenary and at Duc Than. 1 and 2 Troops were deployed in the north of the province and were operating out of FSB Debbie, while 3 Troop was deployed with the FSVs from Support Troop in the northeastern sector of the province along Route 328 between Nui Nhon and Thua Tich.

On 2 September at 9.10 pm substantial movement was detected outside the wire at FSB Centenary, and the area was engaged with small arms fire and M79s. At 10.55 pm further movement was detected and three enemy were engaged. 83 Section, led by Corporal Jack Hannah, which up to that time was located outside the base, was requested to move back into the base before being tasked to investigate further movement on the wire at 11.30 pm. On a sweep of the area one enemy was seen to move away after he was engaged with machine gun fire. Results of the engagement could not be determined. At 6.30 am on 11 September, 23 Section, which was the Ready Reaction Force, was located on the top of Courtney hill and was reacted to assist the Tracker Platoon from 4 RAR. The platoon had been in contact with an enemy force on the edge of the Courtney rubber plantation some 3 kilometres west of Route 2. On arrival at the platoon's position the section undertook a sweep of the area, where four bodies were recovered and transported back to Courtney hill for identification and intelligence purposes.

The enemy tried to breach the wire of FSB Robin to the west of Route 2 on 12 September at 11.05 pm. Illumination flares were fired and Callsign 82 engaged the area with .50 cal. machine gun fire after one of the enemy troops was seen running into a nearby stand of rubber trees. Early on 17 September at 1.05 am, heavy enemy movement was detected 300 metres southeast of FSB Debbie. A number of lights were seen moving and the area was engaged with the .30 cal. machine guns from Support Troop's FSVs. At 2 am more lights were detected and the area was engaged with the FSVs 76 mm canon and .30 cal. machine guns, with unknown results.

Route 2, which had previously been regarded as relatively safe for travel, again became a target for the enemy. On 20 September at 7.45 am, as Callsign 10Bravo accompanied by 11 Section, led by Sergeant Peter McLay, moved from Nui Dat to the Courtney hill area, it was ambushed by an enemy force consisting of 20 enemy troops. The enemy's ambush was sited north of Ngai Giao over a 100-metre area, with the enemy located in three different positions. The ambush on the carriers was initiated by the enemy, which fired RPGs at the leading APC, Callsign 11Alpha. The first RPG round missed the vehicle, but the 'splash' from the rocket when it hit the road ricocheted and wounded Crew Commander Corporal Ike Robins in the head. The APCs immediately counterattacked by engaging the area with .30 and .50 cal. machine gun fire, which resulted in one of the enemy ambushing party being killed. One AK47 rifle and a quantity of equipment was also captured.

The next day at 10.15 am the FSVs of Support Troop were deployed approximately 6 kilometres north of Thua Tich on Route 330 when they contacted one enemy soldier moving along an adjacent track. The enemy was engaged and killed and his AK47 rifle captured. Meanwhile, 1 Troop was engaged as a blocking force for D Company 4 RAR around the Nui Le area some 6 kilometres southeast of Courtney hill. Earlier in the day the troop had transported D Company into the area, but when the vegetation became too thick the company commander ordered his troops to dismount and proceed on foot. The troop immediately withdrew when the infantry had dismounted in order to reduce the noise factor created by the vehicles' engines. A short time later D Company ran into a heavily defended enemy bunker system and spent the afternoon in heavy contact with the enemy. By this time the tanks from 1st Armoured Regiment had been withdrawn from service, and it was said that the area was too close for the Squadron's APCs to access. If ever there was any need to emphasise the value of Armour during the war, it was in this action. With the end of Australia's involvement in the war so close but without the close support previously afforded by Armour, this action resulted in five of the 4 RAR infantrymen being killed and another 23 wounded.

That evening elements from 2 Troop, who were placed in an ambush some 4.5 kilometres due west of the 4 RAR contact earlier that day, activated an ambush at 10.30 pm. The claymore mines surrounding the ambushed site were detonated, but results could not be determined. Earlier in the afternoon Lieutenant Ross McCormack's Support Troop, which had been deployed on Operation IVANHOE with 3 RAR, had located an extremely well-camouflaged camp/training area about 5 kilometres northwest of Thua Tich. The complex, which consisted of 24 structures and 10 bunkers, included lecture rooms which were found under some of the larger houses, with the largest measuring 2.5 × 4 metres. These structures were later destroyed by elements from 3 RAR before they returned to Nui Dat, to prepare for the battalion's return to Australia. Meanwhile, various elements from the Squadron continued to deploy in the area, and the following evening at 8.50 elements from 3 Troop engaged an enemy soldier about 700 metres from where Support Troop had discovered the training camp. Results of the engagement could not be determined.

1 Troop, which continued to operate in southern Long Khanh province, was deployed in the Courtney rubber plantation where two of its carriers detonated mines. The troop had been operating in this particular area for several months and regarded the area within the wide expanses of the rubber trees as relatively free of anti-tank mines, so much so that the crews drove at speed through the rubber trees without paying much heed to any danger. On 25 September at 12.30 pm, Callsign 11Alpha, which was leading the troop back towards Route 2, detonated an anti-tank mine. Crew Commander Corporal Ike Robins and the driver, Trooper Kevin Brakewell, were both wounded and evacuated to 1 Australian Field Hospital at Vung Tau. The vehicle sustained extensive damage. As Callsign 12Bravo drove forward to assist it detonated another mine, which threw the carrier against a nearby rubber tree, preventing the vehicle from turning completely over on its side. Crew Commander Corporal Peter Turner and one of the mini-team members were wounded and evacuated while the driver, Trooper Ray Peele, remained on duty. The hole in the ground from the explosion measured 1 × 1.5 metres and demonstrated the effectiveness of the belly armour, as much more serious damage and wounds would otherwise have occurred. Both mines were thought to be chicom block-type devices and were pressure-switch activated. It was believed that mining had been carried out by elements of the enemy's D65 Engineer Battalion and had been in place for approximately 12 months but recently fitted with initiating switches. Although the wounds suffered by those evacuated were not serious, this incident reinforced the suspicion that the enemy were going to continue to attack the Squadron's vehicles, and indicated that the Australians should not take their intended withdrawal from Phuoc Tuy province lightly. Both vehicles were recovered by

23 Section from 2 Troop, which dragged the carriers and their detached belly armour plates back to Courtney hill.

During the month Terry Walker took the opportunity to trial a traditional cavalry reconnaissance concept in the utilisation of the Squadron's vehicles. With the withdrawal of 3 RAR, elements from the Squadron, including the FSVs, were deployed along Route 328 from the junction of Routes 327/328 northwards. As the Squadron was given such a large area in which to deploy, the opportunity was taken to re-organise Support Troop into two cavalry troops using some of the APCs from 3 Troop. Two FSVs were joined by three APCs. This use of cavalry, extending over two weeks, proved a very useful exercise in cavalry troop organisation. The APCs were used as scout vehicles supported by the readily available 76 mm guns on the FSVs, and this proved a viable organisation. Little difficulty was experienced with mobility, which was dependent only on the experience of the FSV crews.[12]

Captain Rodney Earle, who had led 1 Troop during his second tour of duty in South Vietnam, returned to Australia in September 1971. His effectiveness as a troop leader had enabled him to mould a very cohesive troop and successfully engage the enemy. For his efforts, Captain R.M. Earle received the award of Mentioned in Dispatches. The citation for his award reads:[13]

> On arrival in South Vietnam Captain Earle was appointed to command 1 Troop and has continued in that capacity. Immediately after arrival, Captain Earle was deployed on operations and has been on operations constantly since then.
>
> By an excellent display of devotion to duty, practical and theoretical knowledge, and the finest qualities of leadership, he has welded his troop into an extremely effective and professional group. During his period of command, his troop has accounted for 57 enemy killed or captured.
>
> In all matters pertaining to command and control of his troop, Captain Earle has shown a high degree of skill and initiative.

At the beginning of October 1971, 1 Troop and Support Troop were at Duc Than under the operational control of 4 RAR. 2 Troop was at Nui Dat as the Ready Reaction Force while 3 Troop was deployed at Xuyen Loc for village protection; the Cavalry Troop had been stationed at FSB Robin. On 5 October at 10.51 am an APC from 1 Troop detonated an M14 anti-personnel mine approximately 2 kilometres on the eastern side of the Binh Ba rubber plantation. No damage was sustained by the vehicle, nor were any casualties reported among the crew.

The Squadron had been scheduled to depart Nui Dat on 16 October, but in the two intervening weeks it continued to operate as a whole unit, providing security for the Task Force base as the various other units started to withdraw. 3 RAR was withdrawn and returned to Australia, leaving 4 RAR and the Squadron to provide security and protection as well as all the tasks necessary to keeping the Task Force base functional. Ambushing throughout the now diminished TAOR continued on a wide scale, although the protection of Nui Dat became a priority. Intelligence indicated that the number of enemy troops throughout the province had dramatically increased, and the feeling was that the enemy might try to give the Australians a 'bloody nose' before they departed the province. In fact, captured enemy documents indicated that the 33rd NVA Regiment had precisely that objective in mind. To counter this move by the enemy the Squadron adopted a proactive role, with its APCs constantly deployed to show the enemy that the Task Force still had considerable fire power available.

The week preceding the Task Force's departure from Nui Dat saw the Squadron packing up and destroying ammunition that had passed its use-by date and could not be returned to Australia. An advance party was dispatched to Vung Tau to set up temporary quarters at the Peter Badcoe recreational facility, where the Squadron would be based pending its return to Australia. Already some members of the Squadron (mainly National Servicemen) had returned to Australia. For almost a month large convoys had travelled between Nui Dat and Vung Tau as units packed up and moved out. The Squadron's final night, 15 October, saw the entire Squadron back in Nui Dat, which proved both a joyous and nostalgic occasion for the members of the Squadron. Despite protocol, both officers and sergeants were invited into the OR canteen for a farewell party. It was perhaps fitting that, on the evening before the Squadron departed, the men who had borne the brunt of the Squadron's action should be joined by the senior ranks to reminisce and say farewell.

The next afternoon, 2 and 3 Troops and the independent sections, who had spent the entire day protecting the base as the last units packed up and moved, formed up outside the main gates for their final run down to Vung Tau. As had happened in the past, the Squadron was the last unit to leave Nui Dat, having been the first unit to arrive on the establishment of the Task Force base in June 1966. When the Squadron departed, 1 Troop moved over to the 161 Reconnaissance Flight lines near Luscombe airfield and joined troops from 4 RAR, where the now seriously compressed base would be located. Almost overnight, local scavengers moved in and stripped the huts and infrastructure that had once comprised the Australian Task Force base.

The members of the Squadron now in Vung Tau set about cleaning the carriers and packing up equipment for the trip home, while waiting their turn to either catch a flight home or be returned by HMAS *Sydney*.

It had previously been announced that on its return to Australia, the 3rd Cavalry Regiment would be relocated to Townsville and take up residence in Laverack Barracks. The last members of the Squadron, minus 1 Troop, sailed for Australia on 9 December 1971.

Back at Nui Dat, Lieutenant Chris Stephens, who had assumed command of 1 Troop pending its withdrawal in early 1972, deployed his troop on tasks that would ensure the protection and security of the base. While the remainder of the Squadron cleaned its APCs, 1 Troop acted as Ready Reaction Force and provided a 'screen' from the base at Nui Dat for the Task Force now located in Vung Tau. Patrols were undertaken by the troop out as far as Long Tan but no contacts were reported during this period. When the bulk of the Squadron's members sailed on HMAS *Sydney* on 9 December, 1 Troop, which had been titled A Squadron 3rd Cavalry Regiment-Detachment, moved down to the Logistics Base at Vung Tau. The Detachment was housed with the 102 Field Workshop and spent a three-month period providing support for the Logistics Base, which was by this time Australia's only major commitment in South Vietnam; its combat role effectively finished when it moved out of the Task Force base at Nui Dat on 16 October 1971.

Dave Lester, who was one of the three officers attached to the Detachment, recalls that those members remaining at Vung Tau spent a fairly relaxed period as they awaited their return to Australia. While there was no further contact with the enemy, the Detachment was required to remain at a constant state of readiness and conduct patrols to ensure the security of the Logistics Base. The Detachment's vehicle inventory consisted of 12 M113A1 APCs, two M125 mortar carriers, one M577 ACV and six FSVs. The Detachment spent its time cleaning vehicles in preparation for its return to Australia and providing a security presence. A fitness program was undertaken to keep those not cleaning the carriers occupied, while others were placed on forklift operator training courses to help load the remaining stores and equipment onto the ships bound for Australia. The experience of living by the sea at the Logistics Base proved quite a tonic for many members of the troop.

Sergeant Neville Luff, who had already seen one tour of duty in South Vietnam, returned for a second tour in July 1971. Unfortunately, soon after arrival he was returned to Australia suffering a severe illness. He died in the Repatriation General Hospital at Concord, Sydney, on 28 December. During 1971, the Squadron lost two of its members killed in action and one who died as a result of illness. Another 23 were either wounded or injured.

The Squadron's role in the Vietnam War finally ceased on 5 March 1972, when the last remaining members of the Detachment boarded HMAS *Sydney* for the journey home to Australia.

13

Conclusions

The Squadron had spent a total of five years and 10 months in South Vietnam. During that time it was involved in almost every Task Force operation in either an armoured personnel carrier or cavalry role, and saw action in most of the battles in which the Task Force had fought.

The men who served with the Regiment were not all RAAC members, and it would be remiss to conclude this history without acknowledging the part played by vital elements of other corps who served with the squadrons during their time in South Vietnam. Most notable were the Light Aid Detachment (RAEME) fitters, who became just as 'black hatted' as their Armoured Corps counterparts. The engineers from the mine-clearing teams were always reliable, and were only too willing to turn their hands to whatever was needed. Often during an advance when the situation looked dangerous, the APCs would be out in front of the infantry, but in front of the APCs were the 'mini-teams'. The cooks were always vital to morale: one squadron commander especially recalls at the end of one very long and arduous operation receiving a freshly baked basket of salad rolls. The sergeant cook had decided that the men needed a change of diet after an extended period of C rations and took it on himself to dispatch the rolls to his counterparts still out in the bush. Sometimes the cooks would ask to go along on an operation as spare crewmen and they always seemed more dedicated after the experience. Finally, the Vietnamese Army interpreters quickly identified with the squadrons of the Regiment.

During the years of the Squadron's involvement in the war, a large percentage of its vehicles had been involved in mine incidents and anti-tank rocket attacks. The vehicles that were returned to Australia following the end of the Squadron's involvement in the war were near the end of their useful life, and required extensive overhaul. Several vehicles carried both mine and RPG damage. One vehicle on its return to Australia had a 15-centimetre hole in the side of the engine deck where it had been hit by an RPG. It had been retained in service pending an anticipated pullout by the Australian Task Force.

The addition of belly armour in 1970 had reduced the rate of mine incident casualties, but not enough time had elapsed to ascertain its full impact, especially against the larger mines that the enemy were starting to employ. If nothing else, the belly armour afforded APC crews a degree of comfort by ensuring that if they detonated a mine of moderate size there was a good chance that they would survive. At the very least it was felt that crew members would avoid the serious leg wounds and other wounds that crews had suffered prior to the fitting of the belly armour.

Unfortunately, no armour or defence system could be devised to protect the carriers and the crews against direct hits from RPG rockets. These weapons, which were employed extensively by the enemy, remained a significant threat to Regiment members. However, the lack of adequate training of enemy troops prevented these weapons from being deployed to their optimum capability. Very often the RPG weapon would be handed to the most inexperienced troops, with the AK47 rifle being carried by the more senior or experienced soldiers. This weapon allocation meant that inexperienced soldiers were instructed in the operation of the RPG but never given the opportunity to fire a practice round. Very often the RPG operator's initial combat engagement was his first, so an RPG round fired from a distance more than 100 metres stood a reasonable chance of missing its target through sheer inexperience. When ambushes and attacks were sprung from well-concealed positions using this weapon the results were catastrophic.

The final 'official' casualty count for the Regiment during its time as a part of the Task Force was as follows: killed in action, 17; accidental deaths, two; died in country, one; wounded in action, 110; injured in action, 12; accidentally injured, 11. These were significant casualty figures and reflect the dangerous nature of the Regiment's operations. While a small number of members who served with the squadrons in South Vietnam were initially posted to 1 ATF, it has been ascertained that a total of 1016 were posted and served with the 1 APC Squadron and A and B Squadrons of the 3rd Cavalry Regiment during their tours of duty in South Vietnam. It is thus a reasonable assumption that one person in about every seven could expect to be a casualty of the war.

However, while the above casualty figures were those officially listed, in reality the casualty count was much higher. A great proportion of those members who served with the squadrons in Vietnam were involved in mine, rocket attacks and non-combat injuries, which in many instances resulted in wounds and injuries. For example, minor shrapnel wounds, damage to eardrums and back injuries often sustained by crew members in these incidents were never reported, because the crew members themselves feared that if evacuated they might be removed from their troop/section and posted to another troop/section. Many members of the Squadron who rightly should have been evacuated remained with their troop or section with their mates and the people they had grown to know and trust.

I can well relate to this sentiment. When my hand was crushed under a track I elected to remain with the troop to which I was attached as an operator rather than be removed to another, unfamiliar troop. A number of members of the Regiment who contacted me related similar instances. In fact, the pride each member held for his troop was a significant determining factor in the actions of many members of the squadrons that served in Vietnam. To this day members still associate themselves with the troops in which they served, and many reunions have been organised on that basis. As a result of many of the Regiment's members' devotion to duty and regard for their mates, the unreported casualty rate for the Regiment's service in South Vietnam is thought to be much higher than the reported rate.

A number of members of the Regiment received imperial awards and honours for their service in South Vietnam. A summary of these awards is as follows: Members of the Order of the British Empire, one; Military Cross, three; Distinguished Conduct Medal, two; Military Medal, two; Mentioned in Dispatches, 24.

The following members received an Australian Honour Award under the end-of-war list: Commendation for Distinguished Service, J.C. Grey, K.C. Tunbridge, T.F. Walker; Medal for Gallantry, T.H. Arrowsmith; Medal of Gallantry, D.J. Handley. Note: Lieutenant R.K. Hill received the award of the Military Cross for his service with 4/19 PWLH and 1 APC Troop.

The following members of the Regiment received United States and Vietnamese honours: American Army Commendation for Valour, D.E. Pakes; American Army Commendation for Service, F.J. Beattie, G. Millington; Vietnamese Cross of Gallantry–Gold Star, H.J. Coates, R.L.M. Tingley; Vietnamese Cross of Gallantry–Silver Star, E.S. Levy; Vietnamese Cross of Gallantry–Bronze Star, G. Kemble, R.L.M. Tingley

The charter of service imposed on the 3rd Cavalry Regiment was one of the most demanding of all those issued to the Australian units that served in South Vietnam. The casualties sustained and awards received by the Regiment themselves tell the story of what the members endured.

The final chapter of the 3rd Cavalry Regiment's history was

enacted on 14 May 1986, almost 14 years after the unit had returned from Vietnam. On that day at Enoggera in Queensland, His Royal Highness Prince Phillip, Duke of Edinburgh, presented to the 3rd/4th Cavalry Regiment the 3rd Cavalry Regiment's Guidon. Invitations to witness the parade and the accompanying ceremony were sent to every member who had served with the Regiment in Vietnam. Many hundreds of former members, some of whom travelled long distances, arrived to witness this event. In his presentation speech, the Prince paid a tribute to the former members of the Regiment in attendance and those unable to attend—to their bravery and the devotion of their service. Thus concluded the history of the 3rd Cavalry Regiment, which like so many units had already been amalgamated with another unit out of economic necessity. The Guidon, however, will forever bear testament to the Regiment's record of service in Vietnam.

Gallipoli, Palestine, France, the jungles of the Southwest Pacific and the previous role undertaken by the 4th/19th PWLH in South Vietnam are names preceding the Regiment's history. What the 3rd Cavalry Regiment achieved during the Vietnam War upheld the traditions and fighting qualities of its predecessors, and the actions of the men who fought with the 3rd Cavalry Regiment in Vietnam will be forever at the forefront of Australian military history.

The 3rd Cavalry Regiment in Vietnam

Name	Regimental number	Squadron(s) served
Abbott RL	1732920	A & B
Abdoo GC *	216945	A & B
Abolins EV	136578	B
Absalom AR	53227	A
Adams E	210869	A
Adams J	5411525	B
Affleck JR	3797698	A & B
Aitken GA	5715155	A & B
Aitkin G	215620	A
Albert RA *	38338	A
Aldridge LJ	3793924	A & B
Alexander R	217888	B
Allen WL	3787207	A
Allsopp MH	1731830	A
Almond NN	3789278	A
Amtsberg HH	4717527	A
Anderson AC	29579	A & B
Anderson PT	2794969	A
Angus MG	3787025	1 & A
Anton G	3788957	A
Ansty JK *	61355	B
Apps RK *	2788335	A & B
Armstrong BJ	2788587	B
Arnott AE	39119	A & B
Arrowsmith TH (MID)	235254	A & B
Ashman KC	57080	A
Asquith RA	2787813	A & B
Astridge GA	38754	A
Atherton NP	313986	A
Atkins C	3789137	A
Atkinson GE	3787828	1 & A
Atkinson NP	1734730	B
Atkinson P *	217417	A
Auhl GP	213143	A
Ayre G	215445	A
Bailey LA	13979	A & B
Baird RJ	4718295	A
Baker AC	243470	A
Baker DJ	436667	B
Baker KW	5411228	A
Ball ET	38554	A
Ball GG	39779	B
Ball KR	37480	1 & A
Ballance JR	42785	(NZ)
Ballantyne JM	4718982	A
Ballentine GK	37800	A & B
Bandy GW	5717580	A
Banks DP	167115	A & B

Name	Regimental number	Squadron(s) served	Name	Regimental number	Squadron(s) served
Bannister KL	213276	1, A & B	Bloor DG	2141142	A & B
Barclay MJ	4410905	A & B	Blythe RO ⋆	44047	A & B
Barkle J	1732548	A	Boardman KJ +	218336	A & B
Barnes DG	4720150	B	Boccamazzo P	5716570	A & B
Bartlett LJ	2794293	A & B	Bohrnsen P ⋆	43732	A & B
Bartos JC	213604	A	Bone WS	5717512	A
Bastian DM	217352	A & B	Bonnefin KB	214535	A & B
Bateman PJ	3796062	A & B	Bonser LJ	52735	A
Bates I	1411064	A	Booth VJ	216533	A
Batten RA	3788717	A	Boreland RW ⋆	4410363	A
Batterbury JE	5714022	A	Borg TS	313358	B
Baxter MC ⋆	36841	A	Borlace DG +	42809	A
Bayliss GV	243479	A	Bott DN	4720884	A & B
Beaman KJ	534950	A	Bourne DH	235368	A
Beare ND	38403	1, A & B	Boulter JG	38354	A
Beasley RR	2793083	A & B	Bourke J ⋆	218971	B
Beattie FJ	19955	A	Bowen GJ	2412297	A & B
Beauchamp PW	1733712	A	Bowler IR	2789594	B
Beaumont R	217375	A & B	Bowman GJ	2412424	A & B
Beazley EN	216307	A	Boyd WA	312520	A & B
Beazley RP ⋆	5715599	A & B	Boyle WM	313628	A
Bednarski RG	3411838	A & B	Brady BP	4410734	1 & A
Beeton AJ	214587	1	Brady RE	1735315	A & B
Behan AG	3786623	1 & A	Brabant WM	2785068	A
Ben-Avi Z	3179822	B	Brakewell KR	5717522	A
Bennett AS	3789067	A	Brennan S	39707	B
Bennett KS	4720163	B	Briggs LA	216152	A
Berry AR	3791682	A & B	Bright LB ⋆	519146	A & B
Berry KH	15650	A	Brooker CL	1733555	A & B
Bicheno R	38680	A	Brooker JW	215778	A
Billing J	4717762	A	Brookes D	44747	A & B
Bingham LC ⋆	216874	A & B	Brooks DW	42639	A
Binning WH	54918	1 & A	Brown AD	3799345	A
Birch JA	28039	B	Brown DG	2795932	A
Birse RC	218184	B	Brown ML	1735819	A & B
Black BJ	1735119	B	Brown NH	312900	B
Black WN	38502	B	Brown RK	2786511	A
Blackbourn SJ	534337	A & B	Brown PL	2137762	A & B
Blacket CR ⋆	2244171	B	Brumfield KR	44013	A & B
Blackwell CR	6709821	A	Bryant IJ	335155	1 & A
Blackwood PF	114484	A & B	Buckler TC	1200158	A

Name	Regimental number	Squadron(s) served	Name	Regimental number	Squadron(s) served
Buckingham AG ⋆	42471	1, A & B	Casey GR	1735297	A & B
Buckley AP	2785724	A	Casteldine KR	5713799	1 & A
Buffett DJ	218742	A & B	Catterall JW	39966	A & B
Bulkeley JL	214981	B	Chalk AJ	2785659	A
Bull RJ	2795554	A	Chalk DJ ⋆	157567	B
Bullock AG	54601	1 & A	Chant AW	213971	A
Bulmer RR	1202761	A & B	Chapman BK	2792610	A & B
Bunworth L	213922	1 & A	Chapman DJ	1736230	A & B
Burchill IG	1733144	A & B	Chapman RJ	219729	A & B
Burdett KJ	4721595	A	Chard JE	445704	A & B
Burgher WD	44323	B	Cheetham NJ ⋆	5716795	B
Burkenhagen HR	55529	A	Chester BR	16880	1, A & B
Burnell JW	1200259	A & B	Chester GR	114541	A
Burnett DR	5716422	B	Cheyne CL	175466	A
Burnie RA	39896	B	Chigwidden MG	4719258	A & B
Burns AC	1731220	1 & A	Childs RI	1733564	A & B
Burrage DL	2137783	A	Chinnick LM	2788351	A & B
Burrell LR	214573	1	Churchland WF	2790641	B
Burton PT ⋆	1411349	A & B	Cielens MN	43870	A
Bush R	3798345	A	Clapp GW	4717896	A
Butler MJ	2793373	A & B	Clark GW	3799004	A
Byers RG	1735309	A & B	Clarke PS	3411409	A
Byrne MJ	2793958	A & B	Clary WM	219954	A & B
Byrnes PJ	2784402	A	Cleary RD	213515	1 & A
Cabban AL	23650	1 & A	Clements BA	56209	A
Cadzow LJ ⋆	37568	A	Clements PE +	54570	1
Calder WW ⋆	2792359	B	Clifford LI ⋆	42132	1 & A
Callaghan LP	27187	A & B	Clifton DW	3786671	1 & A
Callison DJ	5717142	A	Coates HJ (MBE)	17023	B
Callow J	3787066	1 & A	Cole SJ	3797195	A & B
Cameron BJ	16932	A & B	Cole SL	38656	A & B
Cameron SP	5411495	A & B	Coleman DA	1200230	A & B
Campbell AL ⋆	629166	A & B	Coleman PM	38628	A
Campbell CR	17107	A	Collett RA	4411014	A
Campbell IJ ⋆	5716008	B	Collins DJ	3787452	1 & A
Canuto JG	157616	A & B	Collins EJ (MID)	214099	A
Carlyle H +	43941	A & B	Comrie RK	3788691	A
Carpenter CR	27013	A	Connell JT ⋆	37595	A
Carroll JJ	3798394	A	Conroy DL ⋆	4718111	A
Carter JA (DCM)	38317	1 & A	Conway GJ	2795096	A
Casey AL +	218715	B	Cooper R ⋆	54604	B

Name	Regimental number	Squadron(s) served
Costa TJ	3796129	A & B
Cotton RW	5713809	1 & A
Cowell BA	15465	A & B
Cowley IS	4721816	A
Cox BD	42613	A
Cox GA	2794973	A
Cox IW	2793415	A & B
Cox KP	520118	A
Cox RD	56275	A
Cranston JA *	1201032	A & B
Cressey J	5713811	1 & A
Cribb DG	217563	A
Crisp DM	2141091	A & B
Crockett PW	2412214	A & B
Crossman JF (MID)	38619	A
Croydon GJ	1200903	A
Cullen AG	218953	B
Cullen NJ	215606	1 & A
Cunninghan DP	217130	A
Currell SJ	218182	A & B
Curtain AJ	342561	A & B
Dadd IN	5713630	1 & A
Daley PF	217983	A & B
Dalton AK	3794475	B
Dando B	243440	A
Daniel IC	3794981	B
Daniels WC	2787760	A & B
Dann DW *	6410229	A & B
Davidson J	54739	A
Davies DW * (MID)	215419	1, A & B
Davies RW *	44947	B
Davies WG	42430	A
Davis GK	2794398	B
Davis MJ	35783	1 & A
Davis PT	1733580	A & B
Davison PO	2791118	B
Dean LJ	3787472	A
Dearling CD	45433	A
Decarli D	1203145	A
Dee GC	2785082	A
Delacey JJ	1731106	1 & A
Delaney BJ	37703	A & B
Denison JA	4718123	A & B
DeVere R (MC)	42463	A & B
Deveson JF	3789149	A
Devitt RJ	423328	B
Dewar KI +	5715633	A
Dickson JS	2789430	A
Digweed JF	16265	B
Dillon TJ	1734561	B
Dinys W	411240	A & B
Dobe RJ	1734562	A
Dodson DT	3787351	1
Donnellan MA	4720096	B
Donnelly TB	1735003	B
Donovan CD *	311480	A
Dore PA	3792362	B
Dore PT	3797694	A & B
Douglas JM *	311415	A
Douma JM	3788695	A
Dowd BC	3791788	A & B
Doyle DG +	219663	B
Drinkwater MB	43018	1 & A
Droop PR	3789125	A
Drumgold LJ	216206	B
Dryden RC	215966	A & B
Dufty MJ	217387	A & B
Duggin AJ	3411433	1 & A
Dunhillmartin JP *	3793762	B
Dunlop BW	3793766	B
Dunstan LJ	1734256	A & B
Durkin RJ	2792491	A & B
Duthie JM	216382	A & B
Dyer RL	37296	A & B
Dyson D	3411719	A
Earle BG	3792256	A & B
Earle RM (MID)	335157	A & B
Earnshaw MD	3793148	A & B
Eaton MP *	38332	A
Ebzery IC *	2791702	B
Ebzery R	2794723	A
Edwards PE	37640	A & B

Name	Regimental number	Squadron(s) served	Name	Regimental number	Squadron(s) served
Eilola AF *	1200295	A	Formby DA	53321	B
Elfverson CR	215738	A & B	Fottrill P	1200016	1 & A
Elliott MD *	3794610	B	Fowler RD	16708	A
Ellis TC	217107	A & B	Fox JM	43890	A & B
Elwell LJ *	137795	A & B	Francis LC	1733797	A & B
Enever GK	397717	A	Fraser RC	3791409	A
English RM	2786902	A	Fratus DJ	214632	A
Errington DA	214523	1 & A	Frazer KN	1200808	A
Etchells JH	210824	B	French VA +	1202185	B
Evans ED	36818	A & B	Frisken ER	216384	A & B
Evans JA	4720313	B	Fryer AB	2190424	A
Eyles OF	135725	A	Fuller RJ	54166	A
Fairfax TV	2786610	A	Gammelgaard AW	220286	A
Fanning LE	3794689	B	Gardiner AR	1731293	A & B
Farr JL	4717924	A	Gardiner WS	2790347	B
Farr MK	448284	A	Garvey DK	2785285	A
Farr PR	2789458	A & B	Gazzard DE	36765	A & B
Farrand RL	44280	A & B	Gelhaar WG	16666	1 & A
Fedorowytsch J	38582	A & B	George RG	38608	A
Fenton LO	1733716	A & B	Gibson SR	215617	A & B
Fenton RJ	4410728	B	Gilder RE	1736431	A
Ferguson DP	136590	B	Gillard RJ +	3790395	A
Ferguson IG	235378	A & B	Glass RJ	1201185	A & B
Ferris PR *	2136891	B	Glassford G	3786786	1 & A
Fietz WH	16725	A	Goedhart F	1200025	A
Files GP	1734963	B	Gooch KD	33231	A & B
Finch BW	311562	A	Goodman PC	2788423	A & B
Fischer GI	2795051	A	Gordon RE	2793933	A & B
Fischer PJ	5717517	A	Gourlay GJ	313440	A & B
Fisher JA	3788569	A	Gowie PR	2783655	A
Fisher JE	3109306	A	Graf AB	3786788	1 & A
Fisher RW	167119	A & B	Graham FA	214560	1 & A
Fitzpatrick JJ	37200	A	Graham JA *	312838	B
Fletcher JR *	217520	A & B	Gray TJ	55371	A & B
Flood JR	2786253	A	Greaves RJ	5715845	B
Flower MV	2790218	B	Green NL	5411168	A
Foale NT	4718772	A	Gregg RC	2790574	B
Fogarty JW (MID)	52989	A	Gregory IJ	4719049	A
Forbes AS	4721628	A	Greig RA	53210	1, A & B
Forbes AV	2140951	A & B	Greig WF	311359	1 & A
Ford GR *	2795101	A	Grey JC (CDS)	235191	A & B

Name	Regimental number	Squadron(s) served
Grice AS	3797293	A & B
Grieve BE	38919	A
Griffin BA	2790523	B
Gross RJ	16250	1 & A
Grove DJ	5714885	A
Guest GD	3791176	A
Gullery MJ	826403	(NZ)
Guymer RC	15261	1 & A
Hagerty RE	335096	1 & A
Hague RI	2784383	A
Hall GR	610518	B
Hamilton WR	1735685	A
Hamstead TC	212886	A & B
Handley DJ (MID) *	1203040	A & B
Hann GH	42379	A & B
Hannah JJ	55863	A & B
Hanson RA	2108560	A & B
Hanuszewicz S	37709	A
Hardstaff AJ	37705	A
Hardy BC	311535	B
Harris JC	220678	A
Harris MR	17678	A & B
Harris SD	220657	A
Harrison DR	1411263	A
Harrison R	55476	A & B
Harry GJ	2795168	A
Hartigan GJ	2798326	A & B
Hartley RG	3411749	A
Hartnett LJ	216159	A
Hartwigg KR	42166	1
Harvey J	55234	A
Harvey JH	1733327	A
Hastie KJ	534745	A & B
Hawes RJ	219466	A & B
Hawkins AE	2786921	A
Hawkins WT	1735505	A & B
Hawksworth EA	210445	A & B
Haydock C	43520	A & B
Heading GJ	1735844	A & B
Healy DL *	134164	A & B
Heaney CR	2788375	A & B
Heath DJ	2790505	B
Heggie RT *	411454	B
Heid LJ	3790647	A
Heine B	218014	A & B
Heise ED	5411450	A
Henderson KJ	54163	1
Henderson RH	220551	A
Henley JB	219923	A & B
Henry RJ	1203057	A
Herd RD	55010	A
Herman M	38378	A
Hermanson AJ	4719302	A & B
Herron LM	3786633	A & B
Higgins GJ	37823	A
Hill DE	37880	1 & A
Hill DV	1202702	A & B
Hill MJ	1201349	B
Hill RK (MC) *	51407	A & B
Hillard RB	2791533	B
Hobbs BR	3792383	A & B
Hobbs JH	54972	B
Hocking DL *	3793589	B
Hogan PD	2412571	B
Hogg DF	1200664	A
Holbrook N	45271	A & B
Holden PD	137779	A & B
Holland T +	3786634	1
Hollett J	5713858	A
Hollindale NA	1736446	A & B
Hollis RJ	2783682	A
Holmes PL	1730966	1 & A
Holmshaw BW	1735691	A & B
Holt KG	359215	A & B
Hopkins WV	1736850	A & B
Horne JO	54953	A & B
Howard GK	63509	A
Howard JA	3905025	1 & A
Howard RJ *	3792606	A
Huckin S	54257	1
Hudson AG	28294	A & B
Hudson JN	39498	(NZ)

Name	Regimental number	Squadron(s) served	Name	Regimental number	Squadron(s) served
Huggins JE	5716684	A & B	Judd VD	3794911	B
Huggins PC	2784884	A	Kadow PJ *	423909	A & B
Hughes BB	2787968	A & B	Kealy GR	2207640	A & B
Hughes RF *	51181	A & B	Keating CR	2900589	A
Hull BG	3796880	A & B	Keenan IC	342810	B
Humphreys BR	38340	A & B	Kees RW	37949	1 & A
Hunt PW	2789544	A & B	Keevers EW	22151	1
Hunter II	627857	(NZ)	Keldie JD (MC)	235100	1 & A
Hunter RF	38224	A & B	Kelly FJ	55771	A & B
Hutchieson JJ	2787718	A & B	Kemble GM (MID)	43040	1, A & B
Hutchinson RJ	3112749	A	Kemp EJ	2787442	A & B
Hyam KA	2795548	A	Kennard RS	33647	A
Ingle TP	2782198	1 & A	Kennedy RR *	4411150	A & B
Ingram GG	5717029	A & B	Kershaw RA	42807	A & B
Innes KN	43930	A	Kidd DR	4410962	A & B
Isaacs JV	215775	A	Kilby PB	215255	1
Izatt DJ (MID)	1733339	A & B	King AF	31056	1
Jackson WN	1411171	A & B	King MR	312908	A & B
James RF	39106	A	Kinsella PA	1731644	A
Jeffress BS	2793964	A & B	Kippax PW	216038	A
Jennings WJ	2781446	1 & A	Kirk GJ	2184771	A
Joel SS	5714327	A	Kirkpatrick DA	2792189	B
Johns AF	1202011	A & B	Klimisch WE	39810	A & B
Johnson DW *	219774	A & B	Klopp RW	4410902	A
Johnson IE *	44886	B	Kollias BC	335166	A
Johnson KW	217990	A	Kopacz AJ	3798612	A
Johnson SJ	219928	A & B	Krake DR	3792391	A & B
Johnson TG *	37888	1	Krizovsky AJ	3798599	A
Johnston EW	215559	1	Laidlaw PF	38770	1 & A
Johnston FS	3787260	1 & A	Lambert DW	44091	A
Johnston IL	2790690	B	Lane RD	213459	A & B
Johnstone MW	43872	A	Larnachjones AW	235170	A
Jolliffe GJ	3411782	A	Lavelle RA	3112750	B
Jones AA	2787987	A & B	Lawrence DR	36549	A & B
Jones DJ	37559	1	Lawrence PC	411388	A
Jones DL	5716272	A	Layton CG	3799177	A
Jones JP	38327	A	Layton DJ	3790684	A
Jones KJ	2781368	1 & A	Lazzaro JF *	3786893	1 & A
Jones LG	15567	1 & A	Leak SJ *	217792	A & B
Jones WM	5713672	1 & A	Lee AJ	34214	A
Jorgensen	1733129	A	Leeman S	2795121	A

Name	Regimental number	Squadron(s) served	Name	Regimental number	Squadron(s) served
Legge GE	1201832	A & B	Malone PA +	215983	A
Leishman J	5717223	A & B	Mann PJ *	2412442	A
Leith PJ	2184617	A	Manning PA	3796253	A & B
Lennon GF *	1734758	B	Manning RL	2793547	A
Lennox DT	216502	1, A & B	Mannion JF	38425	A
Lenz GR	2789583	B	Mannion LS	1202278	A & B
Lester DM	30872	(NZ)	Manton PJ	61354	A & B
Levens JD	38170	1, A & B	Marks DH	2184354	A & B
Levy ED (DCM) *	37178	A & B	Marshall BH	2793730	A
Lewington GE	29470	A & B	Marshall CD	2792029	B
Lewis RJ	548890	A	Martin LJ	3791593	A & B
Ley MI	5714723	A	Mason FP	5411523	A
Limond RJ	2784054	A & B	Mason GW *	1200541	B
Lingard RC *	5715690	A & B	Mason JD	3790049	A
Linsell MK	218185	A	Mason LR	1736158	A & B
Little TR	2793193	A	Mason RD	44163	A & B
Locke RJ *	173700	B	Mason TC	217047	A & B
Locke WJ	5717040	A & B	Mathieson ID	39113	A & B
Lockie JP	3789952	A	May KJ	39139	A & B
Losberg D	1201807	B	May RF	43966	A & B
Lowe TT	54283	A	Maycock G	2789621	B
Lowes N	14574	1 & A	Mayes RG	2787260	A & B
Lowry CW	4410632	1 & A	McAnally FW	2412583	A
Luff NF +	28325	A	McAndrew KH	2782432	A
Luxton MC	1733351	A & B	McArthur DP	5714129	A
Lyons PC	5715490	A & B	McCabe BT	5714544	A
MacDonald KB	218425	B	McCallum IM	2782243	1 & A
MacEwan DA	3411833	A	McCarthy JN +	3112702	A & B
Macey RC (MM) *	216833	A & B	McColl CR	2794550	A & B
MacIntosh RD	4720801	A & B	McCormack RB	235392	A & B
Mack JJ	217012	A & B	McCormick JB	3411689	1 & A
Mack TH	44000	A & B	McCrohan DP	3787147	1 & A
MacKenzie RP	36853	A	McDonough EJ	36970	A
Mackin J	5715721	A & B	McDonough RJ	38862	A
MacKinnon AC *	1201511	A & B	McDowell RG	3788041	A
Mackley RF	2791332	B	McEwan IG	5713682	1 & A
MacMichael PN	6708256	1 & A	McFadyen RE *	213984	A & B
Madden NT	6708873	A	McFarlane MC	7130	A & B
Madigan BT	4718486	A	McGlone GJ	55648	A & B
Maginnity CG	2788397	A & B	McGregor CW	215235	1
Maher IP	11177	A	McHatton MG	2785451	A

Name	Regimental number	Squadron(s) served	Name	Regimental number	Squadron(s) served
McInnes GJ	3790934	A	Mitchell KN *	157571	A & B
McKay GW	2784381	A	Mitchell KW	44017	B
McKinnon BW	3793112	B	Mitchell PJ	39328	A & B
McLaughlin ND	2787785	A & B	Mitchell RS	43945	A & B
McLaughlin PB	5717432	A	Mitchinson KL +	4717751	1 & A
McLay PB	43920	A	Moffat WS	214944	1 & A
McLean DA	1736298	A	Moloney JB	2781871	1 & A
McLean DJ	2791238	B	Monaghan PG	1200747	A & B
McLean JB	2794649	A & B	Monk HC	2788077	A & B
McLean KJ	5715312	A & B	Monks WJ	6995	A & B
McLindin CP	3787590	A	Mooney MK	3175884	A
McManimm MJ	1201586	A & B	Morath MJ	2796107	A
McMillan RG	214836	1 & A	Moreton J	56511	A
McNamara BJ	2785900	A	Morgan DJ	38209	A
McNamara PS	4717530	1 & A	Morgan NT	3797440	A & B
McPherson AC	213284	A	Morris BJ	3793290	A & B
McPherson DL	6708259	1 & A	Moss RP	2785112	A
McQuade J *	1201534	A & B	Mostyn J	2127294	A
McQuade J	54494	A & B	Moyle LJ	56135	A & B
Medhurst RE	42810	A	Muir AB	4721888	A
Melbourne GR	313042	A & B	Muir JD	218709	A & B
Mellett GW	3796250	A & B	Mulholland NG	2784266	A
Mercer BM	411699	A	Munro BD	2785936	A & B
Mercer WB	43648	A	Munro GG	3787811	A
Merkel GJ	3794384	B	Murphy AA	37437	1
Meyer WE	42633	1 & A	Murphy AS	5715506	A & B
Micallef S	3410910	1 & B	Murphy GJ (MID)	47015	A
Michalek C	1732181	A	Murphy JP (MID)	36906	A
Mika RL	2786186	A	Murphy PJ (MID)	36432	A & B
Milikins NF	3786844	1 & A	Murray GC	3411521	A
Millar GW	55493	B	Murray TJ	2412552	A & B
Millar WD	5714363	A	Myler PT	6709373	B
Miller JL	17676	A & B	Nancarrow WF	3788648	A
Miller KN	1200670	A	Naylor P *	219860	A & B
Millington GL	54211	A	Neihoff HL	42710	1
Millington NA	5713691	1 & A	Ness BS	55048	A
Mills JD	216742	A & B	Neve BH	1732188	A
Minty FR	37781	(NZ)	Newby F *	216534	A & B
Mitchell BM	53992	A & B	Newman GD	3786764	1 & A
Mitchell C *	55265	B	Newman TP	2412392	A
Mitchell CL *	4719816	A & B	Nichols GK	4719142	A

Name	Regimental number	Squadron(s) served	Name	Regimental number	Squadron(s) served
Nichols PJ	627489	B	Pepper JE	215883	A & B
Nicolson ML	4717545	1 & A	Perejuan AG	55539	B
Noonan RE	3155774	A	Perkins NC	18765	1 & A
Nordeck BC	2793193	A & B	Perrett DP	1737598	A
Norsgaard AA	2792733	A & B	Perry SL	214145	A & B
O'Brien DJ	4191	A & B	Petrovic S	3790118	A
O'Brien DW	2789054	B	Petteit KA	216596	A & B
O'Brien PW	1733161	A & B	Phillips AJ	37157	A
O'Callaghan TP	5715511	A	Phillips CW	2787888	A & B
Ockwell JT	3790079	A	Phillips DJ	2784363	A
O'Donnell LG (MID)	57033	A	Pickering JE	5716885	A
O'Donnell PL	3793548	B	Picton JR	4410604	A
Ogrodniczek WS	2791262	A & B	Pine PD	217065	A & B
O'Halloran SJ	2787523	A & B	Piper RH	218844	B
O'Kearney DC	167130	A	Pirie DG *	2787235	A
Oldmeadow LJ *	1736163	A & B	Pitt BG *	38551	A & B
Olinski S	211021	A	Plunkett LB *	2783791	A & B
O'Neill ET	214627	1	Polkinghorne PW	4719548	A
O'Neill GA	5714973	A	Polucha SJ	1411200	A
Opray SG	1201842	B	Pomroy VI +	3786644	1 & A
O'Reilly JT	16839	1, A & B	Poole RJ	53839	A
O'Rourke WJ	37226	A & B	Poolier DJ	4410752	A
Ortlipp K *	3789414	A	Porter RA	3787166	1 & A
O'Shea JJ	3411209	1	Porter RJ	2792672	A & B
Oxenham JM	13894	A	Potts GJ	5713927	A & B
Oxer RE	4410996	A	Poulsom PA	311501	A
Padovan DJ	36988	A	Powell AE *	5411297	A
Page AC	2785948	A	Power PF	1736895	A
Page DC	2790147	A & B	Prickett MD	54863	A & B
Page TJ	17743	1 & A	Prindable AJ	1202094	B
Pakes DE	312784	A & B	Prior RJ	2782417	1 & A
Parker GR	311311	A & B	Pritchard JW	38722	1 & A
Parker TJ	61467	A	Przeradzki EA	5717663	A
Parker WJ *	54423	B	Pullinger RC *	43470	A & B
Pass AJ	1200212	A	Purcell PF (MID)	2785969	A
Peake GJ	216824	A & B	Purcell RF	2788012	A & B
Pearce GC	243461	B	Quint GN	55076	A
Peatling KW	3794413	B	Rae PJ	218044	A & B
Peele RD	2244245	A	Ramsay PG	5717970	A
Pell RM	38734	A	Ray PE	2136913	A
Penley DW	4718861	A	Read BD	1411291	B

Name	Regimental number	Squadron(s) served
Reddrop WG	3789456	A
Rees DC	1734778	B
Rees DM	2786775	A
Regtop WJ	235256	A
Reinke JR	1735415	A & B
Rewell CG	5717670	A
Reynolds KS	28512	A
Reynolds PB	2793611	A & B
Reynolds WS	2782938	A
Richards BW *	235292	A
Richards RE	213099	1 & A
Rikkerink JG	219854	A & B
Riley LJ	14205	1 & A
Riley NJ	2239815	A
Rivett DL	312753	B
Roach MJ	6709096	B
Roberts BD	243403	A
Roberts DJ *	311385	A & B
Roberts FA (MID)	54548	1 & A
Roberts PJ	3799996	A
Robertson H	13936	A
Robins II *	219002	A & B
Robins BJ	1200889	A
Robinson IK	311522	1 & A
Robinson KW	4718041	A
Robinson NE	4720637	B
Robinson PL	1731700	A
Robinson RJ	1736034	A & B
Roche JF	1733169	A & B
Rolfe DS	48634	A
Ronan RP	2788485	A & B
Rook MK	6709036	A & B
Rooks RE (MID)	235073	A & B
Rouhan RJ *	312545	A
Rowe NJ	3793130	A & B
Roy NF	1736174	A & B
Rule JR	4720833	A & B
Russell RJ	19989	A
Ryall RJ	254768	A
Ryall RJ	2105179	A
Ryan AE	37212	A
Ryan RD	2794240	A
Savage IC	215565	1 & A
Sayer NM *	5715751	A & B
Scales J	36687	A & B
Scammell DW	3786741	1 & A
Schellhorn JW	2785999	A
Schofield WF *	55115	A & B
Schultz PK	2786000	A
Scott WB	3133914	A & B
Scott WT	2793928	A & B
Scutts JR	216872	A & B
Sellwood DJ	1200020	A & B
Sengstock RT	15909	1 & A
Shakespeare WH	5410936	A
Shangie DA	3790710	A
Sharman VJ	2795551	A
Sharp EJ	216006	A
Sheean GL	218111	A
Sheehan JF	3790197	A
Sheppard DW (MID) *	2139599	B
Short KE	213247	A & B
Sidor BB	3794112	B
Siemsen DP	1736224	A
Silvester MR	1732787	A
Simpson RG	3792247	A & B
Simpson SW	2785376	A
Sims WA	2781708	A
Sincock BJ	4720848	A & B
Singletary DC	214405	A
Slocombe BP *	1201981	B
Smith BD	42897	1 & A
Smith BJ	42914	A
Smith CO	218485	B
Smith DC	2791857	B
Smith DR	4411146	A & B
Smith GJ	3794142	B
Smith GJ	1733427	A & B
Smith IC	54799	A
Smith JA	312615	A
Smith KG	18907	A & B
Smith KO	37423	A

Name	Regimental number	Squadron(s) served	Name	Regimental number	Squadron(s) served
Smith LW	1202459	A	Stuart A	22191	A
Smith MR	3177060	B	Studman JS	2239662	A
Smith PA	2792046	B	Sullivan JP	2786027	A
Smith PR	4410865	A	Sutton GJ	213759	A
Smith RM	3786942	1	Sutton NJ	235361	A & B
Smith RR	2795022	A	Swann JJ (MID)	217083	A & B
Smith WG	5713726	1 & A	Systermanns M	37549	A & B
Smits LJ	3411650	A	Taggart R	313959	A
Snowball M	5716364	B	Taylor H	215674	A & B
Sosnowski WS	3791586	A	Taylor JD	3790261	A
Speet AR	37972	1 & A	Taylor KR	2196751	A
Spenceley AW	356405	A & B	Taylor P	311526	A & B
Spinks RJ	220679	A	Taylor RG	2791430	B
Squires RD	16458	A	Taylor RW	3788424	A
Stach B	3792838	B	Teasdale K	2245460	A & B
Stagg CK	3799351	A	Tebby KM	45555	A
Standley GG	518953	B	Telford WR	1736049	A & B
Stanton AD	1733518	A & B	Tetley RC	2782108	1 & A
Starkey LE	213843	A	Thomas BJ	4410975	A
Starr P	219061	B	Thomas IM	4410737	1
Staszynski J	4410950	A	Thomas JM	3788721	A
Staunton G	138342	A & B	Thomas WR	2140788	A & B
Stearman PT	2794591	A	Thompson KD	61483	A
Steele IR	312512	A & B	Thompson LJ	2137821	A
Stent PD *	5716371	B	Thomson GG *	54162	A
Stephens CE	174128	A & B	Thomson PR	4721541	A
Steward C	56012	A & B	Thomson RC	3112898	B
Stewart BF	36722	A	Thorpe BR	5714609	A
Stewart JG	216885	A & B	Tingley RL (MC) *	54702	A
Stewart W	296085	A	Tinson DJ	214628	1, A & B
Stidwell TC	534715	A & B	Tognolini MP +	218453	B
Stirzaker AW	39708	B	Tompkin AJ	5713740	1 & A
Stoddart RA	5717272	A & B	Tonks PM	39080	A
Stones J *	37413	1, A & B	Toohey PJ	2786296	A
Storey RK	40559	(NZ)	Toohey RJ	1734367	B
Storey WJ	2794553	A & B	Townsend JG *	2792506	A & B
Stow P	436142	B	Toy DL	4410954	A
Strachan GW	3786870	1 & A	Traynor IF	312721	A & B
Strickland BJ	213935	A	Trebilco JM	3787227	1 & A
Stroscio G	3799819	A	Trengrove LA	2784326	A
Strudwick PF (MM)	5715553	A & B	Tronc RW	1200678	A & B

Name	Regimental number	Squadron(s) served
Trower C	4718680	A
Tunbridge KC (CDS)	18666	A & B
Tuntin JK	61678	A & B
Turnbull PB	39369	B
Turner AG	48641	A
Turner PE	3787191	1 & A
Turner PW	7143	A & B
Turner WA	2140626	B
Turnham KN *	3790866	A
Umphelby RD	335184	A & B
Van Anholt JW	3799483	A
Vander GJ	37621	A
Van Kuyk BA	2787884	A & B
Vanrysinge GJ	5716920	B
Vapp GG	342825	1 & A
Veall RJ	410789	A & B
Venema CF *	43544	A & B
Vickers CR	1734394	B
Viergever JL	447654	A & B
Vigar GM	43938	A
Vincent DF	43658	A
Vincent PJ	2789956	B
Vipen JR *	219360	A & B
Virgin RJ	42526	A
Voyzey DJ +	2137680	B
Wade DJ	44551	B
Wade RB	36664	A & B
Wagner K	216585	B
Wailes JA	218180	A
Waldeck PP	5715773	A & B
Waldock WC	549658	1 & A
Wales WS	2791312	B
Walker RE	1734430	B
Walker TF (CDS)	13133	A & B
Wallis KR	1201866	B
Walsh TW	111681	A
Ward R	2135570	A
Warden GR	358964	A & B
Warr J	311559	A & B
Warren LJ	1200339	A
Warren R	42437	1 & A
Watson JG	1735277	A & B
Watson PJ	1732823	A & B
Watts DJ	43438	1 & A
Webb BL	26663	A & B
Webb K	216718	A & B
Webb MJ	1203248	A
Webb MS *	38537	A
Webb N	215805	A
Webster GJ	38679	A
Webster NJ	36743	1 & A
Weire JB	3411509	A
Wells RJ	38273	A
Welsh AJ	3786944	1 & A
Wendt DM	1203319	A
West GW	1736065	A
West PN	1202050	A
West TJ	2787004	A
Westgate DP *	219648	A & B
Whelan RC	36890	A
Whiston BJ +	1202024	B
White PR	4720673	B
White RM	3788345	A
White WC	2788937	A & B
Whitney JD	137822	A & B
Wicks RT	15631	1 & A
Widermanski EF	39777	A & B
Wieland LJ	12954	A & B
Wilkie PA	214575	A
Will AG	4718283	A
Williams AL	215950	A & B
Williams DR	48642	A
Williams RJ	3798928	A
Willingham EJ	312677	B
Willis RA	5714225	A
Willoughby GJ	2784405	A
Wilsen RP +	4717841	1 & A
Wilson BS	42657	B
Wilson DJ	137885	A
Wilson G	18291	A &
Wilson J *	36123	1
Wilson JR	2787881	A & B

Name	Regimental number	Squadron(s) served	Name	Regimental number	Squadron(s) served
Wilton PF	216839	A	Wright GI	1202731	A & B
Woo DG	218548	B	Wynd GA	220232	A
Wood AG	2793673	A	Yelland LD	1202928	A & B
Wood GC	3798253	A & B	Youde PW *	43512	A
Wood NC	2781962	1 & A	Young CW	3788443	A
Wood RE	5717958	A	Young RG +	1733547	A & B
Woodford FB	3791603	A & B	Zuccato PP	2784258	A
Worthington DB	2792623	A & B	Zwart D	4720266	A

The LAD

Adams LA	2790179	A & B	Elliott WO	2790510	B
Adams RE	4410769	A	Fidden PG	2789007	B
Alexander W	1736555	A	Flynn P	342737	1
Allen GD	216732	A	Gately PJ	18800	A & B
Armstrong G	58775	A	Gumley GG	4721436	A
Aspin KR	2789374	A	Hermann BR	1734478	A & B
Back WC	2794028	B	Houston JP	54216	1
Baker BJ	2786232	A	Jensen FP	218808	A & B
Bassett LJ	2791710	B	Jones EJ	38677	A
Batchelor DV	64298	A	Kellar KB	217114	A & B
Beggs WV	242569	A & B	Kennedy EJ	214631	A
Beilby WD	29863	1	Kibby JA	18757	A
Blackwell JW	48623	A	Klaasens MJ	4720581	B
Blake VN	18951	A	Lambert DW	44091	A
Blennerhassett PR	342954	A	London JL	33471	A & B
Board PM *	2790755	A & B	Long RA	6708255	1 & A
Brabants PR	55052	A	Lowry DM	42246	A
Bradley CA	2793155	A	Mascord BP	243456	A
Brown LR	3788211	A	McDougal JC	3798656	A
Brown RG	3793452	B	Michael CG	2788799	A & B
Burrows LJ	12178	A	Mikkelsen G	2789045	A & B
Cashin PF	130335	A	Mills RR	15778	1 & A
Caswell WJ	214616	A	Moore RM	18818	B
Choyce HD	54742	1	Morrison AJ	18258	A & B
Coker RJ	53918	1	Morton AD	217588	A & B
Conde RL	173440	B	Moyers EJ	2789156	A & B
Davis GK	2794398	A	Munro IA	2792145	B
Day RL	3789752	A	Murnane GJ	3798712	A
Edgelow AK	3797262	A	O'Connor JM	217068	A
Edmonds DN	18990	A	O'Donnell MF	18941	A & B

Name	Regimental number	Squadron(s) served	Name	Regimental number	Squadron(s) served
O'Hearn GM	2412239	A	Smith DG	216122	A
Olsson RG	5715728	A & B	Smith LR	216952	A
Omond DM	342881	A	Sparrow KR	4802	A & B
Payne L	2792076	B	Stolk M	43673	1
Philip KD	18884	A	Telford DS	2792557	A & B
Pierce RJ	4717557	1 & A	Tink DJ	58776	1 & A
Plummer KA	43933	B	Warbrook LJ	2786493	A
Rice WI	3798815	A	Webb AV	1201679	A
Riley GK	39057	B	Wicks BJ	216591	A & B
Roughley KJ	242656	B	Williams DR	48642	A
Russell DJ	6709614	A	Willing BW	6410227	A
Sainsbury PJ	243297	A & B	Wilton PF	216839	A
Sandars JF	38779	A & B	Winkler R	2786195	A
Sanders NH	4720000	A & B	Wright NG	1734951	B
Saric JZ	39077	A & B	Zyla J	217525	B
Sidor BB	3794112	A			

KEY

+	killed or died
*	Wounded in Action
CDS	Commendation for Distinguished Service
MC	Military Cross
DCM	Distinguished Conduct Medal
MM	Military Medal
MFG	Medal for Gallantry
MOG	Medal of Gallantry
MID	Mentioned in Dispatches
MBE	Member of the British Empire
DSM	Distinguished Service Medal
NZ	New Zealand Servicemen

Every effort was made to ensure that this roll was as complete as possible. However, a small number of members' original posting was to HQ 1ATF. In the circumstances it has been impossible to identify every person who served with the Regiment in South Vietnam. I apologise for any omissions.

Basic specifications for the M113A1 APC

Manufacturer:	American Food and Machinery Corporation
Crew:	Two—Driver, Crew Commander (and 10 passengers)
Length:	4.87 metres
Height:	2.41 metres
Width:	2.69 metres
Weight:	10 500 kg
Maximum speed:	62 kph on land, 6 kph in water
Radius of operation:	480 km on road
Armour:	Aluminium, various, angled, proof against small arms and mortar splinters
Engine:	GMC V6 diesel giving 215 hp

The cutaway illustration shows the basic components of the M113A1. The armament on this vehicle is a .50 cal. machine gun. Note the right-angle drive configuration, with the final drive extending out from the differential at the front of the engine.

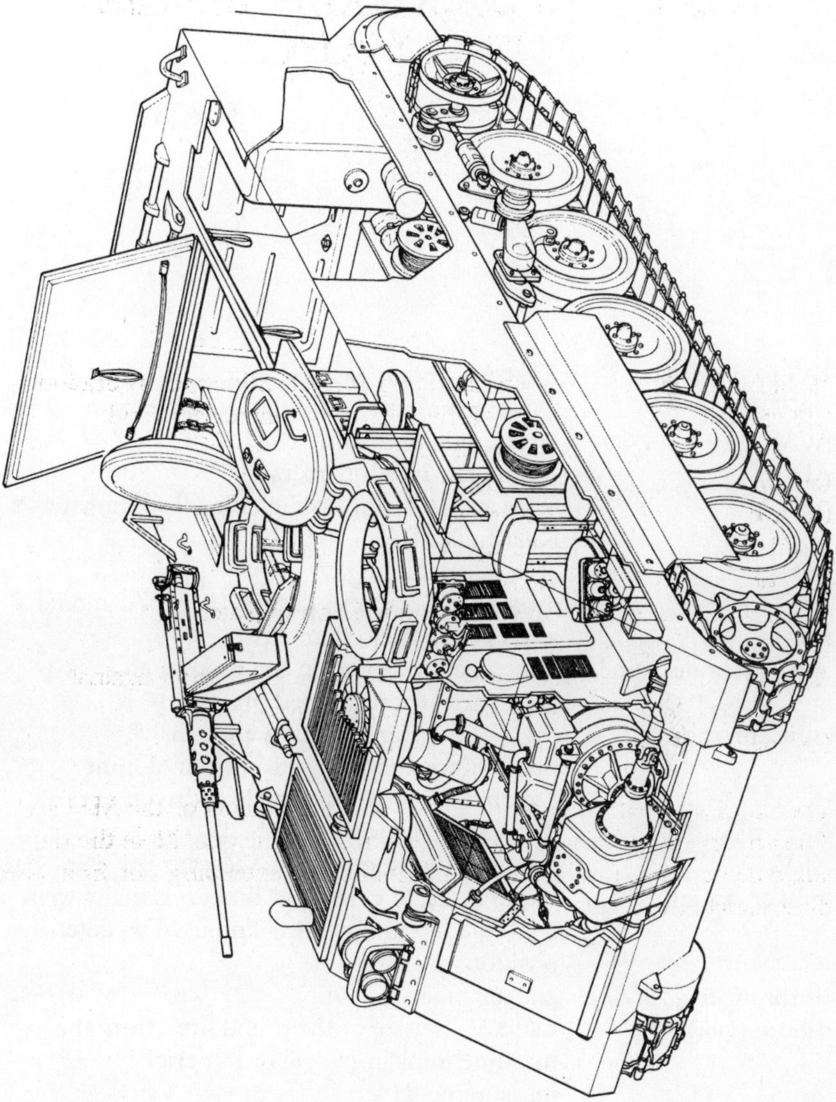

Glossary

1ATF	First Australian Task Force
AATTV	Australian Army Training Team Vietnam
ACV	armoured command vehicle
AHQ	Australian Headquarters
AK47	Russian 7.62 mm assault rifle (also known as a Kalashnikoff)
AO	area of operation
APC	armoured personnel carrier (M113AI model used by the Australian Army)
anti-personnel mine	mine usually buried in the ground and detonated when stepped on
anti-tank mine	mine of substantially larger explosive proportions than an anti-personnel mine. Detonated when the vehicle is driven over a detonating device
ARVN	Army of the Republic of Vietnam
bunker system	constructed of earth and timber. Usually well concealed in jungle areas and used as defensive positions
Bushranger	an Australian gunship
calibre (cal.)	refers to the size of the round fired from the machine guns in metric or imperial measurements
callsign	radio designation assigned to every vehicle in the Squadron. The callsign is based on the pronunciation of the numbers one to ten and

	letters of the Greek alphabet (e.g. Callsign 11A is pronounced One-One-Alpha)
CBU	cluster bomb unit: these 1 pound baseball-size bombs were dropped in lots of 600 or more and were released in such a way as to spread over as wide an area as possible. On hitting the ground they exploded, sending out the smaller steel balls imbedded in their cones
chicom	a brand of explosive manufactured by the Chinese
chieu hoi	an 'open arms' program where the Vietnamese government offered amnesty to Viet Cong defectors
claymore mine	anti-personnel horizontal directional mine
C/S	callsign (on a radio net)
Dinh	Shrine
dustoff	an acronym: dedicated untiring service to our fighting forces. A helicopter used to evacuate casualties
fire mission	artillery bombardment of a specific area for both offensive and defensive purposes
fire support vehicle (FSV)	M113A1 vehicle fitted with a Saladin turret and a 76 mm gun
FSB	fire support base: a base from which artillery and other resources supported an operation in the surrounding area
gunship	helicopter, normally either a UHI (Huey) or Cobra, mounted with mini-guns and rockets
hoi chanh	invitation to members of the Viet Cong to be repatriated by the South Vietnamese government
hoochie	nickname for personal shelter or lodging
HQ	headquarters
KIA	killed in action
LAD	Light Aid Detachment: mechanical and technical unit
lang	village or town
LZ	landing zone
MG	machine gun
MID	Mentioned in Dispatches
M79	40 mm grenade launcher
NDP	similar to a fire support base
nui	hill

NVA	North Vietnamese Army
OC	officer commanding
picket	sentry or guard
PWLH	Prince of Wales' Light Horse
RAAC	Royal Australian Armoured Corps
RAE	Royal Australian Engineers
RAEME	Royal Australian Electrical and Mechanical Engineers
RAR	Royal Australian Regiment
R&C	rest and convalescence
RCL	recoilless launcher (for rockets)
RPG	rocket launcher manufactured in the Communist Bloc. Often referred to as a rocket-propelled grenade
RSM	Regimental Sergeant Major
RTA	return to Australia
SAS	Special Air Service
section	subsection of a troop containing three APCs
Squadron HQ	Squadron Headquarters
song	river
suoi	stream
suppression mission	guns on firing missions to support other troops often had to lower their barrels and fire directly at their own attackers
TAOR	tactical area of operational responsibility
TCV	tarp-covered vehicle
troop	subsection of a Squadron containing four APC Sections
VC	Viet Cong: the South Vietnamese guerrilla army
WIA	wounded in action
WO	Warrant Officer
xa	village or town (smaller than *lang*)

Endnotes

Preface

1 Internal Minute Armour 206/AU40-4: analysis of Australian Army contacts in South Vietnam, 4 March 1971.

Chapter 1

1 Hopkins RNL, *Australian Armour*, 1978.
2 Hopkins RNL, *Australian Armour*, 1978.
3 Cecil MK, *Australian Military Profiles*, Vol 4, 1994.
4 AWM Series O/W 84/5.
5 AWM 952/6/1.
6 Hopkins RNL, *Australian Armour*, 1978.
7 AWM 2/6/1.
8 AWM 2/6/3.

Chapter 2

1 AWM Series 2/6/6.
2 RAAC Bulletin No 50.
3 RAAC Bulletin No 50.

Chapter 3

1 AWM 2/6/8.
2 AWM 2/6/9.
3 AWM 2/6/12.
4 AWM 2/6/8.

5 Cecil, M.K., *Australian Military Profiles*, Vol 4, Victoria 1994.
6 AWM 2/4/1.
7 Private papers, Brigadier G.J. Murphy.
8 AWM 2/4/2 & private papers, Brigadier G.J. Murphy.
9 AWM 2/4/3.
10 AWM 12/4/4.
11 AWM 2/4/5.
12 AWM 2/4/6.
13 Private papers, Brigadier G.J. Murphy.
14 AWM 2/4/7.
15 Private papers submitted by Kevin Ortlipp regarding the action. Private papers, Brigadier G.J. Murphy. AWM 952/4/8.
16 McAulay, L., *In The Ocean's Dark Embrace*, Banner Books, Maryborough, QLD, 1997.
AWM 952/2/9. AWM 952/2/10.
17 AWM 2/4/10.
18 AWM 2/4/11.
19 AWM 2/4/12. Private Papers, Brigadier G.J. Murphy.

Chapter 4

1 AWM 2/4/13.
2 RAAC Bulletin No 55. 3 RAR after-action report.
3 AWM 2/4/13.
4 AWM 2/4/4.
5 AWM 2/4/15.

Chapter 5

1 RAAC Bulletin 57.
2 AWM 2/4/17. McAulay, L., *The Battle of Coral*, Hutchison, Melbourne, 1988.

Chapter 6

1 Cecil, M.K., *Australian Military Profiles*, Vol 4, 1994.
2 RAAC Bulletin No 57.
3 AWM 2/4/18.
4 RAAC Bulletin 57.
5 RAAC Bulletin 57.
6 AWM 2/4/19.
7 AWM 2/4/20.
8 AWM 2/4/21.
9 AWM, Series O/W 84/5.

CHAPTER 7

1 AWM 2/4/22.
2 RAAC Bulletin 57.
3 AWM 2/4/23.
4 AWM 2/4/24.
5 AWM 2/4/25.
6 AWM 2/4/26.
7 RAAC Bulletin No 57.
8 AWM 2/4/27.
9 RAAC Bulletin No 57.

CHAPTER 8

1 Extract from written accounts of the action compiled by Eric 'Blue' Collins et al.
2 RAAC Bulletin 57.

CHAPTER 9

1 AWM 2/5/2.
2 AWM 2/5/3.
3 RAAC Bulletin No 57.
4 AWM 2/5/4.
5 AWM 2/5/6.
6 AWM 2/5/7.
7 AWM 2/5/8.
8 AWM 2/5/9.
9 Cecil MK, Australian Military Profiles Vol 4, Victoria 1994.
10 AWM 2/5/10.
11 AWM 2/5/11.

CHAPTER 10

1 RAAC Bulletin 57. AWM 2/5/11.

CHAPTER 11

1 AWM 2/5/11.
2 AWM 2/5/12.
3 RAAC Bulletin 57.
4 AWM 2/5/13.
5 AWM 2/5/14.
6 AWM 2/5/15.

7 AWM 2/5/16.
8 AWM 2/5/17.
9 AWM 2/5/18.
10 AWM 2/5/19.
11 AWM 2/5/20.
12 RAAC Bulletin No 58.
13 AWM 2/5/21.

CHAPTER 12

1 RAAC Bulletin No 61.
2 AWM 2/5/22.
3 AWM 2/4/29.
4 AWM 2/4/30.
5 AWM 2/4/31.
6 AWM 2/4/32.
7 A cavalry troop (as opposed to an APC troop) consisted of three scout vehicles (M113A1s) and two FSVs. It was on this premise that Major Terry Walker believes that the vehicles were sent to South Vietnam for testing.
8 RAAC Bulletin 62.
9 RAAC Bulletin No 61.
10 AWM 2/4/33.
11 AWM 2/4/34.
12 AWM 2/4/35.
13 RAAC Bulletin No 62.

References

1. Australian War Memorial—commanders' diaries (Number): 2/6/1, 2/6/2, 2/6/3, 2/6/6, 2/6/8, 2/6/9, 2/6/12, 2/6/13, 2/4/2, 2/4/3, 2/4/4, 2/4/5, 2/4/6, 2/4/7, 2/4/8, 2/4/9, 2/4/10, 2/4/11, 2/4/12, 2/4/13, 2/4/14, 2/4/15, 2/4/16, 2/4/17, 2/4/18, 2/4/19, 2/4/20, 2/4/21, 2/4/22, 2/4/23, 2/4/24, 2/4/25, 2/4/26, 2/4/27, 2/5/1, 2/5/2.
   Australian War Memorial—commanders' diaries (Number): 2/5/3, 2/5/4, 2/5/5, 2/5/6, 2/5/7, 2/5/8, 2/5/9, 2/5/10, 2/5/11, 2/5/12, 2/5/13, 2/5/14, 2/5/15, 2/5/16, 2/5/17, 2/5/18, 2/5/19, 2/5/20, 2/5/22, 2/4/28, 2/4/29, 2/4/30, 2/4/31, 2/4/32, 2/4/33, 2/4/34, 2/4/35.
2. Cecil, Michael K. *Australian Military Equipment Profiles, Vol 4: The M113 & M113A1 Armoured Personnel Carriers in Australian Service 1962 to 1972*, Australian Military Equipment Profiles, Melbourne, 1994.
3. Hopkins, R.N.L. (Maj. Gen.) *Australian Armour*, Australian War Memorial and Australian Government Publishing Service, Canberra, 1978.
4. McAulay, L. *The Battle of Long Tan*, Hutchinson, Melbourne, 1986.
5. McAulay, L. *The Battle of Coral*, Hutchinson, Melbourne, 1988.
6. McAulay, L. *In the Ocean's Darkest Embrace*, Banner Books, Maryborough, QLD, 1997.
7. Odgers, G. *Army Australia*, Child & Associates, Sydney, 1988.
8. Private papers of Ian Savage relating to Battle of Long Tan.
9. Private video recording by Adrian Roberts of Battle of Long Tan.
10. Private Papers relating to action during Operation ULMARRA compiled by Kevin Ortlipp.
12. Private papers of Eric Collins relating to the action at Binh Ba.
13. Private papers, letters and interview with Jerry Schellhorn.

14. Private records and letter by Geoff Murray.
15. Interview with Bruce Richards.
16. Interview with Ken Frazer.
17. Private records of Dean Branson.
18. Private records and interview with Ian Bates.
19. RAAC Bulletins: Records Nos 44–62.
20. Clunies Ross, Major A. *The Grey Eight in Vietnam: The History of Eight Battalion, the Royal Australian Regiment, November 1969–1970*, Eighth Battalion, the Royal Australian Regiment, 1971.
21. O'Neill, Robert J. *Vietnam Task, The 5th Battalion in South Vietnam.* Cassell, Sydney, 1968.
22. Battle, M.R. *Year of the Tigers: The second tour of 5th Battalion, the Royal Australian Regiment in South Vietnam 1969–1970*, John Burridge Military Antiques, Swanbourne, W.A., 1970.
23. 9 RAR Association, *9th Battalion, Royal Australian Regiment: Vietnam Tour of Duty 1968–69 On Active Service*, 9 RAR Association, Brisbane, 1992.
24. Newman, K.E. *The Anzac Battalion in South Vietnam, 1967–68*, Printcraft Press, Sydney, 1968.
25. O'Brien, M. *Regulars and Conscripts*, Allen & Unwin, Sydney, 1995.
26. Rowe, J. *Vietnam: The Australian Experience*, Time-Life Books, Sydney, 1987.
27. After-action report 3 RAR for action at Baria, 1 February 1968.
28. Private papers Brigadier G.J. Murphy.

Index

Page numbers in *italics* refer to illustrations.

Last Out
4RAR/NZ (ANZAC) Battalion's second tour in Vietnam
Jerry Taylor

'The role of 4RAR is to seek out and close with the enemy, to kill or capture him, to seize and hold ground and to repel attack by night and day, regardless of season, weather and terrain.'
Extract from 4RAR Standing Orders, 14 January 1970

How did infantry and armour attack a Viet Cong bunker system? What was it that persuaded men to go forward to possible death or wounding, when all their instincts told them that safety lay behind them? Who were the aggressive enemy they faced, and how were they organised, armed, equipped and resupplied? And what were the skills, tactics and techniques needed to live, fight and survive on the jungle battlefield of Vietnam?

Last Out is the story of the training and preparation for war of 4RAR/NZ (ANZAC) Battalion and the Australians and New Zealanders who made up this outstanding infantry battalion in 1970–71. Stand beside the commanders and men as they go into battle; toil with them under their loads of weapons and equipment; and experience through their eyes everything from the one-on-one contact between two opposing scouts, to set-piece attacks into enemy bunker systems supported by tanks, armoured personnel carriers, artillery and aircraft.

When the Battalion makes contact with the 33 North Vietnamese Army Regiment, follow the fourteen-hour action minute-to-minute, and wait in the dark with the surrounded men of ANZAC for the enemy's final attack.

Incisive, sensitive and witty, *Last Out* is a fascinating account of the last battles fought by Australians and New Zealanders in the Vietnam War.

MILITARY
ISBN: 1-86508-561-8